Making and Remaking Italy

Making and Remaking Italy

The Cultivation of National Identity around the Risorgimento

Edited by
Albert Russell Ascoli
and
Krystyna von Henneberg

Oxford • New York

First published in 2001 by
Berg
Editorial offices:
150 Cowley Road, Oxford, OX4 1JJ, UK
838 Broadway, Third Floor, New York, NY 10003-4812, USA

Berg is an imprint of Oxford International Publishers Ltd.

Library of Congress Cataloging-in-Publication Data
A catalogue record for this book is available from the Library of Congress.

British Library Cataloguing-in-Publication Data
A catalogue record for this book is available from the British Library.

ISBN 1 85973 447 2 (Cloth)
1 85973 452 9 (Paper)

Typeset by JS Typesetting, Wellingborough, Northants.
Printed in the United Kingdom by Biddles Ltd, Guildford and King's Lynn.

To Our Mothers
Josephine Amatulli von Henneberg
and
Marian Loomis Ascoli

Contents

Contents

Acknowledgements

This volume had its origins in, and took a good part of its title from, a conference called *Making and Unmaking Italy: The Cultivation of National Identity around the Risorgimento* organized by Albert Ascoli, and held at the University of California, Berkeley, in November of 1997. The conference was sponsored by the Department of Italian Studies, The College of Letters and Sciences, The Graduate Division, the Center for Western European Studies, the Townsend Center for the Humanities, and the Department of Comparative Literature at UCB, and by the Istituto Italiano di Cultura of San Francisco, directed by Dr. Amelia Antonucci. Many others contributed time and energy to making it happen, notably Mr. Michael D'Amato.

Much has happened in the passage from conference to book; only six of the original participants have remained as authors, and their contributions have all been significantly revised to suit the essay form and to further the purposes of the collection. Four essays have been added that the editors felt were important to fulfilling those purposes. We are grateful to all the original participants in the conference, and we owe a particular debt to our ten contributors, who have stuck with us over the sometimes grueling haul these last three years, and whose excellent scholarship has made it all worthwhile for us.

We owe individual debts of thanks to many other people, notably Luis Eduardo Guarnizo, Mary Ann Smart, Randolph Starn, and Susan Gaylard. We also wish to thank those at Berg Press most responsible for seeing this project through to a happy conclusion, especially Kathryn Earle, Sara Everett, Maike Bohn and George Pitcher, 'piggy in the middle' and copyeditor extraordinaire. The index was prepared with care and skill by Nora Stoppino. There is, finally, a substantial institutional debt to be acknowledged: the publication of this volume is made possible by a grant of subvention provided by the Ringrose Fund of the Department of Italian Studies, UC Berkeley.

Three of the essays in our collection have appeared previously in print, and we warmly thank those who have permitted us to make use of them here. The chapter of Nelson Moe is adapted from an article entitled

Acknowledgements

"'Altro che Italia!'. Il Sud dei Piemontesi (1860–61)" which appeared in *Meridiana. Rivista di Storia e Scienze Sociali*, volume 15 for 1992, pages 53–89, and which is translated and reprinted with permission of the editors. The chapter written by Millicent Marcus first appeared as a chapter in her book *Italian Film in the Light of Neorealism*, copyright © 1996 by Princeton University Press, reprinted by permission of Princeton University Press. The chapter of Claudio Fogu is a revised version of an essay entitled "Fascism and Historic Representation: The 1932 Garibaldian Celebrations," which appeared in *The Journal of Contemporary History*, vol. 31, no. 2, April 1996, pp. 317–45, copyright © 1996 Sage Publications Ltd, reprinted by permission of Sage Publications Ltd.

This volume is the fruit of an intense and satisfying collaboration between two scholars with very different disciplinary and methodological orientations: further proof, we hope, that a rigorous interdisciplinarity can be a most valuable tool in the study of human cultures. In closing, then, we thank each other.

Albert Russell Ascoli
Krystyna von Henneberg

List of Illustrations

Notes on Contributors

Albert Russell Ascoli teaches Italian literature and culture at the University of California, Berkeley, where he is chair of the Department of Italian Studies. His principal research interests include the formation of modern ideas and practices of authorship and readership, the literary construction of social identities, and interactions between artistic culture and historical crisis. He is the author of *Ariosto's Bitter Harmony: Crisis and Evasion in the Italian Renaissance* (Princeton University Press 1987); co-editor (with Victoria Kahn) of *Machiavelli and the Discourse of Literature* (Cornell University Press 1993); and numerous essays. He is currently completing work on a study of the career of Dante Alighieri, entitled *Authority in Person: Dante and the Emergence of Modern Authorship*.

Andrea Ciccarelli teaches at Indiana University, where he is Professor of Italian and Chair of the Department of French and Italian. His major research interests are in nineteenth- and twentieth-century Italian literature and culture. He has published a number of articles on modern Italian poetry (Foscolo, Gozzano, Futurism, Saba, Quasimodo, Luzi), a book on Manzoni's aesthetic thought (*Manzoni. La coscienza della letteratura*, 1996), and has co-edited a volume devoted to the concept of exile in modern Italy (*L'esilio come certezza* 1998) and another one on European Romanticism (*The People's Voice: Essays on European Romanticism* 1999).

Roberto Dainotto teaches aspects of eighteenth-, nineteenth- and twentieth-century literature and culture at Duke University, where he is Assistant Professor. He has recently published a book, *Place in Literature* (Cornell University Press 2000), and has edited an anthology entitled *Racconti americani del Novecento* (Einaudi Scuola 1999). He is the co-editor (with Eric Zakim and Miriam Cooke) of a forthcoming volume on *Mediterranean Thinking*. His current project is a book on the theorizing of Europe from Montesquieu to Hegel.

Claudio Fogu teaches European History at the University of Southern California (Los Angeles). His research has focused on the relationship among visual modes of representation and the formation of historical consciousness in fascist Italy. On this topic, he has recently published the article 'Il Duce Taumaturgo: Modernist Rhetorics in Fascist Representations of History,' *Representations* (1997). Thanks to a Jean Monnet Fellowship from the European University Institute, Florence, he is currently expanding his research to a study of Mediterranean imaginary in 1930s Europe.

David Forgacs teaches at University College London, where he is Professor of Italian. His main research areas are the cultural history of modern Italy and history of the media. His publications include two editions of Gramsci's writings (1985, 1988), *Rethinking Italian Fascism* (ed., 1986), *Italian Culture in the Industrial Era, 1880–1980* (1990; 2nd Italian ed. 1999), *Italian Cultural Studies* (ed., with Robert Lumley, 1996), the chapter on 'Spettacolo: teatro e cinema' in the Garzanti *Guida all'Italia contemporanea, 1861–1997* (1998) and a book on Rossellini's *Roma città aperta* in the BFI Film Classics series (2000).

Adrian Lyttelton teaches at the Università degli Studi di Pisa, where he is Professor of European History. He is the author of *The Seizure of Power, Fascism in Italy 1919–1929* (Weidenfeld & Nicolson/Princeton University Press, 1988), and the 'The National Question in Italy,' in *The National Question in Europe* (Porter and Teich, eds, 1993), as well as other essays. He is currently editing the volume *Italy 1900–1945* in the *Oxford History of Italy*.

Millicent Marcus teaches at the University of Pennsylvania, where she is Mariano DiVito Professor of Italian and Director of Film Studies. Her specializations include Italian cinema and medieval literature. She is the author of *An Allegory of Form: Literary Self-Consciousness in the 'Decameron'* (1979); *Italian Film in the Light of Neorealism* (1986); and *Filmmaking by the Book: Italian Cinema and Literary Adaptation* (1993). She has also published numerous articles on Italian literature and on film, and is currently working on a book on recent Italian cinema, and on an interdisciplinary collaborative project (with Lucia Re and others) entitled *Italy 1919*.

Nelson Moe teaches in the Department of Italian at Barnard College, Columbia University. He specializes in nineteenth- and twentieth-century

Italian cultural studies, with a focus on the *Mezzogiorno* and questions of national identity. He has published articles on a wide range of topics including modern Italian fiction and poetry, Gramsci, feminism, film, and cultural theory. His book on representations of the south in nineteenth-century Italy is forthcoming from the University of California Press.

Silvana Patriarca has taught modern European history at Columbia University and is now on the faculty of the University of Florida, Gainesville. She specializes in the social and cultural history of modern Italy and is the author of *Numbers and Nationhood: Writing Statistics in Nineteenth-Century Italy* (Cambridge University Press, 1996). She has also written on the social history of industrialization in the countryside, on peasant memoirs, and on gender and occupational categories. She is presently at work on a book tentatively entitled *The Uses of Identity: The Present and the Past of the Discourse on Italian Character*.

Lucia Re teaches Italian at the University of California, Los Angeles. She specializes in nineteenth- and twentieth-century Italian literature and culture. Her interests include *fin-de-siècle* early modernism and the avant-garde, the relationship between Futurism, Fascism and feminism, gender issues in nineteenth-century and twentieth-century literature and art, and comparative theories of gender and feminism, especially contemporary Italian feminist thought. Her translation into Italian of *Borges: A Literary Biography* by E.R. Monegal received the 1982 Comisso Prize. Her book, *Calvino and the Age of Neorealism: Fables of Estrangement* (Stanford 1990) was awarded the MLA Marraro prize. She has recently completed a book entitled *Women and the Avant-Garde: Experimentalism, Gender and Politics in Modern Italian Culture*. Her translation into English (with Paul Vangelisti) of Amelia Rosselli's *War Variations* is forthcoming.

Mary Ann Smart teaches in the Department of Music at the University of California, Berkeley. She has published articles on various aspects of early nineteenth-century opera, including Donizetti's mad scenes, the role of female characters in Verdi's patriotic operas, and the collaborations between nineteenth-century opera composers and their leading ladies. She is author of the extensive entries on Bellini and Donizetti in the *Revised New Grove Dictionary* and editor of the critical edition of Donizetti's last opera, *Dom Sébastien*, which was premiered at Bologna's Teatro Comunale in December 1998. Her book *Resonant Bodies: Music and Gesture in Nineteenth-Century Opera* will be published in 2002.

Krystyna von Henneberg has worked as a journalist on African and Asian development, technology and human rights. She has taught at Stanford University, and is now an Assistant Professor in the Department of History at the University of California, Davis. Her research focuses on the social impact of modern architecture and urban planning, and the legacies of modern imperialism in Europe and Africa. She is completing a book entitled *The Construction of Fascist Libya: Modern Architecture and Urban Planning in Italian North Africa*, and is also engaged in a study of the relationship between nation-building, tourism and planning, both in Italy's colonies and within the Italian nation. Her next project, tentatively titled *Empire Lost and Found*, deals with the conflicted memory of Italian colonialism as expressed in post-war urban public space, monuments and culture.

Introduction: Nationalism and the Uses of Risorgimento Culture

Krystyna von Henneberg and
Albert Russell Ascoli

The aim of this volume is to analyze how Italian national identity has been imagined, implemented and contested before, during and after the period when a unified political entity known as Italy took shape. Our goal here is not to retell the well-known story of national unification. Myriad scholarly works precede us, including a number of recent and noteworthy additions to the field both in Italian and in English.[1] Indeed, it is precisely the existence of a large historiography about modern Italy that makes this volume possible. Our focus here is on something larger, and at the same time more flexible and diffuse. We probe the role of culture, broadly construed, in making and remaking a nation. In particular, we examine how images of the Italian Risorgimento, the founding era of Italian national unity, have been used by artists, politicians and intellectuals over the course of Italian history up to the present day. This repeated appropriation of the Risorgimento to support widely divergent ends suggests the ways that elites reinvent the past, using cultural means to promote nationalist goals. It also broaches wider questions about the origins and stability of nationalist discourses. How, we wish to ask, are nations and national identity forged, contested and reforged? How are canonical texts and events sacralized, or demystified, to support competing visions of national unity? How are marginal voices (female, lower-class, regional) excluded or appropriated within such visions? We believe that the posing, and provisional answering, of these questions will be of interest to scholars and students of Italy and European cultural history, as well as to those working in larger theoretical terms on issues of nationalism and national identity. The Italian case, we believe, is of exceptional interest in these ongoing debates, although, for reasons we describe below, its importance has not been sufficiently acknowledged to date. Our volume seeks to remedy this crucial omission.

We have deliberately cast our net wide, in terms of time, disciplines and sources. Arranged in roughly chronological order, the articles in this collection trace a historical trajectory of cultural debates over Italian national identity from the aftermath of the Napoleonic occupation, through unification, the fascist and post-World War II eras, all the way up to the present. This 'long view' allows us to chronicle the changing and often contradictory purposes to which the imaginative figure of the Risorgimento, as well as others like it, have been put, historicizing legends that have often been treated as sacred or immutable.

The volume is also multi- and interdisciplinary, with contributions from scholars of history, literature, culture and music. The chapters thus bring a wide variety of methods and styles of interpretation to bear on the relation between culture and nation-building, trespassing beyond what are still surprisingly strong disciplinary boundaries between scholars working on modern Italy. This interdisciplinarity extends to our own collaboration as editors. The volume has offered us a chance to debate the role of nationalist discourses in our own disciplines of history and literary studies. In particular, it helped us reflect on the ways that cultural texts can be freed from their service to teleological narratives, including arguments about Italian exceptionalism, restoring to them both agency and flexibility. From the other side, it has sharpened our sense of the nexus of historical events, social formations and broadly cultural discourses within which such texts can and should be located.

Finally, contributors to this volume scrutinize a wide variety of sources, including public spectacles, paintings, museums, philosophical treatises, journals, educational practices, operatic libretti, films and historical novels. While focusing principally on elite culture, the articles also address the place of widely disseminated, or marginalized, social texts. Contributors not only address the internal structures of individual works, but also analyze the social and political relationships and strategies these works express, relating them to a wider constellation of ideas and conflicts about Italian unity.[2]

The Problematic Nation and the Problem of Nationhood

Making and Remaking Italy has two broader goals. First, it seeks to contribute to a new body of revisionist scholarship, pioneered by several of the authors in this volume, that historicizes and rejuvenates debates about nationalism and state-building in Italy. As Silvana Patriarca underlines in Chapter 10, in Italy the breakdown of political frameworks inherited from the immediate post-World War II era has recently inspired a new interest in the sources of Italian unity. Motivated in part by what Patriarca calls 'anxieties and concerns about the dangers of disintegration'

(p. 299) as well as the rise of supranational forces embodied in the European Union, such works revisit the problem of an essential Italian identity, unsettling assumptions about Italian national development long cherished by Left and Right.[3] Several recent anthologies on topics ranging from Italian colonialism, to Fascism, to the so-called 'Southern Question' similarly challenge accepted periodizations and stereotypes about Italian history, and explore their role in legitimating postwar political parties and arrangements (see esp. Bosworth and Dogliani 1999; Schneider 1998; Allen and Russo 1997; Forgacs and Lumley 1996; Del Boca 1991).

Such efforts to think past long-standing ideological frameworks have an earlier precedent in the contributions of revisionist scholars of Italian social, cultural and economic history dating back to the 1970s. The thrust of many such works has been to re-evaluate the state as the source (or culprit) of invention and social transformations. Several authors have analyzed how groups outside the state have shaped or coopted nationalist projects and discourses to suit their own ends. Some have employed the methods of art and architectural history, literature and anthropology, sociology and oral history to discover an Italy organized along lines quite different from those imposed or imagined by classic political ideologies or parties.[4] Still others have used concepts of race, gender, space and memory to deconstruct Italian political culture, challenging the tendency to cast leaders or political institutions as sole protagonists of Italian national development. Such works do not constitute an erasure of politics per se, but rather a broadening of the concept to include new actors and processes, reworking the line between state and economy, public and private, and center and periphery (Porciani 1997; Isnenghi 1994, 1996, 1997a, 1997b; E. Gentile 1993; Berezin 1997; Falasca-Zamponi 1997). *Making and Remaking Italy* extends this line of inquiry. Several contributors locate debates about nationalism in a variety of artistic or literary spheres that are either independent of, or imperfectly controlled by, the centralizing logic of the state. Perhaps more importantly, contributors show the power of cultural elites to intrude on the more ordered or pragmatic visions of nation-building espoused by political leaders – visions that have often been retroactively purified and elevated by more conventional political historiography. A cultural approach, we believe, can reveal elements of unpredictability and fluidity in the making of nationalist narratives that many nationalists themselves prefer to ignore.

Our second, and related, goal is to bring 'the case of Italy' into an ongoing debate about nationalism both within and outside Europe. In particular, we wish to move beyond traditional concerns with ranking nations as precursors or latecomers, an approach that has often led to Italy's invisibility in comparative and theoretical discussions about nation-building (Petrusewicz 1998; Agnew 1997; Davis 1994; Lyttelton 1991). In both the history and historiography of modern western Europe, Italy has long been designated as an exception. In the centuries when nationhood was first established as the European ideal, the Italian peninsula remained divided into regional states, many of them under the direct or indirect domination of the great European powers. Even after the formal constitution of a national state from between 1859 and 1870, the history of the peninsula was described as an invidious spiral of political failures, casting continual doubt on the substantiality of a political 'Italy.' Such images persisted well into the twentieth century, reinforced by such factors as Italy's north–south divide, the rise of Fascism, and widely held beliefs about Italian political instability, lawlessness, moral backwardness or, lately, the south's lack of 'civic traditions.'[5]

Historiography and politics have naturally played a role in the construction of Italian exceptionalism. The creation of linear, celebratory accounts of nation-building, based most famously on the experiences of England, contributed to Italy's perceived backwardness: many scholars proposed models of economic and political development that few countries (including, ultimately, England itself) could live up to. As John Davis has pointed out, scholars have lately 'drawn aside coy ideal-type veils to reveal the markedly heterogeneous social endowments of the most "advanced" nineteenth-century European societies.' This, as Davis suggests, has contributed to 'replotting Italy's path to the twentieth century' along less exotic or obscure roads (1994: 291–2).

Equally important have been persistent geopolitical divides in traditional scholarship about Europe. Scholars of western Europe could label Italy a unique case only to the extent to which they ignored the experiences of numerous southern and eastern European nations, whose paths to and definitions of nationhood and modernity differed considerably from those described in the idealized histories of the Great Powers. By expanding one's sample to include other nations, from Turkey to Poland, Italy could be made to seem if not typical, then at least not deviant – while 'Whiggish' England could come to seem peculiar indeed. Indeed, comparisons with Balkan nations, particularly in the last turbulent decade of the twentieth century, may well help mute statements about Italy's inherent fractiousness, while also encouraging a more careful search for the sources of nationalist violence and separatism in post-cold war Europe generally.[6]

Similar geopolitical divisions have long existed between Europe and the rest of the world, with similar consequences for an understanding of

Italy. With the exception of scholars of fascism or migration, academics were reluctant to study Italy alongside countries in Latin America, Africa, Asia, or the Middle East. Italian anxieties about gaining or retaining membership in the inner circle of heavily industrialized European nations nurtured a long-standing taboo against such comparisons, even when it came to studying Italy's own Mediterranean neighbors. Comparisons to Africa, as Nelson Moe's contribution reminds us, were long (and are still) considered to be derogatory. But comparative research linking European nationalism to that of the rest of the world can produce useful theoretical insights into practices of nation-building across borders, and through empires, as much recent scholarship reminds us. Comparisons between Italy and Mexico, or between the Italian and American south, to mention only two examples, could yield novel directions for research in a variety of fields.[7]

Seen in this light, Italy's path to nationhood no longer needs to be treated as exceptional (although we will continue to insist on its *specificity*). Indeed, Italian history can prove useful for exploring a variety of topics in comparative perspective, ranging from regionalism and political *trasformismo*, to the pursuit of political and social ends by cultural means. Indeed, Italy's relevance as a historical and cultural case, we argue, lies precisely in its contested and 'uneven' path to modernity. In particular, it is the contrast between the fragility of the political nation on the one hand, and the cultural conviction of 'Italianness' on the other, that makes Italian history useful to scholars re-evaluating the impact and reception of other nation-building projects.

As far as this volume is concerned, a study of Risorgimento imagery can provide a useful introduction to the contradictory and constitutive role that cultural icons and history play in solidifying, or subverting, hegemonic visions of the nation. How and why elites struggled to create a vision of Italian unity despite obvious political odds; how they charged and changed political and cultural symbols; and what criteria (both conscious and unconscious) they used to create a sense of Italianness – all raise questions about the changing nature and boundaries of national identity that are relevant to scholars of nationalism and culture in a variety of periods and fields.

These questions have a direct bearing on the political situation in Europe today. The current reshaping of boundaries and identities has led to a re-evaluation of the claims and legitimacy of nation-states and national cultures. The breakdown of European empires has rendered nationalism a powerful and unpredictable force for political and cultural self-reinvention. Indeed, Europe seems to be revisiting some of the uncertainties of the Risorgimento era, or of the periods immediately following the two World Wars, each of which was shaped by the dual forces of decolonization and new nation-building. The discrediting of postwar European political systems and leaders has also helped to make nationalism a powerful tool in the hands of groups who are outside, or alienated from, the inner circles of the state; the many radical claims to reasserting cultural authenticity constitute a familiar and powerful means for challenging and reconstituting political authority. The questions 'what is a nation?' and 'who or what is part of the nation?,' posed so eloquently by Ernst Renan some one hundred years ago, are once again at the center of attention in countries ranging from Germany to Russia to the former Yugoslavia (Renan 1990).[8] Such changes have made scholarly re-evaluations of the origins of nationalist ideals and legends more urgent and relevant than at any time since the end of World War II. It is with these concerns in mind that our volume brings the case of Italy onto center stage. By exploring the relation between culture and nationalism, we hope to offer new insights into the struggles being waged in European nations, and in European historiography, today.

The Risorgimento as Foundation Story

All nations – especially new or troubled ones – demand foundation stories. At the same time, no foundation story is ever straightforward or unambiguous. The very idea of the Risorgimento, which forms the focus of this volume, is a case in point. The term has traditionally been used to designate the period from 1815 to 1870, the years leading up to the constitution of a unified nation-state with its capital at Rome. It was first coined by the late eighteenth- and early nineteenth-century authors Vittorio Alfieri, Ugo Foscolo and Giacomo Leopardi, on analogy with the earlier period of cultural rebirth and acknowledged Italian greatness known as the Renaissance. Long before its formal constitution as a nation-state, 'Italy' had a well-defined linguistic and cultural shape imposed on it by the economic and political elite of the peninsula, and by the foreigners who periodically invaded or toured it or both.

The notion of an Italian 'resurgence' was used to suggest the immanent and inevitable nature of the Italian nation, whose foundations were understood to lie as far back as the Roman Republic and Empire, or, at least, the founding of a Rome-centered Christian church in the early centuries CE. The ideal existence of this nation had been prefigured – supporters of unification affirmed – in the emergence from the thirteenth century onward of a language and a culture common to the governing elites of the various political entities that dotted the Italian peninsula before 1859. This common culture was symbolized, for example, by the works of Dante – or, as Andrea Ciccarelli points out in Chapter 2, by the many and often contradictory versions of Dante offered up by generations of nationalist intellectuals. The culturally and linguistically pure Italy imagined, or hoped for, both abroad and at home contrasted markedly with the cultural and linguistic diversity of the peninsula. Cultural Italianness, in this sense, was a form of selective and largely elite consciousness that ennobled some traditions, while excluding many others. It was on the basis of this consciousness that certain Italians and foreigners came to agree on the idea of consistent and continuous existence of a national Italian culture and 'character.' And it was this consciousness that the nation-builders of the Risorgimento struggled to translate into political fact, despite deep divisions and differences separating region from region, class from class, one 'Italian' from another.

From the start, the Risorgimento, with its emphasis on ensuring historical continuity, embodied the paradoxes of building anew what was supposed to exist inherently. Thus, for example, Risorgimento leaders faced the challenge of institutionalizing ideals that in the Romantic imagination had been defined as mainly moral and spiritual, or of establishing authority over movements that had only recently used revolutionary means to overturn their rulers. Even the most persuasive images of Italy as a unitary nation were not always sufficient to transcend class, regional or gender inequalities. At the best, the relation of the elites that had 'made Italy' to the revolutionary fervor on which they had uneasily drawn prior to unification was difficult. At worst, the aspirations of radical leaders such as Giuseppe Garibaldi and Giuseppe Mazzini on behalf of subaltern groups and social ideals seemed to have been betrayed, as the brilliant communist leader and thinker, Antonio Gramsci, would argue several decades later.

The idea of re-creating a national territory based on a quasi-sacred understanding of Italy's geographical and linguistic boundaries was especially slippery. The identification of territory, culture and polity was not always easy to sustain, given Italians' mixed loyalties and diverse languages, as well as the not-too-distant and frankly unsentimental landswapping that had produced such polities as the Kingdom of Piedmont-Sardinia (Lyttelton 1996; Gambi 1994). The metaphor of the dormant, and pre-existing nation proved especially problematic when it came to the south. As Moe describes in Chapter Four, incorporating the territories of the Kingdom of the Two Sicilies into the new nation led northern elites to produce elaborate studies of an Italy that many of them, including the architect of Italian unity, Camillo Cavour himself, had never set foot in, and only dimly understood. Such representations, with their denigrating and quasi-colonialist approach, tended to increase rather than bridge the divide between north and south, producing lasting fissures and stereotypes that continue to exercise influence today.

The effort to translate a cultural or historical ideal into a political fact also proved difficult, and led to a blurring of the boundary between culture and politics. The division of the peninsula among various occupying forces, and the absence of a stable, pre-existing state, or even a royal house that could be said to wholly represent the putative Italian nation, helped turned culture into a powerful weapon in making the new nation, or at least, in molding elite opinion in its favor. To the extent that political activity was deemed dangerous or insufficient (and it has rarely been sufficient) to 'make Italians,' literature and the arts became crucial venues for challenging the existing political order, and for defining and prop-agating notions of Italianness. Adrian Lyttelton, Ciccarelli and Mary Ann Smart in Chapters One through Three analyze the role that painting, literature and opera played in disseminating a variety of often contrad-ictory nationalist messages in the period preceding unification.

As far as unification was concerned, the difficulty lay in wedding such disparate cultural challenges into a coherent, and practical, political vision: for writers and artists, like revolutionaries, are neither stable nor obedient actors. The invention of Italianness, as carried out by intellectuals without direct responsibility for the waging of war, or for political administration, could often differ considerably from that required or envisioned by generals or politicians. As both Lyttelton and Smart aptly suggest, nationalism in the hands of artists could be more subtle, hesitant, ambivalent and opportunistic – above all, more influential, and not as easily domesticated to Realpolitikal objectives – than the nationalism of state-builders. Of course, once the political nation had taken shape those state-builders proved consistently adroit at transforming such 'marginal' figures into iconic representatives of *italianità,* as the cases of Manzoni, Verdi and, notably, the rebel turned official poet Giosue Carducci, certainly attest. The politicization of culture thus had its risks, but also its uses.

These ambiguities were not unique to the Italian case. The problem of constituting a legitimate political leadership, and of forging legitimate, unitary traditions in the face of often dramatic opposition, competition or apathy, was common to other nation-states and empires at the time. Nation-building has never been a linear or natural process, even in those countries that came to constitute models of progress or organization, and to which Italian elites often negatively compared themselves. So too, the

Risorgimento's peculiar mix of politics and culture, with all the creativity and problems that territorial fragmentation and foreign occupation entailed, had clear counterparts in other submerged or emerging European nations, particularly in central and eastern Europe.[9] Nor were the paradoxes inherent in Risorgimento nationalism necessarily a sign, or even a harbinger, of weakness, as many commentators retrospectively made them out to be. The tension between tradition and invention, conservatism and radicalism, that underlay Italian nationalist ideals would, on the contrary, provide a source of dynamism and invention for generations of ambitious elites. Defining, returning to, or carrying out the promises of the 'authentic' Risorgimento – however differently that Risorgimento might be defined by different groups at different times – would prove to be the ideological *terra firma* of many of Italy's most important philosophical, political and cultural innovators. If nationalism was not a replacement for religion, then, as many scholars have argued, it borrowed many of its characteristics. The construction of an uncertain *patria* was endorsed by a constant redeployment of its image, and an ever-more layered retelling of its origins. In this sense the Risorgimento, with its charged but ambiguous status, had much in common with the French, Mexican and Russian Revolutions. The strength of Risorgimento ideals, like those of these other legendary movements, lay precisely in their malleability, and hence their availability for cultural and political reinterpretation.

Indeed, well after unification was achieved, the Risorgimento remained a vivid, potent – and changeable – legend. The achievement of a nation-state, and the political and cultural opportunities that accompanied it, invited more, not less debates and polemics over the past. Despite the optimistic visions of nineteenth-century nationalists, unification exposed or even deepened existing divisions by language, region, class, gender and – in the case of the south – ethnicity. Italianness, at least for those living within the newly constituted borders of Italy, no longer had the advantage of being an oppositional identity or ideal. The question: What did it mean to be Italian? was now superseded by more difficult questions: what did it mean to be Italian (or less than Italian) within an Italian nation-state? What kinds of institutions and icons were needed to mend or suppress existing rivalries and mistrust? To what extent had Italy's political leadership traded formal nationhood, great-power status, or even economic growth for justice or equality, and what would be the long-term consequences of doing so? We have already seen that Moe addresses some of these issues in Chapter Four. Lucia Re also tackles them – in terms of gender – in Chapter Five, where she discusses women and writing in late nineteenth-century Italy. The emergence of a flourishing intellectual culture, based on book publishing, newspapers and the promise of education and growing literacy, raised new questions about who was or not included in this new public sphere, and on what terms. Re concludes that the construction of a liberal national culture led to a devaluation of women's writing. Unification, she suggests, ironically served to institutionalize, rather than attenuate, women's exclusion from the world of letters and public opinion.

Doubts about the achievements of the new nation led generations of political and cultural elites to revisit Risorgimento legends, reworking national history to alternately naturalize or question the legitimacy of existing political and social structures. Indeed, political fragility, as historian John Gillis has noted, tends to 'intensif[y] commemorative efforts.' When 'the conflicts of the present seemed intractable, the past offered a screen on which desires for unity and continuity, that is identity, could be projected' (Gillis 1994: 9).[10] Risorgimento history, with its unitary ideals, became a potent tool for arguing about past and present arrangements by both the left and the right. In the Liberal era, differing visions of the Risorgimento, and hence of the nation's problems and future, fueled debates over everything from suffrage, to migration, to colonialism, to the decision to enter World War I. As Claudio Fogu shows in his Chapter Six study of Italy's 1932 Risorgimental celebrations and monuments, fascist-era elites contrived their own ambiguous relationship with nationalist history. Fascist officials, and the artistic elites who interpreted their directives, coopted the boldest language and imagery of Risorgimento revolutionaries, while at the same time claiming to overcome the problems they bequeathed. The Risorgimento became the foundation for debates between the dominant idealist and Marxist schools, embodied in the writings of Benedetto Croce and Gramsci, as well as what Roberto Dainotto presents as the more brooding dialectical reflections of philosopher Giovanni Gentile.

After World War II, the need to explain Italy's plunge into dictatorship and to address the problem of continuity between the historical phases of the Italian state (successively, liberal, fascist and democratic), spurred renewed interest in an analysis of the nature and achievements of the Risorgimento. Like Germans, embroiled in their *Sonderweg* debate,[11] Italians were faced with the question of whether the period of national foundation had contained the seeds that gave rise to Fascism, or whether Fascism could be characterized as an aberration, a 'parenthesis' in the phrase of the liberal philosopher and historian, Benedetto Croce. And this was not only true in high-political and academic discourse: the stories, characters, and imagery of Risorgimento still had a powerful resonance in postwar popular imagination. As David Forgacs and Millicent Marcus show in Chapters Eight and Nine, films about Garibaldi's Sicilian campaign, or the Austrian occupation of Venice, could be readily interpreted by the Italian public as explicit comments on the contemporary political order. Finally, today, as Patriarca explains in Chapter Ten, Risorgimento lessons and failures remain the subtext for heated political debates in both politics and academia, including recent discussions about immigration, race and citizenship.

In each of these periods, the Risorgimento has been endowed with various, often contradictory, qualities which their proponents have nonetheless presented as immutable and essential. Indeed even in cases where the Risorgimento was seen in a negative light, one senses the overwhelming drive to erect an eminent, national precedent for contemporary issues. Local, regional and even international problems have thus frequently been understood to be explainable principally via a story about nation-building or its failures (Riall 1994: esp. 23, 68, 72–4). The sheer – and continuing – multiplication of images and arguments based on nineteenth-century history is a testament to the ability of nationalist narratives to absorb, assuage or sublimate a wide variety of political and cultural aspirations and anxieties. As the chapters of this volume attest, streets, monuments, operas and paintings became sites for working out political battles and nationalist themes. Risorgimento history formed a crucial part of the nationalist project of educating Italians to Italianness, second only to classical Roman history and Latin in shaping a sense of cultural tradition and grandeur. It was not only crisis or uncertainty that elevated Risorgimento icons. Emigration, and distance, were also crucial factors. Risorgimento heroes and myths flourished in places as far away as Argentina and Australia, consoling symbols of what the nation might have been, and creators of transnational patriotism. Even Pacific marine life was provided with its own Italian revolutionary in the shape of a fiery orange Garibaldi fish (*Hypsypops rubicundus*). To scholars of nationalist imagery, there is something irresistible in the warning, reprinted in a recent National Audubon Society guidebook, that 'Garibaldis are protected by law in California, and may not be taken for either sport or commercial purposes' (McConnaughey and McConnaughey 1985: 420).[12]

How, as scholars of politics and culture, are we to understand these historical reworkings? On the one hand, such a panoply of images could easily be read as a form of trivialization or fossilization – a Risorgimental 'heritage industry' of dubious taste or accuracy. The many images of the Risorgimento might thus be read as a peculiar form of political kitsch, with little relevance to national politics and movements. Indeed, faced with a multiplicity of competing histories and legends, scholars may be pushed in the direction of an uncritical or ironic relativism that threatens the possibility of any coherent national narrative.[13] In such cases, one risks not seeing the historical building for the social construction. On the other hand, revisiting images of the Sicilian Vespers and the Lombard league, of Dante and Garibaldi, may seem like a return to older nationalist, intellectual scholarly traditions, which stand accused of inflating the significance of high politics and culture in Italian nation-building at the expense of deeper, structural processes. As Lucy Riall has pointed out in her recent survey of Risorgimento writings, in the past twenty years or so, revisionist scholars have questioned the significance of the Risorgimento altogether, stripping it of some of the grand teleological and explanatory power it held for generations of Italianists. Scholars of nineteenth-century Italy have placed several traditional assumptions on their heads, 'endorsing an account of nationalism that sees it as a consequence, not a cause of nation-state formation,' and making the legitimacy or even relevance of the Risorgimento difficult to account for (Riall 1994: 65–6).

While its centrality as a turning point, or causal force in Italian political history has been rightly relativized, the Risorgimento's enduring role as a cultural icon, and as a framework for political and cultural debate, has yet to be thoroughly explored. In Riall's words, 'in order to deconstruct national myths, we have first to understand their meaning and impact,' including the 'emotional and political appeal' that people endow them with (Riall 1994: 82). This means taking them seriously, not as trivial inventions, or as religious truths, but as windows into contemporary arguments and assumptions about what the nation is, and what it should or could be. It also means broadening the concept of nationalism to include ideas and images that are not necessarily nationalist in origin, but that utilize nations and nationalism as vectors for other more prosaic and not necessarily nationalist goals, from philosophical or artistic reflection, to the waging of cultural rivalries, to self-advancement. Asking how and why symbols and strategies are used, by whom, and for whose good, is crucial to unpacking monolithic and linear accounts of nation-building, and for understanding the sources of conflict and change. As Adrian Lyttelton argues in Chapter One, 'the way in which the national past is reconstructed is not a matter of political or cultural indifference. It is the terrain of a vigorous contest between rival groups, and the outcome of this contest is important for the direction taken by national culture. . . . If we allow that there is no single objectively valid perspective from which national history can be viewed, then the plurality of interpretations and their ideological significance does not imply that they are arbitrary, but rather that they are important' **(see p. 29)**. It is this plurality, and this importance, that we seek to address in the pages that follow.

Outline of the Volume

The volume is composed of ten chapters. The collection proper opens and closes with individual discussions that mark the historical boundaries of our inquiry – the post-Napoleonic and post-cold war eras in Italy, respectively – and define many of the issues central to that inquiry. Between them lie two major sections dedicated, respectively, to the nineteenth and the twentieth centuries.

In our first section Adrian Lyttelton – the great historian of modern Italy – studies major trends in the 'cultural politics' of the period leading up to unification. Lyttelton describes how selective reinscriptions of episodes from earlier Italian history and culture were made into polemical vehicles for a wide range of nationalist visions. He looks in particular at the nationalist interpretations of the Sicilian Vespers, the Lombard League and other memorable episodes from Italian peninsular history as they are represented in the works of historians, novelists and, above all, painters. This discussion gives clear definition to the volume's overall concern with the intersection between political history and cultural artifact, around the central question of national identity.

The next section, 'Whose Italy?,' focuses on the period extending from shortly before the formation of the Italian state to the crisis point of World War I, when the first great 'remaking' of the nation took place. Though the four chapters in this section have distinct interests and foci, they all bring out significant disparities between the 'official story' of Risorgimental nation-building as retrospectively told and retold by an official culture (particularly by the new national educational system), and the diverse and divergent experiences of individuals and classes of people. In the chapters by Ciccarelli and Smart this takes the form of probing beyond the clichés that have been used since shortly after the foundation of the Italian state to suggest a seamless convergence between canonical figures from the aesthetic realm (Dante and Verdi) and the new political order. Moe and Re in their chapters similarly challenge the ideologically-charged assumption that state-formation took place through an untroubled cultural assimilation of disparate groups (regionally southern Italians; women) into a unified 'body politic.'

Andrea Ciccarelli's chapter is in many ways complementary to that of Lyttelton. He analyzes the 'politics of culture' by addressing a central, specifically literary topic: the polemical fortunes of Dante Alighieri. He starts with the early pre-Risorgimento, examining the cases of the four major 'Romantic' writers of Italy – Alfieri, Foscolo, Leopardi, Manzoni – who are variously credited with providing a strong repertory of images and narratives upon which the movement for national unification could draw. He then moves through the programmatic formation of an Italian national culture immediately after the events of 1859–70, looking at Francesco De Sanctis' placement of Dante in his politicized vision of peninsular literary history. Finally, he analyzes the attacks made in the period just before World War I by Futurists and the cultural journalists of *La Voce* on the stultifyingly past-oriented official cultural of national Italy embodied in the cult of 'Dantism.' Ciccarelli offers a twofold vision of how the literary past was used for present political purposes: as a canonical panorama of monuments in honor of the status quo, but also as a dynamic model for imagining and creating the future.

Mary Ann Smart's chapter addresses perhaps the best known example of Risorgimento 'cultural politics': the myth of Giuseppe Verdi's supposed representation of nationalist sentiments in the aria 'Va pensiero' from *Nabucco* and in other choral outpourings from his early operas. Smart persuasively demystifies the schematic equation of Verdi with the Risorgimento. At the same time, she reopens the question of the political-social significance of Verdi's operas in a more complex, less individualized or 'heroic,' vein. Specifically, she separates the mythical Verdi who came, like Manzoni, to personify the New Italy after unification from the working composer who both engaged and disengaged from the nationalist project in the period leading up to the founding of the state. Smart is also concerned with how an Italian culture of revolution and incipient national identity can be linked to – and divided from – the paradigmatic case of revolutionary France. The differences between France and Italy, Smart argues, can be located mainly in the roles accorded to female characters as emblems of patriotism in opera.

The next chapter, by Nelson Moe, moves us up into the very heart of the political Risorgimento, the period when the newly constituted nation-state, which initially included only the north and central portions of the peninsula (minus Venice and Rome), was in the process of deciding to annex the south. Moe goes behind the scenes into the private corresp-ondence and secret diplomatic documents of the 'piemontesi,' including Cavour himself, to reveal the violent tensions that lay beyond the process of assimilation, analyzing inter alia the discourses of disease and racial difference which divided two large areas of 'Italy' imaginatively even as they were being forced into literal union. Moe thus focuses attention on the fate of the southern regions, whose earlier history was quite distinct from that of the rest of the peninsula, and whose differences, perceived and/or actual, have continued to the present day to pose a challenge, and a threat, to the Italian state (seen most notably, though not exclusively, in the emergence of the 'Northern League' in the late 1980s and early 1990s). Specifically, Moe examines the political rhetoric and governmental practices by which southern Italy was cast as deviant by the ruling elite of the new Italian state. He depicts national unification as a process of uneven development and unequal incorporation, with strongly racialized and even colonial overtones. Rather than serving a unifying function, he argues, the attempts to define a generalized 'Italianness' proved to be an exclusionary and hierarchical process that pathologized internal differences.

Finally, in the last chapter of this section, Lucia Re focuses attention on women writers and intellectuals who were at once included and excluded from the new Italian state, and who struggled to define a space for their own cultural activities within its often very limiting confines. Re shows how representations of women, particularly pictorial and literary, helped place them in problematic relation to the instruments of culture and education by which the New Italy sought to define and impose itself. She gives particular prominence to the material and symbolic obstacles that stood between women and the prestigious public role of 'author,' stressing in particular the frequent recourse (by men, but also by women) to opposed categories of (male) intellect and (female) 'passion,' which, she argues, perpetuate exclusionary practices. Re closes by considering how women writers, especially Matilde Serao and Sibilla Aleramo, sought to break with, and insert themselves into, the masculine model of literary and cultural production in the early part of the twentieth century. Using gender analysis to challenge conventional wisdom about the democratizing role of education and literacy promoted by the Italian state, she persuasively demonstrates the ways that restrictions on women's writing served the elite, and largely masculine, project of establishing control over a new nation.

The second major section, 'Remaking the Risorgimento,' also contains four chapters, each of which studies some aspect of the diverse ways in which Risorgimental concerns and imagery have been appropriated during the twentieth century in the name of reviving, dismantling and/or reconfiguring the ideal Italian entity which so evidently failed to come into being between 1859 and 1870. Three of these – by Dainotto, Fogu and Forgacs – dwell on the complex fascist manipulations of the Risorgimento and its protagonists. Two – by Forgacs, again, and Marcus – study filmic examples of post-World War II efforts to overcome the fascist legacy and refound 'Italy' through yet another appropriative return to the myths of resurgence.

Claudio Fogu focuses on official, institutional representations of the period of initial unification, in particular during the celebration in 1932 of the fiftieth anniversary of the death of Garibaldi. Through a close reading of visual sources – commemorative statuary and celebratory parades – as well as official speeches by *Il Duce*, he explores how the Fascist regime sought to legitimate itself as the heir of Garibaldi and the Risorgimental revolution, while presenting itself as the basis for a future nationalist project that would break with the failures of the pre-fascist Liberal state. His chapter closes with an important meditation on the distinction proposed by Mussolini himself between the 'historical' (passive and nostalgic 're-presentations' of the past) and the 'historic' (dynamic and future-oriented shaping of history). Fogu thus calls attention to a basic tension internal to the very notion of a 'cultural politics' as deployed by the 'unifiers' of Italy and their heirs, fascist and otherwise. He throws into generalized relief the dialectic, adumbrated by Lyttelton and Ciccarelli, through which cultural imagery becomes the vehicle for defining the impossible relation between past and future 'Italies.'

Roberto Dainotto's chapter studies the writings of Giovanni Gentile – the preeminent philosopher and ideologue of the Fascist regime – to suggest how the idea of a Risorgimental 'making new' was inextricably linked to the notion of *tramonto* (sunset). This concept can be seen as an implicit rebuke to the Mussolinian opposition discussed in the preceding chapter, since it implies that the 'historical' and the 'historic' are inevitably, even tragically, joined. For Gentile, the metaphor of resurgence and rebirth is saturated by a sense of inevitable loss, and betokens a cyclical process through which national identity emerges, is eclipsed and must then be renewed. Dainotto's study brings to light issues of regional vs national identity also raised by Moe, reconceiving an apparent opposition as a dynamic reciprocity. In Gentile's thought, as Dainotto understands it, Italian nation-building was doubly predicated on a model of local, regional identity and on the suppression of such identities. (The *tramonto* of Sicily is the precondition for the birth of 'Italy,' even as, in some sense, Sicily represents an ideal toward which Italy might strive.) Thus the Fascist Gentile nonetheless anticipates an accommodation of national to regional identities particularly relevant in our own times, when regionalist-separatist voices (especially that of the 'Northern League') are making themselves heard again in the Italian peninsula.

The chapters by David Forgacs and Millicent Marcus focus on filmic interpretations and appropriations of the Risorgimento from Fascism into the postwar period. Forgacs begins by considering fascist-era films which depicted Risorgimento themes in a way that glorified the contributions of Mussolini's regime. In this sense he, like Fogu, is concerned with fascist appropriations of Garibaldi and other icons of national identity. Forgacs, however, then draws upon Ernesto LaClau's notion of ideological 'articulation' to confront the thorny question of how these films, along with their directors, were 'recycled' in the postwar period. In the first instance, this chapter suggests that, just as fascist filmmakers critiqued and 'remade' the Risorgimento, so postwar, anti-fascist intellectuals (whether 'republican' or 'communist') appropriated and reforged Risorgimental images for their own apparently very different purposes. More crucially, he puts in relief the perplexing fact that despite those ideological differences, the images and the strategies deployed in pre- and postwar appropriations of the Risorgimento are not only similar but – in specific (and symptomatic) cases – identical.

By contrast, Millicent Marcus sees director Luchino Visconti's Risorgimento epic, *Senso*, as offering an analysis of the failures of national unification which differs decidedly from the fascist version of that history. In the original nineteenth-century novella of Boito, *Senso* was an apolitical story of destructive love. But in Visconti's cinematic treatment it becomes an indictment of an aristocratic governing class unable to put aside its private desires for the greater good of the nation. Visconti, Marcus argues, was drawing on a specifically Marxist understanding of the Risorgimento as the exclusionary triumph of an elite, a position articulated (from the prisons of the Fascist regime and in direct opposition to it) by Gramsci. In this interpretation, *Senso* becomes a vehicle for contesting the postwar, Christian Democratic 'remaking' of Italy from a Marxist perspective. Marcus's reading of Visconti's reading of a nineteenth-century novella could be seen as emblematic of the process and the problem this volume addresses throughout. She directly addresses the reciprocal shaping of politics by culture and culture by politics in an open-ended series of revisionary 'pentimenti' or refigurations. By the same token, the overt conflict between private desires and public duties in *Senso* clearly points to a perennial dilemma of Italian political culture, indicating the ties that bind and the fractures that separate the world of artistic representations from the political-social order.

The volume's closing chapter is presented from a contemporary perspective, one that is keenly aware of the latest attempts to reconstitute 'Italy' once again and of the forces – regionalist and other – which contest them. Silvana Patriarca traces a history which connects nineteenth-century discourses – for instance that of Vincenzo Gioberti – about the failings of a specifically Italian 'character' to a spate of recent books and essays treating Italian identity from an apparently more sophisticated perspective, and under the pressures of the post-cold war resurgence of nationalism. However, while acknowledging the importance of the newer contributions, and above all of Giulio Bollati's long, influential essay on 'L'Italiano' (The Italian), Patriarca reveals how a late twentieth-century focus on national identity remained rooted in essentializing discourses of 'character.' She draws particular attention to the recurrent theme of Italy's failure to seek and to achieve 'modernity,' and shows how poorly such claims accord with basic social-historical realities.

By focusing on the problem of identity, a concept around which political and cultural forms of *italianità* most explicitly converge and clash, Patriarca's discussion invites us to reconsider the terms and the stakes involved in the recurrent, obsessive return to the desire for a putative national Risorgimento and for a 'modernity' that will not lose contact with a meaningful historical past. Patriarca's authors' drive to 'recapture' the Risorgimento is, after all, not that different from Francesco Hayez's painterly return to the Sicilian Vespers, as described by Lyttelton. Each of the chapters in this volume confronts this process of simultaneously inventing and overcoming the past in the name of re-claiming an original, essentially utopian 'Italian' identity (or character). The process, they reveal, is a common tie which binds together figures whose ideological investments are as diverse as those of Manzoni, Mazzini, Cavour, Garibaldi, Gentile, Croce, Gramsci, Visconti, Bossi and Bollati. Indeed, the ongoing contest to assert that the 'true' Risorgimento conforms to one's own vision to the exclusion of all others is what guarantees that 'Italy' will never be 'made' in any definitive or conclusive way. But, seen from another perspective, it is precisely this perennial affirming and contesting – making, unmaking, remaking – of a forever resurgent 'Italy' that constitutes the dynamic matrix of a modern nation-state.

Notes

1. There is a vast amount of scholarship on this topic. A useful companion to this volume, which ably reviews historiographical trends and debates in the field, is Riall 1994. See also E. Gentile 1997, Levy 1996 and Levra 1992.

2. One relevant area which has not been treated extensively, but which deserves significant attention, is the place of the Catholic Church in the cultural politics of 'Risorgimento.' This includes such pivotal factors and events as Pio IX's ambivalence early in the process of unification; the papal stance, from 1871 on, against Catholic participation in the political life of the new Italian state; the Lateran pacts of 1929; the continuing alliance of Church and State after World War II; and so on. It also embraces the direct polemical interventions of the Church and its cultural and political affiliates in nationalist and then national politics, as well as the responses to such interventions from a range of alternative lay positions. More generally, one should note the pervasive and complex presence of the language, categories and cultural practices of Catholicism in the discursive articulations of national identity (e.g. the 'resurrectional' motif buried in the metaphor of Risorgimento itself). These issues are touched upon in our collection (and particularly by Adrian Lyttelton in Chapter One) but we have been unable to give them the kind of attention they so clearly deserve.

3. Patriarca's Chapter Ten in this volume enumerates and discusses a number of these works, including Rusconi 1993, Lepre 1994, Ottone 1995 and Galli della Loggia 1998. Also notable is Romano 1994.

4. Recent work dealing with the power of cultural and scientific elites include Patriarca 1996, Stone 1998 and Adamson 1993. The uses of anthropology and oral history to revise notions of state-building and consensus are best exemplified in Doumanis 1997, Passerini 1987 and Kertzer 1980.

5. These issues were taken up in such classic and controversial works as Gerschenkeron 1962 and Banfield 1958. Newly refurbished claims about southern involution are presented in Putnam 1993.

6. Discussions of the nationalist and separatist dilemmas in the former Yugoslavia can be found in Denitch 1994, Glenny 1996 and Wachtel 1998.

7. Classic comparative works include Anderson 1983, Hobsbawm and Ranger 1983 and Gellner 1983. The insights provided in several other comparative works are also illuminating for the Italian case. See Eley and Suny 1996, Joseph and Nugent 1994, Brubaker 1996 and Hobsbawm 1990.

8. Renan's much-cited address on the subject was delivered at the Sorbonne in March 1882.

9. For revealing treatments of the cultural politics of nationalism in southeastern Europe and the Balkans, see Karakasidou 1997 and Wachtel 1998.

10. The remark is directed at commemorations of the American and French revolutions, whose complexities are reviewed by Gillis in his 1994 essay.
11. The *Sonderweg* ('Special Path') debate was an explosive political and academic discussion over the nature of Germany's nineteenth-century bourgeois revolution and its implications for subsequent German political development. Useful introductions to this topic include Blackbourn and Eley 1984 and Maier 1988.
12. Our thanks go to marine biologist Dr. Gianna Casazza for the reference.
13. For the dangers and rewards of studying popular nationalist culture, see Lowenthal 1998 and Buruma 1999. Useful works on nationalism and commemoration include Hobsbawm 1983 and Gillis 1994. For the Italian case, see Isnenghi 1996, 1997a, 1997b; Labanca 1992.

References

Adamson, W. (1993), *Avant-Garde Florence: From Modernism to Fascism*, Cambridge, MA: Harvard University Press.

Agnew, J. (1997), 'The Myth of Backward Italy in Modern Europe,' in B. Allen and M. Russo, eds, *Revisioning Italy: National Identity and Global Culture*, Minneapolis: University of Minnesota Press, pp. 23–42.

Allen, B. and M. Russo, eds (1997), *Revisioning Italy: National Identity and Global Culture*, Minneapolis: University of Minnesota Press.

Anderson, B. (1983), *Imagined Communities: Reflections on the Origin and Spread of Nationalism*, London: Verso.

Banfield, E.C. (1958), *The Moral Bases of a Backward Society*, New York: The Free Press.

Berezin, M. (1997), *Making the Fascist Self: The Political Culture of Interwar Italy*, Ithaca: Cornell University Press.

Blackbourn, D., and G. Eley (1984), *The Peculiarities of German History: Bourgeois Society and Politics in Nineteenth-Century Germany*, Oxford: Oxford University Press.

Bosworth, R.J.B. and P. Dogliani, eds (1999), *Italian Fascism: History, Memory and Representation,* London and New York: MacMillan and St. Martin's Press.

Brubaker, R. (1996), *Nationalism Reframed: Nationhood and the National Question in the New Europe*, Cambridge: Cambridge University Press.

Buruma, I. (1999), 'The Joys and Perils of Victimhood,' *New York Review of Books*, April 8: 4–9.

Davis, J.A. (1994), 'Remapping Italy's Path to the Twentieth Century,' *Journal of Modern History* 66 (2): 291–320.

Del Boca, A., ed. (1991), *Le guerre coloniali del fascismo*, Bari: Laterza.

Denitch, B. (1994), *Ethnic Nationalism: The Tragic Death of Yugoslavia*, Minneapolis: University of Minnesota Press.

Doumanis, N. (1997), *Myth and Memory in the Mediterranean: Remembering Fascism's Empire*, London and New York: MacMillan and St. Martin's Press.

Eley, G. and R.G. Suny, eds (1996), *Becoming National: A Reader*, Oxford: Oxford University Press.

Falasca-Zamponi, S. (1997), *Fascist Spectacle: The Aesthetics of Power in Mussolini's Italy*, Berkeley and Los Angeles: University of California Press.

Forgacs, D. and R. Lumley, eds (1996), *Italian Cultural Studies: An Introduction,* Cambridge: Cambridge University Press.

Galli della Loggia, E. (1998), *L'identità italiana,* Bologna: Il Mulino.

Gambi, L. (1994), 'Geography and Imperialism in Italy: From the Unity of the Nation to the "New" Roman Empire,' in A. Godlewska and N. Smith, eds, *Geography and Empire*, Oxford: Blackwell, pp. 74–91.

Gellner, E. (1983), *Nations and Nationalism*, Oxford: Blackwell.

Gentile, E. (1993), *Il culto del littorio*, Bari: Laterza.

—— (1997), *La grande Italia: Ascesa e declino del mito della nazione nel ventesimo secolo*, Milan: Mondadori.

Gerschenkeron, A. (1962), *Economic Backwardness in Historical Perspective*, Cambridge, MA: Harvard University Press.

Gillis, J.R. (1994), 'Memory and Identity: the History of a Relationship,' in J.R. Gillis, ed., *Commemorations: The Politics of National Identity*, Princeton: Princeton University Press, pp. 3–24.

Glenny, M. (1996), *The Fall of Yugoslavia: The Third Balkan War,* New York: Penguin.

Hobsbawm, E. (1983), 'Mass Producing Traditions: Europe 1870–1914,' in E. Hobsbawm and T. Ranger, eds, *The Invention of Tradition*, Cambridge: Cambridge University Press, pp. 263–307.

—— (1990), *Nations and Nationalism since 1780: Programme, Myth, Reality,* Cambridge: Cambridge University Press.

—— and T. Ranger, eds (1983), *The Invention of Tradition,* Cambridge: Cambridge University Press.

Isnenghi, M., ed. (1994), *L'Italia in piazza: I luoghi della vita pubblica dal 1848 ai giorni nostri,* Milan: Mondadori.

——, ed. (1996), *I luoghi della memoria: Simboli e miti dell'Italia unita,* Bari: Laterza.

——, ed. (1997a), *I luoghi della memoria: Personaggi e date dell'Italia unita*, Bari: Laterza.

——, ed. (1997b), *I luoghi della memoria: Strutture ed eventi dell'Italia unita*, Bari: Laterza.

Joseph, G.M. and D. Nugent, eds (1994), *Everyday Forms of State Formation: Revolution and the Negotiation of Rule in Modern Mexico*, Durham, NC: Duke University Press.

Karakasidou, A.N. (1997), *Fields of Wheat, Hills of Blood: Passages to Nationhood in Greek Macedonia 1870–1990*, Chicago: University of Chicago Press.

Kertzer, D. (1980), *Comrades and Christians: Religion and Political Struggle in Communist Italy*, Cambridge: Cambridge University Press.

Labanca, N. (1992), *L'Africa in vetrina: Storie di musei e di esposizioni coloniali in Italia,* Treviso: Pagus Edizioni.

Lepre, A. (1994), *Italia addio? Unità e disunità dal 1860 a oggi*, Milan: Mondadori.

Levra, U. (1992), *Fare gli italiani: Memoria e celebrazione del Risorgimento*, Turin: Comitato di Torino dell'Istituto per la storia del Risorgimento.

Levy, C., ed. (1996), *Italian Regionalism: History, Identity and Politics*, Oxford: Berg.

Lowenthal, D. (1998), *The Heritage Crusade and the Spoils of History*, Cambridge: Cambridge University Press.

Lyttelton, A. (1991), 'A New Past for the Mezzogiorno: New Approaches to the History of Southern Italy,' *Times Literary Supplement*, 4 October: 14–15.

—— (1996), 'Shifting Identities: Nation, Region and the City,' in C. Levy, ed., *Italian Regionalism: History, Identity and Politics*, Oxford: Berg, pp. 33–53.

Maier, C.S. (1988), *The Unmasterable Past: History, Holocaust, and German National Identity*, Cambridge, MA: Harvard University Press.

McConnaughey, B.H., and E. McConnaughey (1985), *National Audubon Society Nature Guides, Pacific Coast,* New York: Alfred A. Knopf.

Ottone, P. (1995), *L'Italia è un paese civile?*, Milan: Mondadori.

Passerini, L. (1987), *Fascism in Popular Memory: The Cultural Experience of the Turin Working Class,* Cambridge: Cambridge University Press.

Patriarca, S. (1996), *Numbers and Nationhood: Writing Statistics in Nineteenth-Century Italy*, Cambridge: Cambridge University Press.

Petrusewicz, M. (1998), 'Before the Southern Question: "Native" Ideas on Backwardness and Remedies in the Kingdom of the Two Sicilies,

1815–1849,' in J. Schneider, ed., *Italy's 'Southern Question': Orientalism in One Country*, Oxford: Berg, pp. 27–50.

Porciani, I. (1997), *La festa della nazione. Rappresentazione dello stato e spazi sociali nell'Italia unita,* Bologna: Il Mulino.

Putnam, R. (1993), *Making Democracy Work: Civic Traditions in Modern Italy,* Princeton: Princeton University Press.

Renan, E. (1990 [1882]), 'What is a Nation?', rpt. in H.K. Bhabha, ed., *Nation and Narration*, London: Routledge, pp. 8–22.

Riall, L. (1994), *The Italian Risorgimento: State, Society and National Unification,* London: Routledge.

Romano, S. (1994), *Finis Italiae. Declino e morte dell'ideologia risorgimentale: Perché gli italiani si disprezzano*, Milan: Vanni Schweiller.

Rusconi, G.E. (1993), *Se cessiamo di essere una nazione*, Bologna: Il Mulino.

Schneider, J., ed. (1998), *Italy's 'Southern Question': Orientalism in One Country,* Oxford: Berg.

Stone, M. (1998), *The Patron State: Culture and Politics in Fascist Italy,* Princeton: Princeton University Press.

Wachtel, A.B. (1998), *Making a Nation, Breaking a Nation: Literature and Cultural Politics in Yugoslavia*, Stanford: Stanford University Press.

Part I
Refiguring the Past

1

Creating a National Past: History, Myth and Image in the Risorgimento
Adrian Lyttelton

Why do nations need a history? Any form of identity requires memory. To make the answer more historically precise, I think one can say that the need to create a national identity out of the materials furnished by the records of the past arises out of the crisis of earlier forms of collective memory. Secularization and the decline of 'sacred history' as a way of interpreting the world are one part of the story. This does not mean that religion cannot be conceived to be an essential constituent of national identity. Another aspect (equally the product of the Enlightenment) is the demand for a new 'civil history' which would not be that of kings, rulers and battles but of peoples, or societies, and their culture. Specifically, in the Italian case, the Napoleonic cyclone shook the foundations of belief in the old territorial states. Particularly important was the final extinction of the republican tradition, with the end of Venetian and Genoese independence. Not, of course, that local, 'municipal' identity and the *piccola patria* ceased to be important. Indeed all the evidence suggests that, in one form or another, they remained the primary focus of loyalty for most inhabitants of the Italian peninsula. But their adequacy as a basis for political identity had been undermined. Nor should one imagine that the larger and more viable territorial states – Piedmont, Naples, even Tuscany – could no longer provide a framework for political action. Still, even in these states, dynastic continuities were decisively challenged by the new conceptions of citizenship and political community diffused by the French Revolution.

What history can nations use, or choose? Some theorists of nationalism have suggested that it does not much matter. In his brilliant treatise on *Nations and Nationalism*, Ernest Gellner admits that nationalism uses 'the pre-existing, historically inherited proliferation of cultures or cultural wealth, though it uses them very selectively, and it most often transforms them radically' (Gellner 1983: 55). However, he goes on to add that: 'The cultural shreds and patches used by nationalism are often arbitrary historical inventions. *Any old shred and patch would have served as well'* (ibid.: 56; emphasis mine). This deliberately provocative assertion of Gellner's cannot fail to disquiet the historian. This chapter, while not contesting the first half of Gellner's statement, will argue that it *does* matter what 'shreds and patches' are available and how they are used to stitch together the national cloth.

There are two aspects of Gellner's argument that need consideration. In the first place, he admits that nationalist writers must choose from a repertoire which has already been shaped by tradition. This tradition already has a shape to it, which nationalists have to respect, even if and when they try to transform its significance. For example, the historic conflict between imperial Rome and the barbarians could not be viewed in the same way in Italy and Germany. Thus I would argue that the 'invention of tradition' (Hobsbawm and Ranger 1983) is typically a process of filling in the gaps in the record, and of meeting already existing expectations.[1] Some 'inventions' are more persuasive than others, and audiences often prefer to hear what they already know, or suspect. If, in fact, there is a sense in which the national past of 'Italy' can be said to have been truly 'invented,' it consists in the translation of events and personages from a local to a peninsular context. I would still prefer the term 'construction,' however, because the materials were not new, only the uses to which they were put.

Obviously, the new 'national' interpretation of such materials was a source of anachronism. It might be argued that this anachronism was a more or less serious distortion of understanding according to the extent to which national history served as the vehicle for other values, such as liberty and economic progress, and avoided a unilateral obsession with the themes of unity and independence. To be specific: in Italy during the Risorgimento, the critical public for national propagandists was that of the educated middle classes; although democrats recognized the need to reach out to the masses, even for them the first priority had to be to constitute the cadres of the national movement from among those whose education already predisposed them to receive the national message favorably. In fact, conscious attempts to produce a national history for the masses became important only after unification had been achieved. In the Risorgimento, national myth-makers, therefore, were not addressing a passive or uncritical audience, and this imposed some limits on invention. Gellner thus asserts too radical a disjunction between modern nationalism and previous national development. As another leading student of nationalism, Miroslav Hroch, has written, '*the nation-forming process is a distinctively older phenomenon than the modern nation and nationalism* [Hroch's italics]: any interpretation of modern national identity cannot ignore the peculiarities of pre-modern national development, or degrade it to the level of a mere myth' (Hroch 1998: 74; see also Smith 1991: 71–2).

In the second place, the way in which the national past is reconstructed is not a matter of political or cultural indifference. It is the terrain of a vigorous contest between rival groups, and the outcome of this contest is important for the direction taken by national culture. It matters whether parliament, the monarchy, the city or the folk community is cast as the protagonist of the story. If we allow that there is no single objectively valid perspective from which national history can be viewed, then the plurality of interpretations and their ideological significance does not imply that they are arbitrary, but rather that they are important. The attention which historians (and even, in this period, writers and artists) attached to 'knowing the facts,' even if often partial and naive, is a sign that establishing the truth of the historical record was typically seen at least as a necessary prelude to conveying the desired national message. There was a common assumption that historical knowledge was a good in itself, because it involved rescuing the nation's memories from oblivion. Naturally, I would not like to deny that current political conflicts and circumstances often determined the success of interpretations of the past. As I will show more amply later on, it was the failure of the 1848 revolutions in Italy which determined the passage from a hegemonic narrative centered on the city to one centered on the monarchy. But successful narratives do not spring from nothing, and unsuccessful narratives do not simply disappear. If we pay attention to the continuities of historical culture as well as to its ruptures, then the persistence of themes and motifs will come into view.

How do these broad issues apply to the case of the Italian Risorgimento? My first concern will be to show how the romantic revolt against classicism introduced a new way of looking at the past, new conventions of representation, and a new, positive evaluation of the Middle Ages. I shall go on to explain how the new concern with continuity and the search for national origins generated controversy over what could be regarded as the true turning points in ancient and medieval history, and what their significance was. In the first instance, if Roman history lost its unique privileged status as a treasure house of examples and precepts, the fall of the Roman Empire before the barbarians and, to a lesser degree, the rise of Roman dominion over Italy were still critical for defining the sense of a national history.

Another focal historical controversy was the conflict between 'neo-Guelph' defenders of the role of the Papacy in Italian history, and 'neo-Ghibellines' who identified with its enemies. This controversy in turn gave rise to another, intermediate position, always influential, which held that both Guelphs and Ghibellines had exemplified the unfortunate tendency of the Italians to divide themselves into warring factions. These divisions had contemporary political correlates in, on the one hand, the Church's troubled relationship to the national movement and, on the other, the Piedmontese monarchy's claims to rise above traditional peninsular factionalism.[2]

The question of factionalism reminds us that the central difficulty in constructing a national past in Italy lay in the existence of many separate regional or municipal histories. As in all national histories, however, the struggle against the foreign invader inevitably held a central place, and episodes in which Italians had successfully rebelled against foreign dominion provided the focus for national history and mythology. I will focus on two individual cases of national construction based on materials drawn from the medieval period: the Lombard League of the late twelfth century against the German Emperor Frederick Barbarossa; and the revolt of the Sicilian Vespers against French rule a hundred years later. Both illustrate particularly well the transformation of regional history into national history.

At the same time, because the national movement conceived itself as fighting for liberty as well as independence, even the resistance to domestic tyranny took on positive significance. The strong civic and republican tradition in the medieval and Renaissance city-states of central and northern Italy was, of course, of particular value to democrats. But even those who were firmly convinced of the necessity of a constitutional monarchy in the present could be proud of the city-states' contribution to European civilization and the rise of the bourgeoisie. This was all the more true since foreign historians and writers took the lead in a new interpretation of the Italian civic efflorescence, which situated it as a decisive moment in the development of European society. For instance, as I will explain more fully below, the final overthrow of the Florentine Republic in 1530, even if it led to the rule of the domestic dynasty of the Medici, could still be treated as a paradigmatic case of the heroic if unsuccessful fight for independence, since the conquest was achieved by a Spanish and Imperial army, and was generally viewed as the last act in the drama of Italy's loss of liberty and independence during the Renaissance.

In its choice of materials for study, this chapter is not concerned only or even primarily with the history of Italian nationality as it was depicted by contemporary historians, for in the diffusion of a sense of the national past, historical novels and drama, paintings, and opera played a major role. They reached a much larger audience than did the historians, and they were primarily responsible for creating a mood of passionate participation in which patriots looked to the distant past to inspire action in the present. Themes and motifs circulated between the different media, in response both to political concerns and cultural fashions. I lay particular emphasis on historical painting, because the generally negative aesthetic judgement that has been passed upon it has tended to obscure its importance as a medium for arousing public interest.[3] More precisely, after generally considering the role of romantic culture in the choice and elaboration of nationalist themes in the early nineteenth century, I will turn to the literary, artistic and other examples mentioned above.

The Roots of Romantic Nationalism

Recent Italian historiography has made great efforts to remedy the previous neglect of the problems of nation-building and national identity (see esp. Lanaro 1988; Spadolini 1994; Soldani and Turi 1993; Gentile 1997; Tobia 1991; Levra 1992; Porciani 1997). But this literature has concentrated almost exclusively on the period after 1861. In a recent discussion, Umberto Levra issued a timely reminder that 'making,' or 'inventing' Italians was a process which did not begin with unification. He suggests that the period of the Risorgimento should be looked at not only as the story of the achievement of political independence and unification, but 'from the perspective of the invention of a common tradition, of the aggregation of images in order to represent the identity of Italy as a nation' (1994: 23).

We all know that the problem in Italy was a particularly hard one. Even by comparison with such aspiring nations as Germany, Poland or Hungary, Italy was handicapped by a lack of unifying political institutions in the past. There was no national tradition of sacred monarchy.[4] Only ancient Rome was a possible point of reference. But the Roman tradition was both too local and too universal to serve as a satisfactory foundation for national identity, although the relationship of national history to Roman history remained a key problem.[5]

In this search for tradition, romantic historical culture was to play a crucial role. Romanticism was undoubtedly part of a wider European phenomenon. The European romantic movement posed a new problem for Italian culture and for patriotic self-definition. Mme de Staël's call to look to the north, to Germany and Britain, to revive a sterile tradition with 'new colors' and 'alien beauties' served as a catalyst (Bellorini 1943: 4–9; see also Thom 1995: 273). Italian intellectuals discovered Shakespeare, Schiller and Goethe. But its Italian forms were also the specific product of a situation in which direct political action was difficult or impossible, and yet sufficient tolerance existed for cultural analogs of such action to be expressed. This romantic nationalism was most vigorous in the 1820s. After the new revolutionary failures in 1831, the use of cultural analogs became more difficult.[6] Political disillusionment stemming from the repeated failures of national and liberal rebellions and conspiracies contributed to a change of mood. So did aesthetic criticism of the superficiality of the romantic fascination with the details of the past. Yet the decline was only relative, and the years leading up to the 1848 revolution marked a new upsurge of historical interest.[7]

Some Italian patriots indignantly rejected romanticism as a northern innovation, on the grounds that the prestige of German culture might seem to reinforce the restored Austrian hegemony, and insisted that Latin classicism was not only a universal but a national heritage. Yet the upshot of the great *querelle* of the 1820s between romantics and defenders of classicism made clear that these were not winning arguments. To those who suspected romanticism as a German innovation, it was easy to reply that the etymology of the word 'romantic' pointed back towards the romance languages and their importance in the production of new literary forms (Visconti 1943: 437). Perhaps more importantly, classicism was discredited by its association with the Napoleonic regime and with the heritage of the French Revolution. In both phases, the French had identified themselves as the heirs of the Romans. It was among the older generations that identified either with Napoleon or with the Jacobin revolutionary tradition that the cause of classicism was most vigorously upheld. For the romantics, instead, the Roman model, whether it appeared under the guise of Brutus or of the Imperial eagles, had played out its last act in the saga of the *grande nation*. Indeed, they argued, it was the consciousness of the French Revolution as an epochal change which rendered irredeemably obsolete the assumptions and the vocabulary of classical drama, even in the hands of a master like Vittorio Alfieri (Visconti 1943: 441–3).

The seduction of romanticism was partly that it was new and could be used as a metaphor for the revolt against established authority: but also that it underwrote the preoccupation with the search for the sources of the peculiarity of 'national genius.' On the one hand, in attempting to rival the vigorous romantic literature of Germany and England, Italians found an impetus for breaking the classical mold. On the other hand, along with the willingness to accept innovation and modernity, the romantic turn implied a rediscovery of the historical sources of national individuality. The Janus-faced nature of liberal romanticism, looking back to the Middle Ages and forward to the age of steam, corresponded with the similar ambivalence which was everywhere characteristic of nationalism.

The romantic turn from the ideal of Rome to the medieval origins of modern Italian identity gave new importance to the Catholic Church as a source of national coherence. The post-Napoleonic critique of Jacobinism, as exemplifying the destructive potential of secular, abstract reason, had brought with it a new appreciation of the historic role of Christianity. This should not be written off as a reactionary phenomenon, linked exclusively to the restoration of the old order in Church and State. It was equally true for liberals and even for those who, like Giuseppe Mazzini, thought that the time had come to transcend the existing forms of religious belief.[8] The Milanese liberals associated with the short-lived journal *Il Conciliatore,* led by the aristocrats Federico Confalonieri and Lodovico Di Breme, saw Christianity as an essential prerequisite for the progress of Europe, which, therefore, could not be adequately interpreted by classical schemata or represented in classical symbols.

Thus from a formal perspective as well, the eternal Italy of the classicists was seen as a mask for decay: according to the significant simile of Ermes Visconti 'classicism is dead and finished like the Venetian Republic' (Visconti 1943: 469). Cultural independence could no more be secured by adherence to ancient forms than political independence by loyalty to ancient institutions. This implied the search not only for new themes but for new conventions of representation: the course of history could not be confined by the unities of time and space of classical tragedy. Shakespeare had been able to deal with history in a way that Racine had not, and the great tragedian Alfieri had been less successful than Schiller in depicting the atmosphere of Philip II's court because he had been restricted by classical prescriptions.[9] Classical conventions of dignity and decorum, which reproduced the social hierarchy on the stage, were even more clearly obsolete. Whether in literature or art, secondary figures – attendants, soldiers, crowds – and accessories – costumes, furniture, weapons – were essential for the creation of the atmosphere of the epoch without which the true significance of events that took place *in history* could not be understood.

With this in mind, romantic critics – both of literature and of painting – argued for the dethronement of the hero or the central figure. Observance of the classical conventions of epic poetry, for example, would not allow the poet to give due emphasis to the popular and collective dimension of great historical events. The writer who wished to make a modern epic out of the First Crusade would not allow his attention to be monopolized by its noble leaders. Instead, he would focus on the actions of Peter the Hermit,[10] 'who, without wealth or power, by the sole authority of his character, excited populations and realms to the holy war, prepared it and forwarded it with a life combining the paladin and the popular leader *(capo popolo)*, the fanatic and the philanthropist' (Visconti 1943: 443).

The Case of Francesco Hayez

This recommendation was not addressed to painters; but it was surely not by chance that the most famous of Italian romantic painters, Francesco Hayez, chose Peter the Hermit as the theme of one of his most popular paintings, *Peter the Hermit Preaches the Crusade* (see figure 1.1), which had a great success with the Milanese public at the annual exhibition of the Brera Academy in 1829. A reviewer commented that the viewers

Figure 1.1 Francesco Hayez, *Pietro l'eremita predica la Crociata* (Peter the Hermit Preaches the Crusade; 1829)
Milan, Private Collection
Photo: L. Carrà, Milan

seemed as if they were listening to Peter themselves (Mazzocca 1994: 198; Pinto 1974: 138, 179–80). One of Hayez's best friends was the poet Tommaso Grossi, a leading figure in the romantic movement, and close to the writer Alessandro Manzoni. Grossi was the author of an epic poem on *I lombardi alla prima crociata,* published in 1826 and illustrated by Hayez in an important series of lithographs. As Hayez actually painted a first version of *Peter* in 1826, it is reasonable to suppose that Grossi's work was his main source of inspiration. However, the audaciously democratic conception of *Peter* was not repeated in the later works of Hayez on crusading themes. Peter is absent, too, from Verdi's operatic version of *I lombardi,* for which Temistocle Solera wrote the libretto.[11]

Hayez's painting was singled out for praise by Giuseppe Mazzini in an article on 'La peinture moderne en Italie' (Modern Italian Painting) published in 1840. He described Hayez as 'the leader of the school of historical painting, which national thought demanded in Italy,' an artist whose 'inspiration emanated directly from the people,' and who knew how to convey the social ideals of the epoch. 'The century gives him the "idea", and the idea the "form"' (Mazzini 1915: 293–4; English version in Mazzini 1841). He commended the setting of the scene in the Alps, which gave a sense of 'contact with the infinite' (ibid.: 301), a typically romantic view of landscape. The Alps had also become politically significant. In his novel of amorous and political suffering, *Le ultime lettere di Jacopo Ortis*, the poet Ugo Foscolo had invested them with patriotic meaning, as the guardian of Italy's natural frontiers. Mazzini compared Hayez's painting to one of the masterpieces of romantic drama for its portrayal of a rich variety of human groups: 'It is Schiller's *Wallenstein's Camp* under a more sublime banner.' He particularly singled out for praise the focus on the conflict between public duty and family affections, a key theme of the period (Mazzocca 1994: 196–8, 394). Above all, the painting conveyed 'the enthusiasm and conviction' of Peter (ibid.: 301–3). The dramatic unity of the whole was secured by the idea of the 'spirit of God which raises, like a wave, this immense European population to hurl it upon Asia' (Mazzini 1915: 303–4; see also Pinto 1974: 179–80).[12]

While an opponent of the Catholic Church in the present, Mazzini had a positive view of the function of medieval Christianity. He saw Peter, I think, as a precursor of his own mission, as one of the 'social apostles' of the new epoch, which was to be one of faith, but a secular and democratic faith. The genius-prophet, according to Mazzini, is characterized by 'rapid and energetic gestures,' and Hayez's Peter answers to this description (Mazzini 1976: 1.3).[13] The emphasis on Peter reveals a tension in the representation of national history. For all the new stress on secondary figures, a hero was still essential for full dramatic impact, in painting as well as in literature. But Peter was a new kind of hero, not an exemplar of timeless virtue and dignity, but the embodiment of the forces of a particular epoch. In Germany, too, images of the great popular preachers were considered by democrats to be particularly significant (Falkenhausen 1997: 193).

One must recognize that only a part of the vast production of historical painting, prose or poetry had a serious civic purpose or ideological motivation, in accord with the prescriptions of the Lombard romantics, or of Mazzini. The taste of the public imposed its own requirements. The fashion for historical scenes, and in particular the vogue for the immensely popular historical novels of Walter Scott, created new stereotypes and stock scenarios. Opera librettos,[14] historical novels and paintings had to provide entertainment as well as instruction, and this meant adhering to the new romantic conventions of plot and situation which could be as constraining in their way as the old classical formulas. As with twentieth-century historical movies, the inevitable question was: where's the love interest? Julian Budden writes of opera librettos: the historical hero 'always has a private, family reason for action as well as a patriotic one. This was an essential feature of the nineteenth-century melodramatic tradition, without which the audience's sympathy could not be guaranteed' (Budden 1978–81: 2.177).[15] And even novels which *did* have a serious political purpose often sacrificed clarity and cogency to the complications of thwarted love and mysterious intrigue.

In all the genres, but perhaps particularly in painting, the conflict between public duty and love or family affection was a typical structuring device. Although the sacrifice of personal affections to public duty was an ancient trope in the representation of virtue, the theme assumed a new salience with the growth of the sentimental cult of the family. There was a shift of emphasis. For the classical tradition, suppression of domestic attachments was an unequivocal sign of austere and disinterested virtue. But according to the new romantic ideology, virtue had to be grounded in feeling, and love of family was a necessary foundation for love of country. So the clash between the two took on a new poignancy. We can see this in another picture by Hayez, with a lengthy explanatory title: 'Pietro Rossi, lord of Parma . . . invited to assume the command of the Venetian army . . . is begged with tears by his wife and daughters not to accept the enterprise' (1818–20 [see figure 1.2]). Hayez asserted that the idea of painting this obscure episode in fifteenth-century history came to him from reading Sismondi's *History of the Medieval Italian Republics,*[16]

Figure 1.2 Francesco Hayez, *Pietro Rossi* (1818–20)
Milan, Pinacoteca di Brera
Photo: Archivio Fotografico Sopraintendenza B.A.S. Milano
Courtesy of the Ministero per i Beni e le Attività Culturali

although the actual scene depicted is taken from a different source. On Hayez's bookshelves, the place of works on classical mythology was taken by histories, chronicles and treatises on medieval and Renaissance costumes, furniture and armor. In spite of the obscurity of the episode in fifteenth-century history which it depicted, *Pietro Rossi* was the painting which really launched the romantic historical movement in Italian art (Haskell 1978: 4–5). It was praised both for its sentimental pathos and for its break with academic conventions in the posture of the figures, which required the spectator to make an imaginative effort in order to read their physiognomy.

'History painting,' once dominated by classical themes and references, had been renewed from the later eighteenth century on by painters who represented events and heroes taken from national history or literature in appropriate costume and settings. However, Italy had lagged behind in this development. Hayez was Venetian by birth, and his early style drew on the great Venetian masters of the Renaissance; their use of color and their realism were seen as antidotes to an idealized, frigid, linear classicism. Since the seventeenth century, the Venetian assertion of the primacy of color over *disegno* had been associated with liberty and unorthodoxy. But, ironically, in Hayez's day Venetian taste was too conservative to accept his innovations in style and content. Milan, economically and politically dynamic, and the center of literary romanticism, was much more receptive, and exhibitions at the Brera galleries served to make Hayez's paintings known to a wider bourgeois public. However, the decisive impulse in establishing Hayez as the protagonist of a new movement came from the closely knit world of the liberal Milanese aristocracy.[17] In his autobiography, Hayez candidly admits that he was himself not fully aware of the cultural significance of the *Pietro Rossi* painting:

> Meanwhile at the Exhibition my painting had won great applause, perhaps more than it merited. Thinking about it later, I came to understand from the way in which they made me these compliments that I had, as it were, embodied in my work the dominant idea of the moment, which was causing a very lively polemic among the leading men of letters, that is to say the supremacy of romanticism over classicism. These new friends of mine believed that this had been my intention, but . . . I must confess that the change introduced by me into the composition came from a purely artistic sentiment, without a preconceived idea. (Mazzocca 1994: 137–8)

Hayez was arguably guilty of false modesty in underestimating his own originality. Still, his account brings out the dominant influence of the Lombard romantic *milieu* in the cultural construction of a vision of history in which the national past took precedence over the classical heritage.

The political connections of Hayez's patrons confirm the association between romanticism and the liberal opposition to the Hapsburgs. The purchaser of the *Rossi*, Count Pallavicino Trivulzio, was tried and condemned for his part in the 1821 conspiracy headed by Count Federico Confalonieri. Another condemned conspirator, Count Francesco Teodoro Arese, competed unsuccessfully to buy the *Rossi,* and later commissioned a painting of the *condottiere* Carmagnola, the subject of a tragedy by Manzoni. This painting also exploits family pathos in its portrayal of Carmagnola's farewell to his wife and children before his execution. Manzoni addressed a poem to Hayez congratulating him on the success of his painting at the Brera exhibition; it had aroused feelings of 'wonder and pity,' and had rescued his verses from 'oblivion' (Mazzocca 1985: 13). Even allowing for Manzoni's talent for self-deprecation, his poem is an important testimony to the popularity of the new historical painting.

Arese was the object of a fine portrait by Hayez, which commemorates his spell in prison (*Count Francesco Teodoro Arese in Prison,* 1828 [see figure 1.3]). His behavior under interrogation had been less than heroic, and he had served a shorter prison term than other convicted conspirators;

Figure 1.3 Francesco Hayez, *Ritratto del conte Francesco Teodoro Arese Lucini in Carcere* (Portrait of Count Francesco Teodoro Arese Lucini in Prison; 1828)
Milan, Private Collection
Archivio Fotografico Electa

the portrait emphasized his status as a victim of persecution. Hayez went to great trouble to obtain the actual chains which Arese had worn from his jailer in order to give his portrait greater authenticity (Mazzocca and Gozzoli 1983: 103).[18]

Hayez's *Conspiracy of the Lampugnani* (1826–29 [see figure 1.4]) which daringly represents the conspiracy of young Milanese nobles to assassinate Galeazzo Maria Sforza in 1476, can be read as a manifesto

Figure 1.4 Francesco Hayez, *La congiura dei Lampugnani* (The Conspiracy of the Lampugnani; 1826–29)
Milan, Accademia di Brera
Photo: Archivio Fotografico Sopraintendenza B.A.S. Milano
Courtesy of the Ministero per i Beni e le Attività Culturali

publicizing the Milanese patricians' historic attachment to liberty and their alliance with freedom-loving intellectuals. A prominent place in the painting is taken by the humanist Cola Montano, held to have inspired the conspirators by his defense of tyrannicide.[19] Before the 1820s the Lampugnani conspiracy could have been construed as an incident in the history of Milan, but in the new climate of opinion its libertarian message assumed a national significance (Pinto 1974: 192).[20] The continuity in the patriotic heritage of the Lombard nobility was asserted even more clearly in a painting commissioned from Hayez by the Brescian nobleman Count Fenaroli in 1834. This work commemorated the death of his ancestor, Ventura Fenaroli, in an unsuccessful conspiracy against the French occupying forces during the war of the League of Cambrai (1512). One might have thought that the Fenaroli family, who had been prominent supporters of the Napoleonic regime in Italy, which had destroyed the Republic of Venice, would have found it incongruous to celebrate an anti-French and pro-Venetian conspirator. However, recalling the family's heritage of political sacrifice might, in fact, serve to sustain the interpretation of collaboration with Napoleon as inspired by patriotic motives (Mazzocca 1994: 237–8).

The Middle Ages were now seen as the critical period for the formation of national identities, in all of Europe. Yet in Italy serious romantic critics claimed that they did not wish to give a privileged place to the Middle Ages as against modern times, only as an alternative to classical mythology. For them, the romantic genre was not identical with the taste for Gothic gloom. Modern times were rich enough in dramatic events. However, their portrayal ran up against several difficulties. In the first place, censorship made direct reference to recent political history risky if not impossible. Political meanings were more safely conveyed under historical disguise. A more intrinsic objection to a focus on modern times was that in the great upheavals of the revolutionary and Napoleonic era, Italians had not been independent actors, or at least were so only in secondary roles. In the eighteenth century, the leader of the struggle for Corsican independence, Pasquale Paoli, had been a patriotic icon. His myth was revived in the Risorgimento (see Cini 1998), but Corsica was too peripheral and too much associated with Napoleon to be a major element in the construction of a national past. There was no other candidate for the role of an Italian George Washington: examples of heroic virtue in the cause of Italian independence had to be sought in the more distant past. Some romantics went further, arguing that passions and emotions shone out more clearly and in a more immediately dramatic form in an age when behavior was not regulated by a dense network of laws and institutions, or by ingrained habits of civility, but by the code of honor. Classicist critics did not fail to point out the contradiction between the romantics' enthusiasm for civil progress and their curious partiality for 'the ferocious anarchy of chivalrous times.'[21] It was not easy for the intellect and the imagination to stay in step.

Sismondi and the New Historiography

In her polemic, Mme de Staël, with more accuracy than tact, pointed out an essential truth: for Italy culture and the literary language was all: 'Other nations can look to glory in war or politics; the Italians must acquire prestige from culture and the arts' (cited in Guglielminetti 1976: 253). So literary and cultural history took on a particular importance. However, politics came back in if one faced up to the problem of how to explain the decadence of the Italian genius, once incontestably the beacon for European civilization. The answer had to be in the conjoined effects of despotism, foreign rule, and the suffocation of free thought by religious conformity. This interpretation reflected back on the history of the arts and literature itself, which could be scanned for evidence of civic vigor or incipient decline.

Francis Haskell has noted that the great Genevan historian of the Italian communes, Sismondi, in spite of some Protestant inhibitions about surrendering to aesthetic pleasures, opened up new horizons for art history when he posited a connection between creativity and political liberty (Haskell 1993: 214–16). His *History of the Medieval Italian Republics,* published in Paris in 1807 and translated into Italian soon thereafter (1968 [1809–18]), was the first work of synthesis which brought the history of the Italian city states together in one unifying narrative. He stimulated Italian pride by demonstrating that the medieval republics of Italy had led the way in the revival of European civilization and in the growth of political liberty. Sismondi's inspiration can be traced in the critical writings of the young Mazzini. Without liberty or independence, Mazzini wrote, Italian literature could only be – as it had indeed come to be – 'an erudite, academic and courtly pastime,' doomed to sterility by its alienation from real life (Mazzini 1976: 1.12). The great age of Italian literature had come to an end with the extinction of republican freedom. So the study of art and literature led back to the primacy of politics. It was necessary both to meet Mme de Staël's criticism, by showing that Italy did have her own political achievements to be proud of, and at the same time to recognize that they were flawed in a way which explained the loss of liberty and independence.

There are many other testimonies to the immense attraction exercised by Sismondi's portrayal of the heroic age of communal independence and its decline. Hayez kept a notebook in which he jotted down scenes and incidents mentioned by Sismondi that might serve as subjects for painting. If Sismondi's claim for Italians as pioneers in the development of political liberty had a tonic effect, for his more meditative readers his analysis of the causes of decline had a subtler fascination. In the *Conciliatore*, the short-lived mouthpiece of Milanese liberalism, its editor, Lodovico Di Breme, outlined the most important themes of Sismondi's masterpiece: first, 'everything which concerns ... the principles and the agents of our civil corruption . . . notably the education of the nobles,' and, second, '[t]he comparison of the ancient doctrines of freedom among the Italians with those professed to-day' (Di Breme 1966: 509). Here Di Breme is referring to Benjamin Constant's famous distinction between ancient and modern liberty. Ancient liberty assumed the active part-icipation of all citizens in the public life of the city and did not recognize the autonomy of private interests. For Sismondi, the political liberty of the Italian republics, like that of their classical ancestors, had its gravest shortcomings in the failure to protect the civil liberty of the individual. Yet compared with his friend Constant, Sismondi the Genevan patriot was more ambivalent, more nostalgic for the immediacy of civic patriotism in the small-scale community.

Di Breme's only major criticism was that in his epilogue, Sismondi had not given due weight to the civil and intellectual revival of the eighteenth-century Lombard Enlightenment, exemplified by the great economist and advocate of humanitarian legal reform, Cesare Beccaria, who achieved worldwide fame with his treatise on crimes and punishments (*Dei delitti e delle pene)*. This was a characteristic theme of progressive liberalism, concerned to reassert the moderate tradition of autochthonous Enlightenment against both French ideological imperialism and reaction-ary condemnation of all progressive ideas as foreign imports. Di Breme and other liberal aristocrats and intellectuals also expressed pride in the specific Lombard contribution to *incivilimento* (the civilizing process). Until 1821 it was even possible for some moderates to hope that the Hapsburgs might resume their patronage of reform, in which case the French Revolution could be written off as an unfortunate parenthesis. Yet Di Breme did not deny that Italian culture, and particularly Italian intellect, had become marginalized in relation to the general process of civilization. The 'middle way' pursued by Lombard intellectuals, under the influence of the French ideologues, did not reject romantic innovation, but was reserved about those features of romanticism which conflicted with the tradition of Enlightenment (Thom 1995: 278). The leading jurist and philosopher of history Gian Domenico Romagnosi accepted that the romantics were right in their attack on a narrow-minded devotion to the classics, which was threatening to reduce Italian to a dead language. But he warned them to beware in their turn of imitating the more superficial features of German romanticism. The Germans had a right to nourish their national pride with memories of 'gloomy and silent forests,' but Italians could look back to a different and richer heritage: 'the primordial origins of Italian civilization, with its temples, with the Latin altars and public squares, with its political customs, and with the marvels of mythology' (Romagnosi 1943 [1818]: 417–21).[22] For Romagnosi it was the reciprocal influence of literature and the continuous process of *incivilimento* which should be the guiding thread of historical interpretation.

But where was this history to start? The romantic identification of the Middle Ages as the critical period for the formation of national identity did not go unchallenged. From the Neapolitan intellectual Vincenzo Cuoco's *Platone in Italia* onwards to Gioberti's *Primato*, a bold attempt was made by some writers to incorporate the classical past in national history and to ground claims for Italian primacy in civilization on the pre-Roman, Italic and Etruscan past. The mythical nature of this indigenous culture, which its enthusiasts argued had taught the Greeks, rather than the other way around, should not obscure the existence of a real historical problem. To what extent was the tradition of the city-state grounded in the continuity of municipal life going back to pre-Roman times? Both the interest in primitive Italic antiquity – as in the researches of Giuseppe Micali, author of the influential *L'Italia avanti il dominio dei romani* (1810) – and the attention paid to the free communes expressed a repudiation of the Roman heritage provoked by Napoleon's identification with imperial Rome.[23] The later revival of the idea of Rome obscures the fact that in its origins the Risorgimento was predominantly anti-Roman or, at least, designed to combat the fixation on Rome's imperial glory. In particular, Sismondi's history was written with the aim of combating the Napoleonic system, even though he recognized the positive aspects of Napoleon's regime in Italy. Romagnosi occupied an intermediate position, as a Napoleonic functionary who was nonetheless critical of French centralization and wished to reaffirm the virtues of the Italian traditions of municipal self-government and confederation (Thom 1995: 278–9). He held that, in spite of the bureaucratic excesses of the later Roman Empire, the heritage of Etruscan and Italic civilization, together with Roman law, had survived the barbarian invasions and had provided the foundation for the communal revival of the Middle Ages.

This thesis of continuity was challenged by Manzoni in his *Discorso sopra alcuni punti della storia longobardica,* first published in 1822. He proposed a much less irenic view of the relations between conquerors and conquered. As with the Franks and the Gauls, or the Normans and the Saxons, so vividly portrayed in Scott's *Ivanhoe,* the relations between Lombards and Romans had been those of dominance and subjection, not of the painless assimilation of the invaders by the native culture.[24] Manzoni was concerned particularly to combat the argument, which goes back to Machiavelli's *Florentine Histories* (Machiavelli 1990 [1525]: bk. 1, ch. 8; Romagnani 1985: 235–40), that it was a misfortune for Italy that the Lombard conquest of the peninsula had not been complete, and still more that the alliance between the Papacy and Charlemagne had destroyed the Lombard kingdom, thus inaugurating the fatal symbiosis between the temporal power and foreign intervention which had doomed to failure all subsequent attempts at political unity. Manzoni did not deny the continuity of Italian history, but the continuity was that of an oppressed and conquered people. Moreover it was not the tradition of ancient Latin civilization which had survived and which had ultimately civilized the barbarians, but that of the Roman Catholic Church.

Manzoni made a considerable contribution to the creation of the 'neo-Guelph' school of Italian history, which defended the national mission of the Papacy. It is true that he did not share the contemporary program of the leading political doctrinaire of the neo-Guelphs, Vincenzo Gioberti, who argued in his *Primato* for the creation of an Italian Confederation under the leadership of the Pope. Manzoni had no interest in the preservation of the temporal power of the Papacy, and no sympathy with Gioberti's idea of the Italians as a chosen people. However, I believe that his influence can be traced, for example, in the widely-read writings of the Piedmontese historian and politician Cesare Balbo. Balbo drew the conclusion that Christian nations can sicken but not perish, because Christianity provides the moral resources needed to overcome defeat. He added that Italy had lost its independence when Renaissance decadence had taken the place of the Christian spirit of the Middle Ages. It was possible, so to speak, to appeal from the present Papacy, the heir of the Counter-Reformation, to the great Popes of the Middle Ages, who had combined the defense of religion with that of Italian liberty, allying with the free communes to resist the German emperors. Echoes of this message can be found in Manzoni: the hero and heroine of his best-known work, *I promessi sposi* (The Betrothed) are symbols of the Christian people's capacity to survive oppression through faith in God's providence.

Balbo's was the basic idea of the neo-Guelph historians, in opposition to the neo-Ghibellines, who argued that the medieval Emperors, even if of German origin, had represented the cause of Italian unity against its perennial enemies, municipalism and the Church. The neo-Ghibellines could appeal to the authority of Dante, and their interpretation had perhaps superior plausibility for southern Italy, where the downfall of the imperial house of the Hohenstaufen and the conquest of Naples by the French army of Charles of Anjou, supported by the Papacy, initiated a period of catastrophe.[25] Many democrats accepted Machiavelli's view that the Papacy had been the most insidious enemy of Italian unity, and consequently sympathized with the neo-Ghibelline thesis. Yet the neo-Guelphs attracted superior literary and historical talents, and their interpretation had the great advantage that it seemed to provide historical legitimacy for a reconciliation between the Church and the nation.

Where did Sismondi stand in this debate? As a Genevan Protestant, he was particularly concerned by the corruption provoked by two centuries of Counter-Reformation hegemony. His strictures on 'Catholic morality' provoked a famous polemic with Manzoni (Manzoni 1992). However, Manzoni himself and other liberal Catholics, open to the influence of the severe and unorthodox spirituality of the Jansenist school of theology, did not deny that the alliance between a particular form of Catholicism – which made large concessions to popular superstition – and despotic power had been profoundly corrupting for both spiritual and civil life. The separation of Church and State could be seen as a necessity grounded in the whole history of Italy since the Council of Trent, as well as in the contrast between the decadence of Italy and Spain and the fortunes of northern Europe.

Yet not all patriots were reconciled to such a severely austere and personal version of the Catholic faith. For was not the Papacy the only really unitary force in Italian history? If the Papacy could be reclaimed for Italy, then at a stroke doubts about the continuity and unity of Italian history could be resolved. And, as Gioberti was to assert, it would not be necessary to invent a universal mission for the Italian nation, as Mazzini aimed to do; it was there to hand. The reconciliation between Rome and the Italian nation would restore to the latter its rightful primacy in European civilization.

The Lombard League

The dangers of the Giobertian view for both liberalism and Catholicism hardly need to be stressed. It could lead to a nationalization of the Church and a clericalization of the nation, as was to seem possible at times under the Fascist regime. In the nineteenth century it proved, perhaps fortunately, simply unrealistic. But the neo-Guelph view of history had a seriousness which cannot be reduced to Gioberti's mystique of primacy. The struggle for liberty and independence of the communes had been critically indebted to the medieval Church and the medieval Papacy. Papal patronage had been essential in the one great example of cooperation against the foreign enemy, the Lombard League against Frederick Barbarossa. The idea of the League as a precursor of the modern movement for national independence goes back to the latter's very origins. It was cited as a precedent by the representatives of the four provinces which constituted the Cispadane Republic in October 1796.[26] In his 1801 celebration of the Peace of Lunéville, which confirmed the independence of Lombardy from Austria, the leading patriotic journalist Giuseppe Compagnoni referred back to the peace of Constance, which had concluded the struggle between the League and the Emperor. 'The Emperor Frederick finally understood that no kingly force could oppose with success peoples determined to be free.' The Cisalpine republicans were 'the grandchildren of the Lombard Confederates' (Fubini 1970: 401).[27] Sismondi represented the League as the high point of his drama, a heroic alliance to defend 'the liberty of Italy.' Like the Athenians, the Swiss, the Dutch and the Americans, the Lombards had shown that a federation of 'small states, in which the sentiment of the *patria* has all its vigor' was an invincible defense against despotism. It was easy to catch the contemporary reference in his judgement that 'power founded on terror cannot be stable, until the nation is completely demoralized' (Sismondi 1968 [1809-1818]: 1.7, 25–6). However, for Sismondi the League was also a missed opportunity, the moment when the chance was lost to transform an alliance into a federative republic.

The impact of Sismondi's narrative on intellectuals was immediate, preceding even the translation of the *History* into Italian in sixteen volumes between 1817 and 1819. Cesare Balbo wrote – but never published – a 400-page historical novel on the *Lega di Lombardia* in 1816, and the romantic liberal Silvio Pellico, who became famous for the book he wrote on his experience as a political prisoner under Austria, planned to write a tragedy about Barbarossa. In his early writings, Mazzini declared that the sixteen years from the foundation of the League to the Peace of Constance were 'worth more than whole centuries of Rome' – an important example of the anti-Roman tendency I noted earlier (Sestan 1991: 229).

However, the real popularity of the theme dates from the publication in 1829 of the poet Giovanni Berchet's verse romance, which acknowledged the inspiration of Sismondi. Berchet, in exile in Paris, contrasted the virtues of 'the most glorious epoch of Italian history' with 'our supine tolerance of servitude' (Brunello 1996: 17–18). What particularly caught the imagination was his depiction of the critical moment of the oath taken by the confederates in the abbey of Pontida (now, ironically, adopted as a holy place by Umberto Bossi's antiunitarian Lombard League). It was celebrated as the realization of an alliance between civic virtue and mercantile enterprise on the one hand and papal guidance on the other, since the League had been concluded under the auspices of Pope Alexander III. Giuseppe Diotti's painting, *The Oath of Pontida* (1836 [see figure 1.5]), places a strong emphasis on the role of the Church: the statue of the Pope is prominent and the abbot occupies the center of the composition. More significant still is the figure of the friar who rebukes the impatience of the group of laymen on the right, who are demanding immediate vengeance. The Church appears as a moderating force which prevents discord from breaking out among the confederates.

This interpretation resembles that of the Catholic liberal Cesare Cantù, one of the most prolific authors of the Risorgimento period, in his verse romance *Algiso,* published in 1828 (Brunello 1996: 18; Cantù 1923). Cantù published a criticism of Diotti's painting, in which he praised the

Figure 1.5 Giuseppe Diotti, *Il giuramento di Pontida* (The Oath of Pontida; 1836) Milan, Galleria d'Arte Moderna
Photo: M. Saporetti Milano

'extraordinary poetry' of the work, but was highly critical of the historical authenticity of its details. The statue of Alexander III could never have been sculpted by a twelfth-century sculptor and 'the oath-takers are writing in modern handwriting with modern pens, on a book made in a modern way.' Moreover, perhaps an understandable concession to didactic clarity, the delegates are signing the names of their cities, whereas historically they signed their own personal names (Pinto 1974: 317–18). Probably one reason why Diotti was found wanting in these respects was that he belonged to an older generation of artists, still wedded to the traditions of neo-classicism, and his turn to national history lacked conviction. In fact, the gestures of the three figures on the right, whom Cantù criticized as disturbing the harmony of the historic scene, are a clear citation from David's famous pre-revolutionary painting of the Oath of the Horatii.

The Neo-Guelph interpretation of the Lombard League culminated in the *History* published by the patriotic Benedictine Padre Tosti in February 1848, and dedicated to Pius IX. Tosti's elevated rhetorical composition is also notable for the accentuation of the motif of nationalist hostility to the Germans: Barbarossa is frequently referred to simply as 'the German,' and the destruction of Milan is 'in the German manner,' '*alla tedesca*' (Fubini 1970: 412). In the depiction of the subsequent victory of the League over Frederick Barbarossa at Legnano, the central image was that of the *carroccio,* a kind of communal Ark of the Covenant, which served both as the symbol of the commune of Milan and as a military rallying-point. The *carroccio* appeared during the festival for the celebration of the concession of the Piedmontese Statute, granting constitutional government, on 27 February 1848, complete with trumpeters in medieval costume and the significant addition of the flag of Savoy (Brunello 1996: 19).[28] Cantù had to explain its deeper meaning: it was the symbol of the agreement of religion and liberty, of the 'force which union gives to the weak,' and the testimony that an untrained volunteer army could defeat the greatest of German emperors.

Nevertheless, the popularity of Pontida and the League remained greatest in Lombardy, and it was associated with the early phase of the 1848 revolution, when religion and the volunteer movement, Pius IX and Garibaldi, seemed to be working for the common cause. The Piedmontese liberal, General Durando, and Garibaldi each gave the oath of Pontida their own inflection: for the first, the theme of papal support for the 'war of independence' was predominant, while Garibaldi stressed the 'brotherhood' – a word with revolutionary and Mazzinian overtones – of the Lombard cities. (Brunello 1996: 19–20). It is particularly significant that the divorce between Pius IX and the national movement was matched by a shift in the symbolic meanings of the history of the League. Pontida was a symbol too impregnated with Catholicism to survive the breach, and Verdi's *Battle of Legnano,* first performed in January 1849 in Rome in an atmosphere of revolutionary enthusiasm, preferred to ignore the scene, in spite of its evident dramatic possibilities (Budden 1978–81: 1.390ff.).[29] It is interesting that the opera openly confronts the theme of Italian disunity, when the citizens of Como resist the patriotic appeals of the protagonists and end by exulting at the prospect of the destruction of Milan.

The competition between rival interpretations of the League's history reached a spectacular climax in 1876, on the 700th anniversary of the battle, when Catholics and radical democrats staged rival celebrations. The main Catholic celebration was held at Pontida, the democratic at Legnano. Moderate liberals, embarrassed, did not take part in either of the celebrations, and there was even a timid attempt in their respectable periodical *La Nuova Antologia* to play down the significance of the battle. The democratic version attracted strong support from the workers' societies of Milan, still Mazzinian in orientation, while the Catholic version would seem to have been more successful in the rest of Lombardy. No episode demonstrates so clearly how even the moments of relative unity in Italian history were subject to conflicting interpretations linked to contemporary politics (Brunello 1996: 21–3).

If we look at historical novels and paintings, I think that we can see that the excitement aroused by the Lombard League was at its height before 1848, and declined thereafter, with the loss of faith in democratic and federalist solutions. However, the theme never disappeared from the repertoire. Cristiano Banti, a convert from the academic to the *macchiaiolo* style,[30] painted a version of the Battle of Legnano whose audaciously modern style as well as its content was meant as a democratic gesture.[31] Democrats and republicans identified with the free communes in their polemics against the moderates.[32]

The Sicilian Vespers

The different experience of the Kingdom of Naples, with its strong monarchic tradition, was difficult to assimilate to a vision of history centered on the free communes. Southern intellectuals, even when they accepted the Italian national ideal, were predominantly absorbed by their own past; indeed the term 'nation' was still often used to refer to Naples, not Italy. This was even more true of Sicily, which in fact proclaimed its independence in 1848. Sicilian autonomists pointed to the continuous existence of their own parliament from the Middle Ages, only suppressed after the Bourbon restoration in 1815, as a symbol and guarantee of national continuity. But the fierce resentment of government by Naples which was provoked by the Bourbons' centralizing policies could also stimulate a desire to dissociate Sicily from the rest of the south. In this perspective the history of the Sicilian parliament, at least in its origins, could be read as the expression of a political and even economic vigor which had more in common with the northern cities than with Naples. This interpretation gave some plausibility to the hope that Sicily could protect her autonomy by becoming an equal and respected partner in a future Italian federation, or confederation.

The national imagination seized on one episode in Sicilian history, and the sequence of events which led up to it, as of particular significance. Next to the Lombard League, the most popular theme for patriotic celebration drawn from the Middle Ages was the Sicilian Vespers. The relationship between historiography and literary or artistic genres is in this case more complicated. The whole sequence of events leading from the battle of Benevento (1266), in which the last of the Hohenstaufen, Frederick II's illegitimate son Manfred, met his death, to the subsequent conquest of Naples by Charles of Anjou, and then to the Vespers, was marked out for special significance by the frequent references to its protagonists in Dante's *Divine Comedy*. The Hohenstaufen were, strictly speaking, a German imperial dynasty. But Frederick II was Italian in the maternal line and, unlike other emperors, had chosen to rule from an Italian rather than a northern base. In addition, since Manfred's illegitimacy debarred him from the imperial title, the Kingdom of Naples under his reign could be regarded as virtually independent, as it had been under the earlier Norman kings, and essentially 'Italian.' The victory of Charles of Anjou over Manfred at Benevento was then interpreted as a national tragedy because it marked the destruction of an independent Italian monarchy by a foreign invader. And the subsequent revolt of the Sicilians against French in the Vespers became a model of resistance to foreign domination.

Here again, it was probably Sismondi who did more than any one else to reawaken interest. The Tuscan democrat Francesco Domenico Guerrazzi, later a protagonist of the 1848 revolution, who briefly became prime minister of Tuscany in 1849, published his turgid but immensely popular historical novel, *The Battle of Benevento*, in 1827. It was republished in 40 editions down to 1915, or almost one every two years. Guerrazzi concentrated his attention on the first, unequivocally disastrous, phase of the story, in which Naples lost her independence to the French. As an anti-clerical democrat, Guerrazzi fastened on an episode which illustrated his favorite theme of the alliance between the Papacy and the foreign invader. This was the dominant motif of the neo-Ghibelline national interpretation, but it cannot be said that Guerrazzi followed this line of thought with any consistency. His sensationalism and his determination to show the whole period as very, very wicked curiously got in the way of a straightforward patriotic interpretation of the fall of the independent Kingdom of Naples and the death of Manfred.[33] For he accepted the stories spread by thirteenth-century Guelph propagandists that Manfred had been guilty of murdering not only his half-brother, but his father, the great Emperor Frederick II himself. So the loss of the Kingdom appears as the just chastisement for Manfred's sins, notwithstanding the fact that in other respects he shows all the noble and royal virtues of a hero.

The patriotic significance of Guerrazzi's novel lies instead in the remorselessly dark picture of a Kingdom betrayed by the treachery of its own barons.[34] There is an anti-feudal, democratic edge to this portrayal, which may explain why Guerrazzi lays on the gloomy tones so thickly. The whole age was vitiated by feudal oppression. This was certainly a more simple-minded and less modern view of the Middle Ages than that derived from a close reading of Sismondi. The popularity of tales of dark deceit and treachery, following a stereotype already popular outside Italy in the Renaissance, as I have already indicated, can be regarded as an autonomous fact. But when the misdeeds were those of princely and seigniorial families such as the Visconti in Milan or the Medici in Florence, it could still be claimed that the depiction of corruption served a patriotic purpose, in warning the people against the misdeeds of the powerful and the moral consequences of the loss of liberty.

The Sicilian Vespers, on the other hand, could be interpreted as the first successful struggle for national liberation from foreign rule and occupation. One might assume the episode presented problems from the neo-Guelph perspective, since the Papacy continued to support Charles of Anjou against the Sicilian rebels. However, because the Empire was not involved, the Guelph-Ghibelline dichotomy was of secondary import-ance. In 1822 Hayez exhibited a painting of the popular rising of Palermo in 1282 (*The Sicilian Vespers* [see figure 1.6]). The theme was chosen by Hayez himself, and his knowledge of the dramatic incident which sparked it off derived, once again, from Sismondi's history (Mazzocca 1994: 100). The occasion was provided by a procession to the Church of Santo Spirito on Easter Monday. The French had prohibited the Sicilians from bearing arms. In Hayez's summary: 'While a beautiful and noble lady was walking

Figure 1.6 Francesco Hayez, *I vespri siciliani* (The Sicilian Vespers; 1822)
Milan, Private Collection
Photo: Archivio Motta

to the Church a Frenchman insolently rummaged in her bosom under the
pretext of verifying if she was carrying hidden arms: the young woman
fainted in the arms of her spouse, and one of her brothers killed the
Frenchman with his own sword. I seized the moment, the single point of
insolence and revenge, which is the origin of the massacre' (Mazzocca
1994: 150–1).[35]

If the choice of theme was Hayez's own, and demonstrates his historical
interests and his patriotic commitment, the identity of the patron undoubtedly influenced his choice. Marchesa Visconti d'Aragona was a notable
supporter of the arts, and in 1834 she was to commission another historical
painting of clear patriotic significance, *Francesco Ferrucci at Gavinana*,
by Massimo d'Azeglio.[36] The Marchesa D'Aragona's husband had been
accused of participation in the *carbonaro* conspiracy of 1821, though he
was acquitted (Mazzocca 1994: 149).[37] Presumably there is also a
reference to the Aragonese connection of the family, since the ultimate
result of the Vespers was to replace French rule in Sicily by that of the
Kings of Aragon, who came to the aid of the rebels. The central female

figure was modeled on one of the Marchesa's closest friends; here, as elsewhere, Hayez's inclusion of portraits of contemporaries in historical scenes brought the past nearer to the present. The participation of fashionable members of society as models can be linked to the great vogue for *tableaux vivants*, in which scenes from famous paintings and novels were enacted live against a suitable backdrop.

Although the composition centers on the personal drama of 'insolence and revenge' there is a clear depiction in the background of mob violence, which contemporaries must have found daring, especially since it followed shortly after the Sicilian revolution of 1820. The German critic Schorn in the *Kunstblatt*, while praising Hayez's free and almost calligraphic execution, suitable to a scene which was all 'shouting, anxiety and fury,' and finding the movements of the figures 'extraordinarily lively and true,' complained that some of them lacked nobility (Mazzocca 1982: 61). The Italian translator of the article commented that this lack of decorum was 'not strange, but right,' since the painter was representing a popular uprising. One may note that, as in the painting of Peter the Hermit, a priest, in this case a Capuchin monk, appears as an agitator who incites the people to action. This may reflect a real hope that the lower clergy might side with revolution, as many in fact had done during the revolutions of 1820 in Naples and Sicily.

There is an interesting contrast between this version and the later one which Hayez painted in 1844, and exhibited in 1846 (*The Sicilian Vespers* [see figure 1.7]; see Mazzocca 1994: 290–1). Here Hayez has abandoned the dramatic concentration of the earlier painting, and though the moment is still the same, the emotional tone is quite different. It is the moment of calm before the storm: even the members of the central group are much less emphatic in their gestures, the mannerist quotations have disappeared, and the mood is one of 'solemn calm' and melancholic reflection on the oncoming tragedy, rather than anger. The mood is heightened by the reflective attitude of the two women spectators on the left. If you think of the operatic equivalent, it would be an *adagio*, instead of the earlier painting's *presto*. It seems as if the older Hayez was more ambivalent about revolutionary violence. The new version is more concerned, instead, with historical and topographical accuracy. Indeed, Hayez visited Palermo to acquaint himself with the landscape and the results of this knowledge can be seen in the correct siting of the church, which in the thirteenth century was outside the city, in the authentic Sicilian style of the architecture, and in the characteristic shape of the mountain. These choices may again have been influenced by the milieu of the patron, who, this time, was a Neapolitan noble of liberal views, Vincenzo Ruffo, Prince of

Figure 1.7 Francesco Hayez, *I vespri siciliani* (The Sicilian Vespers; 1844–46)
Rome, Galleria Nazionale d'Arte Moderna
Photo: Archivio Motta

Sant'Antimo. One should remember that the Sicilian revolution of 1820 had been directed against Neapolitan rule, and an endorsement of the popular fury of Palermo might not have been well received in Naples, although Ruffo himself was more concerned that the historical details should be rendered accurately. But the major explanation for the difference of mood is to be found in Hayez's own evolution. His earlier enthusiasm for revolution had cooled,[38] and in the aftermath of the visit to Milan by the new Hapsburg emperor, Ferdinand I, he had been the recipient of lavish patronage from the imperial government (Mazzocca 1982: 113–16).[39]

By this time, Hayez and his patron would certainly have been acquainted with the history of the Vespers by the Sicilian historian Michele Amari, first published in Sicily in 1842, and then in a much enriched edition in exile in Paris a year later. This undoubtedly quickened interest in a theme which had never lost its popularity, and may have also stimulated the requirement of greater historical accuracy; ironically, however, the spirit of Amari's work was closer to that of Hayez's earlier, more radical version. For Amari, the Vespers were the first act in an epic of popular heroism which showed that the south (or at least Sicily) had not lagged behind the north in its determination to expel the foreign invader, and in its capacity for organization.

Amari had noted that foreign historians tended to view the whole story of the Vespers with some skepticism. It was the attribution of the Vespers to a deep-laid master conspiracy by the exile Giovanni Da Procida, Frederick II's former minister, that aroused suspicion, and when Amari came to investigate it, he found that this part of the story was indeed incredible. He did not deny the importance of Procida's diplomatic role, but he pointed out that this was only relevant to events *after* the initial rising, with the Aragonese intervention and support from the Byzantine Emperor Michael Palaeologus. Instead what Amari found was much more interesting. He discovered a spontaneous popular outbreak, which did not, however, exhaust its significance in the massacre of five thousand Frenchmen, which Amari found it hard either to approve or to condemn. The initial violence was only the prelude to a democratic revolution which showed that the Sicilians were no less capable than the Lombards, and indeed more so, of uniting against the foreign oppressor. Particularly remarkable and worthy of emphasis was the close alliance between the communes of Messina and Palermo, whose rivalry in more recent times had been a recurrent obstacle to Sicilian unity. The revolution in its first phase had substituted the importance of feudal ties by an alliance between the communes; Amari intends to show that there were more resemblances between Sicily and the Lombardy of the League than was commonly thought.

Two further points need to be made: one, which in a sense emerges even at the relatively unsophisticated level of the painting and the opera libretto, is that history reinforces an appreciation of the savage and spontaneous revolutionary potential of the Palermo mob. In fact, in less than a century, Palermo experienced no fewer than five revolutions, a record not matched by any other European city except Paris. Amari explicitly states that the modern Sicilian people has retained the spirit of the thirteenth century, and that the memory of the Vespers has helped to keep this alive: 'The unknown killer of Drouet, with a single blow restored Grecian virtue to the people of Palermo, and the latter to the whole island . . .' (Amari 1843: 138). And, he insisted, 'our people proudly preserves until to-day the memories of that ancient fierce virtue' (ibid.: 136). Amari claimed that his knowledge of present-day Sicily had helped him to understand the past: 'perhaps because I was born in Sicily, and in Palermo, I was better able to understand the uprising of 1282 as it was born, sudden, uniform, irresistible, desired but not planned, decided and made by the turn of a glance' (ibid.: viii).[40]

The second problem to which I would like to draw attention is that of dual national identity. Amari was a Sicilian patriot, and references to the 'Sicilian nation' are frequent in his work.[41] Polemically, he remarked that those who accused him of showing too much 'municipal spirit' should remember that Sicily was rather large for a municipality. He pointed to the role of the Sicilian Parliament as quite unique in Italian history, or indeed, he claimed, in the Europe of its day. Yet Amari did not wish Sicilian nationalism to be seen as exclusive of patriotic concern for the whole of Italy. With rather less evidence, he argued that anger against French domination was a general Italian phenomenon, and that the Sicilians, at least initially, viewed other Italians as brothers in distress.[42] The moral was again of a liberal-federalist kind: the cause of Sicilian autonomy and that of Italian independence were not opposed but associated.

At another level, one may note that Amari's 'revision' of the Vespers failed to destroy the popularity of the Procida myth. In the tortuous and confused plot of Verdi and Scribe's *Vêpres siciliennes*, Procida is the only character who stands clearly for patriotic values, and it is not by chance that 'O tu, Palermo, patria adorata' became the opera's most famous and popular number. It was difficult for Verdi to make Procida into a noble character for a Parisian audience, especially since Scribe portrayed him as an *agent provocateur* who incites the French to molest Sicilian women in order to bring about the revolt and massacre. Verdi, indeed, protested vigorously against the risk of confirming the stereotype of the treacherous Italian conspirator: 'M. Scribe, in altering Procida's historical character, has made him – according to his favorite system – a common conspirator with a dagger in his hand. For God's sake, there are virtues and crimes in the history of every people and we are no worse than the rest. In any event I am Italian above all and come what may I will never be an accessory to any injury done to my country' (Budden 1978–81: 2.177).[43]

One problem with the Vespers as icon of Italian national identity may have been that there was something alarming and altogether too contemporary about popular violence in Palermo: the opera could not even be performed in Italy without changing the historical setting, and in the version staged in Paris the Vespers start only as the curtain falls. But to a large extent Verdi succeeded in giving the opera a positive national significance, by portraying Procida as a figure moved by an implacable patriotic resolve. At least in Sicily, the music of the *Vespers* was both popular and charged with political meaning. As Garibaldi's redshirts advanced on Palermo in 1860, they were greeted by town bands playing selections from Verdi's opera (Boime 1993: 57). The six hundredth anniversary of the Vespers in 1882 provided an opportunity for the Sicilian leader Francesco Crispi, then in the opposition, to commemorate the event as part of his campaign to foster 'the cult of great memories' in order to promote national education. Although Crispi denied that this was his intention, his speech was interpreted as an attack on France, at a time when tensions between the two countries were high over the questions of Tunis and Egypt. Crispi also emphasized the anti-papal message and altogether omitted any reference to Sicilian, as opposed to Italian, motives for the revolt. This is another example of how unification changed the context within which the narrative of the national past was constructed (Duggan: forthcoming).

Renaissance Examples

Space does not permit me to examine in depth other key episodes in the construction of a national past. Briefly, however, I should like to mention the question of the Renaissance and the loss of Italian independence.[44] One of the most successful historical novels of the period was *Ettore Fieramosca*, published by the Piedmontese nobleman Massimo D'Azeglio in 1833. Painter, writer and politician: no one represented the many strands of Risorgimento culture as well as D'Azeglio. He was a friend of both Cesare Balbo and Manzoni, who encouraged his efforts as a writer. D'Azeglio's novel centered on the 'sfida di Barletta,' a duel which took place in 1503 during the war between France and Spain for the control of the Kingdom of Naples. The duel was fought between thirteen Italian knights in Spanish service, and thirteen French knights, or rather twelve plus one; the odd man out is the villain, Grajano d'Asti, who is Italian but fights on the French side.[45] Grajano stands for the pure mercenary who fights for whomever pays him, and is amazed that anyone should behave differently. By stigmatizing Grajano as a 'vile traitor,' D'Azeglio is able to minimize the significance of the fact that the hero and his friends are *condottieri* fighting in Spanish service. Their captain, Prospero Colonna, harangues them before the duel: 'I see amongst you Lombards, Neapolitans, Romans, Sicilians. Are you not all equally sons of Italy? . . . Are you not faced with foreigners who call Italians cowards?' (D'Azeglio 1970 [1833]: 260).[46] D'Azeglio explains almost ingenuously that he chose a Piedmontese as a villain to show that he was superior to the municipal spirit (ibid.: 285). In view of D'Azeglio's later harsh remarks on the Neapolitan character, it is equally worthy of note that the hero is from Capua. *Fieramosca* is the simple novel of patriotic unity, without a social moral.[47] It is somewhat ironic that D'Azeglio is best remembered for his judgement 'having made Italy, it remains to make the Italians.'[48]

Other incidents from the later period also lent themselves to literary dramatization. The siege of Florence, which put an end to the brief revival of the Republic (1527–30), was taken as the culminating episode in the Italian wars, when the spirit of liberty was finally extinguished. The siege of Florence is perhaps the only episode which attracted two major historical novelists. Guerrazzi's *Assedio*, which was considered too inflammatory to be published in Italy when it first appeared in 1836, again took a strongly democratic viewpoint. It was the intrigues of the magnates which had betrayed the Republic, heroically defended by the people, with the aid of great men such as Machiavelli and Michelangelo. The *Assedio* was just as popular as the *Battle of Benevento*. In 1834, D'Azeglio was already at work on a historical novel about the siege of Florence, and in the same year he painted his picture of the Republican general Francesco Ferrucci's last battle at Gavinana, for the Marchesa D'Aragona. Ferrucci, the military commander who had fought for the Florentine Republic in 1530, and who had been the victim of a treacherous assassination in the moment of his defeat by greatly superior forces at Gavinana, was a paradigm of the hero who dies in defense of his country. D'Azeglio's novel *Niccolo de' Lapi* finally appeared in 1841, and can be read as a moderate rejoinder to Guerrazzi. Its hero, significantly enough, comes from a family of wealthy silk merchants. With two famous writers competing to provide dramatic incidents, and with the added attraction of the presence of exemplary Great Men, the siege of Florence was the most popular of all episodes for historical painting, though no single example succeeded in achieving real fame. Verdi keenly desired to write an opera about the siege in 1849, but was foiled by the impossibility of avoiding censorship.

The assumption that 1530 marked the end of Italian liberty reveals the bias of the national historical vision towards Florence. It ignored the continued importance of Venice, the greatest of the Italian republics. In general, the patriotic vision of the Middle Ages found Venice surprisingly awkward to handle. In the construction of the national past the Venetian state oddly plays a secondary role, except in the *Promessi sposi,* where it appears as a haven for the hero Renzo, escaping from the horrors of Spanish Milan. Ironically, Venice's very success, her status as a great power, may have made the city hard to incorporate in any unified scenario. The problem of Venice certainly illustrates the arbitrary exclusions which were a feature of the national reinterpretation of the past. But it can also be taken as an example of the persistence of literary and historical traditions, given the success of Florentine writers from the fifteenth century onwards in portraying their native city as the heartland of Italian liberty and cultural achievement. Following the lead of Byron's tragedy, *The Two Foscari*, Hayez's paintings from the mid-1840s on emphasize the dark and sinister side of Venetian government. Patriotic critics complained, reasonably enough, that the stability and comparative excellence of Venetian government was neglected, even though it had been long been regarded as a model. Of the two dominant themes of Venetian history, it was empire, not republican liberty, which was eventually appropriated for the construction of the national past. In the later nineteenth century, when domination over the Adriatic and Dalmatia became key objectives for Italian expansion, the Venetian heritage assumed a central importance for Italian nationalism. It was D'Annunzio, above all, who popularized the theme of Venice's maritime supremacy as an inspiration for the naval ambitions of the new Italy (Chabod 1990: 299–300).

Until 1848, historical revivalism had mainly concentrated its attention on the rise and fall of the free communes. Even serious historians did not often challenge the vision of the princely *signorie* of the later Middle Ages as a manifestation of decadence, characterized by cruelty, treachery and assassination. The Renaissance as a whole suffered from the stigma associated with political defeat, and its cultural glories were sometimes explained as the survival of an earlier and happier period. In the Middle Ages Italian liberty had at least been vigorously defended. Although the Italians' penchant for internecine warfare was generally deplored, the spirit of communal independence was not necessarily regarded as incompatible with the national idea. The idea of a league of Italian states seemed easier to reconcile with the course of Italian history than that of an unitary, centralized state, although Mazzini regarded the former solution as hopelessly inadequate.[49] Democrats and liberals, however, disagreed over their evaluation of constitutional monarchy. Could the existing monarchic states be accepted if they introduced constitutional government? Or, as Mazzini suggested, was the republic the only solution in line with the true traditions of Italian liberty? Were decentralization and federalism the best way of reviving the creative spirit and enterprise of the communes, as Carlo Cattaneo believed? All these solutions could be supported from within a historical tradition that basically accepted Sismondi's paradigm.[50]

After 1848, instead, following lines first laid out by Cesare Balbo, neo-Ghibelline and neo-Guelph history both gave way to a third version of the national past, centered on the providential role of the Savoy dynasty. Civic history lost ground to dynastic history, and the rise of Piedmont during the centuries elsewhere marked by decadence and foreign rule, from the mid-sixteenth to the eighteenth century, became a major theme.[51] Leading members of the Piedmontese ruling class, like Cesare Balbo and the influential jurist Ferdinando Sclopis, were well aware of the importance of history in legitimizing the Italian role of Piedmont and the Savoy dynasty. Their major problem, until the 1840s, was that of overcoming the resistance of King Charles Albert and the reactionary members of the Piedmontese bureaucracy, who refused to grant free access to the royal archives. They were particularly hostile to research into the medieval Piedmontese Estates, which might have suggested precedents for constitutional government. Piedmontese historians, in fact, were much more restricted in their freedom than those of the states under Austrian influence. However, in the 1840s, with the conversion of Charles Albert first to cautious support for the Italian national cause, and then to the reluctant acceptance of a constitution, these obstacles to the development of an Italian historiography centered on Piedmont were removed (Romagnani 1985). Still, Piedmont was not Italy, and the alignment of official historiography on the Savoyard thesis, which was not really codified till after unification, was not, I think, matched by a similar success in the more popular genres.

Conclusion

I have suggested some of the connections between historiography and literature or art, but in doing so I may have inadvertently blurred their differences. I would suggest that the new historicist mentality, which insisted on a vision of the past as one of continuous development, although it undoubtedly influenced critics and writers as well as historians, did not replace an older way of looking at history. This was the tradition of *Historia magistra vitae*, or history as a storehouse of moral examples. For the true romantic historian, the hero was above all the figure who succeeded in intuiting and expressing the passions and needs of his epoch and people; but historical novels and paintings were more apt to resort to stereotypes of timeless virtues and vices. For the opera librettist, historical scenarios were often interchangeable, and among composers Verdi was rare in his attention to historical specificity and verisimilitude. Among historical novelists, few followed the example of Manzoni in making ordinary, lower-class people the protagonists, and in his refusal to create a hero. The figure of the hero as a model for emulation was essential for national literature.

Even so, the repertoire of heroes and noble actions underwent significant changes. Where the virtues of the hero are inextricably linked to the historical situation, then we have something new (Mascilli Migliorini 1984). Religious imagery was appropriated and transformed for the national cause. The romantic stereotype of the inspired dreamer who foresees the national future is a secular version of the figure of the evangelist or the prophet. One can see this in Faruffini's portrait of *Cola di Rienzo* contemplating the ruins of Rome (1855 [see figure 1.8]), which isolates the figure against the landscape of the Roman Campagna, lit by

Figure 1.8 Federico Faruffini, *Cola di Rienzo che dalle alture di Roma ne contempla le rovine* (Cola di Rienzo Contemplating the Ruins of Rome from Above; 1855) Milan, Private Collection
Photo: Finarte

the rays of sunset.[52] The language of martyrdom could be freed from its religious context and used against the Church.[53] A new and important category of heroes was that of 'the heretics and the great victims of persecution' (Pinto 1974: 38). This is really an altogether new type of heroism, which is not explicable except in the context of a belief in historical progress, and the struggle of science and free thought against persecution. It could be subsumed under a more general anti-clerical interpretation of Italian history, which gained ground after the split between the Papacy and the national movement, and became even more important after 1860, when it helped to sustain an alternative democratic vision of the Italian past. Arnaldo da Brescia, Savonarola, Giordano Bruno and Galileo confronting the Inquisition all served as examples of the struggle of free thought against repressive authority. The diffusion of these images of dissent was not confined in the later nineteenth century to the educated classes. Historical examples and myths were an important part of the new popular urban culture. The popularity of Guerrazzi's novels, republished in cheap editions for a new mass readership, was at its height in the last decades of the nineteenth century. In this way, the image of Italy's Risorgimento as essentially bound up with the cause of free expression, science and progress, survived, even in the age of *Realpolitik*.

However, the Risorgimento vision of the past came under increasing criticism for its rhetorical and outdated character, and was increasingly divorced from creative innovation. Patriotic history painting came to seem unsatisfactory to a younger generation of painters – the *macchiaioli* – who turned to stylistic innovation and contemporary themes as a way of expressing their democratic commitment.[54] Somewhat later, in the last decades of the nineteenth century, scientific historians started to question patriotic myths, and novelists and opera librettists rejected the conventions of historical melodrama. As the national past became an object of official celebration, it invited radical criticism and reinterpretation. The tension between memory and myth, crystallized around easily recognizable and accepted images, and the creative exploration of the meaning of the past for the present, is a universal and inescapable problem.

Acknowledgements

My thanks are due to Ancilla Antonini and *Index* for their assistance in locating the illustrations. I am indebted to Dr. Martin Thom for his careful reading of the draft manuscript, and for his valuable comments. I would also like to thank Krystyna von Henneberg for her indefatigable labors in making the piece ready for publication.

Notes

1. Welsh bardic lore and Scottish clan tartans may have been 'invented,' or reinvented, but they supplied an already existing demand, and that demand resulted in part from the interruption of a genuine popular tradition.

2. The issue of factionalism was one of the foundations of the Piedmontese interpretation of Italian history, which identified the rise of the Savoy monarchy as a happy exception to a history of division and disloyalty, a rise which predestined its kings and institutions to be the essential instrument for unifying Italy in the present. The failure of the 1848 revolutions discredited federalism and seemed to confirm the idea that only a strong monarchy could unify Italy. Since Piedmont, formerly suspect as a repressive, bigoted, absolutist regime, was the only Italian state to preserve a liberal constitution after 1849, it became the focus for Italian hopes. The apologists of the Savoy monarchy were able to point to the skill and determination with which its princes had defended their independence since the sixteenth century.

3. In this connection it is significant that Austria's leading statesman, Count Metternich, went out of his way to try to win over the most important historical painters in Italy. The importance of patronage to the painting of nationalist subjects will be discussed later on.

4. For the importance of this tradition in the pre-history of other European nations, see Reynolds 1997; Strayer 1971; Beaune 1991.

5. See Giardina 1997 (3–116), especially p. 50 for criticism of the teleological view of Italian nationhood. The Italian ethnic consciousness which emerged in the first century BCE was weak and was subsequently overshadowed by the Empire. Note also the discussion in Brunt 1998: 91–112. For the modern superimposition of the image of Rome on that of Italy and its implications, see Porciani 1993: 1.400, 422–8.

6. For instance, the Florentine group which founded the *Archivio Storico Italiano* in 1841 concentrated on publishing historical documents (as against the 'cultural historicism' of the 1820s). This was in part a reaction to the alarming primacy of German scholars, who were beginning to make inroads into Italian archives, but it was also due to the restrictions on freedom of expression, which now affected even historical arguments. See Porciani 1979.

7. After Italy's unification in 1859–60, the production of edifying historical images and literature received the official encouragement of the state and leading politicians as a means of legitimating the new

state. The dimensions of this chapter do not permit a detailed examination of this phase of cultural production.

8. Mazzini, as we shall see later on, shared the positive evaluation of the Papacy's role in the Middle Ages, but had no hopes or desires for reconciliation in the present.

9. See Visconti for the comparison of Alfieri's *Philip II* with Schiller's *Don Carlos*. Alfieri would have succeeded better in conveying the atmosphere of the epoch if, like Schiller, he had set the principal characters in the context of the Spanish court: 'if the Queen appeared under the surveillance of the etiquette of her ladies in waiting, if the Duke of Alba appeared together with courtiers copied individually from history' (1943: 466–7).

10. Peter the Hermit was the most famous among the preachers who mobilized support for the First Crusade, declared by Pope Urban II at Clermont in 1096. He was the spiritual leader of the People's Crusade, which was in fact a disastrous failure. There seems to be no clear evidence that he ever preached in Italy, although Italians did participate in the People's Crusade. The Lombards took little part in the original crusading expedition of 1097; they contributed a large contingent to the expedition of 1100–1101, which was cut to pieces by the Turks in Asia Minor and never reached Jerusalem. In reality, it was only the naval republics (Pisa, Venice and Genoa) and, of course, the Normans of southern Italy, who contributed decisively to the First Crusade's success.

11. One of the most famous scenes in Grossi's poem – the description of the thirst of the Crusaders before Jerusalem – was both the object of a painting by Hayez and the occasion for one of the climactic moments of the opera, the chorus *O signore dal tetto natio*.

12. See also Stendhal's judgement, quoted by Mazzocca (1994: 196): 'how much credulity on these faces. This painter teaches me something new about the passions which he paints.'

13. To be exact, Mazzini viewed Peter the Hermit as having played an analogous role to the first generation of romantic rebels: 'like Peter the Hermit, they had raised the standard of a crusade . . . without understanding its consequences' (Mazzini 1976: 1.73).

14. The need to invent new forms for the new epoch was expressed in regard not only to literature and painting, but also to music. Mazzini's remarkable essay on *The Philosophy of Music* argued that the individual operatic aria must yield in importance to the chorus, as the expression of the collective spirit (Mazzini 1977 [1836]). On this subject, see Chapter Three in this volume.

15. Numerous passages in Verdi's correspondence illustrate this point. For the comparison between opera and film, see Budden (1978–81: 1.21): 'The opera of the 1830s was the cinema of a hundred years later. Audiences wanted the film of the book, or the play as the case might be . . .'
16. For Sismondi, see pp. 42–9.
17. Bourgeois outnumbered aristocrats among Hayez's patrons, but the latter accounted for more of the important commissions of historical paintings. *Peter the Hermit* was commissioned by the Genoese banker and ship owner Francesco Peloso, whose portrait Hayez had painted in 1824. Although he was a businessman, Peloso came from a noble family which had cooperated with the French after 1796. His preferences as a patron show a patriotism which was characteristically colored by local, civic pride. The Crusades could be linked to Genoa's glorious maritime past and Peloso also commissioned paintings of Columbus; see Mellini 1992: 391–407.
18. Other important patrons of Hayez included Countess Vittoria Visconti D'Aragona, *née* Trivulzio, a well-known opponent of Austria, and the mother of the more famous Cristina di Belgioioso, and Countess Teresa Borri Stampa, Alessandro Manzoni's second wife.
19. The *Congiura dei Lampugnani* was commissioned by Countess Stampa.
20. Literary interest in the 1476 conspiracy dates back to the Enlightenment period; Alessandro Verri published a tragedy in 1779 entitled *La congiura di Cola Montano*. Hayez drew on both Sismondi and Machiavelli for his knowledge of the Milanese conspiracy; it is probable that he read Verri as well.
21. Carlo Londonio, *Cenni critici sulla poesia romantica* (1817), cited in Guglielminetti 1976: 265.
22. Romagnosi, however, admitted that modern Italians were not pure descendants of the Latins, but had undergone a mixture with 'the peoples of the north.' Romagnosi's interpretation was basically maintained by the leading theorist of democratic federalism, Carlo Cattaneo (1972 [1858]).
23. For Micali, see Treves (1976: xxiii–xxiv, 295–308); for Micali's eulogy of pre-Roman Italic federalism as a 'salutary restraint on the spirit of conquest,' see Treves 1976: 314.
24. Manzoni's interpretation was much influenced by the French historians Augustin Thierry and François Guizot; see De Lollis (1987: esp. 51), for Thierry and Walter Scott.
25. See pp. 52–9 on the Sicilian Vespers.

26. The Cispadane Republic (which invented the Italian version of the tricolor) was formed by the alliance of the cities of Reggio and Modena (formerly constituting the Duchy of Modena), and Ferrara and Bologna (formerly part of the Papal States). It was united with the Cisalpine Republic (Lombardy) in July 1797.

27. Compagnoni emphasized that the League had not been restricted to present-day Lombardy, but had extended roughly to the borders of the Cisalpine Republic.

28. The Lombard League might seem to be foreign to Piedmontese traditions. Certainly it had nothing to do with the Dukes of Savoy. Fortunately, however, cities which now belonged to Piedmont (Asti and Tortona) had taken part in the wars against Barbarossa, and the defense of these cities was a theme favored by Savoy propaganda as showing their contribution to the common cause. In addition, Alessandria (named after Alexander III) was actually founded by the League as a refuge for those dispossessed by the imperial invasion.

29. The librettist, Cammarano, was responsible for the choice of theme, after Verdi had considered the possibility of an opera based on the career of Cola di Rienzo. The latter subject had already been treated by Wagner in 1842.

30. The *macchiaioli* were a group of painters centered on Florence whose technique substituted linear contours and chiaroscuro by 'blotches' (*macchie*) of color. Although they are not strictly comparable with the French impressionists, their work aroused similar hostility from defenders of the academic tradition. See Boime 1993.

31. Similarly, the Tuscan government awarded a prize to Amos Cassioli's *Battle of Legnano* in 1860.

32. A rough census of historical paintings and novels seems to suggest that medieval themes were at their most popular before 1848, while the Renaissance gained in popularity thereafter. In part, this may reflect a turning away from overtly patriotic themes. But depictions of Renaissance luxury and corruption may also have assumed greater relevance in a period of post-revolutionary pessimism.

33. Guerrazzi (1827: 12): 'I will tell a story of crimes, atrocious and cruel crimes.'

34. The French leader Monforte exclaims 'We shall have Italy without striking a blow' (Guerrazzi 1827: 399).

35. The church which was the object of the procession is wrongly identified by Sismondi as the cathedral of Monreale (Mazzocca 1994: 150–1). See Porciani 1998: 206–8, for the connection made here

between the 'private' motive of the defense of female and family honor, and the 'political' motive of national revolt.

36. For D'Azeglio, Florence and Ferrucci see pp. 60–1.

37. A second version of the *Vespri* was painted for Arese; see p. 41 for a discussion of the Arese portrait.

38. This does not mean that Hayez was just an opportunist, however; in 1848 and after, he once again took sides unequivocally with the patriots against Austria. It must be remembered, in fact, that in the years before 1848, some Milanese intellectuals, such as the federalist democrat Carlo Cattaneo, later to be one of the leaders of the 1848 Milanese insurrection, believed that it was possible to obtain national autonomy within the Hapsburg Empire.

39. On his visit to Vienna Hayez was personally received by the two leading figures in the imperial government, Metternich and Kolowrath, both of whom personally commissioned paintings from him. His most politically compromising commission was the 'Allegory of the Political Order of Francis I of Austria,' painted for the Palazzo Reale in Milan.

40. The preface from which this quotation is taken was not reprinted in the subsequent Italian editions. In the preface to the fourth edition (Florence 1851), Amari distanced himself from the climate in which the book had originally been composed: his history 'was born from the fervent passions of Sicily before 1848,' and 'our aims then were different from the form of political regime to which we aspire today' (Amari 1851: 7).

41. It was an important part of Amari's thesis that before the French occupation Sicily had not been inferior to the north in culture or in industry. Indeed, it was the first center of the invention of a 'courtly' vernacular, as Dante had recognized. And if Sicily had remained self-governing, instead of having to submit to a new set of foreign conquerors, it would have retained its prosperity. He admitted, however, that the revival of the baronage – due to the endless civil and foreign wars – had led to a decline of the communal and popular forces so important in the revolution.

42. See especially Amari 1843: 104: 'Municipal love of country which so much helped and so much harmed Italy, by nature abhorred foreign domination . . . so amidst the tumult of municipal passions, the secret voice of Latin national sentiment spoke to the heart.'

43. The earlier controversy about Mazzini's so-called 'theory of the dagger,' in which he was accused of advocating assassination, is relevant here.

44. National history was ambivalent, if not actually hostile, towards the Renaissance, whose cultural achievements had to be balanced against its evident political failings. From this perspective, Machiavelli and Michelangelo assumed particular importance as creative geniuses who had resisted the trends responsible for political and social decadence.

45. There was a real Grajano d'Asti, but there are good reasons for regarding him as French rather than Italian.

46. For Grajano d'Asti, see the dialogue between him and the hero Fieramosca (D'Azeglio 1970 [1833]: 83); Grajano tells him that he serves the French because unlike the Italians they pay regularly. Fieramosca objects: 'And isn't Asti in Piedmont? And is Piedmont in Italy or France?,' and Grajano replies: 'I serve whomever pays me. [*Servo chi mi paga, io*]. Don't you know, my fine young man, that for us soldiers where there is bread, there is the *patria*.' The phrase invented for Grajano by D'Azeglio paraphrases the well-known proverb *Franzia o Alemagna purché si magna* (France or Germany? it doesn't matter as long as we eat), while at the same time parodying the eighteenth-century patriotic trope that where there is liberty, there is the *patria*.

47. See De Sanctis (1897: 336): the novelty of the book was that it had both a 'historical frame and a patriotic content.' He notes that D'Azeglio does little with the figure of Cesare Borgia, even though he plays an important and suitably villainous role in the book's plot by abducting the heroine. 'Give Guerrazzi that fact . . . and you would see what use he would make of the episode, how many notes he would sound of rage and hatred against internal tyranny. But D'Azeglio is not much concerned with internal tyranny . . .' As a member of the Piedmontese school, 'he chiefly wished to fix the attention of the Italians on the fact of Italy the slave of the foreigner.' In fact, it can be argued that the beginning of *Fieramosca* contains a coded reference to Guerrazzi's *Battle of Benevento*. The incident which sparks off the challenge to the French is a scornful reference by a French baron to that battle: 'the Italians gave us more trouble with their frauds than with their swords' (D'Azeglio 1970 [1833]: 34). By defeating the French, Fieramosca vindicates Italian honor not only against the foreigner, but against Guerrazzi, who has put too exaggerated an emphasis on the treachery of the Neapolitan barons. *Fieramosca* was easily adapted to the needs of fascist propaganda by Alessandro Blasetti in his epic film of 1938: see Landy 1986: 190–4. Landy, however, does not mention D'Azeglio's novel. For more on Blasetti, see Chapter Eight in this volume.

48. What D'Azeglio actually wrote was somewhat different: 'the Italians have wanted to make a new Italy, but themselves to remain the old Italians' (D'Azeglio 1966 [1867]: 1.17).
49. See Croce (1930 [1921]: 1.121) for the political role of historians in 1848; the revolution of 1848 was 'the great attempt' of the Catholic-liberal school 'to put their historiography into action' (Manzoni, Troya, Capponi, Balbo, Tommaseo).
50. See the interesting comments of the art critic Pietro Selvatico (1851) on the reasons for the end of 'medievalism': 'the people had looked to it for the free commune and the corporations, the nobles for their ancient honor, and the more honorably deluded spirits for religion' (cited in Maltese 1992: 86). It had been destroyed by 'philosophy,' which had opened the way for socialism, and only the family was left as a theme capable of inspiring idealism.
51. The civic tradition, however, was vigorously maintained by Cattaneo (see note 22), and after 1860 it gained renewed importance as a cultural theme for the democratic left, because it was linked to the call for decentralization within the now united state of Italy.
52. Faruffini was a democrat and a friend of the Cairoli brothers, who became leading patriotic heroes. Ernesto and Giovanni were killed fighting in Garibaldi's 1867 expedition against Rome (commemorated in another of Faruffini's paintings), and the third brother, Benedetto, became prime minister in 1878. Faruffini dedicated a photograph of *Cola* to Benedetto Cairoli. The word in the book which Cola marks with his finger is 'Brutus.' The painting was exhibited at the Brera, and bought by the Milan Società delle Belle Arti (Olson 1992: 183–4 [cat. n. 58]).
53. In 1848 Atto Vannucci defined the canon of patriotic 'martyrs' in a successful work: see Mascilli Migliorini 1984: 162–3.
54. See the comments of Diego Martelli and Domenico Signorini, cited in Barocchi 1972: 268–9, 285 *et passim*. Signorini complained that 'All the examples of love of country in painting have come to bore me somewhat, because I do not find great merit in making liberal pictures when there is no danger and when even the reactionaries are liberals.'

References

Amari, M. (1843), *La guerra del vespro siciliano*, 1st edn, Paris: Baudry.
—— (1851), *La guerra del vespro siciliano*, 4th edn, Florence: Le Monnier.

Barocchi, P. (1972), *Testimonianze e polemiche figurative in Italia: L'Ottocento dal bello ideale al prerafaellismo,* Messina-Florence: G. D'Anna.

Beaune, C. (1991), *The Birth of an Ideology: Myths and Symbols of the Nation in Late Medieval France,* Berkeley: University of California Press.

Bellorini, E., ed. (1943), *Discussioni e polemiche sul Romanticismo,* Bari: Laterza.

Boime, A. (1993), *The Art of the Macchia and the Risorgimento: Representing Culture and Nationalism in Nineteenth-Century Italy,* Chicago: University of Chicago Press.

Brunello, P. (1996), 'Pontida,' in M. Isnenghi, ed., *I luoghi della memoria: simboli e miti dell'Italia unita,* Bari: Laterza, pp. 15–28.

Brunt, P.A. (1998), *The Fall of the Roman Republic and Related Essays,* Oxford: The Clarendon Press.

Budden, J. (1978–81), *The Operas of Verdi,* 3 vols, Oxford and New York: Oxford University Press.

Cantù, C. (1923), 'Algiso o la Lega Lombarda,' in M. de Rubris [pseud.for M. Rossi], ed., *Novelle romantiche,* Turin: UTET.

Cattaneo, C. (1972 [1858]), *La città considerata come principio ideale delle istorie italiane,* ed. M. Brusatin, Padua: Marsilio.

Chabod, F. (1990), *Storia della politica estera italiana dal 1870 al 1896,* Bari: Laterza.

Cini, M., ed. (1998), *La nascita di un mito: Pasquale Paoli tra '700 e '800,* Pisa: Biblioteca Franco Serantini.

Croce, B. (1930 [1921]), *Storia della storiografia italiana nel secolo XIX,* Vol. 1, 2nd edn, Bari: Laterza.

D'Azeglio, M. (1970 [1833]), *Ettore Fieramosca,* Florence: Vallecchi.

—— (1966 [1867]), *Things I Remember,* trans. E.R.Vincent, London: Oxford University Press.

De Lollis, C. (1987), *Alessandro Manzoni e gli storici francesi della restaurazione,* Rome: Istituto storico italiano.

De Sanctis, F. (1897), *La letteratura italiana nel secolo XIX,* ed. B. Croce, Naples: A. Morano.

Di Breme, L. (1966), *Lettere,* ed. P. Camporesi, Turin: Einaudi.

Duggan, C. (forthcoming 2001), *Francesco Crispi,* trans. G. Ferrara, Bari: Laterza.

Falkenhausen, S. von (1997), 'L'immagine del "popolo": dal centralismo al totalitarismo in Italia e in Germania,' in O. Janz, P. Schiera and H. Siegrist, eds, *Centralismo e federalismo tra Otto e Novecento: Italia e Germania a confronto,* Bologna: Il Mulino.

Fubini, M. (1970), 'La Lega Lombarda nella letteratura dell'Ottocento,' *Popolo e stato nell'età di Federico Barbarossa*, Proceedings of the XXXIII Congresso Storico Subalpino, Turin: Deputazione subalpina di storia patria.

Gellner, E. (1983), *Nations and Nationalism*, Oxford: Blackwell.

Gentile, E. (1997), *La grande Italia: ascesa e declino del mito della nazione nel ventesimo secolo*, Milan: Mondadori.

Giardina, A. (1997), *Italia romana: Storie di un'identità incompiuta,* Bari: Laterza.

Guerrazzi, F. (1827), *La battaglia di Benevento*, Livorno: Bertani.

Guglielminetti, M. (1976), '"Decadenza" e "progresso" dell'Italia nel dibattito fra classicisti e romantici,' *La restaurazione in Italia: Strutture e ideologie* (XLVII Congress of the History of the Risorgimento), Rome: Istituto per la storia del Risorgimento italiano.

Haskell, F. (1978), *Arte e linguaggio della politica*, Florence: Studio per Edizioni Scelte.

—— (1993), *History and its Images,* New Haven: Yale University Press.

Hobsbawm, E. and T. Ranger, eds (1983), *The Invention of Tradition*, Cambridge: Cambridge University Press.

Hroch, M. (1998), 'The Social Interpretation of Linguistic Demands in European National Movements,' in H.G. Haupt, M.G. Muller and S. Woolf, eds, *Regional and National Identities in Europe in the XIXth and XXth Centuries*, Hague-London-Boston: Kluwer Law International.

Lanaro, S. (1988), *Italia nuova: identità e sviluppo 1861–1988*, Turin: Einaudi.

Landy, M. (1986), *Fascism in Film*, Princeton: Princeton University Press.

Levra, U. (1992), *Fare gli italiani: Memoria e celebrazione del Risorgimento*, Turin: Comitato di Torino dell'Istituto per la storia del Risorgimento.

—— (1994), 'Nazione e stato nazionale in Italia: Crisi di una endiadi imperfetta,' *Passato e presente* 12 (33): 13–30.

Machiavelli, N. (1990 [1525]), *Le istorie fiorentine*, Florence: Le Monnier.

Maltese, C. (1992), *Storia dell'arte in Italia*, 2nd edn, Turin: Einaudi.

Manzoni, A. (1992), *Osservazioni sulla morale cattolica*, Padua: Banca Antoniana.

Mascilli Migliorini, L. (1984), *Il mito dell'eroe*, Naples: Guida.

Mazzini, G. (1977 [1836]), *Filosofia della musica: Estetica musicale del primo Ottocento,* ed. M. de Angelis, Rimini: Guaraldi.

—— (1841), 'Modern Italian Painters,' *London and Westminster Review* 35.

—— (1915), *Scritti editi ed inediti*, Vol. 21, Imola: Galeati.

—— (1976), *Scritti politici*, Vol. 1, ed. F. Della Peruta, Turin: Einaudi.

Mazzocca, F. (1982), *Invito a Francesco Hayez*, Milan: Rusconi.

—— (1985), *Quale Manzoni? Vicende figurative dei 'Promessi sposi,'* Milan: Il Saggiatore.

—— (1994), *Francesco Hayez: Catalogo ragionato*, Milan: Motta.

—— and M.C. Gozzoli (1983), *Hayez*, Milan: Electa.

Mellini, G.L. (1992), *Notti romane e altre congiunture pittoriche tra Sette ed Ottocento*, Florence: Vallecchi.

Olson, R.J.M., ed. (1992), *Ottocento: Romanticism and Revolution in Nineteenth Century Italian Painting*, New York: American Federation of Arts.

Pinto, S., ed. (1974), *Romanticismo storico*, Florence: Centro Di.

Porciani, I. (1979), *'L'Archivio Storico Italiano': Organizzazione della ricerca ed egemonia moderata nel Risorgimento*, Florence: Olschki.

—— (1993), 'Stato e nazione: l'immagine debole dell'Italia,' in S. Soldani and G. Turi, eds, *Fare gli italiani: Scuola e cultura nell'Italia contemporanea*, Vol. 1, *La nascita dello stato nazionale*, Bologna: Il Mulino, pp. 385–428.

—— (1997), *La festa della nazione: Rappresentazione dello Stato e spazi sociali nell'Italia unita*, Bologna: Il Mulino.

—— (1998), 'Italien: Fare gli italiani,' in M. Flacke, ed., *Mythen der Nation: ein Europäisches Panorama*, Berlin: Koehler and Amelang, pp. 199–222.

Reynolds, S. (1997), *Kingdoms and Communities in Western Europe, 900–1300*, 2nd edn, Oxford: The Clarendon Press.

Romagnani, G.P. (1985), *Storiografia e politica culturale nel Piemonte di Carlo Alberto*, Turin: Palazzo Carignano.

Romagnosi, G.D. (1943 [1918]), 'Della poesia considerata rispetto alle diverse età delle nazioni,' in E. Bellorini, ed., *Discussioni e polemiche sul Romanticismo*, Bari: Laterza, pp. 417–21,1st published in *Il Conciliatore*, Sept. 1818.

Sestan, E. (1991), 'Legnano nella storia romantica,' in G. Pinto, ed., *Storiografia dell'Otto e Novecento*, Florence: Le Lettere, pp. 221–40.

Sismondi, J.C.L. (1968 [1809–1818]), *Storia delle repubbliche italiane nel Medio Evo*, Vol. 2, ed. S. Lerner, Rome: Avanzini and Torraca.

Smith, A.D. (1991), *National Identity*, London: Penguin.

Soldani, S., and G. Turi, eds (1993), *Fare gli italiani: Scuola e cultura nell'Italia contemporanea*, Vol. 1, *La nascita dello stato nazionale*, Bologna: Il Mulino.

Spadolini, G., ed. (1994), *Nazione e nazionalità in Italia*, Bari: Laterza.

Strayer, J.R. (1971), *Medieval Statecraft and the Perspectives of History*, Princeton: Princeton University Press.

Thom, M. (1995), *Republics, Nations and Tribes,* London: Verso.

Tobia, B. (1991), *Una patria per gli italiani: Spazi, itinerari, monumenti nell'Italia unita (1870–1900),* Bari: Laterza.

Treves, P., ed. (1976), *Lo studio dell'antichità classica nell'Ottocento,* Turin: Einaudi.

Visconti, E. (1943), 'Idee elementari sulla poesia romantica,' in E. Bellorini, ed., *Discussioni e polemiche sul Romanticismo*, Bari: Laterza, pp. 441–3.

Part II
Whose Italy?

2

Dante and the Culture of Risorgimento: Literary, Political or Ideological Icon?

Andrea Ciccarelli

School books on Italian history teach that the period known as the 'Risorgimento' runs roughly from 1821 to 1870. In other words, from the failure of the first open conspiracies against the newly restored Austrian government in Milan and elsewhere to the annexation of Rome into the Kingdom of Italy which had been established in 1861. Analyzed from a cultural perspective, however, this same temporal definition may be broadened in either direction. Such flexibility is particularly evident when we focus upon literary figures and cultural events which contributed to shaping awareness of the nature and significance of unification. In this chapter I intend to explore the ways in which the exaltation of the historical past, in particular of Dante as cultural icon, permeated nineteenth-century Italian culture of 'Risorgimento.' And I will consider how it entered into the vital intellectual debate concerning the need to modernize Italian culture, from after the unification all the way up through World War I and even to the rise of Fascism.

A closer analysis of this cultural phenomenon – and in particular of its ambivalent position between the sphere of literature and that of ideology and politics – requires me to make a fundamental critical distinction. On the one hand there are a very few intellectuals who set out – with at best partial success – to recuperate the essence of Dante's poetic project. On the other hand is the widespread glorification of the poet as a national icon, visible, for example, in the proliferation of statues of Dante in the *piazze* of Italian cities, beginning with the one built in Florence in front of Santa Croce (1830) and ending with the one inaugurated in Trent in 1896. In other words, we should differentiate between the instrumentalization of a canonical author for institutional purposes (i.e. political propaganda for an ideal national unity) and the engagement of a very limited number of nineteenth- and early twentieth-century writers with Dante's poetic values (which were not only aesthetic, but also ethical and political). Still, it is possible to identify several intellectuals who saw Dante's moral-political example and that of his nineteenth-century literary counterparts as integral components of their own nationalist views and political goals, and in whom these two different cultural operations seem to coincide or, at least, to overlap.

This is the case with Giuseppe Mazzini's interpretation of early nineteenth-century literature. Before unification Mazzini was persecuted, arrested and exiled by both the Kingdom of Piedmont and the Austrian Empire because of his populist and republican ideas. And, in spite of his fundamental role in spreading unitarian values during the Risorgimento, such persecution was continued after unification by the new Italian Kingdom which considered him dangerous because of his republicanism. (Mazzini was arrested the last time in 1870, and then released; he died in 1872 in Pisa, where he had moved after abandoning all political activity.) Mazzini viewed literature mostly in light of his own political ideas and aspirations. Three of his early writings are significant in this regard: *Dell'amor patrio di Dante* (1826–27; On Dante's Love of His Country), *Sopra alcune tendenze della letteratura italiana del XIX secolo* (1829; On Some Trends in Nineteenth-Century Italian Literature), and *Ai poeti del secolo XIX* (1832; To the Poets of the Nineteenth Century). In the first Mazzini presents Dante's patriotic love for his native city of Florence as a national emblem for all Italians; in the second he links Dante's ethical perspective to that of the 'new' literary models; and in the last, with romantic fervor, he incites the new writers to let poetry become the voice of the people. In these essays, Mazzini inaugurates a cultural parallel between Dante and contemporary peninsular writers on the grounds of shared ethical conviction rather than of aesthetic qualities. He sees Dante as an example – in fact *the* example – of Italian integrity because he refused all moral compromise with the political power of his times. And he draws an analogy to the writings of some late eighteenth- and early nineteenth-century writers, especially with those of Vittorio Alfieri (1749–1803) and Ugo Foscolo (1778–1827).[1]

Mazzini's comparison between Dante and the 'new literature' did not arise in isolation; rather it stood as the culmination of a cultural situation fermented in the last decades of the preceding century. It is well known that the history of Italian literature up to the late eighteenth century had betrayed very little Dantean influence, either in tone or in style. The Italian literary tradition had been mainly lyrical and, as such, had followed a predominantly Petrarchan path. Pietro Bembo, the great promoter of the Petrarchan model, had argued during the crucial Renaissance debates on the Italian literary language that Dante was to be admired for his ethical vision and for his powerful imagination. But as far as providing an imitable model for a poetic style, a 'classical' language, and a thematics of love, Petrarch's *Canzoniere* remained the principal reference point for Bembo as for most subsequent Italian writers. In fact the sonnet, Petrarch's favorite poetic genre, became the most common lyric form in Italian.

Only under the influence of the Enlightenment in the late 1700s did Italian authors begin to feel that the Petrarchan style, which had nourished European poetry for centuries, was ill-equipped to express their new ideas about society and to communicate emergent civic and national interests. Petrarchism lent itself to the expression of personal emotions such as pain at the loss of love and of youth, but it did not foster the narrative style necessary to the dramatization of civic and political ideas or to the representation of "objective" historical realities. Dante's poem, of course, was a much more appropriate model for this task. In order to register fully the profound intellectual consequences implied by this shift of cultural perspective from the Petrarchan model to the Dantean, we must reflect further upon the aesthetic and ideological implications inherent in this choice. To accept tradition means to embrace what is already known and highly valued. It often implies the rejection of change. Ideologically speaking, such a position leads to the categorical denial that what has been experienced and consecrated in the past can open onto something new and positive.

A 'Petrarchan' world-view is based precisely upon this persuasion: the endless search for the perfect lyric form is fueled by the certainty that memory (with its attachment to the past) represents the only faculty that can remove humanity from an ever-changing, uncontrollable reality. Life is simultaneously revealed and concealed by lyric form: only through the creation of memorialized beauty can one mask the pangs of present reality. But, of course, the search for perfection is paradoxically a sign of its absence. The objective of literature thus becomes the pursuit of a symbol – happiness – that can exist only when resuscitated in memory. Action is banned from Petrarch's poetics, because it implies, epistemo-logically, the exploration of new experiences and the production of new ways of understanding. The concept of life as an experience of growth, as a journey which can lead to something different and unique, is excluded by such an aesthetic attitude. Petrarch's perfect form thus becomes the mirror of despair, of resignation.

Dante's cultural lesson, on the other hand, implies precisely the opposite point of view. The metamorphic nature of reality is not avoided but rather pursued, notwithstanding the inevitably painful surprises which such pursuit brings with it. From this point of view, the instability of experience includes the possibility of change from a negative to a positive mode of existence. No matter how overwhelming they may seem at any given moment, evil and sorrow are conceived of as mere fractions of human life. They are not fully coincident with it, as they are in a Petrarchist perspective. Dante's narrative style reflects a thirst for discovery and the urgency to communicate the knowledge of such discoveries. In this universe, memory is not relegated to the task of endlessly recreating a fixed past, but is projected dynamically toward the future. Hope, not desperation, motivates Dante's aesthetic vision, while action and exploration are its epistemological means.

Nevertheless, the claim that the dynamic concept of literature embodied by Dante prevailed over the Petrarchan one from the end of the eighteenth century forward is only partially sustainable. It is difficult to argue that the majority of the authors who ostensibly revived the Dantean ethical-political line of Italian literary culture were committed to pursuing Dante's own primary poetic aims. If we examine the major lyrical figures who, beginning with Mazzini, have traditonally been identified as the new models for the 'rebirth' of Italian culture in the early nineteenth century – Alfieri, Foscolo, Leopardi and Manzoni – we are forced to conclude that most of them, however profound their overt appreciation of Dantean aesthetics, do not fully engage with its ethical-political imperative.[2]

Of the eighteenth-century figures, it is Alfieri who most shaped the cultural imagination of his time in this respect, bringing Dante back within the mainstream of Italian literature. Alfieri's severe biographical legend, nurtured during his self-imposed exile and fed by his expressions of love for freedom and for justice, is the closest Italian culture could come after so many centuries to resuscitating an actively 'Dantean' climate.[3] Alfieri's poetics concentrated upon the conflict between political power and personal freedom. Books such as *Della tirannide* (1777; On Tyranny), *Del principe e delle lettere* (1786; On the Prince and Literature), as well as some of his tragic dramas (*Saul, Filippo, Agamennone*) boldly asserted his rejection of despotism and of absolute power, and earned him the reputation of moral severity that led to comparisons with Dante. Alfieri's life, both as he lived it and as he narrated it, was that of an exiled intellectual defying political oppression in all its forms. He left his native Piedmont because of its retrograde system of justice, which had remained untouched by the reforms the Enlightenment had brought forth elsewhere in Europe. He then abandoned Paris because of the excesses of the French Revolution, which he had initially praised in a famous poem (*Parigi sbastigliato*; Bastille-less Paris). He finally chose Florence, the city which symbolized Italian civilization more than any other, as the only place where his restless intellect could find itself in cultural symbiosis with the great spirits who had given birth to the Italian tradition. Internal analysis of Alfieri's literary production uncovers the signs of an unresolved frustration which ultimately left no room for moral-political engagement and reduced him to self-imposed isolation and stoic renunciation of any active contact with reality. Unable to develop a practical perspective to complement his theoretical commitment to the struggle against tyranny, Alfieri ultimately rejected the present moment, abdicated any hope of change, and found relief only in lyrical introspection. His works mirror the existential state of an author whose aesthetic faith is solely entrusted to the tragic absolutism of poetry, supported by a spiritualized eroticism that still falls fully within the old Petrarchan tradition.

Like Alfieri, Foscolo is seemingly more Dantean in his biography – notably his exile and tempestuous life – than in his poetic practice. Thanks in no small part to Mazzini, Foscolo's exile (he abandoned Milan in 1815 for Switzerland and then for England, where he later died) became the symbol of political and cultural resistance to Austrian oppression. This was true even though the decisions of other intellectuals – such as those who published the journal *Il Conciliatore* – to stay in Milan and undertake cultural battles in the face of harsh Austrian censorship, were probably more effective in promoting the political cause of nationhood.[4] Foscolo's love of country and his passion for past glories of Italy are well represented in the famous passage of his poem *Dei sepolcri* (1807) celebrating the tombs of great Italians in the Florentine church of Santa Croce. However, Foscolo's poetic vision is profoundly pessimistic. It is based upon the persuasion that justice cannot be found either in human nature or in the natural world, and therefore that there is little consolation to be found in political action, just as there is little possibility of effecting real change.

This attitude is made clear in his epistolary novel, *Le ultime lettere di Jacopo Ortis* (The Last Letters of Jacopo Ortis) which was partially inspired by Goethe's *Sorrows of Young Werther*. *Ortis* takes place in the period immediately following the 1797 Treaty of Campoformio by which Napoleon ceded Venice to Austria, dashing earlier hopes which Italian reformers had placed in him. It recounts the life and death of a young Venetian patriot who is driven to suicide both by his sorrowful love life and political desperation. Thanks to its explicit view of Italy trapped between two foreign oppressors (France and Austria), this novel marks the beginning of the literary Risorgimento, especially in its depiction of a radically fragmented Italy, a country whose parts can be 'sold' by one oppressor state to another. It is this political thematics that has consistently called forth, in the wake of Mazzini, a parallel between Foscolo's patriotism and Dante's. However, the book offers little in the way of constructive action to support the larger implications of such a comparison. In fact, as a political manifesto *Ortis* is notable principally for the openly frustrated absence of any hope for human redemption in social terms. Jacopo Ortis reaches the conclusion that life is ruled exclusively by fraud and by force. Thus the only real human virtue is passive 'compassion,' since any attempt at a more active exercise of virtue is inevitably put at the service of those two (Machiavellian) rules of political life. Action is excluded from the very first page of the novel. In the opening letter the main character – who is wanted by the Austrian police, but who is still at liberty – defines himself as a desperate soul awaiting prison and death. Jacopo Ortis seems absolutely unable to move beyond his impossible political and psychological situation. All his attempts end up as circular motions that bring him back to his original desperate position: from the first to the last page there is never any sense that his 'journey' might lead him somewhere else.

Since we know better than to identify an author's wishes with those of his characters, we might argue that *Ortis* should be taken on its own terms as a novel, and not seen as the expression of Foscolo's perspective. That this *is* Foscolo's own poetic vision, however, is confirmed by its consistent reappearance in his other works. For instance, in the tragedy *Ajace* (1811) the protagonist, much like Jacopo Ortis, kills himself when he realizes that what he had intended as heroically patriotic actions were misused by those in power, who turned them to very different purposes. This analysis is ratified in Foscolo's important essay on the limits and the origins of justice, delivered at the University of Pavia in 1809. In this work, heavily influenced by Machiavelli and Hobbes, Foscolo states that if we look at nature correctly, we find that brute force and selfish instincts are natural 'laws' of life, while justice is an abstract concept that cannot exist unless imposed and maintained by force. The writer concludes that 'l'uomo è un animale essenzialmente guerriero e usurpatore' (humans are essentially warriors and usurpers [cited in Tongiorgi 1994: 427]). This concept recurs in elegantly synthetic form in one of Foscolo's unfinished poems, *Preghiera* (Prayer), probably sketched just before or right after his decision to leave Italy in March 1815.[5] This lyric is markedly Hobbesian – one line claims that 'I popoli . . . sono necessariamente in guerra fra loro' (the nations are necessarily drawn to war against each other) – and it forcefully reiterates the poet's ideological pessimism, coloring it as a providential plan, as if unhappiness were the allotted fate of humanity: 'Poiché tu Dio Signore per i tuoi misterj/ Hai voluto che i Popoli siano sempre in guerra' (Because, you, Lord God, for your mysterious reasons, have desired that the nations must be ever at war [cited in Di Benedetto 1991: 279–80]). In the end, Foscolo's works do not represent injustice and unhappiness as merely painful stages of life, but rather as its essence (see Ciccarelli 1998).

The third of the great pre-Risorgimento poets, Giacomo Leopardi (1798–1837), shows open sympathy for Dante's poetry and for his stoic attitude in cultural matters, as can be seen from his letters to Angelo Stella at the time he was composing his commentary on Petrarch's *Canzoniere*. But even Leopardi does not to reach the core of Dante's beliefs about poetry. The poem *Sopra il monumento di Dante*, for instance, represents an homage which is not so far from the Alfierian model, or from the exalted patriotic rhetoric of Foscolo's *Dei sepolcri*, the same rhetoric which would serve nationalistic propaganda so well even into the fascist period:

> O Italia, a cor ti stia
> far ai passati onor; che d'altrettali
> oggi vedove son le tue contrade,
> non v'è chi d'onorar ti si convegna.
> Volgiti indietro, e guarda, o patria mia,
> quella schiera infinita d'immortali,
> e piangi e di te stessa ti disdegna (7–13).

> (O Italy, let it be your care to do honor to those who have passed away; since your precincts are now widowed of any such, and there is no one now who deserves to be honored. Turn backward, and gaze, o my father-land, at that infinite crowd of immortals; and weep, and feel contempt for yourself.)

Leopardi's creative spirit certainly has dantesque traits, particularly in its rebellious and original reconsideration of inherited poetic subjects, but his innovations are still lodged within the legacy of Petrarchan lyric. For Leopardi, once the squalid reality has been exposed, there is no reason to explore or search further. Given the absence of positive, or even simply different, points of reference external to the self, Leopardi's poetic practice remains content only to explore the poet's own soul ('il proprio petto'), a cruel fate that he accepts without withdrawing from reality. On the contrary, he calls upon his readers to recognize life for what it is, and to endure its stings; but, again, his poetry envisions no potential for any variation of the *status quo*.

The inability of Leopardi and his predecessors to recover the Dantean perspective stems from the incompatibility between their deep pessimism concerning human nature and Dante's hope for a positive solution in the struggle with life. These authors do not believe in the possibility of change; they already know the result of life's journey: all metaphorical departures, all poetic investigations of reality, for them amount to useless repetitions of identical cycles. Many of the romantic and patriotic authors who seemed to choose a less traditional, experimental approach to literary form, in order to express for a broader public the desirability of social change leading to Italy's political independence, still did not really accept this basic ingredient of Dante's aesthetic universe. In most instances, Dante remained the Foscolian 'ghibellin fuggiasco': an ethical model of stoically patriotic virtue or, as in the case of Leopardi and a few others, a stylistic example of fertile poetic invention.

Unlike his counterparts, Alessandro Manzoni's (1785–1873) seems to follow Dante's aesthetic vision quite closely. Manzoni's *Promessi sposi* (1827; revised 1840) is a historical novel which in some sense shares Foscolo's pessimistic meditations on justice and on the fragmentation of Italian culture after the French Revolution. And yet, the novel puts forth the model which Manzoni believes essential to the formation of a modern nation: the definition and promulgation of a unified cultural identity for inhabitants of the Italian peninsula, starting with the creation of a standard language (see Manzoni 1990: 335–415). Manzoni's book does not promote – and, in fact, often ridicules – heroic postures and stoic virtuosity. It insists on education. It bans violence, but asserts the author's firm persuasion of the necessity of a 'just' war for any nation which is oppressed. It advocates a balanced political system based upon a realistic free-market economy, which would banish social oppression along with demagogical and ineffectual economic regulations. It argues for the right of every nation to be given the opportunity to seek and to express its own cultural identity, so as to locate itself within an ideal international system which is respectful of the cultural autonomy of each individual nation. Some of these points were anticipated by Foscolo's *Ortis*, but without any conviction that they could become reality. Manzoni's deep historical pessimism, on the other hand, is similar to Dante's; it does not foreclose the possibility of solutions. Let us take as an example the crucial episode of his novel, when the desperate male protagonist, Renzo, searches for his fiancée, Lucia, in Milan (chapters 34–5).[6] Having lost touch with her, Renzo hears that Lucia may be in the 'lazzaretto' of Milan, the plague-house where people infected with the black death are confined. At this point, Renzo encounters his old spiritual advisor, Padre Cristoforo, one of the Capuchin monks assigned to the 'lazzaretto.' Padre Cristoforo, seeing that Renzo is still filled with hatred for all his many misfortunes, asks him to confront the truth of his life, and takes him to see his old nemesis, don Rodrigo, who lies dying in the *lazzaretto*. The plague-house represents hell and death, with its demonic guardians, the 'monatti,' who rob the dead before burying them; but it is also a purgatorial place of rebirth, reflected in the angelic figures of the Capuchin monks who care for the sick and dying. This double condition mirrors Renzo's suspension between desperation and hope. In response to this situation, he encounters a spiritual guide, Padre Cristoforo, just as the 'lost pilgrim' Dante encounters his guide, Virgil, at the beginning of the *Divine Comedy*. The very phrasing used to describe the encounter echoes the end of the first canto of *Inferno*, where, in the last line, Dante summarizes his fearful yet willed decision to undertake a journey in Virgil's company. Manzoni's 'E presa la mano di Renzo . . . *si mosse*. Quello, senza osar di domandar altro, *gli andò dietro*' (chapter 35) clearly echoes Dante's 'Allor *si mosse*, e io *li tenni dietro*' (*Inferno* 1.136; emphasis mine). The pessimistic elements which inform Foscolo's and the others' works are present in Manzoni's as well; but the apparently more conservative Manzoni depicts them realistically as *phases* of life, but not as *the necessary result* of life, just as Dante does in his poem. In Manzoni's literary vision action and change are given the epistemological dignity of favoring a final situation very different than that in which the novel began.

Manzoni himself became a living icon, as the only one of the three great writers of the early nineteenth century to live into and beyond the time of unification. Even before his death, the *Promessi sposi* was adopted by the political establishment as an educational tool to impose unitarian values – one religion, one language, one nation. Like Dante, Manzoni was turned into an example, a static embodiment of the moral values of a single, dominant class. His profoundly critical treatment of power – both at the political and at the judiciary level – and his explicit advocacy of social change were omitted from the official view of the *Promessi sposi*. The book became the staid mirror of political moderation, rather than an incitement to much-needed social, educational and economic reforms.

If the works of contemporary writers like Manzoni could be read in a way that divorced them from their full intended meaning, and thus exploited solely for moral-political imagery useful to the national cause, it is not surprising that the figure of Dante entered the last part of the nineteenth century not as a model of ethical vigilance to guide the dynamic formation of a new nation, but as a means for propping up the political establishment that governed the Kingdom of Italy. The rebellious intellectual who had courageously refused the cultural limitations and the impositions of the Florentine government that ruled his homeland was not a particularly useful role model for a recently unified state struggling to construct a newly positive identity. Ideologically and politically motivated readings of Dante's life and works concentrated instead on their anticipation of other historical events of the Risorgimento that had particularly captured the popular imagination, especially those involving the many intellectuals who had been either incarcerated or forced into exile for their patriotic ideas.

This cultural phenomenon was indirectly enhanced by the writings of one of the most influential intellectuals of the century, Francesco De Sanctis (1817–1883). His famous *History of Italian Literature* (1870–71) inaugurated innovative ideological and cultural trends, but also lent itself to subsequent rhetorical exploitation by virtue of its insistence on a direct parallel between Dante and the major nineteenth-century literary figures. De Sanctis conceived the history of Italian literature as, almost from its inception, the history of a decadence or falling away. For De Sanctis, this decadence began when Petrarch invented the figure of the 'artist' – the 'man of letters' – and in so doing involuntarily split the *ethical* consequences of writing off from the aesthetic act. In other words, De Sanctis stressed the existence of two opposed traditions within Italian literature, one connected to an ethical view of writing (Dante's, resurrected by Alfieri and company) and the other to a purely aesthetic concept of poetry (Petrarch's).

The limits of the DeSanctian interpretation of the Italian literary tradition were imposed by his strict coordination of the development of that tradition with the ethical and civic life of the 'nation-to-be' over the centuries. In fact, prior to the French Revolution and the formation of the short-lived regional republics during Napoleon's Italian campaign (the Cisalpine Republic, the Ligure, the Romana and the Partenopea, all of which quickly came under strict French control), there had been no properly 'national' political awareness in Italy – not even at a theoretical level. Peninsular authors had not written, therefore, *for* or *within* that 'national entity' which was yet to come into being.[7] Alfieri and other eighteenth-century writers who deplored the absence of a national constituency (Giuseppe Baretti [1719–89] and Pietro Verri [1728–97], for instance) were late exceptions, and even they lamented more the absence of a pan-Italian culture uniting the various states of the peninsula than that of a unifying political entity. It was only after the Restoration, when Austrian control was extended over the entire peninsula (given that the Papal States and the Kingdom of Naples, though technically independent, were natural allies of the Austrian interests), that many intellectuals realized that unification was probably the best way to achieve political independence.[8] From an exclusively literary-critical point of view, therefore, we might actually turn De Sanctis' ideas around and insist on appreciating the fact that Italian literature achieved creative greatness, *despite* the perennial political, ideological and ethical crises that afflicted the peninsula over the centuries. But it is precisely De Sanctis' view that artistic culture and literature in particular should be seen as an integral, indivisible mirror of social reality that concerns us here. It is this idea which contributes to the radical divergence between the official promotion of the principal Italian authors as ethical models for a unified Italy, and their real cultural effectiveness, or lack thereof, in the formation of a national entity in which society and politics on the one hand and intellectual-artistic culture on the other truly intersected.

When De Sanctis outlined his idea of Italian literary history, including the promotion of Dante as an archetype *of* and *for* the civilization of Italy in his own day, he certainly did not intend to offer an easy rhetorical model that would allow his contemporaries to rest on past laurels. On the contrary, for De Sanctis Dante was uniquely important because he did what he did *in his own time*. De Sanctis did not intend to promulgate abstract nationalistic ideals that would keep alive the flame of the Risorgimento in post-unification Italy. In fact, his intellectual goal was exactly the opposite: he wished that the new Italy could close the idealistic chapter of Risorgimento, and move on toward a less academic, less rhetorical, and more concrete modernization of Italian society and culture. Taking Leopardi's suggestion, though turning it from the personal toward the collective, De Sanctis encouraged Italy to explore her own soul – not to look back and rest on past glories, but to take her own pulse and to determine what was needed to build a more efficient nation.

This impulse is clear in the last pages of the *History of Italian Literature*, in which De Sanctis incites the new nation to look forward, and not backward as was unfortunately more customary:

> Continua l'enfasi e la rettorica, argomento di poca serietà di studi e di vita. Viviamo molto sul nostro passato e del lavoro altrui. Non ci è vita nostra e lavoro nostro. E da' nostri vanti s'intravede la coscienza della nostra inferiorità.

> (The posturing and the rhetoric continues, suggesting that we are not particularly serious about our studies and our lives. We live off our own past and the work of others. We lack any real life or work of our own. And in our boasting [about the past], one can detect the consciousness of our inferiority.)

Paradoxically, however, De Sanctis' great fresco of Italian literature as Dante's *orphan* still reinforced the tendency to look to the past and even to memorialize the Risorgimento itself as the most recent manifestation of national glory. His interpretation stressed the possibility of drawing parallels, not only between Dante and Foscolo or other literary figures, but even between Dante and the historical protagonists of Risorgimento (Garibaldi, *et al.*). If Dante was to be understood, above all, as the distant 'father' of national Italian civilization, it seemed only logical, in the climate which followed unification, to compare him directly to the new 'fathers' of political Italy. After unification, the antithesis between the canonization of Dante as the prototype of the glorious resurgence of Italy, and the actual cultural lesson implicit in his rebellious poetics, sharply increased. From being the effigy of a dynamic political and artistic struggle for the independence of Italy, Dante became more and more the emblem of a political establishment (the new Italian Kingdom) that was in search of unequivocal and popular models to widen social consensus.

It is not surprising, then, that the generation of intellectuals who took up De Sanctis' lesson just before World War I had to face up to the abuses inherent in the rhetoricized glorification of the past, and of Dante in particular. The issue was sufficiently pressing that Dante and Dantism became a direct target of various journals and thinkers who wanted to modernize Italian culture by freeing it from the idealizing rhetoric of Risorgimento. It is no coincidence that most of these debates broke out in Florence, Dante's native city and the capital of the unified Italian state between 1864 and 1870. Unlike other cities, such as Milan, which had played a major role in the Risorgimento, Florence's economic structure was not industrial.[9] It was, in fact, from Milan that F.T. Marinetti (1876–1944) would later spread futurism – with its direct artistic response to industrial culture – to the rest of Europe, beginning with the publication of the first of the futurist manifestos (*Fondazione e manifesto del futurismo* [1909]). The contrast with Milan is instructive: Florence's many prestigious cultural institutions (the National Library, the Crusca and Fine Arts Academies, and so on), along with her numerous artistic and architectural monuments, favored her role as the emblematic center of Italian literary, cultural, intellectual and academic traditions. At the same time, given both her cultural heritage and her lack of a modern industrial base, Florence's appeal was linked with a profound orientation toward the past.

It was in keeping with this powerful cultural legacy, therefore, that Florence sponsored the proliferation of cultural reviews and journals in the decade preceding World War I. Among the most important of such journals was *Il Leonardo* (1903–7), founded and directed by Giovanni Papini (1881–1956). Even more influential was *La Voce* (1908–16), founded by Giuseppe Prezzolini (1882–1982), who – except for a brief parenthesis in 1912 – was its director through the end of 1914, when the literary critic Giuseppe De Robertis took over. Finally, the most famous of these mostly literary-artistic journals was *Lacerba* (1913–15), founded by Papini, and co-directed by the painter Ardengo Soffici (1879–1965) and the poet Aldo Palazzeschi (1885–1974).[10]

Like *Il Leonardo* before it, *La Voce* stood out for its polemics against academic culture, represented in Florence not only by the university, but even more by cultural institutions such as the Dante Society (*Società dantesca*) and its prestigious publication, *Il Bollettino della Società dantesca italiana*, devoted to promoting and reviewing academic Dante studies. Like that of the futurists, Papini's and Prezzolini's aversion to the academic world was based in the conviction that Italian culture needed to be 'modernized,' liberated from the cult of the past which they saw being fostered by the traditional scholarly and academic centers. This attitude accounts for their virulent attacks on anything that represented an impediment to the development of innovative cultural activities, whether artistic or critical.[11] For these writers, 'modernization' went hand-in-hand with an anti-academic attitude which from time to time implied targeting classical authors in order to get at contemporary scholars, intellectuals or institutions found 'guilty' of spending their cultural energies on the past rather than the present and the future.

Despite sharing a commitment to 'modernization,' the critical approach of the intellectuals of *La Voce* differed in fundamental ways from that of the futurists. Futurism was born as a literary movement that soon extended to other art forms (after the first *Manifesto* dedicated to literature by Marinetti in February 1909, others followed: one on futurist painters in February 1910; on musicians in January 1911; on sculpture in April 1912; and on architecture in July 1914 [all in De Maria 1973]). Futurism's theoretical and polemical writings were conceived mostly to define and to defend its artistic turf. By contrast, *La Voce* (as *Il Leonardo*) was conceived as an intellectual review with a broad range of interests, and did not have to advocate definite artistic or aesthetic theories.

La Voce quickly acquired national stature because of the importance of its contributors and the broad spectrum of debates it fostered around literary, cultural, educational and political issues.[12] The journal launched the careers of a number of young and then unknown writers and intellectuals, among whom were Scipio Slataper (1888–1915) and Renato Serra (1884–1915).[13] At the same time, the journal published essays by well known historians and politicians such as Giustino Fortunato (1848–1932) and Gaetano Salvemini (1873–1957),[14] and it sponsored crucial philosophical debates, such as the one concerning the nature of 'idealism' between Benedetto Croce and Giovanni Gentile. Finally, the eclectic nature of the journal is confirmed by the contributions of a wide variety of important contemporary intellectuals: the economist Luigi Einaudi (1874–1961; later to become first President of the Italian Republic [1948–55]); the politician, thinker and, later, prominent anti-fascist Giovanni Amendola (1882–1926); the literary scholar and writer Emilio Cecchi (1884–1966); the poet Clemente Rebora (1885–1957); and many others.

These facts help us to understand how and why, despite the temporary consonance between Papini and the futurists in 1913, the voice of *La Voce* differed significantly from that of futurism in its treatment of historical themes and literary figures. The acrimony of their polemics was no less than those of futurists but, with a few exceptions, was not similarly aimed at proving the superiority of a 'new' and distinct aesthetics. Their criticism of canonical culture did not preclude the possibility of studying and discussing the past, including the period of Risorgimento, understood as a crucial component in the formation of the historical situation in which these young writers saw themselves operating. On the one hand, they expressed a fiery opposition to the nostalgic view of the Risorgimento; on the other, they made attempts to recover its ethical mission which, in their view, had been left incomplete from both the cultural and the political standpoint.

As regards the latter project there was no single and rigorous position shared by the writers of *La Voce*. Some were more inclined to overlook the political shortcomings of the Risorgimento, insisting instead on the necessity of reviving its spiritual and cultural missions. Others paid more attention to the political aftermath of the period of unification (primarily Italy's unfulfilled claims on Trent and Trieste, both still under Austrian control), insisting upon a connection between political questions and artistic-cultural ones. The first position was represented above all by the 'Florentine' group of *La Voce*, especially by Papini, Soffici and Prezzolini, who were careful to separate their contemporary political concerns from Risorgimento rhetoric. This stance was also adopted by other contributors to the journal, such as Salvemini and De Robertis.[15] Papini, for instance, in an article of 1 July 1909, stressed that the time for wars was over, despite the thorny problem of Trent and Trieste, and it was instead a moment to concentrate on resuscitating the Risorgimento's cultural mission: 'Fino al 1870 il problema del Risorgimento è stato militare e diplomatico e oggi è problema di pensiero e di cultura' (Up to 1870 the Risorgimento was a military and diplomatic matter, today it is a problem of thought and culture). In sum, for Papini the Risorgimento's cultural goals were still an open problem, but they had very little to do with geopolitical issues.[16]

The standpoint of Scipio Slataper however was entirely different. Slataper was from Trieste, and he had chosen to attend the university at Florence precisely because of what the city symbolized: the essence of 'Italian' civilization. Slataper was critical of the meager cultural efforts of his native city, which he imputed to a commercial tradition that had slowly dissipated any real cultural and educational energies. The young writer made no mystery about his uncomplimentary opinion of Trieste in a series of articles for *La Voce*, beginning in February 1909 with a piece entitled *Trieste non ha tradizioni di cultura* ('Trieste Has No Cultural Traditions'). Nonetheless, his perspective on the political status of the Risorgimento in regards to Trent and Trieste diverged significantly from that of Papini and the others.

This difference was reflected in Slataper's more flexible interpretation of the political use of Dante as an icon of Italian unity. With his article 'I figli di Segantini,' published 9 December 1909, Slataper entered a debate that had been involuntarily opened by Gottardo Segantini, son of Giovanni Segantini, the well known painter from Trentino. The controversy had been triggered when Gottardo, at the inauguration of a monument devoted to his father in their hometown of Arco, near Trent, toasted the Austrian emperor for having favored his father's career. This episode ignited strongly nationalistic commentary against Gottardo, much of it in the newspaper *Il Giornale d'Italia*. Gottardo then sent a letter to the newspaper, explaining that his gesture should be seen as a simple, loving tribute, and affirming that his father's paintings were not the works of an *Italian* painter per se, but of an artist *super partes*. In the 18 November 1909 issue of *La Voce*, Ardengo Soffici took advantage of this polemic to profess that art was not to be judged for its supposed 'patriotic' meaning but only for its aesthetic value, and he accused Italy of having neglected Segantini's works.

Slataper agreed with this last point, but he disagreed with Soffici about the distinction between politics and art, and he placed the whole matter in a very different context:

E qui l'amico Soffici non seppe mettersi nello spirito di quei trentini che, aspirando all'annessione con l'Italia, è naturale infondano uno scopo politico in un significato, per i regnicoli, puramente artistico. Oggi si fa bene a ridere di Dante precursore di Mazzini, ma nel '48 chi ci rideva era in fondo uno che non sapeva vivere le necessità storiche del suo tempo (Slataper 1988: 347).

(And here my friend Soffici did not understand the spirit of the Trentinos who, hoping to be annexed into Italy, infused with a political meaning something that was purely artistic for those who belong to the Italian Kingdom.

Today we may well laugh at the idea of Dante as a forerunner to Mazzini, but one who laughed at it in 1848 did not understand how to live out the historical necessities of his time.)

Slataper's rebuttal of Soffici's view is important for two reasons. The young writer from Trieste admits that his historical interpretation may appear out of touch with the cultural reality of contemporary Italy ('Oggi si fa bene a ridere . . .'), but, in dating the connection between Dante and Mazzini to 1848 ('ma chi ci rideva nel '48 . . .'), he also suggests that the political and cultural climate in Trentino is still close to that of the first war of independence. In other words, for somebody like Slataper who could not call his native city 'home,' the outmoded equation between culture and politics, between Dante and Mazzini, was still full of significance. This is why, in the same article, he recalled the 'political' importance assigned to the Dante monument in Trent: 'Nel 1896 si inaugurava a Trento il monumento a Dante. Tutti sanno cosa significhi' (In 1896 Dante's monument in Trent was inaugurated. Everybody knows the significance of such an event).

Slataper's comments demonstrate the vital role still played by unitarian ideals in geographical areas where the Risorgimento had not yet had its full political effect. Moreover, they prove that Dante was still the strongest vehicle of communication for any message concerning the political Risorgimento. But if Slataper's standpoint was qualified by self-criticism and by his awareness that this view could be easily abused, this was not true of many other authors who relied on the rhetorical links between Dante and the Risorgimento. Dante, even more than Manzoni, was the figure most often misused in the patriotic oratory inherited from the previous century. So misused, in fact, that the controversies surrounding their names was even felt abroad. For instance, an Italian living in America in 1905 wrote two anonymous letters to the *Rivista popolare*, a journal edited by the Sicilian congressman Napoleone Colajanni (1847–1921; one of the first scholars of marxism in Italy), to accuse Dante and Manzoni of immorality, and of many other 'Italian defects' that were being propagated by the Dantists and the Manzonians.[17]

To give an idea of the strength and fascination of the equation between Dante and the Risorgimento beyond the specific context to which Slataper refers, let us briefly examine an article published in 1906 in the *Bollettino di studi danteschi* by its director, Giacomo Parodi, one of the best known Dante scholars of the time. Parodi's article reviews a number of essays that attack Dante and Dantism. Some had been published in England, in the *Westminster Review* and the *Contemporary Review*; others were by

Italians. Parodi notes immediately that, while the English essayists criticized Dante's poetry itself, the Italians were attacking the 'Dantists,' not the poet. This observation confirms indirectly that the real object of the reaction to the cult of Dante in Italy, was not Dante per se, but the ideologically motivated uses to which he was put.

One of the texts rebutted by Parodi was *La coltura italiana*, a book published in 1906 by Papini and Prezzolini. This volume did not merely focus on Dante and Dantism, but addressed a broad spectrum of other traditional targets, Manzoni and 'Manzonism' among them.[18] In their book, Papini and Prezzolini explicitly blame the Dante scholars belonging to the positivistic philological school of the 'metodo storico' (historical method), an approach whose technical and specialized focus had, they complained, diverted attention from the need for comprehensive reforms of the educational system in which Dante played such a crucial role (Papini and Prezzolini 1906). Parodi, a strong supporter of the 'metodo,' agreed about the general cultural deficiencies of post-unification Italy and about the many bombastic and unscholarly uses to which Dante's name had been put, but he also insisted on the scholarly seriousness of the 'metodo storico' as one of the best means of bringing Italy back into the mainstream of European culture. Finally, Parodi added that contemporary cultural interest in Dante was justified on the grounds that his ethical teachings had been revived by the 'fathers' of Risorgimento, further asserting that Dante was a 'national' treasure whose 'spiritual brothers' could only be Italians: 'I fratelli spirituali di Dante [. . .] sono tutti italiani, da San Francesco d'Assisi [. . .] fino a Giuseppe Mazzini e [. . .] Garibaldi' (Parodi 1906: 140–1; Dante's spiritual brothers are all Italians, from St. Francis of Assisi to Mazzini and to Garibaldi).

The ideologically 'Risorgimento' roots of Parodi's view of Italian cultural history are further revealed when he specifies in the same article that the qualities that make Dante and his *fratelli* exceptional are not to be found on 'Germanic soil' (1906: 140). It is precisely against such historiographical abuses that Papini and Prezzolini had directed their essay attacking Dantists in *La coltura italiana*, and it is because of the contamination of the serious scholarship with nationalistic propaganda that they dragged anyone involved in Dante studies, either professionally or ad hoc, into their battle (Papini and Prezzolini 1906).[19] The measure of the hostility they felt toward Dante studies can be seen in another article by Prezzolini in *La Voce* of 13 June 1914, which again depicts the 'metodo storico' as a useless critical approach, unprepared to develop any efficient educational project in the service of the true interest of post-unification Italy. The article summarizes the reasons which had driven Prezzolini,

Papini and others to criticize the 'metodo storico.' According to Prezzolini, the 'metodo' had given rise to a generation that 'oscillated between the spirit of 1870 and that of 1910' (cited in Romanò 1960: 677), that is, it had confused and slowed down the *making* of Italy as actually intended by the best Risorgimento thinkers and patriots. This was because the pedantic 'metodo' negated intuitive thought, and could thus not encourage, strengthen and spread the intellectual dynamism necessary to develop the conscience of the adolescent Italian nation. In fact, Prezzolini pointed out that in 1914 De Sanctis could still be viewed as a new author, because his understanding of Dante's place in Italian culture had been neglected precisely in the name of the 'metodo storico.' Prezzolini clearly believed that De Sanctis' hope for a true 'modernization' of Italy and its culture, as we earlier saw it expressed in the last pages of his *History of Italian Literature*, had not yet materialized (Romanò 1960: 676–86).

In short, the polemics about Dante were the expression of an anti-academic and anti-traditionalist impulse. In fact, Papini, Prezzolini, Soffici and other writers connected with *La Voce*, *Lacerba* and similar Florentine journals, insisted that the Dantists were incapable of a genuine under-standing of Dante's poetry. This critical stance is particularly evident in Papini, who eloquently expressed his convictions in the title of one of his articles: 'Per Dante contro i Dantisti' (For Dante and against the Dantists).[20] For Papini, Dante's most important lesson had been to show the way to creativity and experimentation, while, by contrast, the com-placencies of official Dante scholarship were obstacles to the development of anything really new and thus genuinely dantesque.[21] Occasionally Papini even implied that his and his friends' intellectual battles were closely comparable to Dante's (see, for instance, *Le due tradizioni* [1912; The Two Traditions] or *Dante vicario d'Iddio* [1907; Dante Messenger of God]). Dante is portrayed as misunderstood and isolated by the official culture, which lacked the intellectual courage and profundity to embrace his ethical views.

This critical attitude presumes that the defiant writers of *La Voce* were actually closer to understanding and embodying the most vital aspects of Dante's lesson than any scholar or philologist could ever be. In other words, despite their anti-Dantism – or rather, precisely because of it – intellectuals like Papini and Prezzolini confirmed that Dante, in the years which preceded World War I, was still a crucial reference point for any cultural battle which sought an aesthetic renewal grounded in ethical principles. The debate about the (mis)use of Dante was, in sum, the sign of a paradox: the *real* lesson transmitted by Dante (originality; the possibility of change) was also the antidote to the cult of Dante and the past.

Marinetti himself had a part in these debates. Futurism, by definition, was compelled to attack the cult of the past. Like Papini and Prezzolini, Marinetti despised and vilified the official culture of Dante studies, although he did not engage in direct critical debates concerning Dante's poetics, or attack specific scholars or schools of scholarly thought. A typical and significant *Manifesto* expressing this position is the one entitled *La Divina Commedia è un verminaio di glossatori* (The Divine Comedy is a Worm-Ranch for Commentators), in which Marinetti explicitly suggests that the deplorable status of Italian culture is well represented by Dante commentators who, like worms, feed upon the *corpus* of a dead author. The same basic idea, differently expressed, returns in other *Manifestos*, such as the one against the 'Professors' (*Contro i professori*).

Aside from the theoretical propaganda of futurism, however, Marinetti's own poetic approach to Dante and to the recuperation of his creativity was very different from that of Papini and company. Futurism's main goal (as articulated by Marinetti in the years before World War I) was to propound a new way of looking at the world, one that broke free from the traditional conception of art as the celebration of nature, taken as a symbol of what cannot be grasped and understood by humans. In contrast, futurism was to be a new aesthetics inspired by the dynamic aspects of modern, mechanized, life – by its movement, its speed, its ever-changing realities, and by the possibility of comprehending and shaping nature via the new machines invented in the preceding decades. To embrace this new aesthetics, one had to believe in the power of fantasy as a tool for moving forward into the future, and not just as a vehicle for the repetition of an existing tradition.

Marinetti believed this to be the essential characteristic of Dante's poetics, and he saw Dante as the foremost example of a pure and primitive creative strength able to eradicate the doubts raised by the traditionalists in relation to the futurist project. In his response to the objections directed against his *Manifesto tecnico della letteratura futurista* (1912), where he insisted on the need to 'hate intelligence' and instead to choose intuition as the only real way to break with tradition, Marinetti justified his claims by asserting that Dante, along with Edgar Allan Poe, had already preceded him on this path (De Maria 1973: 85). Dante's aesthetic vision, according to Marinetti, was not dependent upon syllogistic reasoning, but rather drew upon a faith in the intuitive power of poetry and in the innovative generativity of his own creative vision. Marinetti's poetic production betrays a fascination, on the one hand, with the metaphorical journey to the stars that Dante imagines in the *Divine Comedy*, and, on the other, with Dante's powerful belief in his poetic mission and his relentless drive to achieve it. Marinetti's works show this pattern from his early poems such as *La conquête des étoiles* (1902) to the *Areopoema di Gesù* (written in the 1930s). Marinetti shares Dante's desire to yoke fantasy and reality and thereby to reach, or to form, a new perceptual dimension. In other words, Marinetti's and the futurists' belief in the possibility of renewing art in accordance with the continuous and dynamic changes of life found a clear precursor in Dante's creation. In Marinetti's case, of course, access to this new creative dimension is enabled by the fascination of the new machines (see Ciccarelli 1996).

Despite their bitter and often violent proclamations concerning the need to destroy the cult of the past and of national glory, the intellectuals who gave life to the cultural debate before World War I were able to distinguish between the stultifying politicization of a national icon and the vital lessons which that same icon could still offer to them. The rebellious writers who tried to renew Italian culture, rejecting and vilifying the exaggerated celebration of the past, and of Dante above all, were actually affirming an essential belief in the relevance of Dante's aesthetic to the twentieth century. If the fundamental lesson that Dante offered – which was passed on to modern times also through Manzoni's hidden Dantism – was the need to have faith in the exploration of reality, to embrace experimentalism, and to believe in the ultimately positive value of change, then Papini and his friends, on the one hand, and Marinetti and futurism, on the other, owed Dante (and to a lesser degree Manzoni) much more than they ever cared to admit.

With the rise of Fascism after World War I, the contrast between the rhetorical use of the past on the part of the official culture, and the actual lesson filtered from the classics of Italian literature into the new cultural scene would be amplified. Futurism and Fascism did travel together for some years: the cult of technology and modernity, the rhetoric of violence, the simultaneous contempt and fascination for the masses, the exaltation of a nationalistic sense of racial superiority, are characteristics shared by Mussolini and Marinetti, and the movements they headed. But it is also obvious, as Prezzolini had already asserted in 1923 (De Maria 1973: 286), that the discrepancies between the exigencies of a political regime in search of consensus and those of an artistic movement based on the 'destruction' of the past, would eventually become insurmountable.

Fascism, in fact, sought to foreground its distinctively modern political attributes, and therefore devoted much attention to the innovative qualities advocated by futurism and by the other intellectuals who stirred the cultural debate before World War I. (Many of the contributors of *La Voce* and *Lacerba* worked for governmental cultural enterprises during the early years of Fascism.)[22] Fascism's interest in modern art and architecture, for instance, is certainly a sign of this legacy. On the other hand, Fascism needed and wanted to place itself within the classical tradition of Italian history and culture, and thus celebrated everything (from ancient Rome to the recent victory in World War I) and everyone (from Dante to Garibaldi) that represented the national greatness of the country, very much contrary to the wishes of the futurists and the *vociani*. Once Fascism became an unassailable dictatorship, this last tendency prevailed. Marinetti and Papini were soon nominated to the Italian Academy by Mussolini, and Marinetti – the futurist who wanted to burn academies and museums – was chosen to direct the literary section of the Academy (1929). The latter choice reveals the new political regime's cultural double standard. In making Marinetti the director of the literary branch of the Academy, Mussolini attempted to preserve a fresh and dynamic literary image for Italy. But, at the same time he underlined his political resolution to control and to regulate an aesthetic movement like futurism which, ironically, was originally born as the 'destroyer of rules.'

Notes

1. In fact, Mazzini would later publish Foscolo's political writings (1843–44). After an initial favorable evaluation of romanticism, Mazzini modified his view, and condemned the more spiritualizing aspects of the movement. His political interpretation of Italian romantic authors, however, helped to mold the identification between romanticism and Risorgimento. It is in the wake of this interpretation that in 1860 the patriot and thinker Carlo Cattaneo could still praise Foscolo more for his political and moral legacy than for his literary accomplishments.
2. Here, I refer to the canonical authors who have been recognized over and over as the literary protagonists of their time. It is obvious that other authors and intellectuals, such as Carlo Goldoni, Giuseppe Parini, and Ippolito Nievo, also contributed significantly to the phenomenon of 'rebirth' in Italian literary culture at this time.
3. In this vein one should not overlook the works of Vincenzo Monti (1754–1828), although his recuperation of Dante could be dismissed as merely, superficially, stylistic. The fact that Monti's intellectual project was weakly grounded and that his patriotic interests were

changeable (his works celebrate, with equal ease and apologetic ardor, the Papal States, the French Revolution, Napoleon, and the Austrian Empire) kept his Dantism at a very superficial level. The distance between Monti's ethical world and Dante's is evident. And yet, Monti's poems, because of their descriptive structure, which is necessary to the apologetic celebration of their various subjects, privilege a dramatic narrative style and draw heavily upon Dante's powerful language. Monti's example had little impact on the intellectual formation of nineteenth-century Italian writers, but it did suggest to the next generation of poets that they should not disregard Dante as a stylistic model. This influence is evident, for instance, in Manzoni's early works, where the distinctly dantesque tone is certainly filtered through Monti.

4. Dionisotti (1988: 63–71) has shown that Foscolo's exile came about almost entirely as a personal decision that had more to do with his private needs (particularly his long involvement with the Napoleonic army) than any political necessity. Rather, the intellectuals who stayed in Italy, especially in Milan, and endured the censorship of the Austrian Empire offered less visible but more practical and efficient service to the political cause of unification.

5. On the dating of this text, see Di Benedetto 1991: 279–86.

6. The novel is set between 1628 and 1630, during the Spanish domination of Milan, which becomes a metaphor for the Austrians who controlled Milan in Manzoni's time. Manzoni pretends to find an unpublished manuscript that narrates crucial events in the lives of a couple of young Lombard peasants, Renzo and Lucia, who suddenly receive the unwanted attention of powerful people and of the corrupt judiciary system. Throughout the novel, Manzoni develops a parallel between the important historical events of the period – the Thirty Years War involving Spain, France and the German states; the Black Plague that devastated Europe; the many economic and political revolts and so on – and the private lives of the two peasants persecuted by those in power.

7. I am not claiming that the concept of Italy originated only in the nineteenth century. It is sufficient to recall Petrarch's famous canzone to Italy (*Canzoniere* 128). However, except in a very few cases (including, perhaps, Machiavelli), the idea of national 'unity' was advanced solely as a means for expelling foreign invaders, and, later, governments, from the separate states of the Italian peninsula, and not with the aim of creating a unified political entity or a single, centralized state.

8. This view is clear, for instance, in Manzoni's unfinished essay comparing the French revolution and the Italian wars of independence (*Saggio sulla Rivoluzione Francese del 1789 e la Rivoluzione Italiana del 1859*). Manzoni maintains that it was the absolute domination of the Austrian Empire over the entire peninsula after the Restoration that persuaded the Italians that partial solutions, such as the regional republics, would not be sufficient and would fail again (Manzoni 1963: 309–21).

9. The industrialization of Milan certainly played a major role in fostering the fascination of Marinetti and of the other futurists with technology. Of course, the first *Manifesto* of futurism was published in the Parisian newspaper *Le Figaro*. Marinetti grew up in Alexandria, Egypt, where he attended French schools, and he later graduated from high school in Paris. He finally went to Italy – his family having moved back to Milan – to attend university. Nonetheless, there is no doubt that futurism was a 'Milanese' enterprise, conceived and developed in Marinetti's home in Milan which, beginning in 1905, had become a point of encounter for those interested in writing non-traditional literature.

10. In its first year of life, *Lacerba* was strongly connected with futurism. However, after an initial cooperation between the three editors of *Lacerba* and the original Milanese futurist group led by Marinetti and Boccioni, there was a clamorous falling out. The three 'Florentines,' especially Papini, claimed that futurism had departed from its artistic mission – which was to create art outside pre-established categories – and had succumbed to Marinetti's own ambition and to the imposition of a rigid set of artistic rules (see De Maria 1973: 276–86). *Lacerba* had the merit of publishing many important futurists' texts, and also that of offering a forum for the first works of poets such as Ungaretti and Campana.

11. A good indicator of the position of these intellectuals who opposed traditional nineteenth-century culture, is found in Guillaume Apollinaire's famous *Manifesto-sintesi*, published in *Lacerba* in 1913. The French poet places in a single derogatory list categories such as 'literary critics,' 'professors,' 'philologists' (those who live off the past or others' works, in other words), and cultural icons such as Dante, Shakespeare and Manzoni. In another list, of course, he exalts contemporary artists and writers (published in De Maria 1973: 120).

12. In addition to the many important contributors to *La Voce*, it is useful to think about who the *readers* of the journal were. For instance, the young Antonio Gramsci was a careful reader of the review, as we

know from his comments on the function of *La Voce* in Italian culture in his *Letteratura e vita nazionale*.

13. Slataper was author of the book of lyrical prose, *Il mio Carso* (1912), concerning the mountainous area in Trentino which would become a major battlefield during World War I. Serra was best known for his *Esame di coscienza di un letterato* (1915; The Conscience of a Man of Letters), a pamphlet on the necessity, apparently contradictory for an Italian liberal intellectual, of accepting Italy's entrance into the Great War. Ironically, Slataper and Serra both died in battle, just a few months apart and in the same war zone.

14. In the pages of *La Voce* Salvemini helped spread awareness of what came to be called the *questione meridionale* (the Southern Question). He ended his cooperation with the journal in 1911, when he founded *L'Unità*, his own paper entirely devoted to politics (he briefly resumed his cooperation with *La Voce Politica*, a series of special issues published between May and October 1915). In the years in which he collaborated with *La Voce*, Salvemini (who later became one of the best known anti-fascist intellectuals and who lived in exile in Europe and in the United States before his return to Italy in 1947) was a professor of History at the University of Messina and then Pisa. The fact that a politician and a scholar like Salvemini would choose *La Voce* for his social battles is a sign of the cultural importance acquired by the journal. For the intellectual history of the various phases of *La Voce* see the introduction by Romanò (1960). On the Southern Question in relation to the Risorgimento, see Chapter Four of this volume.

15. For instance, after Italy entered the war in May 1915, Salvemini published a brief article in *La Voce Politica* in which he listed the casualty reports of the major Risorgimento battles to show the anachronism of using that conflict as a model for understanding what was at stake in the new war (Golzio and Guerra 1962: 768). In 1915, De Robertis, the new editor of the regular issue of *La Voce*, published a piece in which he underlined the cultural and political awkwardness of looking back at the Risorgimento to justify the present war (Scalia 1961: 562).

16. This point of view is characteristic of Papini's cultural attitude in general. He was susceptible to a sort of mystical idea of history, a trait which returns in many of his writings and which would eventually lead to his conversion to Catholicism after World War I. Papini's spiritual understanding of his cultural mission can be traced back to as early as 1905, when, in a letter to Soffici, he claims that he would

like to be the 'spiritual guide' and the cultural 'reorganizer' of the newly formed Italian state (Romanò 1960: 19). This insistence upon connecting Italy with its spiritual/cultural mission is also evident in a 1911 article, 'La tradizione italiana' (*La Voce*, 14 December). In this essay Papini asserted the absence of *one single* Italian cultural tradition and declared that his intellectual duty was to break the cultural code of his times ('Il genio non ha tradizioni ma le rompe' [Papini 1961b: 1220]). Stigmatizing the Libyan war then in progress, he repeated his belief that Italy needed to build a spiritual unity rather than getting involved in other wars.

17. The letters – signed 'X' – appeared in volume 11, issues 8 and 15 of the *Rivista Popolare*. Even Croce himself and Michele Barbi, the most important Dante scholar of the period, complained about the tendency to misuse Dante's name for political or rhetorical ends (Caretti 1976: 300).

18. The other targets of Papini's and Prezzolini's intellectual wrath were contemporary authors such as Gabriele D'Annunzio, whose aesthetics was seen as an obstacle to a cultural renewal, and entire philosophical schools, such as 'idealism.'

19. In order to understand Papini's and Prezzolini's polemical focus on the critical activities of a select few scholars, one must remember that at the turn of the century – in a city of Florence's cultural stature and in a society dominated by a small, traditionalist cultural elite – centers such as the 'Società dantesca' played a major role in determining the city's public artistic and literary agenda.

20. In this 1905 essay, then included in *La coltura italiana*, Papini considered Dante to be the wrong archetype for Italian culture, because as an Etruscan ('spirito etrusco') rather than a Latin character he could not be understood by the Italians (Papini and Prezzolini 1906, cited from Papini 1961a: 298). Papini would later describe himself in the same terms, establishing a parallel between his and Dante's exceptional qualities (both from Florence, both 'Etruscans,' both misunderstood by Italian culture).

21. Soffici held a similar position. In 1913, in a series of articles about the development of 'Cubism,' he argued that the movement's primitive and expressionistic creations were mirrored by Dante's (see Scalia 1961: 136).

22. Marinetti's political activity in 1919–20 contributed to Mussolini's ascent to power. Prezzolini and Ungaretti wrote for the Mussolinian *Il Popolo d'Italia* and worked for the Italian Foreign Office when Mussolini was already Prime Minister. Papini adhered to Fascism almost immediately and wrote for various fascist-related reviews.

References

Caretti, L. (1976), 'Dantismo fiorentino,' *Antichi e moderni*, Turin: Einaudi, pp. 297–312.

Ciccarelli, A. (1996), 'Note on Futurism and Dante,' *Lectura Dantis* 18–19: 30–40.

—— (1998), 'Foscolo, Manzoni and the Culture of Exile,' in A. Ciccarelli and P. Giordano, eds, *L'esilio come certezza: La ricerca d'identità culturale in Italia dalla Rivoluzione francese ai giorni nostri*, special issue of *Italiana* 7: 22–43.

De Maria, L., ed. (1973), *Per conoscere Marinetti e il Futurismo*, Milan: Mondadori.

Di Benedetto, V., ed. (1991), *Ugo Foscolo: Sesto tomo dell'io*, Turin: Einaudi.

Dionisotti, C. (1988), *Appunti sui moderni*, Bologna: Il Mulino.

Golzio, F., and A. Guerra, eds (1962), *La cultura italiana del '900 attraverso le riviste*, Vol. 5, Turin: Einaudi.

Manzoni, A. (1963), *Saggi storici e politici*, ed. F. Ghisalberti, Milan: Mondadori.

—— (1990), *Opere: Scritti linguistici*, Vol. 3, ed. M. Vitale, Turin: Loescher.

Papini, G. (1961a), *Dante e Michelangiolo*, Milan: Mondadori.

—— (1961b), *Opere: Filosofia e letteratura*, Milan: Mondadori.

—— and G. Prezzolini (1906), *La coltura italiana*, Florence: Francesco Lumachi.

Parodi, G. (1906), 'Rassegna critica degli studi danteschi,' *Bollettino della Società Dantesca Italiana* 13 (2): 128–40.

Romanò, A., ed. (1960), *La cultura italiana del '900 attraverso le riviste*, Vol. 2, 'La Voce' (1908–1914), Turin: Einaudi.

Scalia, G., ed. (1961), *La cultura italiana del '900 attraverso le riviste*, Vol. 4, Turin: Einaudi.

Slataper, S. (1925), *Scritti politici*, ed. G. Stuparich, Rome: 'La Voce' Società Anonima Editrice.

—— (1988), *Lettere triestine: Col seguito di altri scritti vociani di polemica su Trieste*, postscript by E. Guagnini, Trieste: Dedalolibri.

Tongiorgi, D. (1994), 'Un nuovo e importante testimone dell'orazione "Sull'origine e i limiti della giustizia" di Ugo Foscolo,' *Giornale Storico della Letteratura Italiana* 3: 412–34.

–3–

Liberty On (and Off) the Barricades:
Verdi's Risorgimento Fantasies
Mary Ann Smart

My title is deliberately ambivalent, in more than one sense. Its first half already points in two directions, both to the war-like central figure of Delacroix's *Liberty Leading the People* and to more domestic variations on that famous emblem of patriotism and femininity. In their incarnations as Verdian heroines, both types will make appearances in the second half of this article. As for 'Verdi's Risorgimento Fantasies,' the phrase is intended to invoke both Verdi's own imaginary constructions of the Risorgimento in his operas and historiographic fantasies projected onto his music over the last century or so. The second of these is perhaps the more important, and, I will argue, sometimes threatens to obscure the first: the variety and subtlety of the patriotic 'fantasies' in the operas themselves. Recently, both documentary research and new approaches to musical interpretation have prompted revisions to the persistent popular image of Verdi as a political composer who served as a senator in the first Italian parliament, and whose operas reflect a similarly straightforward patriotic commitment. New evidence suggests that Verdi's political commitment was somewhat opportunistic and intermittent, and that popular reception of his operas as patriotic symbols was less widespread than has often been thought. But rather than simply revoking Verdi's credentials as a 'Risorgimento composer,' I would suggest that we might welcome such biographical complications as occasions for new interpretive excursions – to seek the political content of Verdi's operas in images more nuanced, and perhaps more culturally rich, than the dema-gogic choruses and allegorical clashing armies that have traditionally been the focus of interpretations of Verdi's Risorgimento sympathies.

Perhaps the best avenue into the realm of 'fantasy' is by way of Verdi's own words, specifically through one of his most famous letters, written to his friend and librettist Francesco Maria Piave in April 1848. Having braved considerable physical inconvenience to return to Milan when news of the *Cinque giornate* reached him in Paris, Verdi was in the grip of a revolutionary excitement that comes through loud and clear in the ring of the opening phrases, which sound as if they could fit quite comfortably into one of Piave's libretti:

> Onore a questi prodi! onore a tutta l'Italia che in questo momento è veramente grande! L'ora è suonata, siine pur persuaso, della sua liberazione. È il popolo che la vuole: e quando il popolo vuole non avvi potere assoluto che le possa resistere. [. . .]
> Tu mi parli di musica! Cosa ti passa in corpo? . . . Tu credi che io voglia ora occuparmi di note, di suoni? . . . Non c'è né ci deve essere che una musica grata alle orecchie degli italiani del 1848. La musica del cannone! . . . Io non scriverei una nota per tutto l'oro del mondo: ne avrei un rimorso immenso consumare della carta di musica, che è sì buona da far cartucce. (Walker 1978 [1962], 229–30)

> (Honor to these heroes! Honor to all Italy, which is now truly great! The hour of her liberation has arrived; be sure of that. The people want it: and when the people want it, there is no absolute power that can resist. [. . .] / You talk to me about music! What has got into you? Do you think that I want to bother myself now with notes, with sounds? There cannot be any music welcome to Italian ears in 1848 except the music of the cannon! I would not write a note for all the money in the world: I would feel immense guilt at using up music-paper, which is so good for making shells.)

The carefully controlled rhetoric here is entirely typical of Verdi's letters, and the shift of tone in the middle of this passage, with the alarming image it conjures of Verdi's autograph scores stuffed into the throats of cannons, may not be quite as disingenuous as it sounds. But whether Verdi's ringing rejection of music's relevance in times of historical urgency was meant as a gesture of respect to the rebels or as a joke, its contrast with the solemnity of those first few phrases invites interpretation.

These contrasting registers could stand for two ways historians have tended to regard the relationship between works of art and political events. The quasi-operatic clichés of the opening – 'Onore a questi prodi!,' 'L'ora è suonata!' – suggest a very direct contact in which operatic formulations can exert an impact on 'real' life, while the flippant rejection of music that follows suggests an unbridgeable abyss between art and history. I will return to this second, more skeptical attitude, but for now I should like to remain in the 'operatic' world of overstatement and coincidence: a methodological world in which intersections between art works and momentous historical events are still – despite postmodernist skepticism – the ultimate object of desire for many historians of culture.

This desire to have the two worlds intersect has given rise to a series of cross-disciplinary pairings, the best-known of which is probably the hackneyed 'Beethoven and Napoleon.' The parallel formulation 'Verdi and the Risorgimento,' while offering a much richer field of inquiry, is perhaps subject to some of the same pitfalls. In such equations generally, the political dimension often crowds out other interesting avenues of interpretation; and in the specific case of Verdi, the equation carries with it an implicit developmental narrative, one that devalues the musical features of the so-called 'Risorgimento operas' (which date roughly from the first ten years of Verdi's long career) to concentrate on their political meanings. Textbooks of nineteenth-century music, for example, unanimously take the political angle as a starting point, and descriptions of the 1840s audiences who 'roared [with] approval' for Verdi's early choruses too often stand in for observations about the actual sound of the music (Plantinga 1984: 300). Even Carl Dahlhaus, whose brilliant history of nineteenth-century music is remarkable for the caution with which it approaches possible links between works of music and social context, is seduced by the Risorgimento narrative. Dahlhaus begins by emphasizing that 'Verdi was a popular composer before he was a significant one' (1989: 206), as if devaluing the early works musically because they were political, and his discussion ends with the familiar idea that Verdi's early choruses 'were received as musical symbols of the Risorgimento by a torn and disrupted nation whose ardor flared up in opera' (ibid.).

One reason for the appeal of this strain of history may be that it resides mostly in a string of engaging anecdotes. Details vary, but these stories tend to concern choruses, and they usually center around a spontaneous outpouring of emotion from a crowd, moments when Verdi's music enabled the populace to express patriotic sentiments that would have been forbidden in any guise except the relatively 'safe,' 'meaningless' medium of song. One typical tale involves an 1846 performance of *Ernani* in Bologna during which the name of the baritone character, the medieval Spanish king, Carlo Quinto, was replaced in the entire last act by that of Pio Nono, yielding lines like 'Sia lode eterna, Pio, al tuo nome' (Gossett 1990: 57). But the best – and best-known – of the Risorgimento anecdotes concerns Verdi's first great success, *Nabucco*. As the story goes, the audience at the 1842 La Scala première demanded an encore of the famous chorus of chained Hebrew slaves, 'Va pensiero,' in contravention of the Austrians' blanket prohibition against encores at public performances. After this, enthusiasm for 'Va pensiero' spread across Italy, sparking not only more encores, but also spontaneous choral outbursts, with Verdi's catchy tune moving entire audiences to burst into song.[1]

Turning from such a narrative to the chorus itself, what is immediately striking is the incongruous atmosphere of calm and repose of both words and music. Even if one were to substitute the Tiber and 'Rome's toppled towers' for the geographical markers of the Biblical promised land, this evocation of a distant homeland conveys little urgency and only a dulled, remote sense of pain:

Va pensiero sull'ali dorate
Va ti posa sui clivi, sui colli
Ove olezzano libere e molli
L'aure dolci del suolo natal!
Del Giordano le rive saluta,
Di Sïonne le torri atterrate . . .
Oh mia patria si bella e perduta!
O membranza sì cara e fatal!
Arpa d'or dei fatidici vati
Perchè muta dal salice pendi?
Le memorie nel petto raccendi,
Ci favella del tempo che fu! . . .

(Fly, thought, on wings of gold / go, settle on the slopes and the hills, / where the sweet airs / of our native land, free and gentle, waft fragrantly. / Greet the banks of the Jordan / and Zion's toppled towers. / Oh, my country, so lovely and distant! / Oh, fond and painful memory! / Golden harp of the prophetic bards / Why hang mute on the willow? / Rekindle the memories in our breast, / Tell us of times past! . . .)

In a sense, the words of 'Va pensiero' enact an imaginative recovery of the lost country, documenting the exile's attempt to reach back to the homeland by means of peripatetic thoughts, breezes and bardic song. In keeping with this poetic desire to call into being the peaceful, familiar landscape, Verdi's music sets up a kind of static musical paradise, immediately establishing a rocking rhythm and a melodic outline that hardly alters throughout the piece. Patterns of melodic repetition create an exclusively musical symmetry and closure, but never attempt to illustrate individual poetic ideas. As a nostalgic invocation of nation 'Va pensiero' is exemplary, but it carries no impulse toward action, change, or movement.

A few years ago, in the course of preparing a critical edition of *Nabucco*, musicologist Roger Parker tried to trace the story of the spontaneous, unruly 'Va pensiero' encore to an original source. What he discovered was that it dates back only to a newspaper review quoted in Franco Abbiati's 1959 Verdi biography; and when Parker turned to

Abbiati's sources, he found that the biographer had more or less invented the passage, cobbling together bits from two different reviews to attribute to 'Va pensiero' an encore that had actually been demanded for another chorus in *Nabucco*, the Hebrew prayer 'Immenso Jeovha.' The routine Biblical sentiments of 'Immenso Jeovha' lack the allegorical potential of 'Va pensiero's pastoral nostalgia; and one only needs to listen to the first few phrases of each chorus to understand why Abbiati might have wanted to manufacture the 'Va pensiero' encore.[2]

This single instance of misapprehension turns out to be emblematic of a larger-scale exaggeration of the associations between Verdi's music and the emerging Italian sense of nation in the 1840s.[3] Reports in the *Gazzetta Musicale di Milano*, the house organ of Verdi's publisher Ricordi, show that in the aftermath of the *Cinque giornate*, when La Scala closed down for several months, opera was replaced by concerts of newly-composed patriotic hymns and military music. But strangely, in the realm where the 'papa dei cori' should have been a leading figure, Verdi's name is nowhere to be found on concert programs. Ricordi's *libroni*, the log-books that record what pieces were printed, tell the same story: during this period the printing presses were dedicated almost entirely to engraving patriotic anthems, but Verdi's name is missing from these lists too. Even more surprising, there is not a single mention in the *libroni* of any reprints of 'Va pensiero' as an independent piece, an inexplicable absence if it had really been receiving such frequent popular performances.

One chorus that Ricordi did print in 1848, Pietro Cornali's 'Canto degli italiani,' can perhaps provide some clue as to what Milanese audiences did want to listen to and sing along with in moments of revolutionary fervor. Published in the last issue of the *Gazzetta Musicale di Milano* to appear before the Austrians returned to Milan (26 July 1848), Cornali's chorus can probably be taken as representative of the reams of such popular pieces published during the year. The text, credited only to 'un toscano,' consists of eight four-line stanzas, and begins with a call to guerrilla action, urging each citizen to seize stones and bits of roofing tile to defend his country against the invader. Internal stanzas celebrate nation-defining moments of the distant past – 'Viva il Vespro di Palermo!' 'Viva il patto di Pontida!' – and the chorus concludes with a ringing affirmation of the power of the Pope and Holy Cross to support the campaign waged by the sword.

> Finchè Italia non sia nostra
> Non si dorma, non si taccia;
> Segua il fatto alla minaccia,

Italiani alla tenzon.
Chi lo schioppo non ha pronto
Piglia un tegolo d'argilla;
Viva il sasso di Balbilla
Che poté più d'un cannon.
[. . . 5 stanzas omitted]
Chi di voi non può la spada
Osi almen alzar la voce
Viva il Pio che la Croce
Fè segnal di libertà.

(Until Italy belongs to us, / we will not sleep, we will not be silenced. /
Suit the action to the word: / Italians into the fray! / He who does not have
his rifle at the ready, / he may take up a piece of tile; / long live the stones
of Balilla, / which can achieve much more than a cannon. [. . .] Those of
you who do not have a sword, / dare at least to raise your voices; / long
live Pio, whose Cross / has been the signal for our freedom.)

Parker has written that 'it is hard [. . .] to be much interested in Cornali's
music, hard even to take it seriously' (1997b: 110).[4] But in the context of
Italians' strange indifference to Verdi's music in 1848, it would seem hard
not to take Cornali seriously, if only for the access this music promises
to popular and revolutionary musical taste. And, indeed, Cornali's music
could hardly be more different from 'Va pensiero.' True, Cornali sets up
a lilting rhythm early on and sticks to it, even using the same chains of
dotted rhythms as 'Va pensiero.' In Cornali's case, though, that repetitive
rhythm is underpinned by a series of assertive repeated chords, forceful
enough to impel brigades forward in a slow march. Most intriguing, where
'Va pensiero' sustains a single mood across the length of the piece, the
'Canto degli italiani' is full of passing dissonances and fleeting melodic
responses to individual words in the poetic text, effects that jar the listener
out of private contemplation and aggressively call attention back to the
meaning of the words. In the second stanza, voices and piano accompaniment suddenly join in a unison tattoo-figure to paint the lines 'chi lo
schioppo non ha pronto / piglia un tegolo d'argilla,' and the stanza ends
with an even more overstated onomatopoeic effect for 'poté più d'un
cannon.' Judged according to any high-art aesthetic, these points of literal
text-music correspondence verge on the absurd, but it may well have been
partly these devices – the way Cornali's music seems willing to take the
text 'at its word' – that made the chorus suitable for revolutionary
occasions. Taken together with the rather sensual layering of a melody
line embellished by frequent chromatic dissonances over a comfortingly

monotonous bass-line, the effect is a skillful combination of soothing, memorable melody with little surges of heightened sensation and surprise. If in the 1840s Verdi's operas seem neither to have alarmed the Austrians much (two of his early scores are even dedicated to Austrian duchesses resident in Milan), nor to have been quite the focus of popular patriotic feeling usually thought, his reputation as the 'vate del Risorgimento' clearly gained strength as the nineteenth century progressed. The senatorial post granted Verdi in the first Italian parliament and his association with Vittorio Emanuele II by way of the (not-apocryphal) slogan 'Viva VERDI' may have represented the beginnings of this process, and it perhaps culminated in the singing of 'Va pensiero' by mourners at Verdi's funeral in 1901. This last 'spontaneous' outburst, which happens to have been led by Toscanini and supported by the chorus and orchestra of La Scala, seems the perfect symbol for a gradual process of retrospective mythologization, in which the music's significance for the Risorgimento is pushed further and further back in time, with the nostalgic/pastoral hymn 'Va pensiero' playing an ever more central role.

One conclusion in the face of this evidence would be to dismiss the equation 'Verdi and the Risorgimento' altogether, to erect in its place the rigorously postmodern (or rigorously modernist?) view that except in a few rare cases art and politics are basically unconnected, or are connected only in incidental ways unworthy of serious scrutiny. But this would be to ignore evidence that Verdi himself at times cared deeply about the part his music might play in articulating a national sensibility, and – perhaps more important – it would overlook evidence in the operas themselves. Even the arch-skeptic Parker has halted his myth-debunking long enough to point out that in later compositions Verdi quite deliberately imitated the musical features that make 'Va pensiero' inherently suitable as a patriotic hymn (Parker 1997b, 48–82). The unison melody and decasyllabic meter that characterize 'Va pensiero' reappeared the following year in a chorus in *I lombardi alla prima crociata*, with poetry by the same librettist as for *Nabucco*, Temistocle Solera, and Verdi returned to the topos in two later operas, as if in a programmatic attempt to invent the patriotic chorus as a new operatic genre.

But there is another variety of musical evidence, one less tied to Verdi's intentions, that could also yield believable contexts for reading the early operas as Risorgimento documents. Parallel to the string of unison choruses across the 1840s runs a recurring dramatic archetype, the figure of the war-like heroine, represented by the well-known figures of Joan of Arc and Lady Macbeth (in operas from 1845 and 1847 respectively), as well as in some less familiar guises.[5] I should like to focus on one of these, the warrior soprano Odabella from the rarely performed 1846 opera, *Attila*.[6] Even more than most of the early operas, *Attila*'s plot invites reading as Risorgimento allegory. It centers around the founding of Venice (or Acquileia, to give it the antique name used in the opera), and on the heroic efforts of the Acquileian citizens to resist the invading Hun forces led by Attila. There are, of course, male characters – a tenor and baritone lead the Acquileian troops against Attila – but none of the male principals possesses a fraction of the aggression or the vocal force of the soprano Odabella. Her vocal style is characterized by large leaps, loud high notes and jagged rhythms, features that blare forth from the first moments of her entrance aria. Where sopranos in the Italian opera of this period are most often introduced alone or in intimate conversation with confidantes, Odabella is first seen (and heard) in the midst of a public scene, leading a group of Italian women taken prisoner by Attila's forces. Her aria, launched by the defiant shriek 'Santo di patria, indefinito amor!,' replies to Attila's question about what can have inspired mere women to such valor; its slow opening section celebrates Odabella's band of 'donne italiche.' Attila is instantly smitten by this forceful utterance, and he replies by presenting her with his sword as a love-offering.

Much of the aria's force derives from the ways Verdi underlines the sharp contrast in Temistocle Solera's poetry between the cowardly Hun women and Odabella's own fearless Italian forces, an opposition laid out in a symmetrical pattern of four plus four lines:

> Allor che i forti corrono
> Come leoni al brando
> Stan le tue donne, o barbaro,
> Sui carri, lagrimando.
> Ma noi, noi donne italiche
> Cinte di ferro il seno
> Sul fulmido terreno
> Sempre vedrai pugnar.

> (When your warriors rush forward / like lions to take up their swords, / your women, o barbarian, / stay in their chariots, weeping. / But we, Italian women, / our breasts girt in steel / you will see fighting / on the reeking battlefield.)

This verbal contrast is underlined musically in what is for Verdi a fairly unusual moment of text/music correspondence. The first phrase of Odabella's melody circles around a single very low pitch, as if lacking the energy to break away. As Odabella describes the lethargy and weakness of the women of Attila's camp, her vocal line is supported by a leaden dactylic accompaniment figure, and the last few notes of the melody seem to mimic scornfully the sobbing of the Hunnish women. Mention of the 'donne italiche' evokes sharp contrast in almost every sense, with Odabella's melody leaping up an octave, acquiring a propulsive accompaniment pattern, and driving downward stepwise with an incisive rhythm.

The linking of music and text and the break in musical texture accompanying the sharp verbal contrast are ideally suited to the aria's function as a public declaration of patriotic pride: the clarity of the musical gesture seems to spring from Odabella's symbolic role as emblem of Nation. Indeed, the sharp outlines of Odabella's aria could be heard as a musical metaphor for the profile of a sculpture, its contrasts functioning as analogues for the fixed features that make allegorical figures of 'Liberty,' 'Victory,' or 'Italia' recognizable in a variety of contexts.

The strange thing is that this particular emblem of Nation, the sculpted, sword-waving woman, is central to the French iconographic tradition, but seems to have been almost unknown in Italy. As anyone who has wandered the streets of Paris knows, warrior women have been a stock image of French patriotic representation since the Revolution and its invention of the fighting peasant girl 'Marianne' (Agulhon 1981). If the icon's most famous realization is in Delacroix's 1831 canvas *Liberty Leading the People on the Barricades*, with its central figure who urges the male troops into action carrying a tricolor banner and a flintlock, by 1848 the image had captured the French artistic imagination so completely that a competition to design a new emblem for the Republic elicited hundreds of entries bearing some combination of Liberty's standard features (see Moulonguet 1994; Chaudonneret 1987). The caricaturist Bertall mocked the uniformity of the submissions in a series of drawings that transposed the familiar draped white robe, raised arm and weapon to a variety of absurd contexts.

Although Italy must have been at least as much in need of a galvanizing national symbol as France, and although Italian cultural trends followed Paris in many other respects, Italian painting during this period is almost devoid of warrior women; indeed, it tends to avoid allegory altogether.[7] Before unification the closest Italian art came to creating a store of national images was the brand of historical painting pioneered by Francesco Hayez, which presented formative events of earlier centuries in guises that invited reinterpretation in terms of contemporary struggles to define a nation and a people. But, with the possible exceptions of the central figure of Hayez's *I vespri siciliani* (The Sicilian Vespers, 1829) and a popular 1849 lithograph depicting Anita Garibaldi's death, the images of women in Ottocento painting are almost exclusively domestic, placed mostly in genre scenes of partings from husbands leaving for the front, and groups of girls reading letters or sewing red shirts.[8]

It may be a mark of Verdi's acute sense for audience taste that, when he was commissioned to write an opera for Rome's Teatro Apollo specifically commemorating the events of 1848, he relinquished the Amazon heroines of his earlier works and instead chose one of these docile, domestic types as his heroine.[9] Like *Attila* and *Nabucco*, the resulting opera, *La battaglia di Legnano*, glorifies the struggle for independence through historical analogy, this time with the role of the foreign aggressor assigned to Frederick Barbarossa. As Adrian Lyttelton shows in Chapter One of this volume, the formation of the Lombard League and its successful resistance to Barbarossa at Legnano was a foundational tale for Risorgimento artists and historians, treated as a climactic moment in Sismondi's *History of the Italian Republics*, subject of an 1816 historical novel by Cesare Balbo, and of Giuseppe Diotti's painting *Il giuramento di Pontida* (The Oath of Pontida, see figure 1.5).[10]

In fact, Verdi's librettist, Salvatore Cammarano, had grafted the story of the Lombard League onto an existing play about a French/English conflict, Joseph Méry's *La bataille de Toulouse* (1828). But the intimate dimension of this plot remained much the same from play to libretto, centered, like most of Verdi's operas, around a conventional love triangle. As the curtain rises, Lida (soprano) loves the tenor Arrigo, but believing that he has died in battle, she has married Rolando (baritone). Predictably, Arrigo returns from the front alive, but by this time Lida has a son; her guilt and torment over her continuing love for Arrigo provide the opera's central emotional conflict.

Given the outlines of this plot, it is not surprising that Lida's vocal idiom sounds nothing like Odabella's. Lida tends to sing in a smoother, more melodic style, with a good deal of vocal ornamentation. What *is* surprising is that the tenderest moment in *La battaglia di Legnano* comes not in a love duet for the adulterous couple, but in a duet for Lida and her husband just before he goes into battle. Rolando charges his wife with the moral education of their son, saying in the introductory recitative 'Tu resti insegnatrice di lui.' The slow movement that follows offers yet another Risorgimento archetype, an alternative to the melancholy of 'Va pensiero' and the fury of Odabella. Rolando's words are all about heritage, and – crucially – they position Lida as vessel or intermediary: ideally blank and passive herself, she conveys father's heroic message to son, and thus perpetuates the Nation.

Digli ch'è sangue italico,
Digli ch'è sangue mio,
che de' mortali è guidice
la terra no, ma Dio!
E dopo Dio la patria
gli apprendi a rispettar.

(Tell him he is of Italian blood, / tell him he is of my blood, / [tell him] that
the judge of men is not on earth, but God! / And after God, teach him to
respect the homeland.)

The music Verdi writes for the two characters seems designed to reinforce
a traditional gender opposition, a contrast most apparent in the choice of
accompanying instrument: below his solo statement Rolando gets French
horns (conventionally associated with the battle and the hunt) playing
insistent repeated notes, while Lida's reply (expressing guilt and sorrow)
is supported by the more introspective timbres of oboe and clarinet,
playing the sobbing figures that she herself takes up toward the end of
the passage.

The depiction of Lida as virtuous mother to the Nation is of course
part of a widespread archetype linking Woman and Nation, one not at all
unique to Italy. But it also calls to mind a more specific context, a passage
from Mazzini's *Filosofia della musica* (1836) in which music is person-
ified as a pure woman with the power to redeem both culture and country:

> Music, like a woman, is so holy with anticipation and purification, that even
> when men sully it with prostitution, they cannot totally obliterate the aura of
> promise that crowns it. Even in the midst of that music which we today
> condemn, there is still a ferment of life that foretells new destinies, a new
> development, a new and more solemn mission. [. . .] You might say that an
> angel, out of the abyss into which he has been thrown, still manages to address
> us as if from paradise. Perhaps in the future it will fall to woman and to music
> to carry a broader responsibility for resurrection than has so far been
> anticipated. (Mazzini 1998 [1836]: 43)

We cannot know whether Verdi had read Mazzini, although it seems quite
likely. The young Verdi was certainly sympathetic to Mazzini's political
cause, and the two men had met in London in 1847 when Verdi was there
to oversee the première of his *I masnadieri* – although little is known
about what transpired during the meeting (Phillips-Matz 1993: 217). But
there is no doubt that Verdi had, by whatever channels, absorbed Mazzini's
message, and the broader cultural message, about the images of women
desired by the Risorgimento. In composing *Attila*, Verdi's priority had

been largely a personal one: the choice of a Gallic Marianne figure as a central image suggests that, far from trying to invent an inherently Italian musical language for the Risorgimento, Verdi was striving for stylistic innovation and cosmopolitanism by way of Parisian artistic models, which offered the only sure avenue of escape from the firmly codified Italian operatic tradition. With *La battaglia di Legnano*, on the other hand, the pragmatic Verdi perhaps took over, and the combination of self-interest and respect for the revolutionary movement became an incentive to give Italian audiences the kind of feminine ideal they knew and loved.

Even stronger evidence of *Battaglia*'s status as a 'Mazzinian' opera is provided by Verdi's treatment of the opera's principal chorus, 'Viva Italia! Sacro un patto.' By far the best-known passage from Mazzini's *Filosofia* is an oracular paragraph that calls out for the 'new' Italian opera to elevate the chorus, that 'born interpreter of the voice of the people,' to the status of a 'collective individuality [. . . with] an independent and spontaneous life of its own' (Mazzini 1977 [1836]: 65–6; Barricelli 1975: 109). Mazzini's wish list was published three years before Verdi's first opera, *Oberto, conte di San Bonifacio*, was premièred to a rather lukewarm reception, but the *Filosofia* has nevertheless often been seen as fore-shadowing Verdi's achievements – this despite the fact that Mazzini himself, set on a firmly pan-European agenda, later proclaimed German composer Giacomo Meyerbeer, who had composed mostly for Paris, as having realized his hopes for operatic reform (Tomlinson 1986–87: 58–60). In his approach to the patriotic chorus in *Battaglia* Verdi appears to have learned the lessons not only of Mazzini, but also of Pietro Cornali and other successful composers of popular revolutionary music. The musical substance of 'Viva Italia! Sacro un patto' is actually far less interesting than that of 'Va pensiero' or any of Verdi's subsequent attempts to recapture that nostalgic style, but it is eminently singable, and march-able. Sung by male voices in unison with the sparse accompaniment of an on-stage brass band, this curtain-raising number convincingly creates the impression of performance by a gaggle of unschooled singers eagerly striding into battle.

Where the 'lesson' of 1848 is felt most strongly, however, is in a reprise of the chorus at the opera's melodramatic climax. At the end of the third act, Lida's husband Rolando (the perennial jealous baritone) discovers her in a tête-à-tête with Arrigo. Believing that the two must be having an affair (which they aren't . . . quite), Rolando locks them in a 'room high up in a tower,' and departs to march into battle with the suicide-brigade to which both he and Arrigo belong, the 'Squadron of Death.' As Arrigo desperately searches for a means of escape, the chorus 'Viva Italia!' is heard offstage, announcing the Squadron's departure for the battlefield. As if driven mad by the sound of this realistic marching music, Arrigo rushes to the window and hurls himself from the balcony in hope of joining his fellow soldiers. (In the next and final act we learn that he survived his leap, fought as a hero and was mortally wounded in battle.) Here the chorus 'Viva Italia!' works as a dramatic agent, its sounds irresistibly spurring Arrigo to action. In other words, in *Battaglia* Verdi dared to eschew musical beauty, and aimed instead to create a kind of music that could be integrated directly into action and that could inspire wild heroic deeds, an attitude that seems like an explicit rejection of the leisurely aestheticization of the notion of *patria* spun out in 'Va pensiero' and the other early patriotic choruses.

These two examples from Verdi's '1848 opera' demonstrate a kind of pragmatism that is usually demonized in the aesthetic realm, and is perhaps denounced with a special vehemence in the field of Italian opera studies, where popular taste is often felt to be all too influential. But perhaps the admission of such concrete considerations into musical and historical interpretation can suggest a way that we can continue to talk about the conjunction of 'Verdi and the Risorgimento' even if we have to relinquish those comfortable anecdotes about 'Va pensiero.' The variety of 'political opera' embodied by *La battaglia di Legnano* may initially seem less exciting than that conveyed by the familiar anecdotes, because it is based not in brave flouting of the censors and spontaneous popular outbursts, but in the canny tailoring of an occasional piece for the public and in the straightforward mirroring of the cultural archetypes demanded by that audience. But if we recall that rousing 1848 letter to Piave, the pragmatism of *Battaglia* takes on a certain nobility and inevitability: rather than giving up composition altogether and saving his music paper to make cartridges, Verdi did his best to approximate the 'musica del cannone' he had longed to hear a few months earlier in the streets of Milan.

Notes

1. For a classic version of this classic story, see Martin 1979: 21.
2. The initial correction of Abbiati's massaged quotation is published in Parker's critical edition to *Nabucco* (Parker 1987). Since then Parker has undertaken more detailed discussions of the musical content and

popular reception of 'Va pensiero' in Chapter 2 of his *Leonora's Last Act* (Parker 1997b) and in a monograph entirely devoted to the question of Verdi's 1848 reception (Parker 1997a).

3. Parker (1997b: 37) has also debunked the anecdote about the insertion of Pio IX's name into *Ernani*, tracing the story to an item in the theatrical journal *Teatri, Arti e Letteratura* reporting that at an 1846 performance of a Donizetti opera, a chorus from *Ernani* with new words honoring Pio IX was inserted between the acts, in a manifestation that was officially planned and announced in advance.

4. Parker reproduces the entire piece in facsimile.

5. Between his first popular success with *Nabucco* (1842) and his attainment of economic and artistic independence with *Macbeth* (1847), Verdi composed eight operas, of which four (*Nabucco*, *Giovanna d'Arco*, *Attila* and *Macbeth*) feature Amazon-like women. But this was by no means Verdi's exclusive mode of representing women during this period, and the other four operas present more conventionally demure heroines.

6. For additional discussion of *Attila* see Smart 1997.

7. As Albert Boime has shown, female allegories of the Nation appeared in novels by Domenico Guerrazzi and Massimo D'Azeglio, but these images do not seem to have been transferred to the realm of visual representation (1993: 48–70).

8. I am thinking of such oft-reproduced works as Vincenzo Cabianca's *La partenza del volontario* (1858), Odoardo Borrani's *Le cucitrici di camicie rosse* (1863) and Gerolamo Induno's *Il ritorno del soldato* (1867), admittedly all from a later phase of Risorgimento activity than Verdi's 1840s images of warrior women. Before 1848, images of contemporary women were almost non-existent, perhaps excluded by the dominant neo-classical idiom. Roberta Olson's catalogue for the exhibition *Ottocento: Romanticism and Revolution in Nineteenth-Century Painting* offers illuminating commentary on several of these post-1848 canvasses (Olson 1992). See also Chapter Five in this volume.

9. On the circumstances of the *Battaglia* commission and première, see Julian Budden 1978–81: 1.389–95.

10. In his nuanced discussion of this and other historical subjects revived by Risorgimento artists, Lyttelton emphasizes that the Oath of Pontida episode celebrated the role of the Catholic Church in uniting the Lombard towns, and thus was a particularly popular subject during the early, Giobertian phase of the Risorgimento. Lyttelton speculates that the strong Catholic overtones that became attached to the oath

may be a reason that Verdi and his librettist omitted this episode from *Battaglia*, which was not premièred until January 1849, after serious disillusionment with Pio IX had set in.

References

Abbiati, F. (1959), *Giuseppe Verdi*, 4 vols, Milan: Ricordi.

Agulhon, M. (1981), *Marianne into Battle: Republican Imagery and Symbolism in France, 1789–1880*, trans. J. Lloyd, Cambridge: Cambridge University Press.

Barricelli, J. (1975), 'Romantic Writers and Music: The Case of Mazzini,' *Studies in Romanticism* 14: 95–117.

Boime, A. (1993), *The Art of the Macchia and the Risorgimento: Representing Culture and Nationalism in Nineteenth-Century Italy*, Chicago: University of Chicago Press.

Budden, J. (1978–81), *The Operas of Verdi*, 3 vols, Oxford and New York: Oxford University Press.

Chaudonneret, M. (1987), *La figure de la République: Le concours de 1848*, Paris: Ministère de la Culture et de la Communication.

Dahlhaus, C. (1989), *Nineteenth-Century Music*, trans. J. Bradford Robinson, Berkeley and Los Angeles: University of California Press.

Gossett, P. (1990), 'Becoming a Citizen: The Chorus in Risorgimento Opera,' *Cambridge Opera Journal* 2/1: 41–64.

Lyttelton, A., 'Creating a National Past: History, Myth and Image in the Risorgimento' (Chapter One in this volume).

Martin, G. (1979), 'Verdi and the Risorgimento,' in W. Weaver and M. Chusid, eds, *The Verdi Companion*, New York: Norton, pp. 13–41.

Mazzini, G. (1977 [1836]), *Filosofia della musica: Estetica musicale del primo Ottocento*, ed. M. de Angelis, Rimini: Guaraldi, pp. 33–77.

—— (1998 [1836]), 'From the Philosophy of Music,' trans. and ed. R.A. Solie, in O. Strunk, gen. ed., *Source Readings in Music History: The Nineteenth Century*, rev. edn, New York: Norton, pp. 43–52.

Moulonguet, N., curator (1994), *Allégories de la République: Le concours de 1848*, Catalogue for a 1994 exhibition at the Assemblée nationale, Paris: Imprimerie London.

Olson, R.J.M., ed. (1992), *Ottocento: Romanticism and Revolution in Nineteenth-Century Italian Painting*, New York: American Federation of Arts.

Parker, R. (1987), 'Historical Introduction,' in *Nabucodonosor, The Works of Giuseppe Verdi*, Series 1, Vol. 3, Chicago: University of Chicago Press.

—— (1997a), *'Arpa d'or dei fatidici vati':* *The Verdian Patriotic Chorus in the 1840s*, Parma: Istituto di studi verdiani.

—— (1997b), *Leonora's Last Act: Essays in Verdian Discourse*, Princeton: Princeton University Press.

Phillips-Matz, M.J. (1993), *Verdi: A Biography*, Oxford: Oxford University Press.

Plantinga, L. (1984), *Romantic Music*, New York: Norton.

Smart, M.A. (1997), 'Proud, Indomitable, Irascible: Allegories of Nation in *Attila* and *Les vêpres siciliennes*,' in M. Chusid, ed., *Verdi's Middle Period, 1849–59: Source Studies, Analysis, and Performance Practice*, Chicago and London: University of Chicago Press, pp. 227–56.

Tomlinson, G. (1986–87), 'Italian Opera and Italian Romanticism: An Essay in their Affinities,' *Nineteenth-Century Music* 10: 43–60.

Walker, F. (1978 [1962]), *L'uomo Verdi*, Milan: Mursia, Italian translation of Walker, *The Man Verdi* (1st published 1962).

–4–

'This is Africa': Ruling and Representing Southern Italy, 1860–61

Nelson Moe

In May 1860 Garibaldi's 'Thousand' landed in Sicily, defeating the Bourbon troops on the island by late July and from there moving up through mainland southern Italy to enter Naples triumphantly in early September. The Kingdom of the Two Sicilies was thus conquered and, with the plebiscite of 21 October, united to the northern provinces under the rule of King Victor Emmanuel to form the Kingdom of Italy. The dream of a unified Italy, excepting Rome and Venice, was at last a political reality. Nevertheless, for the Piedmontese who orchestrated this union, governing the ex-Bourbon provinces of southern Italy in the months that followed would prove to be every bit as daunting as conquering them.[1]

The period between the spring of 1860 and the summer of 1861 constitutes one of the decisive moments in the history of the Italian Southern Question. It was during this period that certain relations of force between northern and southern Italy were forged that would have a profound bearing upon the relationship between the two areas for decades to come. If the political, administrative and military aspects of the Piedmontese take-over in the south in 1860–61 have been discussed at length,[2] the question of how the Piedmontese confronted and represented the alien reality of southern Italy has received far less attention. Insofar as the Kingdom of the Two Sicilies was transformed into the southern provinces of the Kingdom of Italy at this time, this was a crucial moment in the process of conceptualizing and imagining the south within the new geopolitical framework of the Italian nation. For the Piedmontese, the pressing problem of the day was not only how to govern the south but how to make sense of it, and, as I shall suggest, this 'sense,' this ensemble of interpretations, descriptions and representations, far from being secondary, actually served as the framework within which decisions of how to govern, administer and control the south were made.

In this chapter I shall examine this process of articulating and representing the south as it manifests itself in the correspondence among the moderate political and military leaders involved in the 'liberation' and annexation of southern Italy during the year between August 1860 and August 1861.[3] I shall analyze the various concepts and figures employed to represent the south, focusing on some of the patterns that emerge within the discursive field constituted by these letters. In conclusion I shall consider the relationship between these representations and the form of rule based on military force that was employed in the south during this period.

'L'Europe finit à Naples . . .'

It will be helpful to begin by addressing a more general set of questions regarding the representation of the south in the nineteenth century. How, and when, did southern Italy become 'the south,' a people and place viewed to be different from and inferior to the rest of the country? How did southern Italy become the nation's 'Africa'? The political 'fusion' of north and south in 1860–61 clearly constitutes a crucial moment in the reconceptualization of the imaginative geography of Italy. But the significance of this juncture can be better appreciated if we situate it within a broader historical and geographical context.[4] Leading scholars of southern Italian history have stressed the longevity and persistence of many commonplaces and stereotypes about the Mezzogiorno in the modern era. Benedetto Croce traced the appearance of the proverbial description of Naples as 'a paradise inhabited by devils' back to the sixteenth century (1927), while both Ernesto De Martino (1961) and Giuseppe Galasso (1982) called attention to Jesuit missionaries' descriptions of the rural south as 'the Italian Indies' and '"the Indies over here' in the decades around 1600. Another authority has argued that by the middle of the eighteenth century many of the 'syntagms, topoi and prejudices' regarding the people of southern Italy were firmly 'organized and consolidated,' constituting a 'cultural patrimony inherited from previous centuries' (Placanica 1998: 173–5).

Undoubtedly the staying power of various commonplaces and stereotypes about the south in the modern era has been considerable. My research into this problem nevertheless suggests that a significant transformation in the cultural representation of the south took place between the mid-1700s and Italian unification. Over the course of this century, I would argue, a distinctly modern vision of southern Italy took shape in Italian and European culture more generally. What developed in particular is a dualistic vision, characterized by an emphasis on the backwardness of southern Italian society and culture on the one hand and on the picturesque qualities of the south on the other. A new vision of the south as a liminal zone between Europe and Africa, and sometimes the Orient, took form as well, often interwoven with the backward and picturesque perspectives just mentioned. Two examples, both by French writers in the early 1800s, will help to illustrate the character of these modes of representation and the interrelationship among them.

'Europe ends at Naples and ends there quite badly. Calabria, Sicily, all the rest is part of Africa' (96).Thus wrote Augustin Creuzé de Lesser in his *Voyage en Italie et en Sicile* of 1806. For this Napoleonic official, who, in the words of one scholar, was 'filled with the conviction of belonging to a superior race charged with renewing the world' (Tuzet 1945: 56), Naples and everything beyond it was the epitome of back-wardness. If his compatriots doubted his word, he wrote, let them come and see for themselves; after a week 'in this famous Sicily, in a country without roads, without bridges, without agriculture, without commerce, without hotels, without any of life's niceties, or the delicacies of society' they would certainly say, 'Let's go back to France' (99). But the roads take the cake: 'it is in this above all that the barbarism of Africa triumphs' (96). From the last decades of the eighteenth century forward, as Africa became the dark continent in the European imagination, 'Africa' was the worst that could be said about the south, one of the preferred ways to mark its difference from Europe and, as we shall see, from an Italy conceived in the image of Europe.

But this very difference with respect to western Europe, this proximity to Africa and Orient, could also be attractive. To those with second thoughts about the supreme value of western European civilization, the 'barbarism' of the south could be seen as picturesque if not exotic. In *Corinne ou l'Italie*, published a year after *Voyage en Italie et en Sicile*, Madame de Staël also highlights Naples' proximity to Africa but from a different perspective: 'One can almost sense the African shore that borders the sea on the other side, and there is something indefinably Numidian in the wild cries heard from every direction' (1955 [1807]: 292). There is something 'very original' about Naples' hybridity, about 'the blending of the savage state with civilization' (ibid.: 290). A tinge of the dark continent, 'the tanned faces' of the Neapolitans, 'give a picturesque quality to the city's populace' (ibid.: 292).

For the sake of clarity, I have cited two texts by foreigners, which offer distinctly contrasting perspectives on the south. But it is important to note, in the first place, that these imaginative patterns were also deployed by Italians, and, secondly, that in many instances the distinction between condemnation and celebration, repulsion and attraction, is far less clear, and the backward and picturesque perspectives more tightly intertwined. As the Neapolitan moderate Giuseppe Massari wrote to Cavour in 1860 upon his return to Naples after more than a decade of exile in Piedmont: 'Naples offers the most bizarre and singular spectacle that one could imagine: that of an anarchy that is at once picturesque and grotesque' (Cavour 1949–54: 3.163).

The point I wish to highlight here is that whereas foreigners and southerners played an important role in the production of these imaginative patterns in the century before unification, Italians from the center-north were relatively uninterested. The reasons for this geographical differentiation of cultural attention can be simply stated: the English, French and Germans took a keen interest in the south because it was different; southerners did so because it was their *patria*. In the latter case, southern intellectuals from the political economist Antonio Genovesi forward often called attention to the backwardness of the Kingdom of Naples in an effort to bring about reform and improvement. For Tuscans, Lombards, Piedmontese and others, neither form of interest was very strong in the century before unification. A survey of the major intellectual and cultural output in the center-north reveals a marked, if unsurprising, lack of interest in the peoples and places of southern Italy.

With the spread of nationalism during the second quarter of the nineteenth century, central-northern perspectives on the south began to change, however. For the first time statisticians, historians, painters, novelists, composers, political thinkers and others made a substantial effort to conceive of Italy as a nation. Their works were variously animated by the desire both to represent the diverse regional realities on the peninsula and to imagine a common bond among them. As the Lombard writer Carlo Cattaneo put it in 1845, the time had come 'to illustrate the *bel paese* piece by piece' (1957: 2.80).[5]

From the viewpoint of the center-north, the largest and most distant of these 'pieces' was the southern Kingdom of the Two Sicilies.[6] The striking fact about the interest in the south that emerged during this period is that it tended to emphasize both the similarities and the differences between southern Italy and the rest of the peninsula. Commonality was the dominant concern. But as Tuscans, Lombards and Piedmontese focused in increasingly concrete terms on the nature of the nation, an awareness that the Kingdom of the Two Sicilies differed from the rest of the country was also accentuated. Partly because few central-northerners ever made it south of Rome, their views were strongly influenced by the representations produced by foreigners and southerners. They too began to represent the south more consistently as backward and picturesque.

But their emphasis on a different south was not simply the result of their passive reception of the views of foreigners and southerners. Central-northerners at this time were actively involved in the reconceptualization of Italy along an imaginative north–south axis. Throughout the Risorgimento, Italian elites were keenly aware that foreigners conceived of Italy as a southern country, backward and picturesque like the Mezzogiorno. And while attempts to defend aspects of Italy's 'southern,' Mediterranean identity were made, the valorization and emulation of 'northern,' i.e. western European, models prevailed.[7] In the minds of most patriots, Italy was to become a nation in ideological, cultural and economic accord with the leading nations of Europe: England, France and increasingly Germany as well.

This tendency was most powerfully expressed by the moderates, especially after 1848–49 when they achieved hegemony within the nationalist movement. As Guido de Ruggiero notes, the moderates aimed 'to raise Italy to the level of the other European nations by a rapid assimilation of the most vital elements in their culture and political institutions' (1981: 299).[8] In the words of their leader, Camillo Cavour: 'We are preparing ourselves for a new life, with the assiduous examination of events taking place in countries that are most advanced in the ways of civilization, with close attention to the great lessons proclaimed from the stages of England and France' (cited in De Francesco 1994: 317–18).

To imagine Italy at mid-century was thus to imagine the country within the context of modern European civilization, with a special sensitivity to the ways in which Italy was perceived as 'southern.' But some parts of Italy were more southern than others. Even as central-northerners led the way in the movement to create an independent and united Italy, they harbored an awareness of differences between conditions in the Kingdom of the Two Sicilies and in the center-north. As the Tuscan statistician Luigi Serristori wrote in the late 1830s, the populations of the Kingdom of the Two Sicilies were '*among the less advanced of the peninsula*' (cited in Patriarca 1996: 138; emphasis in original). In the same years, another Tuscan patriot was reputed to have quipped that 'Italy ends at the Garigliano,' the river which marked the northwest border between the Kingdom of the two Sicilies and the Papal States (Gualterio 1852: 4.3).

After Ferdinand II adopted an isolationist and markedly anti-liberal course in the late 1830s, and above all after the repression of the liberal regime in Naples in 1849, this sense of divergence between the south and center-north increased dramatically. Southern exiles in Piedmont and other parts of the north, assisted by the English parliamentarian William Gladstone, targeted the Bourbon regime as the enemy of both European civilization and the cause of Italian nationhood (Petrusewicz 1998). The Bourbons, it was said, had built a 'wall of China' between southern Italy and the rest of Italy and Europe. To be sure, the focus of this propaganda was the regime itself, often represented in opposition to an innocent, long-suffering people. Yet a decade of denunciations inevitably darkened the social, cultural and economic picture as well. As one anonymous southern writer wrote in an anti-Bourbon pamphet of 1855:

> The traveler who visits that kingdom finds no signs of a civilized people, no institution that is useful and productive, no public or private instruction, no roads, no links among provinces or between the capital and the provinces, no traffic, no commerce, no arts, no industry, no manufacturing. And if it were not for the thousands of monks, priests, two-bit lawyers and vagabonds, beggars and do-nothings; if it were not for the tranquillity and clarity of the sky, the fertility of the soil luxuriant with spontaneous and flourishing vegetation, this traveler would think that he was in one of the countries of Africa made bestial by the most degrading despotism (*Quistione napoletana* 1855: 9)[9]

In the 1850s the image of a backward south was thus accentuated by southerners and foreigners. Central-northerners were, again, less actively involved, usually refraining from such public broadsides, partly out of a sense of patriotism, partly because it was not their most urgent concern. The anti-Bourbon campaign of the 1850s indeed helped to reinforce the view, prevalent in the moderate camp right through the 1850s, that the Kingdom of the Two Sicilies should, at least for the time being, remain intact, separate from the Kingdom of Northern Italy envisioned by Cavour.

What happened to the picturesque view of the south amid these denunciations and denigrations? In many respects, the south was as picturesque as ever – certainly for foreigners, and for southerners and central-northerners as well. One Calabrian exile, whose 1856 anti-Bourbon tract denounced the 'vivid contrast between Piedmont and the Kingdom of the Two Sicilies' (Miraglia 1856: 13) evoked for his northern readers the 'poetic and picturesque world' (ibid.: xvii) of his native land. And when the Lombard writer Ippolito Nievo landed in Sicily with Garibaldi in 1860 he found the island 'more picturesque than I could have hoped' (Nievo 1961: 22).[10] But well into the 1860s, the political and cultural task at hand was nation-building. Picturesque images of the south would have to wait until the 1870s – that is, until the key problems of national unification had been resolved – before they could proliferate in illustrated magazines, in folklore studies, in literature.[11] Until then, representations of the south would tend to be focused on the problem of making this 'Africa' a part of Italy.

We can see then that on the eve of their descent into the Kingdom of the Two Sicilies, the moderate leaders of the nascent nation had already formed some strong views about what they would find south of the Garigliano. Against this background we can now take up the specific forms of representation that were elaborated in the context of the 'liberation of the Mezzogiorno' during the summer and fall of 1860.

The Neapolitans Disappoint the Piedmontese

During the last weeks of August 1860, as Garibaldi and his troops made their way up through Calabria towards Naples, Cavour and his associates were dismayed by the fact that the Neapolitans would not rise up against the Bourbons before Garibaldi's arrival. They were concerned that without a Neapolitan insurrection, Garibaldi's solo conquest of the Bourbon capital would give him overwhelming control of southern Italy, as well as undermining French support for the cause of Italian unity. The Neapolitans, however, despite the work of Piedmontese agents provocateurs, would not budge (Mack Smith 1954: 129–62, as well as Candeloro 1956–1986: 4.473–92). Two remarks made about the Neapolitans on this occasion by Cavour and his envoy in Naples, the Marquis de Villamarina, in some sense mark the beginning of the lengthy 'jeremiad' against Naples and the south that fills the letters exchanged among the moderate political and military leaders involved in the annexation of southern Italy in 1860–61.[12] Cavour writes:

> The Neapolitans' conduct is disgusting: if they won't do anything before Garibaldi's arrival, they deserve to be governed as the Sicilians were by the likes of Crispi and Rafaeli. (Cavour 1949–54: 2.169)

The next day, Villamarina writes back from Naples:

> Is it my fault, dear Count, if the Neapolitans are spineless . . . if they have become, so to speak, brutish? (Cavour 1949–54: 2.176)

Already in these two brief remarks a number of significant elements of the Piedmontese attitude towards the south emerge, elements that would have considerable implications for the way the south would actually be governed by them.

In Cavour's statement, we find a discounting of the political capacities of the Neapolitans, such that they 'deserve' to be ruled in an authoritarian, even violent manner – à la Rafaeli and Crispi, the latter of whom a group of Sicilians claim 'attracted in twelve hours of rule all the hate that the most infamous of the Bourbon henchmen, Maniscalco, attracted in twelve long years' (Cavour 1949–54: 2.55). Villamarina gives Cavour's negative assessment of the Neapolitans' political behavior a further twist, situating it at a level which more directly regards the Neapolitans' character: they have 'no blood in their veins,' a phrase followed by an even more explicit, and commonplace, declaration of the Neapolitans' fall from the ranks of the civil and human – they have become 'brutish.' The two parts of Villamarina's remark, moreover, imply a significant equivocation that underscores many of the statements on the south made in these letters: are the Neapolitans somehow 'naturally' spineless and brutish? Or, as one correspondent writes, is their objectionable behavior rather historically determined, 'the consequence of centuries of despotism and of the confluence of the most tragic circumstances' (Cavour 1949–54: 4.147)?[13]

As we shall see below in greater detail, nearly all the men[14] participating in the leadership of the new Italian state consider the people and society of southern Italy 'corrotto' (corrupted) and 'abbrutito' (become brutish) by centuries of bad government, and thus different from those of the north, Piedmont specifically. Conversely, most, to different degrees, believe that the south, viewed 'through the prism of the old literary view that attributed every sort of natural and climactic advantage to the south' (Romeo 1974 [1963]: 271–2), can be reformed (politically, economically, morally) through the good government of the Piedmontese.[15] Nevertheless, in the various articulations of the south vis-à-vis the north in these letters, one often detects a crucial slippage from a historicizing perspective to one which posits the southerners and south as *essentially* different. As Cavour puts it on one occasion, the Neapolitans are corrupt 'to the marrow.'[16] Thus if the phrase 'they have become brutish,' with its implication of a historical process of barbarization, holds out hope for the reversibility of a process which is extrinsic to the subject, such interiorizing images as 'no blood in their veins' and 'to the marrow' ground that corruption in the subject's very nature, casting more than a shadow of doubt over the hope for reform and redemption.

I will return to this cluster of issues concerning the corruption and barbarization of the Neapolitans below, but let us first look at another response to the same situation in Naples, made by Cavour's faithful associate Giuseppe Massari. Originally from Bari and later Naples, Massari was one of the many Neapolitan political leaders to spend the years between 1849 and 1860 in exile in Turin.[17] Massari played a prominent role in publicizing the 'Neapolitan Question' during this decade (as anti-Bourbon pamphleteer and as a member of the Subalpine Parliament),[18] and we will encounter him numerous times in the pages that follow. Writing to Donna Ghita Collegno in late August, Massari vents his frustration at the Neapolitans thus:

> Oh Naples! How baleful it is to Italy! Corrupt, vile land, lacking that stalwart virtue that distinguishes Piedmont, the invincible wisdom that distinguishes central Italy and Tuscany in particular. Believe me – Naples is worse than Milan. (Cavour 1949–54: 2.137)

Massari clearly extrapolates a good deal more from the uprising manqué against the Bourbons than even Cavour and Villamarina. The specific political situation which prompts this outburst in fact gives way to a global statement about the moral qualities of the different regions of Italy.[19] With a rhetorical flair which, while not infrequent in these letters, nevertheless marks Massari's statements about the south in particular, Massari sets up Naples as Italy's enemy, in opposition to Piedmont, central Italy and Tuscany (which thus implicitly constitute the true Italy).

Among other things, this statement reveals the negative ideological charge built up against Naples in the years before unification, fed in large part by the Neapolitan exiles in Turin, and lying ready to be ignited on occasions such as this. It is in fact just this surplus charge that characterizes so many of the statements on the south in these letters. Furthermore, this letter is the first full-blown example of the logic of binary opposition that structures the encounter between north and south that is staged in this correspondence. Massari draws up a kind of moral map of Italy, divided into regions of virtue (northern) and vice (southern). Naples' very *italianità* is moreover cast into doubt by its description as 'baleful' to Italy (a description which, with reference to the particular moment in August 1860 when the Kingdom of Naples was in fact warring against 'Italy,' is not inaccurate but which linked to the universal characterization that follows ['corrupt, vile, lacking that virtue . . .'] loses its claim to historical specificity).

Meeting the Barbarians

The Neapolitan rebellion manqué in August 1860 thus gave rise to a number of negative characterizations of the society and people of Naples. In the following pages these stereotypes will reappear in different combinations, with different inflections, accompanied by many others still to be considered. One in particular, a cognate of Villamarina's notion – shared by others – that the Neapolitans had become 'brutish,' plays a particularly significant role in the imaginary field being examined: *barbarism*, and its more or less explicit complement, *civilization*. It is just this notion that rings out in one of the inaugural statements of this northern encounter with the south, the 27 October 1860 letter of Luigi Carlo Farini – chief administrator of the south during the first months of Piedmontese control there – to Cavour. In this letter, written just after Farini's arrival in the Neapolitan provinces, Farini describes the famous meeting between Garibaldi and King Vittorio Emanuele at Teano. He then turns his attention to the state of these territories:

> But, my friend, what lands are these, Molise and the south! What barbarism! Some Italy! This is Africa: compared to these peasants the Bedouins are the pinnacle of civilization. And what misdeeds! . . . (Cavour 1949–54: 3.208)

Barbarism and civilization, Africa and Italy, these are the oppositions which structure the articulation of the south in Farini's statement. But it is not so much a statement as a series of exclamations, the dramatic sign of the first moment of northern impact with southern Italy. This land is 'other than Italy,' other than that socio-political unity imagined by the Farinis, Cavours, Villamarinas and other members of the moderate Piedmontese leadership who at that very moment were in the process of consolidating their political hegemony over the democratic forces of opposition.

Farini provides what is probably the most concise expression of the contrast between the barbaric south and civilized (northern) Italy, respectively connoted here in terms of Africa and its implicit Other, Europe.[20] It recurs frequently, however, and, while the specific inflections of the opposition vary according to the context in which it appears, its basic character remains the same. In the following passage of a memorandum on the conditions in southern Italy written by Lady Holland to Cavour from Naples in late October, the emphasis on the 'state of indecency' and lack of civilized infrastructures in the south goes hand-in-hand with the notion that the Piedmontese will have to build a civilization there starting from scratch:

> It is remarkable that in the entire Kingdom of the Two Sicilies the new government will discover that everything remains to be done. . . . All the cities of Naples and Sicily are in a state of indecency, almost inferior to that of the ancient tribes of Africa. The prisons and sites of detention are places

where beasts can hardly be kept. There are no public fountains, no clocks, conditions not in the least fitting for civilized quarters. (Cavour 1949–54: 3.244)[21]

A similar vision of the uncivilized south as a place where society must be built *ex novo* appears in a letter to Cavour written by his Minister of Justice, G.B. Cassinis, while on a government visit to Naples in late November. Cassinis frames the problem in terms of the need to create the 'public conscience' necessary for the 'application' of a constitutional system of government in the south:

> In a certain sense it is necessary to remake the country, to remake or, better, create the public conscience; it is necessary to render these men capable of living under the constitutional system of government. And it would would be something to despair over, to consider impossible, if this very land, so far from the ideas of progress and civilization, didn't offer us special opportunities . . . (Cavour 1949–54: 3.351)[22]

The south is 'so far from the ideas of progress and civilization' (which, again, implicitly characterize the Piedmontese) that it will require a Piedmontese intervention, or as Massari writes on another occasion, 'a massive invasion of Piedmontese morality' (Cavour 1949–54: 3.164) to reform it. By the same token, Cassinis's statement manifests the proprietary or, more precisely, imperial attitude towards southern Italy that is a hallmark of this correspondence, an attitude which in turn relies upon a crucial assumption regarding the stability and autonomy of the Piedmontese. As we shall see more clearly below, the Piedmontese posit themselves in these letters as active, stable and sovereign against a south that is presumed to be passive, subject to change and heteronomous.

The representation of the south as a land of barbarism (variously qualified as indecent, lacking in 'public conscience,' ignorant, superstitious, etc.) is evidently one of the most effective ways to assert its distance and difference from the civilized, Piedmontese north. At the same time it engenders a corollary proposition, the need for and justification of Piedmontese intervention in and reform of the south. The representation of the south in these terms works as a kind of figurative see-saw, such that the lower the south falls in the north's representation, the higher the north rises in its self-representation. The distance and difference of the south from the north is thus one that consolidates the north's self-identity as morally, culturally and technically superior to the south, a sense of superiority resoundingly expressed by Diomede Pantaleoni in a letter to Cavour of 6 November 1860:

Our annexation of Naples and those provinces devastated and ruined by the most absurd despotism is already a bold test to which we have put ourselves, but at least with our force, our greater courage, with our superior intelligence and superior morality, with our experience and character, we can hope to govern and master them. (Cavour 1929a: 1.70)

Or, in this letter to Massimo D'Azeglio of 21 August 1861, with an emphasis on the north's benevolence towards the south:

Believe me, we are not the ones who benefit from this union, but rather those wretched peoples without morals, without courage, without knowledge and endowed only with excellent instincts and a mixture of credulousness and cunning that always delivers them into the hands of the greatest crooks. (D'Azeglio and Pantaleoni 1888: 441)

These assertions of the south's civic ruin ('ruined and devastated provinces') juxtaposed to the north's positive capacity to govern, master and aid it represent one of the key stances taken by the north vis-à-vis the south in these letters. It is a stance characterized by the north's power over the south's dysfunctionality, by its ability to master it.

There is, however, another stance taken by the north, one which reveals another face to the south's difference, and which proves to be a good deal more unstable than the one just considered. This is the stance taken when the south manifests itself to the northern observer as excessively ugly, disgusting, abject. Such manifestations of the south's difference threaten the glowing and gloating sense of northern superiority which fills these letters, calling into question the north's ability to overcome this intense condition of negativity.

The type of representation engendered by this relationship is one in which the negative qualities of the south are articulated minus the assertion of the north's capacity to master and reform them. These representations are among the most emphatic and indiscriminate in this correspondence, recklessly confusing the register of moral judgement and objective description. Reading the following passage from the diary of General Paolo Solaroli after his brief visit to Naples in December 1860, one is left wondering, for example, just what aspects of the Neapolitan people the words 'brutta' (ugly), 'mollezza' (weakness), 'vizio' (vice) and 'sudiciume' (filth) actually refer to:

I shall now say a few words about the often-praised Naples with its lovely climate.

Its population is the ugliest I have seen in Europe after Oporto's, but it surpasses them in weakness and vice, in filth.

[. . .] We have acquired a terrible country, yet it seems impossible that nature could bestow so much upon its land without generating another people (Cavour 1949–54: 5.231–2).

This is of course an explicit reprise of the description of Naples as 'a paradise inhabited by devils.'

Like other statements to the same effect, the insistence upon, indeed obsession with, these negative characteristics calls attention to the subjective state of the author, to the effect this purported reality produces upon him. In contrast to the group of statements considered above in which the capacity to reform, master and govern held sway, in this group the emphasis on the abject nature of the south tends to be intimately associated with the author's sense of being overwhelmed by that state of negativity. According to Massimo D'Azeglio, for example, the north was not up to the Herculean task of cleaning out the 'Augean stables' of the south (see Mack Smith 1954: 134), an image that expresses the notion of the south's superlative filth with a touch of classicism. On another occasion, and in a different figurative register, D'Azeglio writes: 'in every way fusion with the Neapolitans frightens me; it's like going to bed with someone who has smallpox' (D'Azeglio and Pantaleoni 1888: 430);[23] and, one year later, 'As for Naples, with each step we take things only get worse. It's an ulcer that gnaws at us and costs us dearly' (cited in Flora 1961: 100).[24] In each of these statements the south is represented as that which enervates, contaminates, detracts from the north. The south that appears in this abject guise therefore tends to provoke disgust, inspire fear or dismay, as in the statement: 'fusion with the Neapolitans frightens me'; or 'what frightens me above all is the distance between the moral and political life of these provinces and those of middle- and upper-Italy.'

But fear and disgust are only one side of the coin. The very same elements that represent a source of repulsion and dis-ease can, when seen in a different light, constitute a source of attraction and pleasure. Let us look at this form of psychic ambivalence, this complicity of disgust and desire, in a letter by Giuseppe Massari. Shortly after returning to Naples after more than a decade of exile in Piedmont, Massari communicates these 'impressions' to Cavour in a letter of 21 October:

I find myself in an entirely new world, and I want to share my impressions of it with you. Naples offers the most bizarre and singular spectacle that one could imagine: that of an anarchy that is at once picturesque and grotesque: an unholy racket, a continuous shuffling about of people, an uproar that would deafen even Senator Plana, and a filth that would disgust the people of Constantinople. I have always loved and appreciated Piedmont, but after these three days in Naples I adore it. The contrast is indescribable. (Cavour 1949–54: 3.163)

Massari offers here some of the familiar stereotypes regarding Naples: its 'anarchy,' mentioned by numerous correspondents who alternately describe it as Babel or Babylon (i.e. 'the filthy spectacle of this filthy Babylon'), its confusion and clamoring crowds, its filth – described here with a nod to the Orient – which exceeds even that of Constantinople.

It is not, however, so much these commonplaces as the framework for their articulation that merits our attention. First of all, Massari – who, let us remember, is a former resident of Naples – expresses the astonishment of the (assimilated) Piedmontese subject before the 'entirely new' world of Naples. The Neapolitan 'spectacle' is 'bizarre' and 'singular,' at the limits of the imagination. The distance separating Naples from Piedmont is in fact an abyss, the contrast between them 'indescribable.' And out of this contrast and encounter the author's identification with Piedmont emerges consolidated and confirmed: 'I have always loved and appreciated Piedmont, but after these three days in Naples I adore it.'

The most striking feature of the passage, however, is its double-vision of Naples' anarchy, which it labels 'at once picturesque and grotesque.' Naples is grotesque in a way similar to that indicated by General Solaroli and Massimo D'Azeglio – noisy, filthy, disorderly. But by the same token it is picturesque. Massari thus formulaically describes the dialectic of attraction and repulsion that the north engages with its southern Italian Other, both during this period and in the decades that follow. In the statements we have considered, the grotesque, repulsive dimension was the prominent one, but it seems evident that the very insistence upon and often obsession with the south's negative qualities constitute a form of attraction to it. (Charles Dickens' phrase 'the attraction of repulsion' is very much to the point.) As Stallybrass and White observe with respect to the 'low-Others' that bourgeois society defines as dirty, repulsive, noisy and contaminating: 'disgust always bears the imprint of desire. These low domains, apparently expelled as 'Other,' return as the object of nostalgia, longing and fascination' (1986: 191). They return, in our case, as 'picturesque,' that lens through which the south was so often viewed from the end of the eighteenth century forward. To frame the problem in Foucauldean terms, Massari's formulation attests to what could be described as the 'incitement to discourse' that the south offers the north, an incitement which another correspondent expresses in a way that could serve as an exergue not only to these letters but to the discourse on the south as a whole in the first decades following unification:

Your Excellence, please pardon these words dashed off in such fury. This land is too interesting not to discuss at length. (Cavour 1949–54: 4.481)

Two Moral Maps

The mapping of various moral, political and cultural traits onto the geographical axis of north and south is a key aspect of the northern confrontation with the south inscribed in these letters. In the statements we have just considered it was present in a more or less implicit fashion; in others it is articulated in a more open and elaborate manner. The Lombard Count Guido Borromeo (recently appointed to the post of secretary-general of the Ministry of the Interior) formulates it this way in a letter to Ferdinando Riccardi di Netro of 14 December 1860:

> I know this city where I have sojourned for more than two consecutive years and know the perils and snares strewn upon its streets. Accustomed to the severe discipline and scornful honesty of our north, the cowardice, greed, corruption and bad faith that grow exponentially as one descends towards the heel of the boot are appalling. It will take at least two generations before stealing, lying and cheating are considered actions that are not merely prohibited by the Legal Code. Still, it is necessary for someone to assume the role of master and pedagogue. (Cavour 1949–54: 4.71)

Here we find some of the familiar hierarchical oppositions between north and south – between the discipline and honesty of the former and the 'cowardice, greed, corruption and bad faith' of the latter. But what is striking is the cartographical imagination at work in this passage, the way the author envisions an ethical scale of values descending with mathematical regularity as one moves down the 'heel of the boot.' Here too the disastrous conditions in the south are a source of despair for the northern subject, and this sense of consternation in turn leads typically to the adoption of a morally superior stance, that of 'master and pedagogue.'[25]

In another letter we find a somewhat different version of this moral map. If the preceding letter was written by a Piedmontese aristocrat and government official who, by dint of 'more than two consecutive years' of residence in the south, professes the authority to describe it and contrast it with the north, the author of the following quotation is a Neapolitan lawyer and patriot, Tommaso Sorrentino. Sorrentino's text consists of a 'memorandum' to Costantino Nigra, who at the time was serving as secretary to the Lieutenant General of the Neapolitan provinces, Prince

Eugenio di Carignano. In it he offers Nigra a bit of local advice, suggestions for the successful governance of the Neapolitan provinces.

> Consider that Italy from the Alps to the Roman Appenines has one way of life, one thought, one upbringing; from the Appenines to the sea it has another. In the north patriotism predominates, in the south self-interest; there sacrifice is spontaneous, here one works out of egoism; in the north there is reflection, here in the south dancing; there harmony exists, at least in purpose, here discord in everything; in upper Italy one is familiar with political life, in lower Italy it is entirely unknown; up there civic education exits, down here public corruption. (Cavour 1949–54: 4.288)

Whereas Borromeo offers the image of an ethico-cultural scale of values descending from north to south, Sorrentino sets out a more dichotomizing geographical schema. Sorrentino's Italy is divided by the Roman Appenines, on either side of which exists a distinct form of 'life, thought, upbringing.' Sorrentino draws out this dichotomy, repeatedly passing back and forth between north and south, consistently valorizing the former and devaluing the latter. The variations he employs to indicate northern and southern Italy are also significant: after specifying north (Settentrione) and south (Mezzogiorno) at the beginning, he writes 'there' and 'here' twice respectively, then 'upper' and 'lower' Italy, finally 'above' and 'below.' The modulation from the simple indication of 'there' and 'here' to these other terms combined with the emphatic moral contrast between the two places serves to tint the otherwise merely topographical adjectives with a distinctly moral color.

The Wound, the Doctor, the Nation

Both the Lombard Count Guido Borromeo and the Neapolitan Tommaso Sorrentino articulate the social, political and moral reality of the newly-formed Italian nation along the geographical axis of north and south. Borromeo, we saw, concluded his geographical representation with an appeal to reform, a call for someone to serve 'as master and pedagogue' for these morally depraved provinces. Sorrentino concludes on a similar note. At the end of his memorandum he beseeches Cavour to heed his patriotic advice, and closes with this appeal: 'Don't you see the general ill-health of this social body? May you cure it before its condition worsens' (Cavour 1949–54: 4.288). The south is a sick body in need of the Piedmontese cure.

Images of disease and medical treatment constitute one of the most common modes of visualizing the south and its relationship to the north in these letters.[26] The south is frequently figured as a 'piaga' (wound) or 'cancrena' (gangrene) that requires the north's healing treatment. As with other representations considered so far, these are unstable, tending to shift among the political, social and moral domains. The 21 November 1860 letter of the former Sicilian exile in Turin and secretary of the National Society, Giuseppe La Farina, to Cavour from Naples provides a striking example of the use of this medical imagery; at the same time it demonstrates the way the imagination and denunciation of a particular political and administrative reality expands to embrace an increasingly general, 'moral' range of characteristics.

> Here theft in public offices continues just as under the Bourbons and under the Dictatorship [of Garibaldi]; and it will take fire and iron to extirpate this gangrene. Another lethal wound is the greed for employment. The halls of the ministers and stairways are so crowded that it would be impossible for a gentleman to make his way without the help of our Police. It's a form of blackmail, no less irritating, impudent and disgusting than that of the city streets, along which one sees the most horrible and obscene human infirmities put on display as advertising for alms.
>
> But what frightens me above all is the distance between the moral and political life of these provinces and those of middle- and upper-Italy. Except for the name of Piedmont itself, there is not one Piedmontese name that is known here: no one speaks of Piedmont, no one asks of it; its history is unknown, no one knows the slightest thing about its political conditions and laws. In short, the moral annexation [of the south] has not happened. I believe that the King's government should make every effort and sacrifice to increase the communications between these and the older [northern] provinces. . . . The Bourbons surrounded Naples with a Great Wall of China, and the Neapolitans are so used to considering their great city as a world unto itself, that it is necessary not only to invite them but to force them to enter into the common life of the nation. (Cavour 1949–54: 3.356)

La Farina's observation begins with the particular phenomenon of theft in public offices which, figured as gangrene, gives way to 'another lethal wound,' the greed for employment. The concrete manifestation of this greed however entails another shift in perspective, from the general notion of theft and greed to a specific, subjective and anecdotal description of the difficulty a 'gentleman' has in moving along the stairways. The description of this phenomenon, a 'form of blackmail,' shifts in turn to the public streets, forming a comparison between the domain of administration and that of society at large. What links these two spheres is in fact the figure of infirmity itself, and the sense of the abject which underscores the description of both.

Of course what gets lost in this series of figurative associations and shifts in perspective is whatever analytical validity the original description of theft in public offices had; and, as we shall see in a moment, the description eventually concludes in the realm of utmost moral abstraction. But what is equally notable about the cited passage is the movement from objective observation to subjective involvement. The problem of greed for employment seems to be reduced to the problem one gentleman has in moving along the stairways. And what follows leaves little doubt that the gentleman is La Farina himself, for as his description turns to the streets the force of the adjectives – *molesto, impudente, schifoso, orribili, laide* – renders the author's own participation in this scene readily apparent.

The opening of the following paragraph confirms this subjective stance of fear and trembling before the horrors of Naples ('But what *frightens me* above all . . .') at the same time it directs the problem back into the generalizing register of an objective moral dichotomy. The confrontation between this single, 'Piedmontesized' subject and the socio-political reality of Naples thus becomes 'the distance between the moral and political life of these provinces and those of middle- and upper-Italy.' Of the Piedmontese who are to rule these provinces and indeed the entire nation, no one in Naples seems to have the slightest idea. Their military and political conquest of the south has fallen short of the desired 'moral annexation' and thus a concerted effort involving both solicitation and constraint is necessary 'to force them to enter into the common life of the nation.'

The visualization of the south as a wound also raises the question of just what kind of treatment must be administered in order to heal it. La Farina clearly indicates the need for a more violent intervention, both in the opening lines of the passage cited earlier ('it will take fire and iron to extirpate this gangrene') and at the conclusion when he mentions the necessity of force. This certainly contrasts with the more tender treatment suggested by Pasquale Stanislao Mancini of Apulia, who writes to Cavour of 'this homeland of mine lacerated by terrible wounds in need of *loving care*' (Cavour 1949–54: 3.362; my emphasis), as well as with Farini's assessment of the situation in Naples as so grave that it would be impossible 'to make a clean, deep cut in the wound overnight':

> Let me say it to you one more time, the state of this miserable land is appalling. . . . To be sure, we mustn't encourage all the wicked inclinations and abject customs, but it isn't possible to make a clean, deep cut in the wound overnight. The multitudes teem like worms in the rotted-out body of the State: some

Italy, some liberty! Sloth and maccheroni. No one in Turin or Rome will envy us the splendor and dignity of the capital of Italy as long as this one continues to be the capital of sloth and of the prostitution of every sex, of every class. (Cavour 1949–54: 3.328–9)

Equal in importance to the method of treating the wound is the question of who shall be the doctor: clearly the Piedmontese, who more or less explicitly arrogate this function for themselves. The Piedmontese representation of the south as wound and self-representation as doctor provide then yet another way to project a moral and 'operational' (political, administrative, military) superiority over the south which lies accordingly passive and supine as a patient.

The dualism and detachment that this doctor-patient relationship implies is relatively unstable, however, undermined by the presence of another, contradictory figure belonging to the same medical register: that of the *body* of the nation, understood as 'one and indivisible.'[27] The body politic being treated is, in other words, that of the northern doctor himself, and the consternation, if not hysteria, that many correspondents express with regard to the infirm south no doubt derives from an awareness of this fact. The knowledge that Italy's newly-acquired unity depends upon the south's own integrity ('if Italy is to be saved or lost, it will be saved or lost with Naples and in Naples') thus underscores the fear that the south's ills might spread to the north (Cavour 1949–54: 5.404).[28] And it is just this realization that inspires Farini to appeal to the 'great moral authority' of Parliament in a letter written to Cavour soon after his arrival in Naples in mid-November:

If the National Parliament with its great moral authority does not establish a bit of effective authority here, believe me, *the annexation of Naples will become the gangrene of the rest of the state.* I see that the view of these parts of Italy held by the rest of the country does not correspond to the truth. . . . Let's make sure that this phase of the annexation of Naples does not mark the beginning of the moral break-up of Italy! (Cavour 1949–54: 3.328; my emphasis)

The South's First Day in Parliament

The representation of the south as the wound or gangrene of the nation (along with the concomitant figure of the doctor/surgeon) is also present in the first parliamentary debate on the south which took place in Turin on 2–6 April 1861 (Passerin d'Entrèves 1956: 287–310). As the first

national, public discussion of the situation in southern Italy and, specifically, of the recent events connected to the 'liberation' and annexation
of the south, it marks an important episode in the story of the Piedmontese
encounter with southern Italy. There is a significant overlap between the
correspondents of the *Carteggio Cavour* and the participants in the
parliamentary discussion (Massari, Cavour, La Farina, Pantaleoni, Crispi,
Cassinis, Scialoja, Torrearsa, *et al.*). Equally importantly, the project of
describing the south to the Piedmontese leadership, of representing it to
and for them, is similar in both cases. A brief look at this discussion both
allows us to see how the figures of disability and disease used in the
letters are deployed in an affiliated discursive space and brings into focus
the issue that will concern us for the remainder of this chapter – the
relationship between representing the south and ruling it.

In his opening statement Giuseppe Massari, the deputy responsible
for initiating the discussion, presents the problem in these familiar terms:

> When a wound bleeds and is about to turn to gangrene, it is necessary to
> freshen it with the pungent air of publicity, it is necessary, if you want to heal
> it, to treat it with the hot iron of open discussion. (*Discussioni della Camera*
> 1862a: 361)

In his response to Massari's remarks, Minister of the Interior Marco
Minghetti elaborates upon the figure thus:

> The Honorable Massari has, in a sense, acted as a surgeon, revealing the
> principal wounds of the land [the south]; ... I will try to be the doctor
> (*laughter*), indicating the remedies. (*Discussioni della Camera* 1862a: 371)[29]

At the same time, according to one member of Parliament the government has been remiss in its medical duties towards the south:

> In my opinion, the King's government has been like a surgeon that finds
> himself before a tremendous operation to perform, and has not the courage to
> attempt it; he sees all the harm that can come to the patient, yet does not feel
> up to the task. (*Discussioni della Camera* 1862a: 413)

Yet another – Emerico Amari – takes issue with the very representation
of the south as the nation's wound and source of corruption:[30]

> When one speaks of corruption ... we must tell the truth: that is, that we
> have not all been corrupted simply because we were subject to the most corrupt
> of governments. I will say it once and for all, that these two peoples [the

Neapolitans and Sicilians] must not be represented as nothing but some gangrene. No, we are Italians and we have preserved our Italian virtues. We made the revolution, and this suffices to demonstrate our morality. (*Discussioni della Camera* 1862a: 416)

Challenging the prevalent view of the south as corrupt and politically incapable, this parliamentarian from Palermo asserts the active role of the southerners in the struggle for unification ('we made the revolution'),[31] together with their moral integrity which, he claims, cannot be reduced to the corruption of the Bourbons. He shows that what is at issue in this debate (and elsewhere) is the *representation* of the south, the manner in which it will be imagined. And what seems implicit in his plea is that the manner of imagining the south will have a decisive effect upon the manner of governing it. This debate on the south is in other words at once a debate on how it will be represented and how it will be ruled.

Those that contest the representation of the south as the corruption and gangrene of the nation are vastly outnumbered, however. Between Giuseppe Ferrari's motion 'to learn the state of the southern provinces, undertaking a solemn and impartial investigation, aimed at informing both the government and national Parliament' (*Discussioni della Camera* 1862a: 399), and the government motion which authorizes and encourages the government to maintain order there, it is the latter that is overwhelmingly approved.[32] Notwithstanding Amari's protest and Ferrari's motion, the description of the south as corruption and wound clearly retained its currency,[33] and the government thus received its first parliamentary authorization to act in accordance with that figure, to extirpate the gangrene with 'fire and iron' – which is to say in practical terms, to rule southern Italy by means of military force.[34]

The Supreme Argument of Force

Returning to the *Carteggio Cavour*, a similar connection between the description of the south as corrupt and infirm and the prescription of military force to 'cure' and control it emerges distinctly in a letter sent a few weeks after this parliamentary debate, from Prince Eugenio di Carignano – who at the time was serving in collaboration with Nigra as Lieutenant General of the Neapolitan provinces – to Cavour:

. . . because of the demoralized and degraded conditions in which the Bourbon government kept this land, the south is incapable of governing itself. It is necessary to destroy all of its administrations and assimilate it as quickly as possible to the other provinces. . . . Because this land does not understand the word 'nationality,' annexation happened here under the pressure of revolution and with the fear of the revolvers of the Garibaldines and bandits. With this people's ignorance, complete assimilation will not be felt here as it is in other parts of Italy. What's needed here is troops everywhere and in great quantities, send governors and officials from the other provinces of the kingdom, scrupulous people however, and I can assure you that things will go a hundred times better than at present. . . . (Cavour 1949–54: 4.459)

In one seamless whole this passage articulates the negativity of the Neapolitans – their moral depravity, brutishness, political ignorance and incapacity for self-government – and the necessity of ruling them by force. It constructs a kind of logical progression between the past of these provinces (their corruption under the Bourbons), their present (their ignorance and incapacity for self-government) and their near future (the need for 'troops everywhere and in great quantities'). Read together with the parliamentary debate just considered, this letter offers a clear indication of the prevalence of the view of the south both as corrupt and infirm and requiring military force. In conclusion I wish to articulate the relationship between these two instances – of representation and rule – more carefully, situating this relationship in the context of the historical events of 1860–61.

In many of the letters we have considered thus far the imperative mode of commands, orders, instructions and declarations intermingles with the descriptive mode of impressions, observation and representation. While my analysis here has been primarily concerned with statements of a descriptive-representative nature, let us remember that the overall context of these descriptions and representations was that of governing and administering southern Italy. Each of these statements, in other words, possessed an imperative and performative force which affected the socio-political context in which it was deployed.

Another important aspect of this discourse with respect to the practical rule of southern Italy is its role as part of the imaginary and conceptual horizon within which the Piedmontese 'apprehended' the south and consequently acted upon it. At one level the articulations of the south in this discourse also articulated the types of actions that could be taken there. The Piedmontese discourse on the south was an important enabling condition for ruling it. Prince Eugenio's statement above, in which we saw a 'natural,' logical progression from the assessment of the southerners' corruption and incapacity for self-government to the request for 'troops everywhere and in great quantities,' must therefore be read as an integral part of the militarization of southern Italy during this period.

At the same time, this effective, epistolary discourse was itself subject to the historical conditions in which it was enmeshed. The climate of violence that reigned in the south during this period and the increasingly systematic use of military force there themselves formed the matrix out of which the statements we have been considering were produced. We have seen that the Piedmontese undertook the 'liberation' of southern Italy with a well-stocked repertoire of preconceptions and prejudices. But the particularly antagonistic, extreme articulation of this repertoire was the result of the specific form that the initial encounter between north and south assumed.

Now the nature of this encounter had been, from the outset, a violent one. From the landing of Garibaldi's 'Thousand' in Sicily in May 1860, the south was a field of battle, a territory to be won from an enemy power. From that moment, the government, management and imagination of the south took place within the horizon of military conflict. When at the beginning of October 1860, Luigi Carlo Farini enters the Neapolitan provinces alongside King Victor Emanuel to set up a Piedmontese administration there, he arrives with a conquering army engaged in an operation of military clean-up. His first encounter with and representation of this 'other Italy' is thus underscored by violence, as the extended version of the citation considered earlier suggests:

> But, my friend, what lands are these, Molise and the south! What barbarism! Some Italy! This is Africa: compared to these peasants the Bedouins are the very pinnacle of civilization. And what misdeeds! The King [of Naples] gives carte blanche and the rabble sacks the houses of the gentry and cuts off the heads, the ears of the gentleman, and they boast and write to Gaeta [the King]: we killed this many gentleman, and I get the prize. Even the hick women do some killing; and worse, they tie up the gentlemen (that's how they call the liberals) by their testicles, and they drag them that way through the streets, and then chop 'em off. Horrors beyond belief if they hadn't happened right around us in this area. But nothing else has happened for a few days: I've arrested a lot of people; some I've had shot in the back (I hope Cassinis [Minister of Justice] will forgive me); Fanti has published a severe decree. As soon as I arrive in Naples, I'll send you a report with the documents regarding these exploits of the Court of Gaeta, which are wholly worthy of the tradition of Queen Caroline and Cardinal Ruffo. (Cavour 1949–54: 3.208)

To be sure, this is a wartime document, and, seen from the perspective of an imagination-at-war, there is perhaps nothing particularly remarkable about the 'barbarization' of the enemy manifest in this description. But the key problem this passage represents with respect to the formation of a national consciousness is not only how to make Italian citizens out of barbarians but how to bring about a cessation of hostilities, both on the field of battle and in the field of the imagination. Instead of decreasing in the wake of the Bourbon defeat, the militarization of the south actually increased during the years immediately following unification, assuming the dimensions of a civil war. And this continuation of hostilities in southern Italy weighed heavily upon both the political and imaginary relationship between north and south for years to come.

Faced with the socio-political disorder and unrest ensuing from the collapse of the Bourbon kingdom and the revolutionary war in the south, the Piedmontese government adopted what Molfese describes as 'a strictly repressive approach to the solution of the problems in southern Italy, with the near total exclusion of measures of social reform.' The repressive measures adopted were, moreover, of an 'exceptional, exaggerated and indiscriminate severity' (1964: 39, 64). In the political correspondence of 1860–61, and specifically in the autumn of 1860, it is in fact possible to mark a crescendo of 'appeals and incitations to the use of force and repression' (Villari 1961: 269) and to observe the transition from a war conducted against an external threat (the Bourbons) to one conducted against complex and multiple forms of internal political resistance. In the mind of Cavour and others, the military campaign had to be conducted on two fronts: against the foreign threat of the Bourbons, and against a multi-faceted domestic threat, ranging from Garibaldine 'democratic' political opposition to Bourbon-instigated insurgency to 'brigandage.'[35]

Shortly after defeating the Bourbon troops in the areas south of Naples, General Villamarina urges Farini to declare a state of siege:

> It is necessary, in all areas where acts of rebellion have occurred or will occur, that a state of siege be declared, so as to pass judgement quickly and effectively and to give an adequate idea of the force of the King's government. (Cavour 1949–54: 3.152)

Two months later, as the Piedmontese laid siege to the last Bourbon stronghold of Gaeta in early December, Cavour's secretary Isacco Artom writes to Massari from Turin:

> Certainly when Gaeta falls it will suffice to distribute the twenty or thirty thousand soldiers that are now involved in the siege [of Gaeta] into the major centers of population so as to restore material order throughout the Neapolitan state. (Cavour 1949–54: 4.24)

In late December, Antonio Scialoja writes to Cavour of 'the impossibility of establishing a government [in the south] by other means than force, at last for a long time to come' (Cavour 1949–54: 4.143). And the commander of the army in southern Italy, General Della Rocca, reflecting on his decision to administer summary executions in the countryside in January of the next year, writes of 'certain regions where it [is] not possible to govern except through terror' (cited in Molfese 1964: 66).

By mid-July of 1861, with the violence of brigandage and its repression raging throughout continental southern Italy, the south was virtually under military government.[36] A few weeks later, Diomede Pantaleoni, on a governmental 'fact-finding' mission in the south, would write back to Minister of the Interior Minghetti that the answer to the problems for the moment was 'troops, troops and more troops':

> This is a land that can only be held through force or through the terror of force. It has never been held by other means, and if you want them to be on our side, we must show them that we are by far the strongest. (Della Peruta 1950: 78)

Around the same time, finally, Massimo D'Azeglio summed up the political situation in the south thus: '. . . I know nothing about suffrage. All I know is that there is no need of battalions of troops this side of the River Tronto, only beyond it' (1938: 399–400).[37] To the north of the Tronto there was democracy and political freedom; to the south military repression.

One year after the 'liberation' of southern Italy, the south was under a state of siege, and Cavour's words on his deathbed earlier that summer ring out with all their desperate and delirious force:

> No state of siege, not the means of absolute governments. Anyone can govern with a state of siege. I would govern them [the Neapolitans] with freedom and show them what ten years of freedom can do for those lovely lands. In twenty years, they will be the richest provinces of Italy. No, I beg you, not a state of siege.[38]

Viewed through the flames that were devastating southern Italy in the summer of 1861, as well as through the different forms of representation considered in this chapter, the necessity of Cavour's other approach to the south is readily apparent: 'The aim is clear; it is not open to discussion. To impose unity upon the weakest, most corrupt part of Italy. There is no doubt about the means: moral force and, if that isn't enough, physical . . .' (Cavour 1929b: 4.292–3).

Notes

1. Cavour puts it this way in a letter to William de La Rive written just before the inaugural meeting of the first Italian Parliament in February 1861: 'But the task is more laborious and difficult now than in the past. To constitute Italy, to meld together the diverse elements of which it is composed, to create harmony between north and south, presents as much difficulty as a war with Austria and the struggle with Rome' (cited in Artom 1901: 145).
2. For a general overview, see Candeloro (1956–86: 4.415–538 and 5.9–178). More specifically, see Mack Smith 1954; Scirocco 1963; Passerin d'Entrèves 1956: esp. 101–59; Pavone 1964: 73–120; Molfese 1964: 9–129; Villari 1961; and Romeo 1974 (1963): 253–76.
3. The majority of the letters I will be considering are collected in the *Carteggi di Camillo Cavour*, above all the five volumes of the series titled *La liberazione del Mezzogiorno e la formazione del Regno d'Italia* (referred to hereafter as Cavour 1949–54, followed by the volume number).
4. I investigate this broader context in the first four chapters of my forthcoming book, *The View from Vesuvius: Representations of the South in Nineteenth-Century Italy*.
5. Cattaneo makes this statement in his review of the *Annuario Geografico Italiano* which appeared originally in *Rivista Europea*.
6. In 1815–16 Sicily was united to the Kingdom of Naples to form the Kingdom of the Two Sicilies.
7. In his classic essay, 'L'italiano,' Giulio Bollati addresses this tension (Bollati 1972). If anything, however, as Silvana Patriarca argues in Chaper Ten of this volume, Bollati over-emphasizes the anti-northern, anti-modern tendency in Risorgimento culture.
8. On the 'Europeanism' of the moderates, see as well Chabod 1951: 148–50; Salvatorelli 1944: 120–5; Salvatorelli 1975 [1935]: 276–8.
9. Contemporaries attributed the pamphlet however to Francesco Trinchera. *La quistione napoletana*, it must be noted, marks an extreme position, and was vehemently attacked by another southern exile in Piedmont, Francesco De Sanctis. These comments nevertheless reflect a broader tendency, as De Sanctis himself admits in his response to Trinchera (1898: 1.193–9). Petrusewicz discusses this and other debates among southern exiles in Piedmont (1998: 129–34).
10. Although, as Romagnoli notes, Nievo's sense of alienation from the reality of Sicily ultimately prevails (1982: 482–5).

11. I explore the proliferation of picturesque representations of the south in the 1870s in relation to the emergence of the Southern Question in the second half of my forthcoming book. Moe 1999 provides an introduction to this set of problems, with specific reference to Verga.

12. The term 'jeremiad' appears in a letter written by Villamarina a few months later in which he notes that 'all the letters that come from Naples, all the reports that circulate on the affairs and people of Naples end with an interminable jeremiad' (Cavour 1949–54: 3.23–4).

13. Ruggero Moscati sums up this equivocation thus: 'with all the good will in the world, for the Piedmontese ruling classes . . . and for the Neapolitan exiles themselves who returned to Naples 'Piedmontis- ized,' it was difficult to distinguish between that which was an organic imperfection and infirmity of the country and that which was the transitory consequence of a transitory maladministration' (1951: 286).

14. Lady Holland, a friend of Cavour's, is the sole female contributor to this correspondence. Cavour, in response to her criticisms of his policies in the south, writes: 'If you were a man and an Italian, I would entrust the destiny of those provinces to you; but since you cannot govern them, may it please you to enlighten me with regard to their miserable condition' (Cavour 1949–54: 4.411).

15. It is the history of just this 'mythical' notion that Salvadori traces (1976 [1960]).

16. Cavour's words as referred by Hudson to Russell in a letter of 30 November 1860, cited in Mack Smith 1954: 412. In a similar vein, Villamarina suggests in another letter from Naples that history alone cannot account for the degradation of the Neapolitans: 'There is nothing but cowardice here. As an excuse they say that *they have been degraded . . . but why, I ask, have they let themselves be degraded in this fashion? . . .* In final analysis, history shows that all peoples have gone through something like this, yet they haven't fallen into the state of brutishness and *sloth* which has overcome the Neapolitans . . .' (Cavour 1949–54: 1.141; emphasis in text).

17. For a discussion of Massari's activities in Turin during these years, as well as of his return to Naples in 1860, see Cotugno 1931: 154–318.

18. Massari also edited the 1851 Italian edition of William Gladstone's influential anti-Bourbon diatribe, 'Letters to Lord Aberdeen' (Massari 1851).

19. For the highly 'Piedmontisized' Massari, Milan is evidently fair game for criticism as well. This derogatory allusion to Milan (nevertheless favorably compared to Naples) serves to remind us that Naples – the

Mezzogiorno – was by no means the only region to be maligned by the Piedmontese, that indeed the negative representation of the south takes place within a field of multiple regional antagonisms. At the same time, I would suggest that the annexation of southern Italy in 1860–61 constitutes a crucial episode in the formation of a dualistic antagonism between north and south which, while by no means cancelling out the force of other, more specific regionalisms and *campanilismi*, eventually becomes the overarching geopolitical division in the national imagination.

20. In his report to Minister of the Interior Marco Minghetti on the conditions in southern Italy, Diomede Pantaleoni describes the difficulties of traveling in Calabria during the summer of 1861 in a similar fashion: 'One must have forty, sixty bodyguards, go with extra carriages, all armed to the teeth, and travel like caravans in the desert defending oneself from the Arabs and Bedouins. . . . There isn't a word of exaggeration in all this! It's the story, the simple story of the way . . . I myself had to and did travel in those areas' (Alatri 1953: 771). A few years later, A. Bianco di St. Jorioz was even more explicit about the paradoxical nature of the coexistence of 'Italy' and 'Africa' in the same country: 'we are among a people who, although they are Italian by birth, seem to belong to some primitive African tribe' (cited in Croce 1970 [1925]: 240).

21. It is interesting to contrast this description of Naples and Sicily with the encomium of Naples offered by the Milanese federalist Giuseppe Ferrari a few weeks earlier on the floor of Parliament during the 8 October debate on the annexation of the southern provinces. In his speech against annexation and in favor of *confederation* he declaims: 'I saw a colossal, rich, powerful city. . . . I saw better-paved streets than in Paris, more splendid monuments than in the premier capitals of Europe, fraternal and intelligent inhabitants, quick in thought, in conversation, in association, in action. Naples is the greatest Italian capital, and when it overlooks the fires of Vesuvius and the ruins of Pompeii, it seems the eternal queen of nature and of nations' (*Discussioni della Camera* 1861: 936). In light of the Cavourians' representations of Naples, there would appear to be a correlation between Ferrari's federalist political orientation and his respect for the human and civic reality of Naples. This hypothesis must be considered, however, in relation to the case of Massimo D'Azeglio (cf. note 24 below).

22. Consider also the following statement regarding the savage mind of the Neapolitans: 'The people of Naples are profoundly ignorant,

semi-barbarian and superstitious to a degree unequalled in history'
(Cavour 1949–54: 3.332). Again the hyberbolic terms of the affirmation are prominent.

23. As in the previous citation from this collection of letters, the editor
adds an exculpation of D'Azeglio in a footnote: 'These are remin-
iscences of the dreaded Bourbon government. *Absit iniuria* from that
genial people [the Neapolitans], which in fact possesses excellent
and serious qualities.' The editor is clearly at pains to dissipate the
lingering confusion between the political system and the essential
character of the Neapolitans discussed earlier.

24. In the context of the prevalently moderate *Carteggi Cavour* under
examination, D'Azeglio's statements prompt us to consider the extent
to which the denigration of southern Italy is not limited to the
Cavourian entourage or to the moderate leadership but is rather
something that invests other political orientations as well. Professing,
in a federalist spirit in open polemic with the Cavourians, the
Neapolitans' right to political autonomy and self-determination,
D'Azeglio nevertheless presents a vision of the south akin to theirs
in its visceral sense of contempt and disgust. The geographical
imagination, in other words, does not line up neatly with a single
political position but is rather 'overdetermined,' the product of diverse
social, cultural, regional and political formations. For a relevant
discussion, see Bidussa 1992, with specific reference to the uneven
fit between the *grammar* of anti-semitism and the *politics* of anti-
semitism.

25. As the Neapolitan Giovanni Manna noted at this time, it was just
this attitude that prompted a growing resentment among many
southerners, as they realized that the Piedmontese compatriot who
claims to be 'friend, associate, brother, instead aims to be master
and superior' (Passerin d'Entrèves 1956: 64).

26. The medical vision of the south is however by no means limited to
this period and this correspondence. To cite a few examples from
the first decades following unification, in 1863 Alexandre Dumas
writes (with reference to Naples) of 'the necessity of a surgeon' for
'a gravely ill society' (cited in Ragionieri: 1969: 11–12); just after
the conquest of Rome in 1871 Rattazzi speaks of Naples as 'the
bleeding wound that we have opened on our side' (cited in Capone
1991: 121); a few years later Franchetti describes the world-view of
the Sicilians as a 'illness to be cured' (Franchetti and Sonnino 1974:
1.221); and finally Paolo Orano writes in 1896 that the 'race' of
Sardinians 'grows, spreads like rotten, pussy gangrene. This is not

normal generation; it is a breeding ground of assassins, of beasts; it is without doubt an invasion of barbarians' (cited in Salvadori 1976 [1960]: 187). For a general consideration of the analogy between disease and civil disorder in Western political thought, see Sontag 1978: 71–85. The *locus classicus* in the Italian tradition is surely to be found in Machiavelli's *Prince*, chapter 3: 'When trouble is sensed well in advance it can be easily remedied; if you wait for it to show itself any medicine will be too late because the disease will have become incurable. As the doctors say of a wasting disease, to start with it is easy to cure but difficult to diagnose; after a time, it becomes easy to diagnose but difficult to cure. So it is in politics. Political disorders can be quickly healed if they are seen well in advance (and only a prudent ruler has such foresight); when, for lack of diagnosis, they are allowed to grow in such a way that everyone can recognize them, remedies are too late' (1981 [1517]: 39–40).

27. 'L'Italia una e indivisibile' was the phrase that appeared in the text of the plebiscite of 21 October 1860.

28. Or, similarly: 'the entire Italian question is now in Naples. To succeed there is to create Italy' (Cavour 1949–54: 4.72).

29. Massari's medical representation of the south must have seemed particularly fitting to Minghetti. Four months earlier he had communicated to Farini his conviction that 'some soldierly methods would be beneficial medicine for this people' (Cavour 1949–54: 4.76) – a comment which points toward our discussion below of the correlation between such imagery and the use of military force in the south.

30. One of the most eminent and authoritative members of the Sicilian autonomy movement, Amari was the man whose concerns about Piedmontese centralization inspired one of Cavour's most celebrated (and, in retrospect, ill-fated) statements regarding regional self-government: 'Professor Emerico Amari, most learned jurisconsult that he is, will recognize, I hope, that we are no less fond of decentralization than he, that our theories of the State do not lead to the tyranny of a capital over the provinces, nor the creation of a bureaucratic caste that would subject all the members and fractions of the kingdom to the control of an artificial center against which the traditions and customs of Italy would rebel no less than its geographic conformation. I expressed my views on this subject to Professor Amari's brother on a number of occasions, and I have no doubt that as soon as the commotion that a few rabble-rousers are trying to stir up by fomenting personal controversy is quelled, it will

be very easy to reach an agreement on the scheme of organization which leaves the central authority the necessary force to complete its great work of national liberation and grants real self-government to the regions and provinces' (Cavour 1949–54: 4.220).

31. Similarly, in his opening statement on 'the state of the Neapolitan provinces,' Massari begins by refuting the widespread opinion – which he numbers among the common errors about the south – 'that the revolution in the southern provinces was what one would call, with an economic metaphor, the fruit of importation . . . that the national sentiment among the population of southern Italy is sluggish, is weak' (*Discussioni della Camera* 1862a: 361).

32. As Candeloro notes, 'the national Parliament's first discussion of the Southern Question thus did not lead to a change in the government's policy there, which proceeded along the road of administrative unification, without an exact idea of the actual needs of the South' (1956–1986: 5.143). It would be at least another decade before Parliament began to take the conditions in southern Italy seriously as a 'social question.'

33. The 'wound' of southern Italy figures prominently in fact in the opening discussion of the second period of Parliament on 20 November 1861. After a long summer of fighting brigandage, however, Prime Minister Bettino Ricasoli's statement suggests a somewhat diminished faith in the government's medical abilities: 'There is no doctor that can heal the wounds of the Neapolitan provinces with specific remedies. Time is needed to heal them, along with the actions of the government and the efficacy of the laws . . .' (*Discussioni della Camera* 1862b: 6).

34. In response to this militarization of government policy towards the south, and specifically to Minghetti's suggestion that additional troops would be sent there to maintain order, two voices of protest rang out in this debate with particular force. That of Ferrari: 'A single word shook and stung me like an arrow, and though I am to some extent in accord with the Minister as long as he is fighting the Pope and Emperor, when I heard him assure, promise that he would send crack troops to the south, that at this very moment an imposing military force is already encamped at Foggia, at Sora, etc., then I felt myself to be almost personally threatened. What are you thinking, sirs, to send bayonettes from Turin into the old Kingdom [of Naples]? To what end? To police the area? Don't you see the enormous contradiction of your position?' (*Discussioni della Camera* 1862a: 396); and that of Mellana: '. . . I'll say it frankly, I listened with great

distress to those who invoked the supreme argument of force. And with greater distress I heard the Minister of the Interior vaunt this grievous expedient with an air of satisfaction, speaking of it more in an absolutist sense than in that of a free government' (*Discussioni della Camera* 1862a: 437).

35. For an illuminating discussion of the interrelations between the representation and repression of 'brigandage,' see Dickie 1992.
36. General Cialdini assumed full civil and military powers in the provinces of southern Italy on 14 July 1861. Colonel Mazé de la Roche, commander in the area around Campobasso in the summer of 1861, offers this picture of the extent of military rule in one southern Italian province: 'I am, in the district, mayor, judge, commander of the police . . . and I exercise nearly absolute authority over some fifteen towns' (Buffa di Perrero 1888: 80).
37. The Tronto River roughly marked the border between the ex-Kingdom of Naples and the Papal States in the east and, along with the Garigliano to the west, commonly served as shorthand for the divide between northern and southern Italy.
38. As reported by Cavour's niece, Giuseppina Alfieri, in La Rive (1862: 439).

References

Alatri, P., ed. (1953), 'Le condizioni dell'Italia meridionale in un rapporto di Diomede Pantaleoni a Marco Minghetti (1861),' *Movimento Operaio* n.s. 5 (5–6): 750–92.

Artom, E. (1901), 'Il Conte di Cavour e la questione napoletana,' *Nuova Antologia* 4th ser., 96 (Nov.–Dec.): 144–52.

Bidussa, D. (1992), 'La grammatica dell'antisemitismo ovvero il ritorno del complotto,' *La talpa libri*, book review section of *Il manifesto* 3 April: 1.

Bollati, G. (1972), 'L'italiano,' in R. Romano and C. Vivanti, eds, *Storia d'Italia*, Vol. 1, *I caratteri originali*, Turin: Einaudi, pp. 951–1022.

Buffa di Perrero, C. (1888), *Biografia del Conte Gustavo Mazé de la Roche*, Turin: Fratelli Bocca.

Candeloro, G. (1956–1986), *Storia dell'Italia moderna*, 11 vols, Milan: Feltrinelli.

Capone, A. (1991), 'L'età liberale,' in G. Galasso and R. Romeo, eds, *Storia del Mezzogiorno*, Vol. 12, *Il Mezzogiorno nell'Italia unita*, Naples: Edizioni del Sole, pp. 95-193.

Cattaneo, C. (1957 [1845]), *Scritti storici e geografici*, eds G. Salvemini and E. Sestan, 2 vols, Florence: Le Monnier.

Cavour, C. (1929a), *Carteggi: La questione romana negli anni 1860–1861*, 2 vols, Bologna: Zanichelli.

—— (1929b), *Il carteggio Cavour-Nigra dal 1858 al 1861*, Vol. 4, *La liberazione del Mezzogiorno*, Bologna: Zanichelli.

—— (1949–54), *Carteggi: La liberazione del Mezzogiorno e la formazione del Regno d'Italia*, 5 vols, Bologna: Zanichelli.

Chabod, F. (1951), *Storia della politica estera italiana dal 1870 al 1896*, Vol. 1, *Le premesse*, Bari: Laterza.

Cotugno, R. (1931), *La vita e i tempi di Giuseppe Massari*, Trani: Vecchi.

Creuzé de Lesser, A. (1806), *Voyage en Italie et en Sicile*, Paris: Alphonse Pigoreau.

Croce, B. (1970 [1925]), *History of the Kingdom of Naples*, ed. and introd. H.S. Hughes, trans. F. Frenaye, Chicago: University of Chicago Press.

—— (1927), 'Il "paradiso abitato da diavoli,"' *Uomini e cose della vecchia Italia*, 1st series, Bari: Laterza, pp. 68–86.

D'Azeglio, M. (1938), *Scritti e discorsi politici*, Vol. 3, Florence: La Nuova Italia.

—— and D. Pantaleoni (1888), *Carteggio inedito*, Turin: L. Roux.

De Francesco, A. (1994), 'Ideologie e movimenti politici,' in G. Sabbatucci and V. Vidotto, eds, *Storia d'Italia*. Vol. 1, *Le premesse dell'unità: Dalla fine del Settecento al 1861*, Bari: Laterza, pp. 229–336

Della Peruta, F., ed. (1950), 'Contributo alla storia della questione meridionale: Cinque lettere inedite di Diomede Pantaleoni (1861),' *Società* 1: 69–94.

De Martino, E. (1961), *La terra del rimorso: Contributo a una storia religiosa del Sud*, Milan: Il Saggiatore.

De Sanctis, F. (1898), *Scritti varii inediti o rari*, ed. B. Croce, 2 vols, Naples: Morano.

Dickie, J. (1992), 'A Word at War: The Italian Army and Brigandage 1860–1870,' *History Workshop* 33: 1–24.

Discussioni della Camera dei Deputati: Atti del Parlamento Italiano (1861), Sessione del 1860, 2 periodo, 2nd edn rev., Turin: Botta.

Discussioni della Camera dei Deputati: Atti del Parlamento Italiano (1862a), Sessione del 1861, 1 periodo, 2nd edn rev., Turin: Botta.

Discussioni della Camera dei Deputati: Atti del Parlamento Italiano (1862b), Sessione del 1861, 2 periodo, 2nd edn rev., Turin: Botta.

Flora, E. (1961), 'Massimo D'Azeglio e l'annessione delle provincie meridionali,' *Atti del XXXVII congresso di storia del Risorgimento italiano*, Rome: Istituto per la storia del Risorgimento italiano, pp. 96–100.

Franchetti, L. and S. Sonnino (1974), *Inchiesta in Sicilia*, 2 vols, Florence: Vallecchi.

Galasso, G. (1982), 'Lo stereotipo del napoletano e le sue variazioni regionali,' *L'altra Europa: Per un'antropologia storica del Mezzogiorno d'Italia*, Milan: Mondadori, pp. 143–90.

Gualterio, F.A. (1852), *Gli ultimi rivolgimenti italiani: Memorie storiche*, 4 vols, Florence: Le Monnier.

La Rive, W. de (1862), *Le Comte de Cavour: Récits et souvenirs*, Paris: J. Hetzel.

Mack Smith, D. (1954), *Cavour and Garibaldi 1860: A Study in Political Conflict*, Cambridge: Cambridge University Press.

Machiavelli, N. (1981 [1517]), *The Prince*, trans. George Bull, Harmondsworth: Penguin.

Massari, G., ed. (1851), *Il signor Gladstone ed il governo napolitano: Raccolta di scritti intorno alla questione napolitana*, Turin: Tipografia Subalpina.

Miraglia, B. (1856), *Cinque novelle calabresi precedute da un discorso intorno alle condizioni attuali della letteratura italiana*, Florence: Le Monnier.

Moe, N. (1999), 'Il Sud di Giovanni Verga tra la Sicilia pittoresca e la questione meridionale,' in R. Lumley and J. Morris, eds, *Oltre il meridionalismo: Nuove prospettive sul Mezzogiorno d'Italia*, Rome: Carocci, pp. 145–75.

Molfese, F. (1964), *Storia del brigantaggio dopo l'unità*, Milan: Feltrinelli.

Moscati, R. (1951), 'Il Mezzogiorno nel Risorgimento italiano,' in E. Rota, ed., *Questioni di storia del Risorgimento e dell'unità d'Italia*, Milan: Marzorati, pp. 253–90.

Nievo, I. (1961), *Lettere garibaldine*, ed. A. Ciceri, Turin: Einaudi.

Passerin d'Entrèves, E. (1956), *L'ultima battaglia politica di Cavour*, Turin: ILTE.

Patriarca, S. (1996), *Numbers and Nationhood: Writing Statistics in Nineteenth-Century Italy*, Cambridge: Cambridge University Press.

Pavone, C. (1964), *Amministrazione centrale e amministrazione periferica da Rattazzi a Ricasoli (1859–1866)*, Milan: Giuffrè.

Petrusewicz, M. (1998), *Come il Meridione divenne una questione: Rappresentazioni del Sud prima e dopo il Quarantotto*, Soveria Mannelli: Rubbettino.

Placanica, A. (1988), 'Lo stereotipo del meridionale e il suo uso nel Settecento napoletano,' *Bernardo Tanucci, la corte, il paese 1730–1780*, special issue of *Archivio Storico per la Sicilia Orientale* 84 (1–2): 163–85.

La quistione napoletana: Ferdinando Borbone e Luciano Murat (1855), Turin: Tipografia Economica.

Ragionieri, E. (1969), *Italia giudicata 1861-1945: Ovvero la storia degli italiani scritta dagli altri*, Bari: Laterza.

Romagnoli, S. (1982), 'Spazio pittorico e spazio letterario da Parini a Gadda,' in C. De Seta, ed., *Storia d'Italia: Annali*, Vol. 5, *Il paesaggio*, Turin: Einaudi, pp. 431–559.

Romeo, R. (1974 [1963]), *Dal Piemonte sabaudo all'Italia liberale*, Bari: Laterza.

Ruggiero, G. de (1981), *The History of Italian Liberalism*, trans. R.G. Collingwood, Gloucester MA: Peter Smith.

Salvadori, M.L. (1976 [1960]), *Il mito del buongoverno: La questione meridionale da Cavour a Gramsci*, Turin: Einaudi.

Salvatorelli, L. (1975 [1935]), *Il pensiero politico italiano dal 1700 al 1870*, Turin: Einaudi.

—— (1944), *Pensiero e azione del Risorgimento*, 1st edn, Turin: Einaudi.

Scirocco, A. (1963), *Governo e paese nel Mezzogiorno nella crisi dell'unificazione (1860–61)*, Milan: Giuffrè.

Sontag, S. (1978), *Illness as Metaphor*, New York: Farrar, Strauss, and Giroux.

Staël, Mme de (1955 [1807]), *Corinne ou l'Italie*, ed. S. Balayé, Paris: Gallimard.

Stallybrass, P., and A. White (1986), *The Politics and Poetics of Transgression*, London: Methuen.

Tuzet, H. (1945), *Voyageurs français en Sicile au temps du Romantisme (1802–1848)*, Paris: Boivin.

Villari, R. (1961), 'La liberazione del Mezzogiorno e l'unità nazionale,' *Mezzogiorno e contadini nell'età moderna*, Bari: Laterza, pp. 243–79.

–5–

Passion and Sexual Difference: The Risorgimento and the Gendering of Writing in Nineteenth-Century Italian Culture

Lucia Re

Women and the Scene of Writing

In tracing the cultural genealogy of the gendering of writing in nineteenth-century Italy, I will start with a little-known small painting entitled *La lettrice* (The Female Reader) by Federico Faruffini, one of the more interesting exponents of Milanese romanticism. The painting dates from 1864, three years after the official proclamation of the new Kingdom of Italy and seven before the completion of the unification (see figure 5.1). 1864 was also the year of the first International, and of the publication of Anna Maria Mozzoni's impassioned feminist pamphlet, 'La donna e i rapporti sociali' (Woman and Social Relations). The leisurely and apparently harmless appearance of this little scene, like the stage of a Pirandello play, evokes a complex and highly problematic set of questions.[1] In a comfortable bourgeois room, a young woman reads. She is alone. She is looking at the pages of her book with an expression of concentration which indicates that she is not just killing time – she looks interested and focused. The cigarette in her hand, held comfortably at a distance to keep the smoke out of her eyes, suggests both a clandestine and a habitual act. (Smoking was distinctly masculine in the nineteenth century, and no 'proper' middle or upper-class woman would let herself be portrayed while smoking.) The woman is in fact painted from the rear, an unusual perspective that makes the viewer feel like an intruder and runs against the convention of depicting women frontally, and presenting them as 'composed' and feminine. The painting suggests that smoking and reading both are somehow illicit, a forbidden solitary pleasure for this young woman in a scene that we are not really meant to see. Ours is

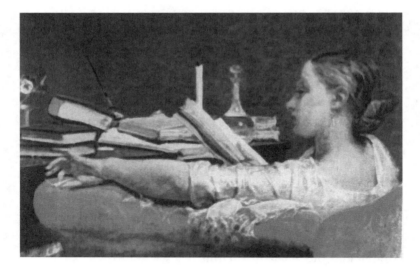

Figure 5.1 Federico Faruffini, *La lettrice* (The Female Reader; 1864)
Milan, Civica Galleria d'Arte Moderna

a surreptitious glance at a private, intimate moment. Not far from the
young woman is a small desk full of papers piled up with books. Among
the books we can see a pen, an ink pot, a candle. These suggest that her
reading may soon turn into writing. Questions arise about the identity
and character of this young woman. Is she an example of women's
emancipation? A well-brought-up young lady who secretly indulges her
passion for forbidden novels and smoking? Or is she a budding Jane
Austen or a Virginia Woolf with a room of her own in which to read and
write in peace?

But perhaps these questions of identity are less interesting than another
one: why are we as viewers more provoked and intrigued by this nineteenth-
century scene of intimacy – of reading and, perhaps, writing – than if we
were seeing an explicitly erotic scene (a naked woman looking at herself
in the mirror, for example)? The response to this question is largely what
this chapter is about. The fact is that naked women and erotic scenes are
a dime a dozen in later nineteenth-century painting and fiction, while the
scene of a woman writing is largely absent, or concealed. There is, to be
sure, no scarcity of images of women reading or of women with books
in nineteenth-century art and literature. One can think of innumerable
examples of tranquil domestic scenes in the realist work of the Italian

macchiaioli, for instance, depicting bourgeois women holding books or with books on their laps or at their side – where the book is an icon of respectable female leisure. In Adriano Cecioni's *La zia Erminia* (Aunt Erminia; *c.* 1867 [see figure 5.2]), for example, the act of reading is qualified as a simple interlude of relaxation in a comfortable bourgeois

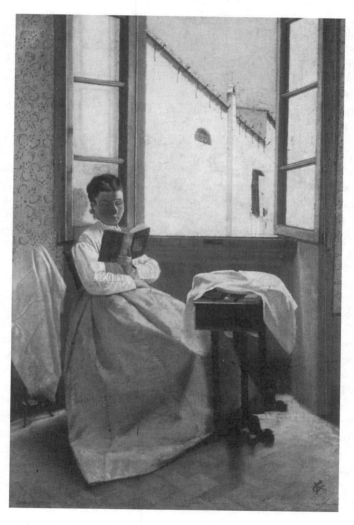

Figure 5.2 Adriano Cecioni, *La zia Erminia* (Aunt Erminia; *c.* 1867) Arezzo, Museo Medioevale e Moderno

interior by the presence of the small sewing table (not yet a sewing machine), where a white cloth appears temporarily perched, as if waiting to be picked up again by the unhurried sewer (or embroiderer).

Or, more disturbingly, we can think of the devastating effects that reading books – or, more specifically, novels and sentimental romances – has on innumerable young women in nineteenth-century Italian fiction. It is a topos that became firmly established after the publication of Flaubert's *Madame Bovary* (1857). Eva, the protagonist of one of the novels by the Marchesa Colombi (one of the most accomplished novelists of the second half of the Italian nineteenth century) is, like Flaubert's Emma, addicted to novels. Eva describes the experience of reading *Atala* by Chateaubriand as something that 'exalts one, makes one feverish. One would like to no longer have a husband, a home, children, in order to wander in the vastity of that desert, under that burning sky, and to be loved that way, and inebriated by that great dream and that desperation' (Colombi 1988 [1887]: 5). But while scenes like this which rehearse the topos of the connection between women reading novels and illicit passion are numerous, what is lacking in nineteenth-century Italian visual as well as literary culture is the connection between women reading and women *writing*. Writing, that is, anything other than letters or diaries. Writing novels or essays or newspaper articles. While portraits abound of men at their desks writing, the equivalent for women is extremely rare.[2] This makes *La lettrice* all the more remarkable, and explains in part its uncanniness. For of course the painting's scene of reading does not speak the scene of writing, it only *alludes* to it and evokes it as a tantalizing but uncertain possibility. The woman writer – literary writer or essayist or professional writer of any sort – is also remarkably rare in fiction written about women, despite the increasing and considerable number of women who, from about the 1880s, actually wrote and published fiction. Among the few and exceptions, Sibilla Aleramo's *Una donna* (1992 [1906]), Matilde Serao's *Fantasia* (1892 [1883]) and Luigi Pirandello's *Suo marito* (1973 [1911]) are particularly revealing in that, as we shall see in the last section of this chapter, they bring to light the reasons why the very act of writing, as an extension and development of the act of reading, is persistently constructed as threatening and subject to various forms of cultural censorship even by its very practitioners.

The Cult of Domesticity and the Politics of Feeling

What is at stake precisely in the question of women reading and writing in Italy in the nineteenth and early twentieth centuries? Writing, reading and thinking were traditionally perceived as male activities in all Western patriarchal cultures, and women writers were universally regarded with suspicion or condescension. Yet the anxiety generated by the very notion of female authorship in Italian culture of the nineteenth and even the early twentieth century appears unusually intense and protracted compared, for example, to that of France or of England. What is specific to the Italian cultural context? What gives to the Italian gendering of writing its particular form? [3]

In attempting to answer this question, let us start with the material fact of reading in nineteenth-century Italy. In 1861, 74.7 percent of the population was illiterate. Among women, the illiteracy rate was 81 percent. In the 1871 census the rate of illiteracy was 75.8 percent for women and 61.8 percent for men. One of the most frequently reiterated goals of 'moderate' politicians (the *destra storica*) in the aftermath of 1861 had been the education of women, which was seen as fundamental to the reconstruction of the new Italian national community. The explicit interest that Risorgimento rhetoric (from both the left and the right) devoted to the education of women before and during the unification was couched in terms stressing the need to free women from their pre-Risorgimento cultural slavery, based on ignorance and prejudices, superstitions and conservative traditions (De Giorgio 1992: 411). The new laws stated the need to provide equal educational opportunities for men and women. But the discourse of literacy and the protocols set up for the education of women were in practice far from liberal. They amounted rather to instruments for social and cultural control.

While at the lowest levels of instruction the gap between men and women narrowed, it remained huge at all other levels. As late as the end of the nineteenth century, formal instruction for most women across all social classes in Italy ended with the completion of primary school grades, while middle-class men had access to higher education. Discrimination often occurred within the same family. The novelist Neera (born to a petit bourgeois family) was sent to a primary school for girls and subsequently, as an adolescent, stayed at home with her aunts doing sewing and embroidery, while all her brothers had the opportunity to attend the university. Until 1888 the teaching of reading to both male and female children was a slow process, spread over several years and separate from the teaching of writing, which sometimes never occurred, especially in the rural areas. Male and female children were assigned suitably different kinds and amounts of readings. The scant readings given to female children in elementary school were carefully selected in accordance to what was increasingly presented by the state as the most desirable mission of woman in the new Italy, namely that of 'angel of the hearth'. In 1860, the official instructions to the elementary school teachers who were to implement the new programs stated that 'for women, culture must have as its only goal domestic life and the acquisition of those notions required for the good government of the family.'[4] This differential notion of education remained prevalent in Italy until the beginning of the twentieth century, and became an integral part of the gendered anthropological theories of positivist thinkers such as Paolo Mantegazza and Cesare Lombroso (Garin 1962: 29–32).

The new Italy, under the leadership of one of the most influential of its moderate intellectuals, Francesco De Sanctis, whose *History of Italian Literature* is to this day considered a classic, and who was appointed minister of education, dealt with the problem of women's education by creating effectively a two-tiered system. Basic literacy was culturally acceptable and even desirable for women, at least for some. But while men had access to upper education all the way to university and professional schools, the few women who were able to continue their studies were channeled toward schools designed just for them – the so-called 'normal schools' and institutes for the training of nursery and elementary-school teachers. The education of children – especially their initial moral and emotional education – was widely perceived as one of the few legitimate professions for women because it was a 'natural' extension of women's influence in the home. True to their name, these schools for women were supposed to normalize and discipline women's instinctive and emotional nature by containing any tendency towards the unruly or the passionate and nurturing a healthy desire for the maternal and for a mothering kind of pedagogy.

Most of the women writers who flourished in increasing numbers in the new Italy in the last two decades of the century, including some of the best-known – Matilde Serao and Ada Negri among them – attended 'normal schools' or similar institutions for women only. But although Serao, Negri and all other major women writers (including Grazia Deledda and Sibilla Aleramo) were essentially autodidacts,[5] the influence of this type of school on their ideological formation was doubtless considerable. Lucienne Kroha has persuasively shown how all of Neera's writing is pervaded by a strong sense of anxiety with regard to her own position as a woman writer, which is at some level always felt to be illicit, a kind of misappropriation analogous to the transgressiveness of her adulterous and passionate heroines (Kroha 1992: 67–85). A telling clue to the role that schooling had in generating Neera's self-loathing can be found in the opening pages of *Confessioni letterarie* (1977 [1891]) where she tells about writing her first story while still at school. (She wrote in secret, during recess.) Significantly, the tale was about a little girl who steals and is dutifully punished for her theft.

The educational practices of the new Italy constituted only one aspect of a widespread discriminatory system. While early feminists such as Anna Maria Mozzoni, who translated John Stuart Mill's *On the Subjection of Women* into Italian in 1870, had hoped that the Italian Risorgimento could also alter the abject condition of women, the post-unification Italian state quickly dispelled that illusion. The new Italian family law delegated all authority to male heads of household. Without their husbands' authorization women were barred from most commercial and legal acts and they could not become their own children's guardians. Adultery was considered a crime for women only. Unmarried women who worked (by the turn of the century they constituted half of the industrial work-force) or had property were expected to pay taxes but could not vote in either local or national elections. By contrast the laws and regulations defining the juridical position of women and their civil rights in several states of the Italian peninsula before the unification were, as Anna Maria Mozzoni and other nineteenth-century feminists insistently and polemically pointed out, in many cases comparatively less discriminatory.[6] Mozzoni observed that the ideal of the 'angel of the hearth' invoked by the legislators of the new Italy to justify their discriminatory policies was anachronistic, as in reality women – especially from the lower classes – had been working outside the home for decades and would undoubtedly continue to do so out of necessity, even though they received salaries inferior to those of men doing the same work. For Mozzoni, the failure of the new Italian civil code to measure up to the standards set by developments in women's rights in countries as diverse as England, Prussia, Austria and the United States constituted a betrayal of the Risorgimento promises of progress for women and the nation at large ('La donna in faccia al progetto del nuovo codice civile italiano' [1865]; cited in Bortolotti 1975: 70). Indeed, as she stated in a memorable sentence echoing John Stuart Mill in her preface to her translation of *The Subjection of Women*, it was from the condition of its women that the degree of *civiltà* of any nation could best be judged (Mill 1870: 9). In 1871 Mozzoni observed ironically that as far as women and the family were concerned, the enlightened despotism of Josef II and Maria Theresa were indeed preferable ('La questione dell'emancipazione della donna in Italia' [1871]; cited in Bortolotti 1975: 77–8).

It is a commonplace of Italian cultural history that the unequal treatment of women in education as well as in other institutional areas of the new Italy can be ascribed to the conservative influence of the Catholic Church and to the persistence, well after the Risorgimento and the unification, of deeply-rooted prejudices in Italian patriarchal culture, which continued to resonate particularly among its most conservative exponents. The 'moderate' forces (the so-called *destra storica*) which ruled the new Italy perpetuated a standard notion of woman as naturally subject to man. She was weak, passive, intellectually inferior, inclined towards sentimentalism and best kept in the home or at most – if unmarried – in the elementary schoolroom. This vision in its most extreme form can be traced back to the work of some seminal conservative Catholic thinkers of the earlier Italian Risorgimento, such as Vincenzo Gioberti, who in 1847 had written: 'femininity resides in an inchoate and confused nature that does not generate reflection and does not manifest itself except in the instinctive form of feeling' (1847: 129–30).

Yet the work of cultural historians such as Bortolotti (1975), De Donato (1983a) and De Giorgio (1992), among others, increasingly indicates that the systems which were put into place in the new Italy to administer and control women's access to reading and writing (as well as their social and cultural position in the new nation) did not just express variations on the old conservative stereotypes. Rather, they deployed those stereotypes in order to elaborate a new, culturally and politically specific gender ideology based on the notion of the separate spheres and on the cult of domesticity, both of which were ultimately rooted in class as well as gender discrimination.

Due to the particular economic and social conditions of the new Italy, and the specific way in which its unification came about, the victorious moderate elites felt compelled to impose with every possible means at their disposal a gender ideology rooted in the confinement of woman to the home as her only proper sphere. The conservative, even reactionary nature of the Italian unification process have been extensively explored by historians. Only recently, however, have the gender system and the control of women's access to reading and writing begun to emerge as central strategies in the post-Risorgimento consolidation of the Italian state and in the struggle for social hegemony in the nineteenth century. As De Donato has shown, in its efforts to pull Italy out of what it perceived to be its economic and cultural 'backwardness' (and to bring it up to the level of progress achieved by the 'more advanced' European nations), the emerging moderate leadership of the Risorgimento found that it 'needed' – and therefore did everything it could in this direction – to cultivate the 'passive virtues' of women (1983a). In the reconstruction of civil society, the moderates' principal aim was to preserve the social order by promoting a harmonious, non-conflictual relationship among the existing social classes. In their view, a stratified but peaceful society founded on the principle of class solidarity, and on the ethics of work, self-sacrifice, parsimony and savings, would eventually make up for the lack of industrial productivity. Essentially an agrarian and mercantile society until the 1880s, Italy lacked the resources generated elsewhere in Europe by industrial capitalism and the exploitation of colonies. In the complex network of ideological apparatuses through which the Italian moderate leadership gradually sought to consolidate its hegemony and to improve the state's economy, the exploitation of women and the idea of 'the home' as a productive space thus took on particular relevance.

In order to implement the desired economic, social and ethical transformation of the new Italian civil society, the reformist rhetoric of the moderates appealed from early on to what it termed the 'moral virtues' and the natural goodness of the healthier members of the social body, with particular reference to middle-class women. The economy of the home, and woman's role in it, were increasingly envisioned as a source of healing for society at large both in terms of women's actual labor in the home, which would hopefully make up for many of the inadequacies in the underdeveloped national economy, and in terms of the habit and ethics of savings, instigated by women through the practice of caring for the family's well-being.[7]

In the education of children, women were expected to be the principal agents for the inculcation of 'good feelings' such as a sense of obedience, respect for authority, parsimony and charity. When subordinates such as servants and peasants were present in the household, women's benign influence would be extended to them. Women were thus entrusted with the delicate mission of forestalling in the microcosm of the home the development of any potential class resentment or conflict, containing any egalitarian or emancipatory tendencies, and promoting harmonious coexistence. Women were supposed to nurture in their husbands a sense of loyalty, duty, abnegation and protectiveness toward the 'nest'.[8] Cultivated in the home, such feelings would hopefully carry over to the larger social body, fostering a sense of national community. This was a particular concern to the moderate leadership because Italy's unification had been substantially forged by a small elite and the citizens of the newly formed nation lacked a strong conviction that they really had anything in common. One of Cavour's chief difficulties was precisely the lack of loyalty and public spirit or political training in responsibility. Thus the leaders of the Risorgimento and its aftermath gave women a crucial political role. In an apparent paradox, it was precisely this political use of women that dictated their exclusion from politics. Women's sphere was to be exclusively the home; like the subaltern masses, women would continue to be excluded from the decisional sites of politics and public life.[9]

The new, politically expedient cult of domesticity which confined women to the private sphere also demanded that they be kept in school as little as possible. Cesare Balbo, one of the principal moderate leaders of the Risorgimento, stressed repeatedly that 'la vera vita delle donne si vuole imparare dove ella si ha da vivere. Il regno della donna è in casa; ivi se son belle, paion più belle; ivi se buone, più buone' (women learn best to live the life that they are going to live in the place where they are going to live it. The woman's realm is the home; there, if women are beautiful they will seem more beautiful; if they are good they will seem better [cited in De Donato 1983a: 47]). Thus feminine beauty and femininity itself are to be nourished in the most 'natural' way in and through the home. A moderate amount of learning – essentially basic literacy and a few clear moral and practical principles – was considered desirable, but after that the fulfillment of her mission as bride, mother and educator of her children and subordinates only required a woman to follow her natural feminine feelings. According to Nicolò Tommaseo (one of the most influential patriots, writers and thinkers of the Italian nineteenth century), a woman should study enough only to learn to express clearly 'part of what she feels in her heart' (Tommaseo 1872: 257). Excessive learning may threaten women's natural grace, charm and docility, or, in short, their femininity. If women have cultivated their *ingegno*, warns Silvio Pellico, they must be 'senza ambizione di farlo comparire' (without desire to exhibit it [Pellico 1834: 70–3]).[10] The need for women to hide their talent, to keep it away from public eyes, extends to the ability or passion for writing. Whatever writing women engage in must remain private.

We begin to see now that the incompatibility between writing, publishing and femininity, and the need to suppress or hide female talent, were part of an ideological construction of gender whose foundations were laid in Italian culture by the very 'fathers' of the nation even before the moment of its birth. This ideological construction became so deeply interiorized in Italian culture that its effects continued to be felt well into the next century – for example, as we shall see, in Sibilla Aleramo's conflictual vision of her own work and her own talent, and in the need she felt 'not to be seen' in the act of writing.

Promoting the Bourgeois Cult of Domesticity

One of the reasons for the often-lamented lack of a great tradition of novel writing in nineteenth-century Italian literature before roughly the last two decades of the century may be found precisely in what was effectively an unofficial campaign against women's education and women's writing, with the exception of basic literacy. The strategic and profound opposition to women's learning anything that may have taken their minds beyond the walls of the family home was an integral part of the Italian cult of domesticity during and after the Risorgimento which stifled or deferred women's interest in fiction writing. As late as 1879, the *Dizionario biografico degli scrittori italiani* registered only 180 women writers compared to 4,525 men (De Giorgio 1992: 377). Ironically, these statistics were often used in fin-de-siècle rhetoric to argue the natural inferiority of women and their lack of artistic talent.

Faruffini's painting, with its scene of feminine reading and perhaps writing, emerges as a transgressive image that counteracts the cultural injunction to suppress or hide women's writing or to keep it strictly within bounds. For the cult of domesticity and the separation of the spheres in nineteenth-century Italy were produced, reinforced, maintained and – occasionally – contested through a variety of cultural practices, discourses and institutions, including literature and the visual arts. The realist art of the *macchiaioli* was particularly engaged in the political discourse of the unification and in the promotion of the cult of domesticity. It provides ample visual evidence of the pervasiveness of the domestic vision of womanhood and of women's role in 'making good Italians' and educating children. Silvestro Lega's *Educazione al lavoro* (Education to Work) from 1863 (see figure 5.3) and *La madre* (The Mother [see figure 5.4]) from 1884, are excellent examples of this rhetoric.[11] Some elements of the first painting may be considered ambiguous; for example the shadow on the floor and the bars on the window, which suggest imprisonment, and the little girl's kneeling position and concerned glance, which add to the severity of the scene and of the mother-daughter bond. Yet the overall meaning of the image and the title are clear: in a middle-class home a mother is doing her duty of educating her daughter by initiating her in a typically female practical task, i.e. making a ball of yarn from a skein. *La madre* has a more idyllic tone and portrays a less austere, more comfortable middle-class domestic scene. What is striking about this painting is that while the woman is engaged in the identical task as in the previous painting, namely making a ball of yarn, the child at whom she

Figure 5.3 Silvestro Lega, *Educazione al lavoro* (Education to Work; 1863)
Montecatini, Private Collection

directs from above her benign but controlling gaze (a little boy wearing
a dress, as was customary at the time) is not helping or looking back at
her, but rather has his back to her and is intently engaged in the act of
writing.

Figure 5.4 Silvestro Lega, *La madre* (The Mother; *c.* 1884)
Montecatini, Private Collection

An 1869 painting by the *macchiaiolo* artist Odoardo Borrani entitled
L'analfabeta (The Illiterate [see figure 5.5]) illustrates the centrality of
the discourse of literacy for the social and gender ideology of the new
Italy. In this portrayal of the domestic ritual of the mistress writing a

Figure 5.5 Odoardo Borrani, *L'analfabeta* (The Illiterate; 1869)
Montecatini, Private Collection

letter on behalf of the illiterate servant, the deferential expression and position of the young peasant woman – whose physiognomy and predicament may remind us of Manzoni's Lucia in *The Betrothed* – underscores her inferior social status. In fact, a number of cultural and political controls are encoded in the painting. For if the young peasant woman of Borrani's painting is a servant to her mistress and must entrust to her even a matter as possibly intimate and private as a personal letter, the mistress's apparent privilege (her freedom to write) is in fact illusory and quite limited. Indeed, as she sits at the small table with pen in hand waiting for the other woman's words, in order to transcribe and possibly translate them, she is only performing one of her feminine duties as bourgeois home-maker – a servant to her own servants, as Paola Masino was later to observe about the bourgeois *massaia* – and following the protocols of respectability. Faceless and anonymous for the viewer, she is only a passive wheel in a well-ordered mechanism, a means to keep things tidy and in order.

Although the hegemonic moderate vision of the Risorgimento favored class solidarity, the model family and the model 'angel of the hearth' were decidedly middle-class. Indeed, it was in opposition to the 'decadence' and 'corruption' of the aristocratic household, with its excessive luxury, its wasteful expenses and its 'soft' lifestyle, that the new bourgeois ideal of the home was set up during the Risorgimento. It became increasingly commonplace to argue, as did G. Calvi in his 1840 essay 'Le donne italiane' (Italian Women), that unlike the aristocratic woman of the decadent past, who wasted her time in theaters and dances, the new Italian woman would find her true dignity and 'glory' not in the vain noise of the world, in public display or the short-lived triumphs of worldliness, but in being known only to the few who have the privilege of being close to her and of admiring her wisdom in the private space of the home.[12] Leading Risorgimento intellectuals such as Cesare Balbo, Silvio Pellico and Nicolò Tommaseo all expressed similar thoughts (De Donato 1983a: 22). The 'decadent' aristocratic woman who frequented society was recurrently associated in Risorgimento rhetoric with licentiousness, the widespread practice of adultery, and indifference to the womanly duties of bride and mother, including the education of the children and the proper management of the household.

In her 1847 pamphlets on the education of women ('Dell'educazione morale della donna italiana' and 'Degli studi delle donne'), Caterina Franceschi-Ferrucci decried the wasteful spending and the unchristian behavior of the aristocracy ('they throw at the feet of dancers and actresses gold enough to feed many families'), and she eloquently put forth the new patriotic, bourgeois ideal of austerity and moral integrity for women.

If women are to become what they ought to be, they should be educated to 'remain solitary to attend to the care of the children and their virtue' in order that 'the new generation might prepare a better fortune for itself and for Italy' (cited in De Donato 1983a: 19). Franceschi-Ferrucci, whose works were published and reprinted several times over the next three decades, theorized with the utmost clarity the division of the spheres. Women were to manage the home, keep it ordered and happy, and make the children into good and useful citizens for the new Italian state. At the same time, she forcefully expounded the view that no woman should be *letterata*.[13] The cultivation of knowledge, reading and writing by women is presented in her work as yet another form of wasteful selfishness, directly related to the licentious erotic behavior and the vanity of the old kind of aristocratic woman. This deplorable kind of woman 'cultivates the mind because she knows that letters and the fine arts make conversation more pleasant and add light to one's native beauty. The peace of the hearth and the austere joys of the family have no value in her eyes . . . She likes the bustle of horses and carriages, the waving of the crowd, the tumult and noise of the streets. She runs to where she hears the sound of musical instruments: you see her often at the theater . . . What does it matter to her if . . . all is disorder and trouble at home, if her husband's heart is growing colder, if a miserable child cries desperately in the unattended cradle?' (Franceschi-Ferrucci 1875 [1847]: 32).

The aristocratic woman Franceschi-Ferrucci evokes is in all likelihood only a specter,[14] for the effects of the new bourgeois ideology, the clear distinction between public and private spheres, and in particular the limitation of women's existence to the latter, became pervasive after the unification, reaching beyond the lives of the middle classes. Indeed many of the forgers of the unification were themselves (from Cavour on) aristocrats who embraced a new middle-class ethic as the best for the new Italy. The new bourgeois ideology extended both upward to the older ruling classes and downward to the lower middle and working classes. Although lower-class women did continue to work outside the home in trade, in cottage industries, in textile mills, and as peasants in the fields, Risorgimento and post-Risorgimento rhetoric on women's domestic role conveniently glossed over this fact.[15]

In Franceschi-Ferrucci's text we can recognize the first indications of that paranoid – yet, as we have seen, politically deeply motivated – ideological discourse on women and on their unnatural, immoral and destructive misappropriation of writing which re-emerges in the figure of the early Sibilla Aleramo and in Pirandello's 1911 novel, *Suo marito*. As a woman writer Aleramo was perceived (and indeed she perceived herself) as anti-bourgeois and transgressive, a social outcast of sorts. She was essentially a democrat, and indeed she was to become a socialist and, later in life, a communist. Yet somehow there was always something of the decadent aristocrat about her – a typology which resonates from Franceschi-Ferrucci's text. Other women writers were similarly cast, or provocatively cast themselves, in similar roles towards the end of the century and at the beginning of the next. The famous Contessa Lara and Annie Vivanti were both examples of how women's writing in Italy could be identified with pseudo-aristocratic 'disorderly conduct' (De Giorgio 1992: 381–2) and with indecorous public exposure.[16]

In Franceschi-Ferrucci's text, the specter of the home's and the family's destruction are associated with a woman's appearing in the public space of the theater and with her selfish indulging of her passions. Even though Franceschi-Ferrucci's woman is not a writer, but rather a reader and a conversationalist, she nevertheless derives pleasure and admiration from books and from exposure to the promiscuous space of the theater. Franceschi-Ferrucci's text also allows us to see clearly the prejudice that will be thematized later in Pirandello's novel, *Suo marito*, namely the notion that what drives women to books and even to writing is fundamentally nothing other than their narcissism. It is not the disinterested love of art that leads Pirandello's Silvia Roncella to writing, but rather (as demonstrated by the kind of popular writing that she practices) the love of her own self-image reflected in the eyes of the crowd.[17] It is a topos that, in the years between Franceschi-Ferrucci and Pirandello, underwent many variations but remained substantially intact.[18]

The Natural Qualities of Women and the Containment of Passion

During the Risorgimento and its aftermath a profusion of essays, articles, poems and novels of the most varied registers, ranging from the most lowbrow to the highest, associated the image of woman with the feminine virtues of the gentle and wise 'angel' of the home. Already by 1852 Carlo Tenca complained about the narrowness and sentimentalism of Italian literature compared to other literatures, and its exclusive and excessive focus on the cult of domesticity and the family, the home and private life (Tenca 1971 [1852]: 264).[19]

But the Risorgimento did not just attempt to forge new social, political and cultural roles for women (and men) in the new Italy. Simultaneously, it also did something much more radical and momentous by attempting to redefine not only what men and women do, but also what they *are*.

The production of an 'idea' of femininity and masculinity, the construction of a cultural notion of what is natural and proper to women and to men, was an integral part of the ideological and political project for the creation of the new Italy. The seminal text on this question is Antonio Rosmini's *Filosofia del diritto* (Philosophy of Right; 1845). What are the natural qualities of woman? he asks. They are 'timida dolcezza, graziosa debolezza, attenta docilità: [la donna] è delicata, tranquilla, casalinga, paziente' (timid sweetness, graceful weakness, alert docility: [woman] is delicate, tranquil, home-loving, patient). Furthermore, she has the 'specialissima necessità di starsene ritirata' (the very special need to stay at home [Rosmini 1845: 301]). Man, on the other hand, has the natural qualities which 'lo rendono atto a comandare, coraggio, forza, attività, mente ferma o certo più sviluppata' (make him able to lead; courage, strength, activity, a strong or certainly more developed mind [ibid.: 301]). Thus, given women's intellectual inferiority, along with their natural affectionateness and need for protection, Rosmini concludes that, 'La condizione naturale della moglie è riposta ... nell'amore disinteressato al marito e nel sacrificio. Il contrario non sarebbe natura della donna, ma vizio; non sentimento della specie, ma individuale, e fattizio' (The natural condition of the wife resides in the disinterested love for her husband and in sacrifice. The opposite would not be the nature of woman, but vice; it would not be the feeling of the species, but rather individual and false [ibid.: 29]). Rosmini's text had profound cultural as well as juridical implications. The new Italy's juridical discrimination against women was in fact based effectively on the notion of the different nature of women and men that is so eloquently phrased by Rosmini.

The prescriptive gender ethos that the moderate leaders of the Risorgimento adopted had as its basic tenet Rosmini's notion that the two sexes are incomplete parts of a whole which can be recomposed through marriage, bringing about the fusion of the male and female individual and their respective qualities. Each of the genders takes on half of the indivisible reality of the individual subject: on the one hand sentiment and feeling (feminine) and on the other hand rationality and intellect (masculine). This fusion was to take place exclusively in the private sphere, however, and it was out of the question to extend it to the juridical and political sphere.

As neat and seductive as this binary gender structure may have been, it was far from innocent, for it was predicated on the notion that reason must triumph over sentiment. Hence the inescapable conclusion is that it was natural for one gender to dominate the other. This corresponded to the natural ability of man to dominate and master his passions by reason, while woman was unable to do so. Indeed her ability to feel (*sentire*) may, if not held in check by reason and masculine authority, and channeled towards the domestic and respectable feelings of spousal and maternal love, degenerate into unruly passion. Passion is the explosion of feeling beyond its legitimate borders; it is by definition excessive, transgressive, dangerous. It is thus the responsibility of men to guard and protect women against the eruption of passion.

As the Italian feminist theorist Adriana Cavarero points out in her essay, 'La passione della differenza' (The Passion of Difference [1995]), in Western culture women tend to be invested with the original sense of the word passion, emanating from its etymology, *patire* ('to suffer,' 'to endure'), which in turn links passion to its cognate, passivity. Women are supposed to be the prey, the passive victims of passions, especially erotic ones. They are predestined victims, as in Flaubert's caricature of Madame Bovary's novel-induced love passion, of storms of the senses, ecstasy and delirium. Unlike men, in other words, women lack the rational means to control themselves. Thus the new bourgeois cult of domesticity of the Italian Risorgimento was promoted not only through a discourse about the nature and the spontaneous inclinations of the genders but also through a regulatory discourse that sought to contain and 'domesticate' female passions, especially the passions that may be aroused by excessive learning and reading. 'Tra l'uomo e la donna è quella differenza che è tra la forza del fare e la virtù del patire' (the difference between man and woman is the difference between the strength of doing and the virtue of suffering) wrote Tommaseo in his 'Degli studi che più si convengono alle donne' (On the Studies That Are Most Appropriate for Women). This 'female virtue' *del patire* comes not from 'cose lette' (things read) but those that are 'meditate col cuore' (meditated through the heart [Tommaseo 1872: 255–7]).[20]

Feeling, Passion and Fiction: The Anxieties of Female Authorship

Nowhere is the ideological work of the regulatory discourse of the passions in the Italian nineteenth century more apparent than in the debate about fiction. The intense exchange during the era of the Risorgimento and in its aftermath on the novel and on the legitimacy of women's reading and writing novels is both a symptom of the gendering of passions and, at the same time, one of its principal cultural sources. Silvio Pellico, who may have been thinking of a certain English tradition of the novel that, since the eighteenth century, enshrined women in the private sphere, found the novel a highly 'moral' genre for women; in an 1819 review article published in *Il Conciliatore*, he encouraged women not only to read, but even to write novels.[21] It seemed to Pellico that women, incapable of political passions and naturally inclined towards 'le virtù private' (private virtues), have more talent than men for uncovering those subtle character traits and feelings required of the novel, and that the 'storia naturale delle passioni segnate dal cuore umane' (the natural history of the passions marked by the human heart) should be their domain as naturally 'romantic' writers.[22] Yet what was initially a positive connection between women, feeling, passion and the novel, came during the course of the Risorgimento to be seen in an increasingly negative light, as women reading or writing novels become more and more suspect.

It is in light of women's vulnerability to passion that Carlo Cattaneo objected – in an essay entitled 'Sul romanzo delle donne contemporanee in Italia' (dated 1863, a year before Faruffini's painting) – to Italian women reading George Sand's novels. These novels, he argues, provoke in women 'that restlessness, that need to rebel against their position in society and to demand emancipation' (Cattaneo 1983: 363). The essay's intentions are ultimately prescriptive in a political as well as a moral and aesthetic sense. In a reversal of Pellico's earlier enthusiasm, Cattaneo thus finally judges the novel generally inappropriate for women readers and/or writers.

The debate on the novel and on the legitimacy of female readership and female authorship in the second half of the nineteenth century often overlapped with the debate on the role and position of women in civil society. These debates were effectively the site of a contest about representation, in which questions of aesthetic representation were deeply enmeshed with debates about political representation, about gender and the representation of gender, and also with pervasive anxieties about cultural and political authority and control. When finally in 1912 the liberal prime minister Giovanni Giolitti broadened the electoral franchise, he granted the vote to all males over twenty-one who had completed military service, including illiterates, but not to women, claiming that female suffrage constituted a 'leap in the dark.'

What exactly was this threatening darkness and what did it have to do with reading, writing and passion? In the debate on women which characterizes the period I am discussing and that grew increasingly intense, brutal and even macabre at the turn of the century and in the first decade of the new century, emancipation was often a synonym for transgression and subversion and it was inevitably associated with reading, writing and books. 'Do not talk to me about the emancipated woman,' wrote Giuseppina Stefani-Bertacchi in 1882, 'Do not show her to me strange, outlandish, eccentric among books and newspapers, among ministers and politicians . . . forgive me but I need to find the woman – that angel of blessing and love – at the bedside of the sick man, of the dying man, at the bottom of a prison, at the foot of the scaffold, in the shadows of a cemetery.'[23] Reading, writing and books in women's hands were seen to be increasingly dangerous and offensive because they were the sign of a social and cultural transformation which, as the frenzied and necrophilic language of this passage indicates, signaled the death of the 'old' woman – here she is indeed represented as a kind of angel of death – and the advent of a new and threatening type of feminine behavior as well as a new political reality.

The questions of women's right to self-representation (which for Giolitti constituted a leap in the dark) played an important role in this context. Beginning in the 1880s, in fact, there was a considerable shift in the politics of the emancipation movement in Italy. Still under the leadership of Mozzoni, it turned from a predominantly philosophical and elitist movement which had attempted to keep a politically neutral position, to a resolutely left-wing movement close to the new socialist party. Mozzoni, who in 1864 had given her support to the First International, believed – incorrectly it turns out – that the socialist constituency would push for equal rights for women, in view of the fact that impoverished and working-class women constituted such a large portion of the labor force. There was a certain interest in women's emancipation among the socialists, especially on the part of its only female leader, Anna Kuliscioff. However, this interest was not shared by her co-leader and companion, Filippo Turati, whose views prevailed.

Emancipation in the collective imaginary was nevertheless connected increasingly with the specter of socialism. This radicalization of women in social as well as political terms threatened to dissolve completely the nineteenth-century scenario of the separate spheres and of women's gentle emotional nature, their exclusive ability to feel and to nurture which subtended the limiting ethics and aesthetics of sentiment. As Anna Kuliscioff pointed out in an article entitled 'Il sentimentalismo nella questione femminile' (Sentimentalism Concerning the Question of Woman [1977 (1892)]), the reassuring scenario of the woman 'angel of the hearth' had been dispelled by an irrefutable social and economic phenomenon. By this she meant the surfacing into the labor force of a whole new class of young women from the impoverished middle and lower middle classes with neither a dowry nor a title, who could not even dream of a modest marriage and were pushed against their will to go to work. These were the women who – among many difficulties and against all odds – became seamstresses, telegraph operators, postal workers and especially school-teachers. Matilde Serao emerged from this exact social group. She learned to read late, studied to become a teacher, and worked for a while as a telegraph operator while also beginning to write novels.

As newly literate masses began to emerge, more and more women like Serao entered the literary arena as well as the *manovalanza del libro*, that is the often anonymous contingent of women scribblers who turned out popular fiction. Serao was one of the few who were financially successful (De Giorgio 1992: 393). 'In Italy, a good seamstress earns more than a good writer, and with less effort' (Jolanda 1909: 522), wrote the fiction writer and magazine editor Jolanda in response to the inquiries of aspiring women writers.[24] Among the ones that achieved a modicum of literary reputation for at least some of their works, we may mention Marchesa Colombi, Emma, Neera, Regina di Luanto, Bruno Sperani (pseudonym of Beatrice Speraz), Contessa Lara, Sibilla Aleramo, Ada Negri, Annie Vivanti and Grazia Deledda.[25] Grazia Deledda was eventually awarded the Nobel prize in 1926, and Serao came close to it. Widely different in many ways, these women writers shared two major features – they were socially and politically committed, and they wrote mostly about and for women. Only a few, however, most notably Marchesa Colombi and Bruno Sperani, were both socialists and feminists. Although ideologically varied, the novel in this period became for the first time in Italian culture the most influential and widely disseminated medium in which women spoke about women. In England and France, novels by women and about women formed a substantial tradition dating back to the early part of the nineteenth century and even to the eighteenth century, to the point that, as Elaine Showalter has remarked, to many it seemed that the nineteenth century was the age of the female novelist (1977). In Italy, however, the rise of women novelists occurred later, and it overlapped with an era of increasing social unrest and the rise of socialism. Anxieties about female authorship therefore tended to intersect with political anxieties, and the increasing production of novels by women was perceived as a sign of both cultural and political crisis. Thus in England, according to Nancy Armstrong, the novel was from the beginning associated with a specialized language for women and operated to conceal political and social tensions by encoding them as differences rooted in gender. In Italy, on the other hand, there was no such depoliticization of fiction. Rather, fiction by and about women became part of a political and cultural struggle at one and the same time.

Of course what Italian women could write, and the reception of their discourse, were still constrained by prevailing discourses on women and by the gendered discourse on writing itself. The novel, particularly the ever-larger numbers of novels by women and the discourse about it, became once again a site in which contradictions, anxieties and opposing ideologies of gender within Italian culture converged and were put into play. A wide range of cultural anxieties about gender stereotypes, sexuality, class, the family and marriage surfaced there, and found different and conflicting solutions.

What was especially threatening in women's reading and writing was embodied in the discourse of a woman such as Matilde Serao. She was immensely successful both as a novelist and as a journalist in the public arena, and, at the same time, was acquainted with the corrupt world of the new Italy's politicians and capable of exposing it and denouncing it in her fiction. Her work threatened the collapse of the binary system of encoding masculinity and femininity along the lines of reason and intellect and the public sphere, on the one hand, vs feeling, sentiment and the sphere of the private on the other hand. I am thinking especially of novels like *La conquista di Roma* (The Conquest of Rome; 1885) and *Vita e avventure di Riccardo Joanna* (Life and Adventures of Riccardo Joanna; 1887). Women writers such as Serao made public the private, opening it up and exposing it to public scrutiny. They thus politicized explicitly what happens in the home, in the living room, in the bedroom and, most crucially, in the hearts and minds of its occupants. The scandal was not that this should be done. The scandal was rather that a woman should have done it.[26]

Novels by women – however conventional at times, especially in their endings and resolutions – articulated suppressed female emotions and expressed the limitations of women's social and domestic circumstances. This was in itself a disturbing fact. The prominence of women in the production and consumption of books also became an alarming phenomenon. A novel in the hands of a woman became a sure sign of subversion. A painting by Umberto Boccioni, entitled *Il romanzo di una cucitrice* (The Novel of a Seamstress [see figure 5.6]), is an interesting early example of the controversial interest in women as potential agents of unrest which was to characterize the futurist political and aesthetic avant-garde. As pointed out by Jolanda, the seamstress and the woman writer both were likely to be exploited and underpaid, the writer perhaps even more than the seamstress. Most women workers in Italy were employed in the production of textiles and clothing, and the women textile workers were among the most underpaid as well as the most active in socialist unions and labor unrest. Painted in Milan in 1908, only two years before the revolutionary *The City Rises* and *Riot in the Galleria* which

Figure 5.6 Umberto Boccioni, *Il romanzo di una cucitrice* (The Novel of a Seamstress; 1908)
Private Collection
Archivio Fotografico Electa

inaugurated the new futurist aesthetics, the painting by Boccioni – who was himself a socialist sympathizer – portrays (still in exquisite divisionist style) a young woman reading by an open window, next to a sewing machine. The novel that the seamstress is reading could very well be a novel by Matilde Serao, Bruno Sperani, or the Marchesa Colombi. The painting has none of the dynamism and multiple perspectives which will soon mark Boccioni's modernist work, and compositionally it appears to echo Cecioni's *La zia Erminia* and other nineteenth-century developments of this same visual theme, as well as a number of Boccioni's own divisionist paintings from this period. Yet the uncanny presence of the machine at the center of the image foreshadows the futurist modernist aesthetics, visually establishing an ambiguous (and soon to be emphatic) correlation between woman and machine. The word *cucitrice* itself is ambiguous, as it could refer to either the woman or the machine. Through its cult of the machine and modernity, futurism will resolutely attack the ideology of domesticity dominant in nineteenth-century Italy, and the futurist woman will be the antithesis of the 'angel of the hearth'.[27]

A clue to the significance of Boccioni's painting comes from the pages of his diary from this period. He was unhappy with it, feeling that the painting was more the culmination of past themes and images than an intimation of things to come, as he had hoped it would be. Yet in the very same days in which he was painting *La cucitrice* Boccioni was himself reading a book, which inspired a most enthusiastic response. It was not a novel but a play, Ibsen's *A Doll's House*. It seemed to him that Nora's liberation, her 'resurrection' as he called it, when she finally decides to abandon her husband and home, was a most striking expression of modernity and of the awakening of an individual's personality.[28] Within only a few years, the window that is still closed in his *La cucitrice* will be thrown open, and Boccioni will break the symbolic barrier between the domestic space of the home, traditionally associated with femininity, and the public space of the street, traditionally associated with the masculine realm. In two remarkable paintings of 1911, *Visioni simultanee* (Simultaneous Visions) and *La strada entra nella casa* (The Street Enters the House), Boccioni will break open the interior space of the home and make us see, through the eyes and mind of a woman looking out, a modernist montage of the urban street scene below her – an electrifying spectacle of which she is now a part. As it happens, Ibsen's *A Doll's House* was also the inspiration for Sibilla Aleramo's novel *Una donna*, which also tells of a woman's liberation and rebirth. Between 1913 and 1914, Boccioni and Aleramo became involved in a tumultuous love affair, and Aleramo flirted for a while with the idea of becoming a futurist herself (Conti and Morino 1981: 87–105).

The Legacy of the Risorgimento and the Monstrosity of Women's Writing

Boccioni's interest in women's creative affirmation, however, was definitely an exception. Although toward the end of the nineteenth century and in the first decade of the twentieth in Italy there were more women writers than ever before, there was not – contrary to circumstances in England and even the United States – a feminization of writing per se.[29] Rather, Italian culture witnessed a renewed masculinization – that is, an attempt to contain women's writing through the ethics and aesthetics of masculinity.[30] What I mean by this is a process of cultural censorship in which an increasingly threatened male establishment of writers, intellectuals and critics reacted to the wave of women's writing in two principal but equally effective ways. Either women writers were not women at all, but rather men – gendered as males so to speak, although biological females – or writing was essentially masculine and therefore what women produced was not writing at all, at least not good writing, but rather a flawed, monstrous or castrated imitation of it.[31]

In a long review essay entitled 'Letteratura femminile' (Literature by Women) published in the prestigious journal *La Nuova Antologia* in 1907, Giovanni Capuana, the chief theorist of *verismo*, writes: 'Should we worry, as some do, of the intrusive competition by women in narrative literature? I do not think so.' (Non lo credo.) He then goes on to expand his theory that 'When there is no need for reflection and imaginative intellect woman can succeed very well,' '[but] the imaginative intellect is masculine' ([ma] l'intelletto immaginativo è mascolino). Therefore, he concludes, let women write, for there is nothing to fear: women can never be original. Intellectually and aesthetically they can only be epigones and imitators. Women artists – whether novelists, painters or even sculptors – exist only because masculine intellects ('intelletti mascolini') have opened the way. No woman in the world has ever done what they have done. Yet women put into their texts something that is all their own, namely, their 'femininity and nothing else' (la femminilità; ma niente di più). And what is femininity? Femininity, Capuana says, should not be understood as a false kind of sentimentalism, or a weakness ('fiacchezza'), but rather as that sense of kindness ('gentilezza'), compassion, tenderness and enthusiasm that is the special characteristic of the heart of woman (Capuana 1988 [1907]: 19–22).[32]

Whenever, as in the case of Matilde Serao, the talent of a woman writer was indisputable (even though she also devoted a large portion of her career to consumer literature), doubts were raised about her femininity. Most memorably, the leading *verista* novelist Giovanni Verga called her an exception to the rule of women being bad writers, but ascribed this exception to a sexual aberration or monstrosity: Serao, he wrote in a letter to a friend, was surely a hermaphrodite (Verga 1980: 157). According to the critic Ugo Ojetti, on the other hand, the *scrittrice* was 'a man condemned to live in a woman's body' (De Caro 1977: 28).

The absence in Italian fiction, despite the ever larger numbers of women who devoted themselves to writing in the later nineteenth century and early twentieth century, of the figure of the woman writer is one of the most remarkable legacies of the gendering of writing during the Risorgimento and its aftermath. It is as if the woman writer were literally a *monstrum*, a monster that had to be kept hidden from sight.[33] One of the few appearances of a woman writer, and certainly one of the most controversial, took place in *Una donna*, the autobiographical novel that Sibilla Aleramo wrote in 1901 and published in 1906 to great scandal in Italy and critical acclaim internationally. In the novel, Aleramo tells of her late self-initiation to the reading of books of literature and sociology (her formal education was limited to elementary school), the experience of beginning to write, and finally her entrance into the active life of literature and journalism. Through all this she reached the decision to walk out of the abusive marriage she had felt compelled to contract with the man who had raped her as a young girl. That she did not tell her story straight, a fact for which she is often criticized (and which she herself regretted), and that she failed to reveal in the novel that when she left her marriage she was already involved in a relationship with another man, is more a measure of her interiorization of the censorship of adultery as an illicit female passion – adultery was considered legally a crime in Italy only if committed by women – than of her feminist commitment.[34] But more striking even than the concealment of adultery is the sense of guilt and self-doubt in connection to the act of writing that emerges in some of Aleramo's correspondence and in her auto-biographical writings, in sharp contrast to the feminist self-confidence of the first novel.

In a passionate letter to Umberto Boccioni dated 4 April 1914, she wrote: 'You know how much I have worked . . . And I have never been a coward . . . I know the value of the soul that creates alone. But . . . I am a woman, I am a mother who has lost her son, I am the child who was violated without knowing. When I cry, it is my entire past, which I have defeated, that avenges itself' (cited in Conti and Morino 1981: 103). A deeply contradictory, divided attitude towards the act of writing is a recurrent pattern in all of Aleramo's work and it also pervades the image of her life that she chose to disclose to the public's gaze. Aleramo was among the first in Italy proudly to claim the status of the professional woman writer and to assert the legitimacy and indeed the necessity of writing as a woman. Yet, partly because of the circumstances of her coming to writing, she also felt that writing was somehow illegitimate and shameful, like the adultery that she felt compelled to hide, and forever marked by the trauma of her abandonment of her child. Aleramo allowed herself to be endlessly photographed and portrayed by, among others, Anton Giulio Bragaglia, the great futurist photographer and film-maker. Yet in leafing through the pages of her 'illustrated life' one is struck by the fact that among the many published photographs of her, both formal and informal, including those taken in different periods by her lovers, first the writer Giovanni Cena (at the time of *Una donna*) and later the poet Dino Campana, none portrays her in the act of writing. Even the public Aleramo, it seems, felt the effects of a cultural censorship which made the act of writing by women seem illicit or too private to be publicly exposed – more private even than the intimate images of the beautiful young Sibilla in bed, her long hair on a white pillow, in the photographs taken by Giovanni Cena.[35] Only in later photographs, from after World War I, is Aleramo portrayed surrounded by books in the rooms where she read and wrote, for example the famous tiny attic in the via Margutta in Rome (Conti and Morino 1981: 220–1). There is only one pre-World War I exception among the photographs published in Conti: an informal anonymous photograph from 1912 (see figure 5.7), where Aleramo is seen standing next to a table covered, much like the table in Faruffini's painting, with books and papers, gazing beyond the camera and holding

Figure 5.7 Sibilla Aleramo in 1912
Anonymous photograph
From B. Conti and A. Morino (1981), *Sibilla Aleramo e il suo tempo. Vita raccontata e illustrata*, Milan: Feltrinelli

a book in her hands. Although she is not seen reading or writing in this image, the table is clearly a writer's table. Reproductions of some of her favorite artworks are on the wall, along with postcard-size reproductions of portraits of Dante and Leonardo.

Matilde Serao's *Fantasia* (1883) is the other novel written by a woman where a woman writer appears as the protagonist. In many ways Serao was the opposite of Aleramo: antifeminist, conservative, very attached to the family and to the traditional values of Italian patriarchy. Yet Serao shares with Aleramo a sense of women's writing as clandestine and somehow illegitimate, although in Serao's case it is not her own writing but that of other women that is deserving of censure. Serao's protagonist, the passionate, highly anti-Manzonian Lucia, is said to be writing secretly a novel by night. From the beginning this nocturnal writing is alluded to as something perverse that must be kept hidden. In a final twist of the plot the 'novel' turns out not to have been a novel at all, but rather Lucia's intimate journal, where she recorded her fantasies and her adulterous desires. Lucia, who has nurtured her morbid passion through writing and cultivating 'la poesia ammaliatrice della parola' (the bewitching poetry of language), eventually seduces Andrea, the husband of her childhood best friend, the virtuous and meek Caterina. In the devastating conclusion, Caterina kills herself in desperation.

Lucia's writing and her deadly adulterous fantasies in Serao's novel are directly inspired by her reading. Reading begets writing which begets death and destruction. This sinister genealogy is not without its self-conscious irony. Serao's novel is an explicit take-off on *Madame Bovary* (Kroha 1992: 99–113). At the climax of the seduction scene, in a carriage near Posillipo, as Andrea embraces Lucia, she points out to him, 'laughing ironically,' that their situation is identical to that of Flaubert's novel. He is taken aback, hurt and surprised: 'Io non l'ho letto' (I have not read it), he says (1892 [1883]: 315). He thought it was love, but it was only imitation literature, Serao seems to imply tongue-in-cheek here. Lucia's flashes of meta-literary irony make her appear intermittently as a projection of the author. Ursula Fanning has argued persuasively that as negative as Lucia's character and her nocturnal, passionate writing are intended to be in the economy of the novel, Serao's own feelings about the character remain ambivalent, and she cannot entirely dissociate herself from her (Fanning 1993: 95–7).

Serao's and Aleramo's texts associate women's writing with autobiographical experience, in particular with a kind of inauthentic female experience that is censurable and connected to the disruption or even the destruction of domestic space. But while Aleramo always wrote about herself, and felt deeply the paradoxes of her position as a woman writer, Serao did not seem to experience any anxiety about her own role as a writer. Serao, unlike Aleramo, often let herself be photographed in the act of writing or working at her desk, in her study or office, surrounded by books. How can this difference be explained? A clue may be found in Serao's assessment of Aleramo. Although she professed to admire Aleramo's talent (and to some extent she clearly did), Serao's review of one of Aleramo's books of poetry deploys a telling metaphor: that of the mythical female monster, the Chimera.[36] Serao plays with the double meaning of the word 'chimera' which, besides referring to the mythical monster, also connotes something like a vain and idle fantasy. Serao states that the myth of freedom ('il mito della libertà') is the motivating force of all of Aleramo's writing, yet this very myth has been Aleramo's chimera, misleading her from the beginning in all her fundamental life choices. Extending the logic of the image even further, Serao insinuates in between the lines that the Chimera and Aleramo's writing are one and the same, a monstrous disfiguration of that which woman should 'naturally' be. What woman according to Serao naturally should be is – simply put – a mother. In breaking her chains in order to pursue her chimerical freedom to write, Aleramo simultaneously gave up her son and hence, according to Serao, her femininity. Writing and femininity are thus seen as antithetical and irreconcilable. The freedom to write may have appeared to make Aleramo into a newly born woman, but that woman, Serao implies, is not really a woman. She is, like the Chimera, a monster.

In decrying the Chimera-like monstrosity of women's writing, Serao may seem to have taken a rather hypocritical stand, for was not she herself a woman writer? Anna Banti, Serao's insightful if rather severe biographer, has an astute explanation to offer for this apparent contradiction. As a woman who had 'made it' in a world of men, Banti argues, Serao, whose friends and associates were the likes of D'Annunzio, Michetti and Scarfoglio, placed herself on the side of the 'strong' sex, ridiculing other women's aspiration to equal rights (Banti 1965: 125–6). Marie Gracieuse Martin-Gistucci takes this hypothesis even further and argues that 'being ugly, and practicing a man's profession, Matilde felt more like a man than like a woman' (1973: 35). Several statements by Serao herself corroborate this interpretation and also shed more light on Aleramo's anguished self-questioning. Serao was notoriously opposed to woman's work outside of the home, for woman in her view was naturally suited only to the domestic roles of wife and mother. She favored special schools tailored for girls alone and their generally feebler mental resources because, she argued, to attempt 'studi del tutto maschili' (wholly masculine studies) would lead to endless sacrifices and tribulations which would surely prove pointless and endanger the health and the natural beauty ('leggiadria') of young women.[37] To Serao, then, not only is beauty, like motherhood, 'natural' to woman, but such beauty can only be preserved in the home. Because she had no beauty, and (presumably) was more intelligent than normal women, Serao felt that she could take on the position of a man, and embark on a profession that would take her outside of the home. (She became the chief editor of her own newspaper after having six children with Edoardo Scarfoglio, whom she divorced in 1901, shortly after launching a press campaign *against* divorce . . .) Serao envisioned her gender position as exceptional, hybrid and bisexual, and therefore, from her perspective, essentially unnatural and monstrous. It is thus not surprising that, while on the one hand she branded Aleramo as a monster who betrayed and disfigured her natural femininity, she felt at the same time a deep attraction for her and a sense of kinship.[38]

The myth of Serao's 'bisexual' or 'hermaphroditic' nature is one that Serao herself helped to spread[39] and, as we have seen, it was conveniently seized upon by the male writers of her generation. When we look at photographic portraits of Serao in her office, at work and writing at her desk (see figure 5.8), the image Serao wants us to see is that of a woman superimposed with that of a man. Only this 'double exposure' gives Serao a sense of the exceptional legitimacy of her position, her being at the same time both man and woman.

As strange as Serao's double-exposed 'hermaphroditic' image may seem (no less 'monstrous' certainly than that of the Chimera with which she identifies Aleramo), the ideology that generates these monsters is thoroughly banal and hence, perhaps, all the more insidious. Serao's stance is hardly original. Her vivid metaphor of the Chimera is only one of the more striking manifestations of the gendering of writing in Italian culture that was first put into place during the Risorgimento, was shaped by the particular social, political and economic circumstances of the formation of the new state, and developed into a long-lasting, enduring ideological construction whose effects continued to be felt in Italy well into the twentieth century (the nineteenth century in many respects did not really end until World War I). As different in terms of temperament, style and politics as Aleramo was from Serao, she was still plagued by the same sense of being a 'monster' of sorts. This was due not only to her sense of guilt for having exchanged her role of mother for that of writer. Extremely beautiful, she – like Serao – identified beauty with femininity, and she was obsessed by the fear that her writing might

Figure 5.8 Matilde Serao at her desk
Anonymous photograph
From B. Conti and A. Morino (1981), *Sibilla Aleramo e il suo tempo. Vita raccontata e illustrata*, Milan: Feltrinelli

somehow obscure her beauty, and obfuscate her femininity by masculinizing her.[40] This question – how can a woman write and still be a woman? – is the compulsive and unresolved subplot in all of Aleramo's works, and it is present in some form in the writing of most nineteenth- and early twentieth-century women writers.[41]

It is uncanny to see how a guilt-ridden Sibilla Aleramo, after the notoriety of her first novel, proceeded throughout her life and her long career as a writer to seek the approval and the moral and aesthetic advice of a number of male censors. The gendering of writing which can be seen in her work required her to do two things at once. On the one hand, she sought to keep writing from the heart, as a woman that is, about her own experiences and feelings, but, on the other hand, in following this very imperative she was ever conscious of and plagued by a sense of stylistic and intellectual inferiority. She attempted compulsively to demonstrate that she was a real woman with real feminine feelings, and not the monster who had forsaken her home. She constantly sought to legitimize herself by writing highly affected and 'passionate' prose, fearing at the same time that what she wrote could not possibly be literature.

Benedetto Croce's devastating letter to her, written in response to her plea for moral and aesthetic counsel, gives the measure of how this gendering of writing operated in practice. The echoes of the Risorgimento cult of domesticity and the normative discourse on passions are unmistakable: 'You are the victim of an illness,' he wrote to her, 'I was able to detect this very clearly when I read your novel [*Una donna*], which I found dominated by a totally false idea of reality and life. . . . You are empty of will and full of passion and instinct. . . . I never believed in the ideal justification which you provided in your novel; because evil is done in the pursuit of pleasure and not by following theories. . . . You wanted to love . . . when your duty should have been . . . sacrifice' (1913; reproduced in Conti and Morino 1981: 83–4).[42]

But Croce's censorship was not merely private or targeted at specific women writers. Croce's gendering of writing in his monumental *La letteratura della nuova Italia*, which was reprinted through the 1950s, contributed perhaps more than any other single critical text to disseminate this proscriptive and prescriptive aesthetic and ethical model for women's writing. In his 1906 essay on Ada Negri (a writer whose themes – political and erotic passion – were particularly disliked by Croce), for example, he asserted that the 'mancanza di elaborazione artistica' (1848: 361) or 'lack of artistic labor' is most particularly a feminine flaw ('difetto femminile' [ibid.: 362]). Not only is the territory of the political and the conceptual proscribed to the woman writer, who according to Croce must limit herself to the domestic sphere of feminine feeling and of the maternal, but it is precisely woman's maternal instinct, her stupendous and all-consuming ability to mother a child that prevents her from successfully giving birth to a fully realized literary or aesthetic work. 'It appears that women,' Croce wrote in the same essay, 'capable of developing within themselves for nine months a germ of life and of bringing it into the world by painful labor, and then of raising it with a patience that is prodigious, are usually incapable of regular poetic labor. Their artistic births are almost always premature: or rather, the conception is followed by an instantaneous delivery and the still-born child is then thrown into the streets . . . I do not mean that there haven't been or cannot be exceptions; but this is the rule' (ibid.: 362). Thus, in Croce's logic, it is precisely that which makes woman by definition a woman, the primary fact of her sexual difference and her ability to mother a child, which also incapacitates her as an artist. Croce thus places the woman writer once again in a double bind, for she cannot be a writer or an artist without abandoning her femininity, and she cannot be a woman and pretend to be an artist at the same time.

Neither Aleramo's nor Serao's novel, however, could be said ultimately to center on the question of women's writing. It was Luigi Pirandello's 1911 novel *Suo marito* (Her Husband) that brought the problem of the woman writer into full view. It was a thwarted appearance, however, which turned almost immediately into a vanishing act. The protagonist of the novel was indeed – unique in the history of Italian literature of this period – a woman writer. Pirandello had reviewed *Una donna* with words of admiration when it first appeared, and there has been some speculation that Aleramo's story may have influenced the plot of Pirandello's novel.[43] But almost immediately Pirandello was forced to withdraw the book from circulation when another woman writer, Grazia Deledda, who thought *her* life was alluded to in the book, threatened to sue. This episode, aside from the 'roman à clef' possibilities, suggests that as usual Pirandello had focused on a particularly sensitive and thorny issue. Its ideological implications were particularly 'scandalous' because they exposed for the first time the most threatening aspects of women's writing for Italian culture.

In *Suo marito*, writing is the secret, private, nocturnal passion of Silvia Roncella, a young woman from a small town in southern Italy. She marries Giustino only because he appears willing to tolerate this *grave colpa*, which eventually develops into a professional commitment to literature and to the theater. As Silvia leaves the domestic sphere and, through her writing, becomes increasingly a public figure in the world of letters, however, the husband begins to feel threatened and emasculated. To regain a more active role, Giustino begins to encourage his wife to write commercial, mass-market works; he finds an apartment for them in Rome, and he becomes her increasingly greedy and demanding manager (Pirandello 1973 [1911]). Mass culture may from its inception have been gendered as 'a woman' (at least according to Andreas Huyssen's argument),[44] but Pirandello's novel astutely implies that the desire that creates and profits from the feminine gendering of mass culture is still the phallic need to control, to master and to exploit the Other's – in this case women's – work.

In his single-minded obsession to maximize profits, the husband puts such pressures on his wife to produce mass-marketable works that their marriage deteriorates. Silvia resents Giustino for inducing her to leave their young child behind in the country with his mother and a nurse so as to have no distractions while she writes and he promotes her work. She is eventually driven into a brief, ludicrous and sexually failed affair with another man – a writer who, unlike the prolific Silvia, seems to have a terminal case of writer's block. The experience is nauseating for Silvia, and she feels incapable of loving any more. Giustino, the husband, is desolate and devoid of any direction. The evening of the opening of Silvia's new play, he watches her secretly from the audience as she appears on stage after the performance to receive the crowd's enthusiastic applause. That same evening their child, who had been living with Giustino's mother, falls ill and dies. At the end Silvia is alone and devastated, and Giustino is a broken man.

In characteristically Pirandellian terms, as Silvia 'creates' art she cannot but 'kill' the life around her and in her. This is, however, not just a case of the tragic predicament of the artist in general. It has a more gendered and culturally specific explanation. At the heart of Pirandello's novel, as brilliant as it is in many ways, is a profound paranoia with respect to the gendering of writing which reached a peak in Italian culture in conjunction with the rise of women writers in the later nineteenth century. In Pirandello's allegory the woman who writes is a woman who castrates; by taking up the pen she somehow usurps the phallus,[45] abdicates her feminine and maternal function, and precipitates the collapse of the domestic sphere, finally causing her husband's, her own and her child's destruction. The scene of Silvia's triumph on the stage and the simultaneous death of the son exhibits an uncanny logic: the work to which the woman gives life with her mind undoes the life that she can create with her body. As in another brilliant work focused on gender roles, the novel *L'esclusa* (The Outcast), Pirandello does not so much subscribe to this binary and exclusionary gender logic as expose its devastating work within the social text.

One of the most insightful intuitions of Pirandello's novel was making Silvia into not just a writer, but a playwright. The staging of Silvia's play and her own triumphant appearance in the theater the night of the opening underscore the way in which writing can take woman away from the home and the domestic, feminine sphere and catapult her into the public, masculine sphere epitomized by the stage. The plot of the novel literally transports Silvia from the enclosed, intimate space of the room inside the home where she secretly writes to the open stage where her secret writing is shamelessly exposed to the public. In fact it is not writing in and of itself that is construed as unfeminine and execrable in nineteenth-century Italian culture. In the paranoid gender logic that Pirandello's novel dramatizes, writing becomes unfeminine when it takes woman away from the domestic sphere. This is also made apparent in *Una donna* when Aleramo tells how her petty and brutal husband at first encouraged her to write at home as 'a distraction' (1992 [1906]: 103). But when her writing began to take a professional turn he reacted by burning all her papers and books. Eventually, however, when the family was in need, he allowed her to write for profit, as long as he could be reassured that all of his wife's work would take place at home where she 'would be isolated' (ibid.: 129). Pirandello's novel seems to seize on this paranoia and magnify it in his novel. From within the enclosed space of the home, writing begins to work as both a conduit to the outside world and a slow-burning time-bomb that eventually will tear the home to pieces.

Aleramo, Serao and Pirandello point to writing by women as clandestine, transgressive and even deadly. We now understand the strangely provocative effect of Faruffini's painting from which we started, the sexual and social threat that is hidden in this apparently idyllic scene – a scene that continued repeatedly and compulsively to be censored or suppressed in Italian culture well into the early twentieth century, even as women's writing became an undeniable reality.

Notes

1. Some of the questions raised by this painting in connection to women's writing in nineteenth-century Italy are briefly evoked in Reim 1991: 9. Although this painting, like all paintings, deploys its own specific visual and formal code and is thus susceptible to a more technical and specific art-historical reading, it also is a cultural artifact that can be read in terms of the larger thematic and ideological issues that it evokes and that connect it to other cultural expressions of the period, including the novel. In this chapter I will therefore cross the line between painting and literature, seeking to explore the ways in which these two different modes of discourse can be mutually illuminating and at the same time help us to understand the culture that they both express and interrogate.

2. The editors of a recent anthology which attempts to cover the entire history of women writers in Italy (Forlani and Savini 1991) came up with an image of a woman writing for the jacket of the book, a painting by Federico Zandomeneghi (a major exponent of the *macchiaioli* school, like Cecioni). But the painting's title is *La lettera* (The Letter). The young woman writer is therefore ostensibly not engaged in the kind of literary writing collected in the anthology. One could argue of course that she might be writing an epistolary narrative. *Ginevra* (1839), one of the most disturbing and fascinating novels of the early

Italian nineteenth-century, written by Leopardi's friend and admirer Antonio Ranieri, is presented to the reader as the transcription of the original manuscript of an autobiographical letter written by the young protagonist shortly before her tragic death. Sibilla Aleramo's novels after *Una donna* are also all in epistolary form or draw extensively on letters. The Marchesa Colombi's *Prima morire* is narrated through a sequence of letters.

3. No comparative study exists as of yet. For the English literary tradition, Gilbert and Gubar's classic *Madwoman in the Attic* (1979) and Showalter's *A Literature of Their Own* (1977) opened the way for a large body of impressive critical work. For Italy, some useful suggestions may be found in the introductions to the Morandini 1980 and Reim 1991 anthologies, and especially in De Donato *et al.* 1983b, De Giorgio 1992 and Genevois 1994. See also Kroha 1992, esp. chapter 1 and the chapters on the Marchesa Colombi and on Neera.

4. 'Istruzioni ai maestri delle scuole primarie sul modo di svolgere i programmi approvati con R. D. 15 settembre 1860' (Cited in Marchesini 1989: 45).

5. See Zambon 1989 for an interesting analysis of how most Italian women writers of the late nineteenth and early twentieth centuries were self-taught.

6. For example, the Austrian code foresaw several exceptions to the rule of the *patria potestà*, and women in the Austrian territory had full rights to dispose of their property without needing to obtain their husbands' permission. Both Lombard and Tuscan women also enjoyed limited electoral rights. See Bortolotti 1975: 51–2.

7. See for example L. Blanch, 'De' necessari legami che ha la domestica con la pubblica economia e degli effetti della prima sul perfezionamento morale' in *Il progresso delle scienze, delle lettere e delle arti* (1832) 1.3.264–76, cited in De Donato 1983a: 30.

8. Marriage is good for men because, wrote Tommaseo, 'il vivere coniugale può rafforzarli negli abiti del risparmio, dell'ordine, della mondezza, de' riguardi affettuosi, e de' nobili sacrifizi' (Married life can strengthen their tendency toward saving, order, cleanliness, affectionate attentions and noble sacrifices [1872: 124 *et passim*]).

9. What differentiates the separation of the spheres in nineteenth-century Italy from its equivalents in English and French culture is precisely its specifically political use in the 'nation-making' process. On the propagation and diffusion of the ideal of the woman of the hearth in French culture, see MacMillan 1981. For an analysis of the English case, see Hall 1979.

10. Silvio Pellico was among the most influential of the Risorgimento patriots and Romantic intellectuals in Milan. A member of the anti-Austrian *Carboneria* secret society, he is best known for his prison memoirs, *Le mie prigioni* (1832).

11. But see Boime 1986 for a rather strained view of the 'feminism' in the *macchiaioli* paintings of the 1860s (62–5).

12. *Rivista europea* 23/24: 455, cited in De Donato 1983a: 18.

13. Ironically, Franceschi-Ferrucci's own daughter, Rosa Ferrucci, was tempted by writing, and authored a number of short stories. In collecting them and presenting them to the reader after her daughter's death, the mother wrote that the stories were not intended as a 'literary work' but as a 'faithful image of her [Rosa's] heart' (*Rosa Ferrucci e i suoi scritti*, ed. C. Franceschi-Ferrucci, Florence 1858; cited in Reim 1991: 18).

14. Albeit an enduring one, which re-emerges for example in Neera's *Lydia* (1887). In the novel, the heroine's superficial and frivolous nature and her inability to forge an enduring love bond and to start a family (she eventually takes her own life after having been deceived by a fortune-hunting Austrian count) are associated with her frequenting the corrupt circles of 'la decadenza aristocratica' (aristocratic decadence).

15. See C.A. Vecchi, 'Progetto a favore degli operai indigenti' (1844), cited in De Donato 1983a: 57, 63.

16. For a more optimistic view of the cultural acceptability of the figure of the woman writer in the later nineteenth century and in the first decade of the twentieth century, see Arslan 1988: 164–8.

17. As it happens, Freud's first essay introducing the notion of narcissism, 'Formulations Concerning Two Principles of Mental Functioning,' was published in 1911, the same year as Pirandello's novel (Freud 1953–73 [1911]).

18. Even the brilliant and puritanical Neera, whose passion for reading and writing were among the purest and most intense of any Italian writer of the nineteenth century (but whose own literary respectability is still today the object of contention), thought that women were driven to writing essentially by a form of thoughtless vanity. In numerous essays and articles, she repeatedly argued that women should not become writers, and that 'excessive' education of women would interfere with their social mission and turn them into neurasthenics. Her sense of herself as a writer was therefore highly conflictual, and her fiction was equally divided, ranging from the conformist and puritanically bourgeois to the daring and subversive.

19. Nicolò Tommaseo's *Fede e bellezza* (Faith and Beauty; 1840) and Neera's *Un nido* (A Nest; 1882) may be seen, respectively, as an early and a late example of this ideology at work in the novel. Both novels foreground the ideology of domesticity and the 'passive virtues' of woman, and at the same time they clearly define the inferiority of women as writers and intellectuals.

20. Yet the period of the Risorgimento was hardly completely uniform or monolithic in terms of gender ideology. Although it eventually achieved a hegemonic status that had repercussions at all levels of civil society and cultural discourse, Rosmini's notion of sexual difference was far from uncontested. Other, alternative notions of gender emerged in Italy in the earlier nineteenth-century, and the position of women was more a matter of debate, negotiation and cultural confrontation than is often assumed. Melchiorre Gioia, for example, in his 1834 pamphlet about the legitimacy of divorce, had disputed the very notion of 'nature' and 'natural order' used to substantiate the need for woman's subjection and self-sacrifice in marriage (cited in De Donato 1983a: 35). The Neapolitan poet and patriot Maria Giuseppina Guacci, in her 'Canzone per le donne italiane' (Song for Italian Women; 1834 [cited in Morandini 1980: 50–4]) stated that women's natural talent – including especially the talent for writing – could be superior to men's, and more daring. Guacci, encouraged by her mother, overcame her father's skepticism (he was an architect and wanted her to work for him as a copyist) and went on to become not only a writer and a patriot but also a leading figure of Neapolitan intellectual life. Gioia and Guacci, among others, provide in effect alternative visions of gender in this period which deserve a separate in-depth exploration.

21. The same argument, and a specific reference to the 'amore della vita domestica' (love of domestic life) in the English novel, can be found in S. Uizielli, 'Sul romanzo storico e di Walter Scott,' in *Antologia* (1824), cited in De Donato 1983a: 73. De Donato 1983a: 68–80 provides a detailed discussion of the controversy on women and the novel during the Risorgimento.

22. Pellico, review of O.R. Sacrati, *Lettere di Giulia Willet* (1818) in *Il Conciliatore*, 7 January 1819 (cited in De Donato 1983a: 40).

23. 'La donna nella famiglia. Due parole alla buona' in *La missione della donna* (1882; cited in Pisa n.d.: 41).

24. On Jolanda and the new magazines for women, especially *Cordelia*, see De Giorgio 1992: 385–90, 393 *et passim*.

25. Most women writers in this period used a pseudonym: Marchesa Colombi (Maria Antonietta Torriani), Emma (Emilia Ferretti Viola), Neera (Anna Radius Zuccari), Regina di Luanto (Anna Roti), Contessa Lara (Evelina Cattermole), Sibilla Aleramo (Rina Faccio). The choice of these pseudonyms deserves a separate study. It often involved elaborate strategies of distancing, masking and even masquerading, directly related to the gendering of writing and to the writers' problematic self-images. It is customary in the critical literature on Italian women writers to provide their 'real' names (and even sometimes to use their real names instead of the pen names), while the same is rarely done for male writers. Gabriele D'Annunzio's real name, Rapagnetta, for example, is mentioned only in biographies.

26. D'Annunzio – who is often held responsible for opening up the boudoir for all to see and for mixing sex and politics – was actually following in Serao's footsteps, and he acknowledged as much by dedicating his novel *Giovanni Episcopo* to her with words of admiration.

27. Even within futurism, however, women remained chiefly associated with sentimentalism and domesticity at least until World War I. Only with the cultural upheaval and the gender trouble generated by the war were women suddenly seen (and began to see themselves) in a different light; writing became once again – at least until the fascist era – an activity that women could pursue professionally without fear of compromising their womanhood.

28. The autograph pages of Boccioni's diary are reproduced in Ballo 1964: ill. 114.

29. The feminization of writing in the nineteenth-century is a label which English and American feminist critics (I am thinking of the great ground-breaking work of Gilbert and Gubar, of course, as well as Showalter 1977, Armstrong 1987 and many others) have used to indicate the increased and irrepressible, successful presence of women writers in the literary arena, with its momentous consequences for the production, structure and reception of literary and social discourse.

30. Giovanni Papini's *Maschilità*, first published in 1915, collects essays and statements written by the author as early as 1910, and is a kind of *summa* of this tendency in Italian culture, as well as the direct predecessor of the fascist rhetoric of virility (Papini 1915).

31. The masculinist ethos was shared by intellectuals from the right and the left, including many exponents of the avant-garde. For the

misogynist attitude towards women writers and the prejudice against any writing done by women prevalent among the intellectuals participating in the journal *La Voce*, including Papini, Giuseppe Prezzolini and Emilio Cecchi, as well as Giovanni Boine and Renato Serra, see Nozzoli 1994.

32. Capuana paid Neera the most heartfelt compliment he had ever paid to a woman writer when he wrote to her – regarding the novel *Il marito dell'amica* – 'What I like most of your book is the "masculine" tone one feels in it.' The letter, dated 15 July 1885, is reproduced in Arslan 1983: 185. Croce sounded a similar note when, in prefacing her posthumous autobiography, *Una giovinezza del secolo XIX*, he wrote of her: 'Neera was not "sentimental" . . . This woman writer showed herself to be a virile thinker' (Neera 1919: x).

33. Women writers appear in Annie Vivanti's *I divoratori* (The Devourers; 1910) and (but we are already in the midst of World War I) in the novella 'Il denaro' (Money) by Ada Negri, which appeared in *Le solitarie* (1917).

34. It was apparently her lover at the time, the writer Giovanni Cena, who talked her into excising from the novel all references to her liaison with Felice Damiani.

35. Cena's photographs, as well as Campana's and Bragaglia's, are reproduced in Conti and Morino 1981.

36. Serao's review of Aleramo's *Momenti* appeared in *Il Giorno* on 23 December 1920. It is reprinted in Conti and Morino 1981: 167.

37. 'Che fanno?,' editorial article published in Serao's journal *Il Giorno*, 19–20 June 1925, cited in De Nunzio-Schilardi 1983: 290.

38. See the letter to Enrico Bemporad, dated 25 May 1920, in Conti and Morino 1981: 166–7.

39. 'Bisexual' in this case refers not to sexual orientation (Serao, unlike Aleramo – who was actually bisexual – was known to be hetero-sexual) but to the kind of double gender position Serao was able to take in her society, assuming traditionally male roles while retaining her feminine role as mother, etc. In a letter to her friend Gaetano Bonovenia (cited in Banti 1965: 21–2), she wrote: 'I write everywhere and about everything with a unique daring; I get ahead pushing and shoving, with the burning and intense desire to arrive with nobody's or almost nobody's help. You know that I do not partake of any of the weaknesses of my sex and move forward like a man.'

40. Aleramo constructed her own bisexual mythic monster to attempt to solve this dilemma, but it was a beautiful one: the androgyne. On

the contradictions in Aleramo's vision of herself as both a woman and an androgyne, in contrast with Virginia Woolf's somewhat similar vision, see Melandri 1988.

41. In her novel *I divoratori*, Annie Vivanti portrays three women, including a writer (Nancy) and a violinist, who sacrifice their desire – erotic and artistic – to their 'natural' destiny as mothers: the children are thus their 'devourers.' Although this novel has been read as being aligned with reactionary patriarchal notions of femininity as mother-hood (e.g. Nozzoli 1978: 12), Vivanti's position, as the title itself indicates, is more complex and contradictory, and Nancy's elaborate masquerade as a fictional *femme fatale* in the novel deserves to be read in a key of ironic self-consciousness.

42. Some interesting observations on Croce's vision of women and their social role can be found in Contorbia 1994.

43. See Angelini 1988: 69. See also Kroha 1992: 143–58, for a thorough reading of *Suo marito* that examines the question of gender and writing. Pirandello's book was republished only in 1941, in substant-ially revised form, under the title *Giustino Roncella nato Boggiolo*. The import and significance of these changes made to the first five chapters (Pirandello died before he could complete the revision) are still to be evaluated, especially in regard to Pirandello's relationship with Fascism and the fascist vision of women's roles. For some preliminary observations see Kroha 1992: 157n 2.

44. According to Huyssen, in a chapter entitled 'Mass Culture as a Woman: Modernism's Other,' the notion gained ground during the nineteenth century that mass culture was somehow associated with women while real, authentic culture remained the prerogative of men. Thus 'woman is positioned as a reader and producer of inferior literature – emotional and passive – while man emerges as the writer of genuine, authentic literature, objective, ironic and in control of his aesthetic means' (1986: 46).

45. Thus Pirandello anticipates Gilbert and Gubar's well-known argu-ment (1979: ch. 1) that in Western patriarchal literary culture the pen is a 'metaphorical penis,' and women writers are perceived and perceive themselves as abnormal and unfeminine. Gilbert and Gubar go on to examine the specific conflicts that this ideology of gender generates in nineteenth-century Victorian culture, with particular attention to women writing in the English literary tradition and to their highly conflictual and anxiety-ridden sense of authorship.

References

Aleramo, S. (1992 [1906]), *Una donna*, Milan: Feltrinelli.

Angelini, F. (1988), 'Un nome e una donna,' in A. Buttafuoco and M. Zancan, eds, *Svelamento Sibilla Aleramo: Una biografia intellettuale*, Milan: Feltrinelli, pp. 64–75.

Armstrong, N. (1987), *Desire and Domestic Fiction: A Political History of the Novel*, Oxford: Oxford University Press.

Arslan, A. (1983), 'Luigi Capuana e Neera: Corrispondenza inedita 1881–1885,' in *Miscellanea di studi in onore di Vittore Branca*, Vol. 5, Florence: Olschki, pp. 161–85.

—— (1988), 'Ideologia e autorappresentazione: Donne intellettuali fra Ottocento e Novecento,' in A. Buttafuoco and M. Zancan, eds, *Svelamento: Sibilla Aleramo: una biografia intellettuale*, Milan: Feltrinelli, pp. 164–77.

Ballo, G. (1964), *Boccioni: La vita e l'opera*, Milan: Il Saggiatore.

Banti, A. (1965), *Matilde Serao*, Turin: UTET.

Boime, A. (1986), 'The *Macchiaioli* and the Risorgimento,' in E. Tonelli and K. Hart, eds, *The Macchiaioli: Painters of Italian Life, 1850–1900*, Los Angeles: The Fredrick S. Wight Art Gallery, pp. 33–71.

Bortolotti, F.P. (1975), *Alle origini del movimento femminile in Italia: 1848–1892*, Turin: Einaudi.

Capuana, G. (1988 [1907]), *Letteratura femminile*, ed. G.F. Chimirri, Catania: CUECM.

Cattaneo, C. (1983), 'Sul romanzo delle donne contemporanee in Italia,' in *Opere edite e inedite,* Vol. 1, ed. A. Bertani, Florence: Le Monnier.

Cavarero, A. (1995), 'La passione della differenza,' in S.V. Finzi, ed., *Storia delle passioni*, Bari: Laterza, pp. 279–313.

Colombi, Marchesa [title] (1988 [1887]), *Prima morire*, Rome: Lucarini.

Conti, B., and A. Morino (1981), *Sibilla Aleramo e il suo tempo: Vita raccontata e illustrata*, Milan: Feltrinelli.

Contorbia, F. (1994), 'Croce e lo spazio del femminile,' in E. Genevois, ed., *Les Femmes-écrivains en Italie (1870–1920): Ordres et libertés,* Paris: Université de la Sorbonne nouvelle-Paris III, pp. 15–32.

Croce, B. (1948), 'Ada Negri,' in *La letteratura della nuova Italia: Saggi critici*, Vol. 2, 5th rev. edn, Bari: Laterza, pp. 344-65.

De Caro, G. (1977), *Matilde Serao aneddotica*, Naples: Berisco.

De Donato, G. (1983a), 'Donna e società nella cultura moderata del primo Ottocento,' in G. De Donato, S. Ghiazza, M. Pagliara, V. Gazzola, G. Borella, W. De Nunzio-Schilardi, G. Zaccaro, eds, *La parabola della donna nella letteratura italiana dell'Ottocento*, Bari: Adriatica, pp. 11–96.

—— and S. Ghiazza, M. Pagliara, V. Gazzola, G. Borella, W. De Nunzio-Schilardi, G. Zaccaro (1983b), *La parabola della donna nella letteratura italiana dell'Ottocento*, Bari: Adriatica.

De Giorgio, M. (1992), *Le italiane dall'unità a oggi: Modelli culturali e comportamenti sociali*, Bari: Laterza.

De Nunzio-Schilardi, W. (1983), 'L'antifemminismo di Matilde Serao,' in G. De Donato, *et al.*, *La parabola della donna nella letteratura italiana dell'Ottocento*, Bari: Adriatica, pp. 277–305.

Fanning, U. (1993), 'Matilde Serao: "Scrivere donna",' in Centre Aixois de Recherches Italiennes, *Les femmes écrivains en Italie aux XIXe et XXe siècles*, Aix-en-Provence: Publications de L'Université de Provence, pp. 91–9.

Forlani, A., and M. Savini (1991), *Scrittrici d'Italia*, Rome: Newton Compton.

Franceschi-Ferrucci, C. (1875 [1847]), *Dell'educazione morale della donna italiana*, Florence: Le Monnier.

Freud, S. (1953–73 [1911]), 'Formulations Concerning Two Principles of Mental Functioning,' in *The Standard Edition of the Complete Psychological Works of Sigmund Freud*, Vol. 12, trans. and ed. J. Strachey and A. Tyson, London: The Hogarth Press and the Institute of Psycho-Analysis, pp. 213–26.

Garin, E. (1962), 'La questione femminile,' *Belfagor* 17: 18–41.

Genevois, E., ed. (1994), *Les Femmes-écrivains en Italie (1870–1920): ordres et libertés*, Paris: Université de la Sorbonne nouvelle-Paris III.

Gilbert, S., and S. Gubar (1979), *The Madwoman in the Attic: The Woman Writer and the Nineteenth-Century Literary Imagination*, New Haven: Yale University Press.

Gioberti, V. (1847), *Il gesuita moderno*, Vol. 6, Lausanne: Bonamici.

Hall, C. (1979), 'The Early Formation of Victorian Domestic Ideology,' in S. Burman ed., *Fit Work for Women*, London: St Martin's Press.

Huyssen, A. (1986), *After the Great Divide: Modernism, Mass Culture, Postmodernism*, Bloomington: Indiana University Press.

Jolanda, E.R. (1909), *Consigli e norme di vita femminile contemporanea*, Florence: Casa Editrice Italiana.

Kroha, L. (1992), *The Woman Writer in Late-Nineteenth-Century Italy: Gender and the Formation of Literary Identity*, Lewiston: The Edwin Mellen Press.

Kuliscioff, A. (1977 [1892]), 'Il sentimentalismo nella questione femminile,' rpt. in M. Boggio and A. Cerliani, *Anna Kuliscioff: Con gli scritti di Anna Kusliscioff sulla condizione della donna*, Venice: Marsilio, pp. 156–60.

MacMillan, J. (1981), *From Housewife to Harlot: French Nineteenth-Century Women*, Brighton: Harvester Press.

Marchesini, D. (1989), 'L'analfabetismo femminile nell'Italia dell'Ottocento: caratteristiche e dinamiche,' in S. Soldani, ed., *L'educazione delle donne: Scuole e modelli di vita femminile nell'Ottocento*, Milan: Franco Angeli, pp. 37–56.

Martin-Gistucci, M.G. (1973), *L'oeuvre romanesque de Matilde Serao*, Grenoble: Presses Universitaires de Grenoble.

Melandri, L. (1988), 'Scrittura e immagine di sé: La "mente androgina" in Virginia Woolf e il tema dell' "estasi" negli scritti di Sibilla Aleramo,' in A. Buttafuoco and M. Zancan, eds, *Svelamento Sibilla Aleramo: una biografia intellettuale*, Milan: Feltrinelli, pp. 75–87.

Mill, J.S. (1870), *La servitù delle donne*, trans. and introd. A.M. Mozzoni, Milan: Felice Legross Editore-Libraio.

Morandini, G. (1980), *La voce che è in lei: Antologia della narrativa femminile italiana tra '800 e '900*, Milan: Bompiani.

Neera (1977 [1891]), *Confessioni letterarie,* in '*Le idee di una donna' e 'Confessioni letterarie*,' Florence: Vallecchi.

—— (1919), *Una giovinezza del secolo XIX*, introd. B. Croce, Milan: Cogliati.

Nozzoli, A. (1978), *Tabù e coscienza: La condizione femminile nella letteratura del Novecento*, Florence: La Nuova Italia.

—— (1994), '"La Voce" e le donne,' in E. Genevois, ed., *Les Femmes-écrivains en Italie (1870–1920): Ordres et libertés,* Paris: Université de la Sorbonne nouvelle-Paris III, pp. 208–22.

Papini, G. (1915), *Maschilità*, Florence: Libreria della 'Voce.'

Pellico, S. (1834), *De' doveri degli uomini (Discorso a un giovane)*, Naples: Gammella.

Pirandello, L. (1973 [1911]), *Suo marito*, in G. Macchia, ed., *Tutti i romanzi*, Vol. 1, Turin: Einaudi.

Pisa, B. (n.d.), *Venticinque anni di emancipazionismo femminile in Italia: Gualberta Alaide Beccari e la rivista 'La Donna' (1868–1890)*, Rome: Quaderni del FIAP.

Reim, R., ed. (1991), *Controcanto: Novelle femminili dell'Ottocento italiano*, Rome: Sovera.

Rosmini, A. (1845), *Filosofia del diritto*, Vol. 2, Naples: Batelli.

Serao, M. (1892 [1883]), *Fantasia*, Turin: Casanova.

Showalter, E. (1977), *A Literature of Their Own: British Women Novelists from Brontë to Lessing*, Princeton: Princeton University Press.

Tenca, C. (1971 [1852]), 'A proposito di una storia della letteratura italiana,' in G. Scalia, ed., *Giornalismo e letteratura nell'Ottocento*, Bologna: Cappelli.

Tommaseo, N. (1872), *La donna: Scritti vari con assai giunte inedite*, Milan: Agnelli.

Verga, G. (1980), *Lettere a Paolina*, ed. G. Rayan, Rome: Fermenti.

Zambon, P. (1989), 'Leggere per scrivere. La formazione autodidatta delle scrittrici tra Otto e Novecento: Neera, Ada Negri, Grazia Deledda, Sibilla Aleramo,' *Studi Novecenteschi* 16 (38): 287–324.

Part III
Remaking the Risorgimento

– 6 –

'To Make History': Garibaldianism and the Formation of a Fascist Historic Imaginary
Claudio Fogu

Had it not been for the celebration of the *Decennale Fascista* (the tenth anniversary of the 'Fascist Revolution'), the year 1932 would have been remembered by most Italians as *l'anno garibaldino* (Garibaldian year). The commemoration of the *Cinquantenario garibaldino*, the fiftieth anniversary of the death of Italy's most popular Risorgimento hero, Giuseppe Garibaldi, assumed proportions which were truly unprecedented, both in terms of the number of commemorative events organized throughout the year and in terms of the involvement and sponsorship by the Fascist government.[1] Undoubtedly, however, the symbolic *clou* of the *Cinquantenario* was a three-day national commemoration which may have constituted the regime's most elaborate attempt at colonizing private time (Berezin 1997), in order to secure a properly fascist consciousness of the recent national past.

This unusually long commemorative spectacle was executed in three public ceremonies, all of which were exhaustively documented by the news media and purposely orchestrated to that end.[2] First was the transfer of the remains of Garibaldi's first wife, the Brazilian Creole Anita Riviero, from Genoa to Rome, on June 1; second, the entombment of Anita's remains in the base of a monument to be built in her memory at the top of the Roman Janiculum Hill on June 2; and, finally, the official inauguration of this monument by Mussolini, on June 4.[3] In view of the ritual and representational wealth of these public events, the *Cinquantenario garibaldino* found itself placed at the chronological and symbolic apex of the most vital phase in the construction of the cult of Fascism: the year of the first fascist *Decennale* (E. Gentile 1996: 33). And, in fact, I have elsewhere argued that the organization, performance and rhetorical encoding of the *Cinquantenario* was semiotically subordinated to that of the *Decennale* (Fogu 1996). However, my purpose in returning here to the Garibaldian celebrations is to address a central tension characterizing the cultural turn in fascist studies between analyses of fascist ritual culture and investigations of fascist image politics.

Recent studies of fascist mass-culture have tended to deliver two alternative images of the fascist phenomenon, supported by contending paradigms of interpretation. Following upon the path opened by George Mosse's inquiry in to the sacralization of politics in nineteenth- and twentieth-century Germany (1975), some scholars have focused their attention on the crucial role played by fascist ritual politics in winning mass consensus to the Italian regime. By contrast, other scholars have sought to give historical content to Walter Benjamin's famous theory of the fascist 'aestheticization of politics,' exploring the intimate relationship between Mussolini's aesthetic conception of mass politics and the involvement of avant-garde artists in the creation of a properly fascist image-politics (Benjamin 1988 [1936]). By and large the former have stressed the cultural continuities between the Catholic mold of Italian popular culture, the cult of the Fatherland elaborated by Risorgimento intellectuals and the institutionalization of Fascism as a proper 'political religion' (E. Gentile 1996; Berezin 1997). The later, instead, have painted a modernist image of fascist mass-appeal anchored to its discursive rhetorics of virility and visual politics of style (Spackman 1996; Falasca-Zamponi 1997).

While highlighting the crucial role of fascist cultural politics in the consolidation of the regime, cultural studies of Italian Fascism have clearly tended to reify an outdated theoretical divide between historicism and modernism projecting it onto their subject of inquiry. They have thus raised without resolving a crucial question: Where can we locate the point of ideological condensation between the cult of Fascism and fascist modernism, fascist ritual- and image- politics?

My close reading of the *Cinquantenario*'s representational strategy proposes an answer to this question on both theoretical and historical grounds. Conceived, organized and performed in order to highlight the historical incommensurability between Garibaldianism and Fascism, the Garibaldian celebrations constituted a crucial step in the elaboration of a properly fascist form of historical imagination simultaneously modernist and deeply resonant with the rhetorical codes inscribed at the heart of Latin-Catholic visual culture. My analysis therefore suggests that the crucial point of intersection between the sacralization and the aestheticiz-ation of politics in fascist Italy may be located in the institutionalization of a modernist politics of historical representation whose mass appeal rested on the longevity and widespread literacy of Latin-Catholic rhetorics in Italian popular culture.

Anita Garibaldi and the Nationalization of Garibaldianism

> I believe that Garibaldi can keep gazing in that direction [the Vatican] because, today, his spirit is appeased! Not only will he not be moved, but the Fascist regime will also raise a monument to Anita Garibaldi in the same area. (Mussolini 1939a [1929]: 53)

Thus in his official presentation of the Lateran Pacts to the Fascist Chamber of Deputies (14 May 1929), Mussolini added insult to injury in response to the Vatican's unofficial request that Garibaldi's monument be moved from the top of the Janiculum hill (Rome). The announcement that the government intended to build a monument in honor of Garibaldi's first wife next to the one built in 1895 in memory of the legendary hero was to serve as an explicit deterrent for an ultra-Catholic interpretation of the pacts as 'a license to put the Risorgimento on trial' (Mussolini 1939b [1929]: 54) as well as an authoritative reinforcement of what had rapidly become the most popular and widely elaborated image of the regime's historical continuity with the recent Italian past: the fascist 'completion' of the Risorgimento (Zunino 1985).

In addition, the building of a monument to Anita was also meant to reaffirm the commitment of the Fascist government to rectifying the symbolic crimes of liberal democracy. In fact, the very same initiative had been launched in 1905 by the *National Inter-Parliamentary Committee for the 1907 Celebration of the Centennial of Garibaldi's Birth*, but, notwithstanding an unusual bipartisan consensus, even after two national competitions among fifty-seven renowned artists for a design for the monument, and a successful popular collection of funds for its construction, the enterprise had failed miserably. The monument was never built and the subscription money never returned, leaving the socialist-republican press a fine opportunity to cite the episode as one more 'scandalous symbol of parliamentary incompetence,' of 'delinquent speculation on the most sincere popular feelings,' and of the 'liberal state's inability to honor its own martyrs' (Greco 1907).

From its beginning, therefore, the building of a monument to Anita was charged with polemical overtones that had no equivalent in the history of fascist consolidation and absorption of Risorgimento cults (E. Gentile 1996: 32-52). But this charge was effectively diffused by Mussolini's decision to delay the construction of the monument in order to place its installation ceremony at the center of the Garibaldian celebrations to be performed in June 1932. Endowed with the ritual solemnity of a national commemoration, the construction of the monument lost its confrontational bite in favor of a more effective exploitation of its symbolic capital. In the first place, by commemorating the Risorgimento hero via the monumentalization of his exotic and heroic wife the regime could capitalize on the symbiotic relationship between Garibaldi and Anita without taking any risk with the more controversial political figure of the revolutionary general. Conversely, the monumental fulcrum enabled the government to concentrate all the activities associated with the national commemoration in Rome and to prohibit any other provincial or spontaneous celebration, thereby endowing the planning itself of all commemorative events with a clear symbolic direction:[4] Garibaldi was to be remembered and celebrated solely for his most nationalistic trait: that is, his romantic love of Rome, which had inspired his heroic defense of the Roman Republic (1849) and the 'sacrifice' of his beloved Anita.[5] And, in this respect, the *Cinquantenario* was certainly aimed at providing a definitive closure to the nationalization not only of the Risorgimento hero per se, but also of his popular cult (Isnenghi 1984).

But, did the Garibaldian celebrations lead to a 'fascistization' of Garibaldi's figure and contribute to the fateful 'absorption' of the cult of Risorgimento into the cult of Fascism (E. Gentile 1996)? To answer these questions I will take a close look at the rhetorical encoding and performance of the celebrations. However, before proceeding in this direction, a preliminary factor that distinguishes this commemorative spectacle from the mainstream construction of fascist ritual culture needs to be emphasized immediately: the primary agent in the organization and realization of the Garibaldian celebrations was neither the Fascist Party nor the 'regime' in abstract, but the *Duce* in person. As Honorary Chairman of the celebration's organizing committee, Mussolini was not only accountable for the strategic marginalization of all non-nationalistic traits of Garibaldi's figure – a feat achieved through the monumentalization of his wife and the centralization of the celebrations in the Eternal City – but he was also personally responsible for all tactical choices regarding the aesthetic form and ritual performance of the commemorative events.

Garibaldianism between Fascist Aesthetic Politics and Mussolinian Imaginary

The first act in the planning of the national commemoration, the selection of the design for the monument, began as early as 1928. However, already in this preliminary phase two fundamental elements can be made out characterizing the organization and performance of the whole spectacle: Mussolini's decision to make the event a personal project for which he exercised an unprecedented control over the details of the celebrations' aesthetics, and a puzzling struggle over the ultimate codification of meaning in the spectacles, between Mussolini and the appointed organizer of the celebrations, Ezio Garibaldi. A faithful Fascist since 1922, Ezio was also one of the seven living grandsons of Giuseppe Garibaldi and a 'war hero' in his own right.[6] Given the confidential relationship established by Mussolini with Ezio throughout the 1920s,[7] Mussolini's choice to capitalize upon Ezio's biographical connection with Garibaldianism was equally instrumental in excluding the party from any decisional role in the organization of the celebrations and in keeping the latter under his direct oversight. And yet, this choice also meant that via Ezio, Mussolini was to come into personal contact and conflict with the 'historical' rhetoric of continuity that had underscored the absorption of Garibaldianism into Fascism's 'sacred history' (E. Gentile 1996: 53–79).

Sometime between February and May 1928, Mussolini instructed Ezio to commission an artist of his choice to make a plaster cast of the monument-to-be and to submit it to him for final approval. Ezio's choice fell upon a relatively unknown sculptor, Antonio Sciortino.[8] As the photographs and correspondence preserved in the archives of the National Federation of Garibaldian Veterans show, Ezio had asked Sciortino to represent a specific historical scene: Anita's forsaking the military camp of San Simón (Uruguay) to search for her missing husband, her twelve-day-old son Menotti clutched to her bosom (see figure 6.1). This episode had taken place in 1840 when Garibaldi led a corps of international volunteers to fight on the side of the Republican forces against Argentinian and Brazilian Conservatives, and it had been described in detail by Garibaldi himself in a memoir published in 1872 (Garibaldi 1932 [1872]). Sciortino had clearly based his design on this most authoritative account; in fact, all of his representational decisions matched Garibaldi's narration to the letter.[9] This monument, however, was never built. On the contrary, Mussolini not only rejected Ezio's choice, but suddenly decided to choose an artist himself. He personally commissioned a handful of artists to produce alternative designs and finally selected that of the oldest, most established and most traditional of all Italian commemorative sculptors, Mario Rutelli,[10] an artist who had been acclaimed (and criticized) during the first decade of the century for the 'sensuality' and 'idealized realism' of his public monuments (Riccoboni 1942: 459).

In contrast to Sciortino's historical representation, Rutelli's first design constituted a purely symbolic depiction of Anita. While the former had

Figure 6.1 Antonio Sciortino, *Anita* (plaster cast; 1928)
Courtesy of the Archivio Società di Mutuo Soccorso Giuseppe Garibaldi

labored to produce an exact representation of a historical scene *as reported* by Garibaldi, Rutelli relied on popular iconography in order to produce a symbol of heroic/exotic womanhood with no concern for historical accuracy. Unlike Sciortino, however, he made his *Anita* immediately recognizable even to the least historically informed viewer by combining a realistic rendering of her exotic physiognomy (oval visage, long hair), with clear signs of fearlessness and tumultuous passion. Anita was thus presented as a sensuous Amazon raising a gun in her right hand, astride a rearing horse, about to launch herself into battle (see figure 6.2). Because this heroic/exotic image of Anita corresponded to the expectations of most Italians, Mussolini's selection of Rutelli's monument over Sciortino's might seem to lend credit to the conclusions of a recent study of fascist commemorative monuments, according to which the regime's choices were solely dictated by the opportunistic desire to favor the 'work least problematic from a figurative point of view, and most likely to have an impact on the public' (Cardano 1984: 223). However, Mussolini was not satisfied with the plaster cast he had approved. During a personal visit to Rutelli's studio he ordered a crucial modification: the addition of the infant Menotti on Anita's left arm (see figure 6.3). And, in this respect, the quality

Figure 6.2 First plaster cast of Mario Rutelli, *Anita* (1929)
Courtesy of the Archivio Società di Mutuo Soccorso Giuseppe Garibaldi

and unprecedented amount of Mussolini's engagement in the realization of an actual work of art suggests that *Anita* was not simply commissioned, but rather conceived, by the *Duce* as an artistic expression of his aesthetic politics.

This kind of aesthetic policing and the addition of the infant Menotti provide a clear clue to the 'narcissistic myth of total control connected to

Figure 6.3 Mario Rutelli, *Anita* (1932)
(Note the addition of baby Menotti leaning on Anita's left arm)
Photograph by author

the idea of the *manly* creator and the motif of autogenesis' that characterized the virilist horizon of Mussolini's aesthetic conception of
politics, just as much as his discursive 'feminization' of the masses
(Falasca-Zamponi 1997: 24). In giving autotelic birth to *Anita*'s son,
Mussolini had forged a seductive and static icon of fascist femininity,
which conjoined the campaign against Italy's declining birthrate and the

ongoing project of fostering the formation of a warrior culture into a well-codified image of fascist womanhood: the warrior-mother (Macciocchi 1976; De Grazia 1992:41–76; Spackman 1996). And, while ultimately functioning as a patriarchal lesson to women *never* to abdicate their fascist femininity – that is, their child-bearing role – the oxymoronic appeal of Anita as a motherly 'Amazon' also had the power to capture the imagination – not the historical one – of its male audience. In the end, it was Mussolini's autotelic creation of Anita's 'heroic motherhood' (rather than the monument per se) that became the symbolic fulcrum of the celebrations, and the sole landmark of the monument's appeal, as we shall see in a moment.

And yet, despite its direct reference to contemporary fascist values, the modified statue also managed to refer very explicitly to the military heroism of Garibaldi, of his spouse, of his descendants, in a word, to Garibaldianism. And, in this crucial respect, a closer comparison of Sciortino's plaster cast and Rutelli's final monument suggests that Mussolini's aesthetic politics were also based on a discriminating concern for the symbolic values produced by different modes of historical representation. With the addition of baby Menotti – and without impinging on the balance of Rutelli's composition – Mussolini detached Rutelli's representation from its original and purely symbolic status by adding to it the referential authority of the same historical scene Sciortino had chosen to depict in his monument. Quite plausibly, Mussolini's appreciation of this historical scene can be related to the commemorative value it might have consigned to public memory: next to the signified of heroic-motherhood, the modified image suggested also Anita's passionate dedication to her husband. But what, then, prompted Mussolini to reject Ezio's initial choice of Sciortino's *Anita* which depicted the very same historical episode he later imposed on Rutelli's design?

With the addition of the babe in arms, Mussolini had clearly pushed Rutelli's idealized *Anita* towards the realist tradition of nineteenth-century historical representation (Bann 1990). As mentioned above, the general public had no difficulty in recognizing the mother-warrior Anita Garibaldi thanks to Rutelli's exploitation of some of her most popularized iconographic traits: the long hair flying behind her, the Colt gun in her right hand and the feminine side-saddle riding posture. Also, the historical value of the scene was enhanced by the narrative relationship between the equestrian group and the two historical scenes depicted by Rutelli in the lateral bas-reliefs on the monument's base, both of which referred to episodes immediately preceding and following Anita's flight from the military camp of San Simón.[11] Sciortino's monument, instead, was not immediately forthcoming in disclosing its historical subject: Anita's facial features were only suggested and none of the traditional iconographic signs associated with her figure were inscribed in the model. Thus, despite its faithfulness to Garibaldi's historical account, Sciortino's monument pushed its historical message – Anita's courageous motherhood – into the background, thereby entrusting the monument's meaning entirely to the appeal generated by its modernist aesthetics.

Without renouncing the main tenets of sculptural realism, this artist was clearly attempting a modernist amalgamation of 'age' and 'newness' signs which gave his *Anita* a powerful appeal to unmediated sensory perception.[12] On the one hand, the weathered appearance of the human figures and the lines of erosion which were visible in the simulated ground at the horse's feet evoked the appeal of age-value. On the other hand, Sciortino replaced the static equine posture found in traditional commemorative monuments with the extremely dynamic one of Anita's horse. The representation of movement and speed, one of the most distinguishing traits of futurist aesthetics, was accomplished through the artist's choice to represent the horse's run in the last suspended moment of galloping: a composition which also evoked that quintessentially modern mode of representation, the cinematic still-frame. This monument, with its mixing of age-signs and cinematic dynamism, attempted to arouse in the viewer a modernist perception of time – a mixture of Bergsonian duration and *élan vital* which gave to its historical referent immanent status. Sciortino's *Anita* was clearly meant to stand for the dynamic immanence of a unique revolutionary tradition: *garibaldinismo*. It suspended this tradition between an absolute past and an absolute future, thereby encoding the historical status of Garibaldianism with the symbolic appeal of everlasting presence.

It was this appealing *making immanent* of Garibaldianism, commissioned of Sciortino by Ezio, that Mussolini first rejected and then sought to marginalize in Rutelli's monument. In other words, Mussolini's addition of historical value to Rutelli's idealized realism was aimed at fixing Garibaldianism in a static and feminine icon which purposely prevented the monumentalization of a much more appealing signified: the dynamism and historical immanence of *garibaldinismo*. And, here, in this first 'semiotic' struggle between Mussolini and Ezio Garibaldi we can already ascertain that the Garibaldian celebrations were not in reality at all about the absorption of Garibaldi in the lictorial pantheon, but rather provided a means of counteracting the epochal assimilation of Fascism and Garibaldianism, which had come to constitute not only one of the most solid and popular columns of fascist historical discourse (Zunino 1985), but also Ezio's most cherished ideological project as self-appointed leader of the Garibaldian tradition.[13]

On the death of his father (1923) Ezio found himself isolated when his elder brothers, Ciotti and Peppino, chose to defy the fascistization of the 'Garibaldian tradition' and proceeded to organize a militantly anti-fascist association of Garibaldian veterans in France. For several years, Ciotti's organization prove to be quite a nuisance for the young Fascist government, for it openly sought to preserve the association of Garibaldi's name with notions of direct action, republicanism, voluntarism, masonry, socialism and political leftism in general. However, its existence also made Ezio's political fortune. In order to silence Ciotti, Mussolini had not only invited Ezio to join the PNF – and personally helped his military and parliamentary career throughout the *ventennio* – but also financed Ezio's political journal *Camicia Rossa*,[14] and supported his project of uniting three generations of Italian *garibaldini* into a single organization: the National Federation of Garibaldian Veterans.[15] It was from this solid institutional basis that Ezio worked unsparingly to propose Garibaldianism as the living sign of a historical continuity between the Risorgimento, interventionism, the Great War and Fascism. But, in the process, he also came to propagandize a daring conception of Garibaldianism as the political 'vanguard' of Fascism (E. Garibaldi 1928). With the threat of antifascist Garibaldianism rendered negligible,[16] between 1928 and 1932, it was most plausibly Ezio's 'relentless effort to preserve a space for himself in the regime and to prove that next to the Blackshirts there was still a need for the Redshirts' (Isnenghi 1984: 540) that stimulated Mussolini's personal engagement with the 'Garibaldian tradition.' However, seen in this larger context, Mussolini's response to Ezio's explicit attempt of giving monumental form to his 'assumption of a parallel dynasty called upon to embody and lead – generation after generation – the "immanent" function of Garibaldianism' (ibid.: 541) also suggests that in Mussolini's aesthetic policing of the monument there also converged ideological concerns that are not reducible to an autotelic interpretation of Mussolini's aesthetic agency. Instead, Mussolini's aesthetic agency should be inserted into a dialogical space connected with the unique challenge that Garibaldianism posed to the Mussolinian core of fascist mass imaginary and the 'spontaneous' evolution of *mussolinismo* into *ducismo*.

From its earliest manifestations, and throughout its evolution into an interrelated myth-cult of the *Duce*, the construction and appeal of Mussolinism had remained not only 'for the most part neither imposed nor solicited by the regime' (Passerini 1991: 79), but also solidly anchored to a structural homology between the 'congenital duplicity' of Mussolini's image, the 'ambivalent mass imaginary' which emerged in the aftermath of the Great War, and the 'double game' that *Duce* and the masses came to play in ritual events (ibid.: 66). As Luisa Passerini argues, it was a dynamic of reciprocal immanence (ibid.: 66), rather than of feminization (Falasca-Zamponi 1997) or transcendence (E. Gentile 1996), that sustained the discursive construction of Mussolini's image, just as much as the dialogical relationship that Mussolini himself came to develop with the imaginary *Duce*, and the development of both in relation to ever new frontiers opened up by the regime's visionary politics.

In fact, between 1915 and 1926, the founding myth of Fascism's 'conservative revolution' had found its immanent incarnation in the biographical codification of Mussolini's image as 'a refuge from the menaces of modernity' (Passerini 1991: 66), its 'uniqueness' celebrated or vituperated as an oxymoron 'capable of containing within itself all oppositions' (ibid.: 39) and its first collective identity established in relation to its representing 'Italianness' itself (ibid.: 61). In the following years (1927 to 1932), the intensified atmosphere of sacrality and rituality within which the regime sought to envelop itself contributed instead to the codification of the reciprocal immanence of *ducismo* and *mussolinismo*. In this crucial phase of reciprocal exaltation between the masses and their leader, we can witness the expansion of Mussolini's image beyond the confines of its earlier identification with Italy, towards an imaginary 'figure that does not succumb to the flux of time and, positioned in an eternal present, embodies the immortal primacy of the Italian spirit' (ibid.: 116). It was at this crucial juncture that the Garibaldian and Mussolinian imaginaries came to collide.

No other figure of a fascist precursor could have threatened the dynamic ambivalence of the Mussolinian imaginary as much as that of Garibaldi. As Mario Isnenghi has rightly noted, Garibaldi's image was endowed with the very same 'congenital duplicity' that Passerini has found in Mussolini's, their common 'reversibility irreducible: from rebel to man of order, from man of order to rebel, in a spiraling movement of promised or menacing potentialities' (Isnenghi 1984: 537). In addition, by constituting 'the prototype of the modern "protagonist"' (Calabrese 1982: 108), the cultural construction of Garibaldi's image had anticipated by several decades the 'culture of personality' that was to sustain that of Mussolini (Falasca-Zamponi 1997: 45–56).[17] Accordingly, any direct representation of Garibaldi would have turned out to be not only inherently unstable and open to antifascist interpretations, but also a direct challenge to the atemporal aura that had come to surround Mussolini's image.

Seen in this context, Mussolini's aesthetic policing of the monument acquires crucial significance not only in the history of fascist aesthetic politics, but also in connection with the whole performance of the celebrations. As I will illustrate below, the continuing struggle between Mussolini and Ezio Garibaldi over the semiotic codification of all ritual events confirms that the celebrations represented more than an opportunity to discipline Ezio's 'fascist Garibaldianism,' and prevent it from sliding into 'Garibaldian Fascism.' They constituted an overcharged site of negotiations between the narcissistic foundations of Mussolini's aesthetic politics, and the movement of fascist mass imaginary towards the assimilation of the cult of the lictor within the cult of the 'historic' *Duce.*

History on Parade: Performance and Reception in the Garibaldian Celebrations

Having reviewed the long process by which Mussolini selected the artist for the monument, we will move now to the final stage of the Garibaldian celebrations: the actual performance of the three-day national commemoration which climaxed with the inauguration of Rutelli's monument on 4 June 1932. This last act contained three separate scenes: the transfer of Anita's body from Genoa to Rome, its entombment at the base of the veiled monument and the unveiling ceremony of the monument. Predictably, all three scenes display the marks of Mussolini's personal direction. Indeed, they unequivocally prove that Mussolini's symbolic repression of Garibaldianism in the choice of the monument's design did not occur merely because of a personal competition with Ezio Garibaldi, but constituted rather the preliminary segment of a complex rhetorical strategy aimed at producing a unique and coordinated historical spectacle.

Let us start from Mussolini's direction of the first scene: the parade which was to convey Anita's remains from the Genoese cemetery of Staglieno to the local train station on 1 June 1932. In a letter dated 19 May 1932, Ezio had made a series of requests aimed at regaining some of the symbolic capital lost earlier in the struggle with Mussolini over the selection of the monument. As before, however, Mussolini would not cooperate. In response to Ezio' s requests he refused to allow an on-the-air radio broadcast of the Genoese ceremony; he also denied a request that Anita's coffin be conveyed in a gun-carriage; he prohibited the Garibaldian veterans who would mount an honor guard over the coffin from bearing arms, or from sharing with the Fascist militia the honor of being on duty to control public order; and, finally, he refused to allow the train, which was to carry Anita's body from Genoa to Rome, to make any stops before its intended destination.

The symbolic weight of all such arrangements cannot be under-estimated. Undoubtedly, the implicit referent for Ezio's requests was the most successful national ritual ever performed in the pre-fascist era: the 1921 burial of the Unknown Soldier in the Roman *Altare della Patria*. Following a proposal made by the Garibaldian Colonel Luigi Douhet, the last pre-fascist government had entrusted the Roman association of Garibaldian veterans (*Società Mutuo Soccorso Giuseppe Garibaldi*) with the organization of this ritual. On this occasion, the train transporting the Unknown Soldier from the northern town of Aquileia to Rome had stopped at every station along its route; and, once in Rome, the coffin had been escorted on a gun-carriage by armed Garibaldians to its final destination (Labita 1990).[18] Therefore, by refusing to allow Anita's coffin to be similarly transported, Mussolini had again sought to prevent the representation of that metonymic relationship between Anita and militant Garibaldianism which Ezio had earlier attempted to monumentalize through Sciortino's design. This time, however, Mussolini's decisions were also animated by a more strategic intention: they were aimed at assigning the whole Genoese spectacle an appropriate symbolic position in relation to the Roman celebrations which were to follow.

Genoa was meant to be a period of respectful silence and mourning; a limited time-space, however, which was not to be extended to the whole nation – not even to the communities along the path of the train carrying Anita towards Roman resurrection. At the same time, the Genoese spectacle was to stimulate the narrative memory of its audience by means of its aesthetics so as to ensure the symbolic historicization of *garibaldin-ismo* as a nineteenth-century phenomenon. Responding to Mussolini's express directions, the core of the parade which accompanied the precious coffin appeared like the central room of a historical museum. Framed between the municipal valets (dressed in their historical uniforms) and the funeral carriage, the Garibaldians – all dressed up in their glorious red shirts and riding on open horse-drawn carriages – were separated from both the Blackshirts and the World War I veterans who followed the carriage. These Redshirts were put on display as *living relics* of Garibaldi's time. The parade's implicit codification of this memory-time was then reinforced by another *coup de théâtre* devised by Mussolini himself: Anita's coffin was carried in a solemnly decorated funeral carriage pulled by four black horses (see figure 6.4).[19] The syncretic combination of living relics and horse-drawn carriage could not have more explicitly referred to the popular memory of nineteenth-century funerals.

Figure 6.4 The funeral carriage transporting Anita Garibaldi's body from the cemetery of Staglieno to Genoa's central train station
Courtesy of the Archivio Società di Mutuo Soccorso Giuseppe Garibaldi

Indeed, as the local newspapers' accounts indicate, the parade's aesthetics determined the reception of this mass-spectacle as a Risorgimento museum in motion.[20]

Il Lavoro described the parade's path to the station as a visual narrative of the Risorgimento itself, going from an 'animated and polychromatic painting recalling the atmosphere of 1848,' to a 'monochromatic and conciliatory passage before the imposing statues of the Prophet [Giuseppe Mazzini], the Gentleman King [Victor Emmanuel II] and the Liberator [Giuseppe Garibaldi],' to a final '*macchiaiolo* scene.'[21] Thus the representational ritual was also imbued with the post-unification experience of mourning, disillusionment and memory. The account of another newspaper, *Il Secolo XIX*, stressed the role of aesthetics in determining the emotional response of the parade's spectators. It repeatedly recorded the abrupt alternation between silence – at the passing of the solemn carriage – and loud cheers – at the passage of the Garibaldians – thereby matching *Il Lavoro*'s laconic description of the parading Redshirts:

> In five carriages, each pulled by two horses, here come the glorious old Garibaldians. Old, truly old, and tremulous, with their eyes fogged by the

passing of time, survivors who have gone beyond their red shirts, their wounds, their medals, their far dreams of youth and glory: and yet, in all of them, the living memory of those distant days.

No other words could have better highlighted the Garibaldians' representational status as living relics of the nineteenth century. Their horse-drawn carriages – themselves relics of a time gone by – put them on display, thereby detaching them from the historical painting they had initially animated. Their age-value was enhanced by the hyperbolic reiteration of their senility. Finally, their historical value as relics was doubled because they themselves served as witnesses to their own relichood.

The press accounts of the Genoese parade testify to the success of Mussolini's stripping *garibaldinismo* of its military symbolism and metonymic association with Anita. They also show how Mussolini was able to frustrate Ezio's attempt to cancel the symbolic distance between the Redshirts and the privileged martyrs of the new Fatherland: the World War I veterans and the Blackshirts. This rhetorical operation resulted from the interaction between Mussolini's orders, the parade's construction of a visual narrative and the only proper ritual performed during the parade's progress to the station: the minute of silence and the *Attenti*! (On Your Guard!) ordered by the leader of a Fascist youth squad as the carriage passed before the local monument to Giuseppe Garibaldi. The public performance of this ritual did not simply fix the link between the Genoese parade and the national commemoration of Garibaldi's death; it also encoded it as a solemn act of 'homage' by the fascist present to the Garibaldian past. Unlike its purely fascist alternative, the *Appello* (Roll Call) – which sought to symbolize a mystical communion between the ritual actor, the onlooking masses and the honored martyr – the ritual of the *Attenti* – which combined silence and the Roman salute in the crowd's response to the Fascist leader's command – was aimed at codifying the distance itself between a present which paid homage and a past which received that homage.

And indeed, the association of Garibaldianism with a past to be honored as historical, and only as such, was definitively enacted in the parade's passage through the Arco dei Caduti – Genoa's triumphal arch recently built in memory of her dead in the Great War (see figure 6.5). Only the *historical section* of the parade – that is, the municipal valets, the funeral carriage, the members of the Garibaldi family and the Redshirts – passed through the arch; the rest, including the Blackshirts and World War I veterans, were ordered to proceed to the station by another route. As the municipal monthly *Genova* aptly put it, this careful choreography

Figure 6.5 The parade's passage under the Genoese *Arco dei Caduti*
Courtesy of the Archivio Società di Mutuo Soccorso Giuseppe Garibaldi

allowed everyone to direct his thoughts toward 'an ideal point, the heroism of two distinct generations that have both devoted their entire existence to the unification of the Fatherland.' Two heroic, but *distinct* generations: the Redshirts passing through the arch, the World War I veterans taking a separate path to the station. Two generations, above all, whose historical value was symbolically connected to a common historical task – the unity of the Fatherland. A task, finally, that the parade's aesthetics and the ritual homage to Garibaldi had already encoded as a nineteenth-century accomplishment, thereby marginalizing the idea of a living continuity between Fascism and Garibaldianism.

The second scene of the final act of the celebrations opened in Rome the morning after the Genoese spectacle, on 2 June 1932. While both the selection of Anita's monument and the performance of the Genoese homage had been characterized by a policy aimed at repressing the contemporary value of *garibaldinismo*, the arrival of Anita's body in Rome coincided with the complete restructuring of such a strategy. Every aspect of the Roman event – from the aesthetics and structure of the parade, to the ritual performed, to the absorption of the viewers into the spectacle – was carefully planned to function as an antithesis to the Genoese codification of memory as mourning and homage. In addition, Mussolini not only continued to play an exclusive role in the planning of Anita's burial and monumental rebirth, but took center stage in the performance of both events. Responding to his precise directions as well as to his actual presence on the spot, the formation of the Roman parade provided a most striking contrast to that nineteenth-century 'picturesque, animated and polychromatic painting' evoked by the Genoese parade-in-the-making. While no general public was allowed to attend the arrival of the coffin at Termini Station, over ten thousand members of thirty-five Fascist associations, including a mixed contingent of Garibaldian and World War I veterans, were ordered to assemble in discrete groups at specific places between the station and Piazza Esedra, so as to proceed in a synchronic and spiraling movement to the formation of the parade.

Indeed, as the maps and accounts published by all Roman newspapers attest, Mussolini's plan for the parade's formation and his own presence during this initial segment of the commemorative event, were crucial for the encoding of its aesthetics (see figure 6.6).[22] Performed exclusively for its own actors, this spectacle was directed at fostering in all a sense of partaking in the symbolic re-presentation of the coming-into-being of the fascist movement, its constitution being portrayed as dependent on a magnetic fulcrum (Mussolini), just as much as on the synchronic and orderly manner of its formation. And, once the formation of the fascist movement had been depicted, Mussolini departed, leaving behind an enthusiastically charged crowd, a collective 'fascist subject,' as it were, ready to function as a magnet for the larger, unorganized crowds it encountered on its path toward its final destination – Rutelli's veiled monument on the Gianicolo.

Once again, the press accounts of the event provide us with an invaluable and clear indication of how much the parade's aesthetics were built upon the assumption of a rhetorical literacy of codes shared by all the performing agents: the *Duce*, the fascist organizations, the crowds, the mass media. Emphasizing the interaction between the parade and its spectators, *La Tribuna* (3 June 1932) described the narrative transformation of its collective subject. From 'a river flowing between banks which can hardly contain it,' the parade is seen as turning into a sort of inverted 'river flooded by its own banks,' until it becomes 'a slow moving mass. . . . A long, most continuous wave. One that appears to have no end' (see

Figure 6.6 The map published by *Il Popolo di Roma* with detailed instructions for the formation of the parade of 2 June
Courtesy of the Archivio Società di Mutuo Soccorso Giuseppe Garibaldi

figure 6.7). Beyond the rhetorical flair of their journalistic jargon, the Roman newspapers depicted the allegorical thrust of the Roman parade as a historical re-presentation of the fascist movement becoming a fascist mass movement. In so doing, these accounts illustrated the rhetorical gap between the Genoese *homage* and the Roman *apotheosis*: rather than stressing the symbolic distance between present and past, earlier codified in the Genoese parade, the Roman parade was solely concerned with representing the abolition of this distance in the development of Fascism from 'movement' to 'regime,' and in the development of its collective subject, from 'fascist subject' to 'fascist mass subject.'

Figure 6.7 A rear view of the parade seen from the beginning of Via Nazionale
Courtesy of the Archivio Società di Mutuo Soccorso Giuseppe Garibaldi

And indeed, the symbolic gap between the two parades was made apparent in the ritual performed before the definitive entombment of Anita's coffin: that is, that fascist 'Roll Call' which had not been performed in front of the Genoese crowd. In contrast to the Genoese 'On your guard!' which had reinforced the parade's ties to nineteenth-century narrative memory and mourning, the Roman 'Roll Call' signaled the eruption of modernist remembrance. Thus, this ritual was structurally connected to the parade's narrative re-presentation of the 'fascist mass subject.' It was *this* collective subject that answered '*Presente!*' to Ezio's shout '*Anita Garibaldi!*' In so doing, the fascist mass subject not only obliterated the residual distance between itself and the past it revived, but foregrounded its own presence as a *maker of history* (see figure 6.8).[23]

What I am trying to point out here is that the Roman parade of 2 June 1932 displayed a modernist conception of subject-object relations aimed at re-presenting 'Fascism' as an event which was incommensurable with any other in history, for, as an event, it entailed the eruption of a new

Figure 6.8 The final moments of the entombment ceremony
(Note Ezio Garibaldi standing behind the coffin, and the many hands raised in the Roman fascist salute after the roll-call)
Courtesy of the Archivio Società di Mutuo Soccorso Giuseppe Garibaldi

subject-agent that *made* the past present. In fact, while the parade's representation of the coming-into-being of the 'fascist mass subject' implied its explicit reference to Fascism (the event), this subject's ritual answer (*Presente!*) simultaneously signaled its own real presence and its unique attribute and function of giving presence to the historical past. And, in the light of this Roman segment of the celebrations, the initial repression of Garibaldianism in the monument's design and in the Genoese homage also appears to have been rhetorically connected to the necessary representation of Fascism as the collective subject which was to make the Garibaldian past present. What was at stake in the encoding of the Garibaldian parades is something like the combination of a Proustian experience of remembrance with a Nietzschean sense of suprahistorical agency; or, put in another way, the implementation of a modernist conception of history seeking to disrupt not only Enlightenment notions of the relations between subject and object, present and past, truth and rhetoric, but, more specifically, the historicist assumption of narrative continuity as *inherent to* historical reality. And here, I want to suggest, the performance of the Garibaldian spectacle assumed a very specific ideological profile that inserted the celebrations at a crucial nexus between the deep-seated longevity of Latin-Catholic rhetorical codes in Italian popular culture and the evolution of fascist modernism toward the elaboration of a *historic* conception of agency, representation and consciousness.

'To Make History'

> No wonder, gentlemen, if side by side the shirkers of war we find the shirkers of history, who, having failed – for many reasons and maybe because of their creative impotence – to produce the event, that is, to make history before writing it, later on consume their revenge diminishing it without objectivity or shame. (Mussolini 1939b [1929]: 117)

Thus, ten days after the 'annunciation' of Anita before the Chamber of Deputies, Mussolini outlined the antithesis between the fascist 'making' and the liberal 'writing' of history in his Senate response to Benedetto Croce's opposition to the Lateran Pacts. In a single stroke, Mussolini produced a spectacle for which the whole fascist intelligentsia had been waiting: a direct intellectual confrontation between the *Duce* of Fascism and the philosophical champion of historicism.

Quite explicitly, Mussolini's sentence (in both the legal and the literal senses of the word) connected Croce's political response to the Concordat to the creative impotence, moral cowardice and intellectual bankruptcy of his recently published *Storia d'Italia dal 1871 al 1915* (1928). Overnight, the equation between Fascism and history-making became a popular motto, and the fascist propaganda machine proceeded to celebrate Mussolini's intellectual stature by highlighting the perfect fit between his political intuitions and the concurrent debate on the 'question of fascist historiography' (De Frede 1983: 123). However, in this occasion, much was left out by the presentation of the *Duce* as intellectual *primus inter pares*. As we shall see, this speech was to bear more on the evolution of fascist image politics in general – and the rhetorical encoding of the Garibaldian celebrations, in particular – than on the fascist *bonifica* (reclamation) of historiography (De Vecchi 1937).

Below the polemical jab directed against the 'lay Pope' of liberalism there lurked the suggestion that the ideological dichotomy between Fascism and liberalism derived from two opposite views of the relationship between *res gestae* and *historia rerum gestarum*. In fact, as Croce recognized in recalling the episode twenty years after the facts, the question raised by Mussolini in his 1929 speech went beyond the 'common objection that I had arbitrarily ended my treatment with 1915,' and concerned his historicist premises that, as for a work of art or a theory in the process of elaboration, 'one cannot determine the character of a new political, social and moral order, and thus form an epoch before a new arrangement has been reached' (Croce 1948: 11). And, in hindsight, Croce implicitly admitted that both his 1928 epochal periodization of liberal Italy and his 1929 refusal to acknowledge the Concordat as an event that forced the historian to 'form an epoch' were 'matters of political activity and not historiography' (ibid.: 12). The rhetorical vertigo of Mussolini's response was thus entirely commensurate with Croce's challenge to the core of fascist aesthetic politics. The accusation of creative impotence moved against Croce's *imboscamento* (shirker-ness) from epoch-making events in the past as well as the present rested on the implicit claim that the creative and discretionary power of forming epochs no longer belonged to the historian as *homo aesteticus-moralis-politicus*. Mussolini's idea of fascist history-making ascribed this power to a presentist conception of epochal agency founded on a collapse of historical consciousness and representation that was embedded in the rhetorical logic of his speech.

To paraphrase Barbara Spackman's analysis of Mussolini's speech-events (1996: 123–33), the rhetorical appeal of Mussolini's polarization of liberal history-writing and fascist history-making rested in its sudden stockpiling of eventfulness, rather than violence, and the whole speech pointed towards the popular-cultural imaginary that had sustained the development of fascist rhetorics of virility. The rhetorical conflation of speech and epochal eventfulness referred the idea of fascist history-making to the notion of historic-ness incorporated, since the dawn of modern historical culture, into the expressions 'historic event,' 'historic site' and 'historic speech.' Although no romance language has ever coined an analog of the adjective 'historic' – and even in spoken English the semantic distinction between the two adjectives is often lost – its discursive compounds (historic event, speech and site) have appeared in all European languages recording a semantic differentiation that late-eighteenth-century historians introduced between the adjectives 'historical' and 'historic,' assigning to the former the meaning of 'belonging to the past,' and to the latter that of 'forming an important part or item of history; noted or celebrated in history' (*Oxford English Dictionary* 1989: 259).[24] The logic of Mussolini's speech-event undermined precisely this historicist conception of historic 'importance,' and foregrounded a presentist conception of 'epochal agency' sedimented in the discursive association of historic-ness to speech, site and event. In other words, Mussolini's answer to the 'question of historiography' associated the formation of fascist imaginary to the emergence of an anti-historicist notion of 'historic-ness' signifying a conception of epochal agency that is not only independent of, but acts upon 'historical' facts, representations and consciousness.

The polarization of liberal history-writing and fascist history-making thus reified a paradigmatic series of conceptual distinctions between 'historical writing' and 'historic speech,' 'historical time' and 'historic site,' 'historical fact' and 'historic event,' into an ontological dichotomy between 'historical' (liberal) and 'historic' (fascist) conceptions of epochal agency, consciousness and representation. To the inscription of liberal ideology under the sign of the 'historical' corresponded the projection of a fascist historic agency not merely 'significant' in the eyes of historians, but rather, that signified history in the present. Mussolini's speech ascribed to Fascism a historic imaginary that conjugated history in the present tense and inscribed historical meaning under the rubric of immanent presence, against the transcendental horizon of historical time.

Lest we dismiss Mussolini's reification of historic-ness as an arbitrary cipher of the populist and virilist horizon of fascist rhetoric, we need to recognize immediately that the historic imaginary it evoked not only resonates with our own 'epochal' notion of 'historic' eventfulness (i.e. a 'turning point in history'; a 'watershed'), but inscribed it within the intellectual field of a modernist rather than merely presentist challenge to historicist conceptions of history.[25] It is not so much that Mussolini's 'historic' calls to mind Nietzsche's antidotes to historicism (the unhistorical and the suprahistorical), and. in the same vein, a whole series of worn-out dichotomies between literary modernism and historicism, spatial form and linear time, speech acts and narrative writing. Recent scholarship on literary, cultural and philosophical modernism(s) has unanimously undermined the theoretical and historical blindness of these polarizations, just as much as the tautological reduction of modernism to some sort of Nietzschean Zeitgeist. The theoretical polarization of modernism and historicism has left its place to a more nuanced kaleidoscope of modernisms and a generational perspective on their historical evolution. Among both literary scholars and cultural historians has emerged substantial agreement on the impact produced by the Great War on (re)orienting a whole generation of modernist writers, artists and philosophers away from a subjectivist critique of historical objectivism, and towards the search for a new 'historical sense' that, in the words of T.S. Eliot, would involve 'the perception, not only of the pastness of the past, but of its presence' (Eliot 1919; cited in Longenbach 1987: 7)

As a significant case in point, Hayden White has recently argued that the historical development of modernist conceptions of history may be understood as a response to 'modernist events' that 'function in the consciousness of certain social groups exactly as infantile traumas are conceived to function in the psyche of neurotic individuals' (1996: 20).[26] The 'events' to which White alludes stretch from the Great War to President Kennedy's assassination (including, naturally, the Final Solution). However, their common 'holocaustal' effect he has summarized in the characteristic revolt of post-World War I modernist culture against all 'realist' theories of historical representation, and the sharp distinction that modernist literature has implicitly posited between 'fact' and 'event.' For White, 'all great' twentieth-century writers and philosophers have therefore offered a modernist answer to the question of history, hinging

> on a new distinctive way of imagining, describing and conceptualizing the relationship obtaining between agents and acts, subjects and objects, a statement and its referent – between the literal and figurative levels of speech, and therefore between factual and fictional discourse. (1991: 49)

We may dispute the elitist ring of White's theory of historical modernism, but any reader of Benjamin's *Theses on the Philosophy of History*, Heidegger's *Being and Time*, Eliot's *The Wasteland*, Mann's *Magic Mountain*, Freud's *Civilization and its Discontents*, or Valéry's *Regards sur le Monde Actuel*, can find traces of a modernist confrontation with the existential incommensurability between historicist conceptions of the relationship among historical agency, representation and consciousness and 'the experience of a different "history"' (White 1991: 51) Among these, we should not hesitate to insert the historic imaginary elicited by Mussolini's speech.

This insertion does not mean that we should consider Mussolini's speech as a quintessential elaboration of 'fascist modernism,' or equate tout court rhetorical logic with intellectual elaboration, or literary experimentation. However, if we accept Robert Wohl's conclusions concerning the political 'temptation' that Fascism constituted for the intellectual 'generation of 1914' (1979) and, consider – with Spackman – Benjamin's own involvement in the 'rhetorics of virility' that character-ized Mussolini's speeches (Spackman 1996: 27–33), we may consider Mussolini's invocation of fascist historic agency as a document that points simultaneously to the rhetorical contiguity between modernist thought and fascist mass culture, and the historical origins of such a contiguity. Unequivocally, the historic logic of Mussolini's 1929 speech moved away from the mid-1920s debate on the 'question of historiography' and gestured instead towards the modernist answer to the 'question of history' elaborated in the aftermath of the Great War by Croce's philosophical nemesis, and Fascism's prime ideologue, Giovanni Gentile. More specifically, the speech pointed to a precise genealogical connection between the ideological framework of *ducismo*, and Gentile's translation of the founding actualist notion of *autoctisi*[27] (G. Gentile 1979 [1912]) into the concept of 'history belonging to the present,' theorized in his essay *Politica e filosofia* (G. Gentile 1918).

The concept of history 'belonging to the present' conjugated in modernist syntax the catastrophe of all past tenses onto the plane of the 'historic present.' In this respect, Gentile's modernist answer to the question of history may be seen as connecting the evolution of a historic semantics toward the identification of 'epochal' and 'historic,' to the 'longevity' of Latin-Catholic rhetorical codes and the survival of the epic and didactic tradition of *historia magistra vitae* in modern historical culture (Koselleck 1985: 28–32). In much the same way as the historic present tense was defined as giving 'vividness' – in the ancient sense of *energeia*, 'real presence' – to a narrative passage about the past, so, even today, we consider an event 'historic' when its 'meaning' appears to give immediate palpability to our epochal representation of the historical record, that is, to what we refer to as our historical consciousness.[28] However, for Gentile, the emergence of this historic form of consciousness was to be traced to the traumatic experience and response of all Italians to the very historic event that had threatened their nationhood: the military defeat of Caporetto (October 1917).

In the last year of the Great War – Gentile argued in *Politica e filosofia* – Italian masses and leaders had experienced history as immanent rather than transcendental. And, in this connection, the immanent catastrophe of the histori(ographi)cal act he proposed sought to exorcise the psychological ambivalence felt by most Italians before an imagined death of the Fatherland (Fachinelli 1979), at the same time as the early ideological compound of Mussolinism and Fascism began attracting the support of war veterans through a 'transposition of the ideal of Fatherland onto an absolute plane, entirely unknown until then' (Fachinelli 1979: 143; Passerini 1991: 66). Thus, the ultimate foundation for Gentile's claim to have produced a more realistic philosophy of history than German historicism was not related to its prescriptive emphasis on the Italian Risorgimento, but to its descriptive ability to ground a modernist notion of style and personality – articulated in the post-war political field by the 'visionary politics' of Mussolini, Marinetti and D'Annunzio – in the emergence of a repressed form of historic consciousness in the Catholic body of the Italian masses (G. Gentile 1918). If the political encounter between the philosopher of actualism and Fascism can be read in line with Gentile's elaboration of a political theology of state, the same cannot be said of the ideological contribution Gentile made to the development of the historic imaginary elicited by Mussolini's 1929 speech. *Politica e filosofia* subordinated the intellectual catastrophe of politics and philosophy to a full scale de-trascendentalization of historical agency at the level of mass consciousness. And, in light of this long digression, I would like to suggest that the deep ideological homology among actualism, Latin-Catholic rhetorical codes and fascist history-making found visual expression in the 'historic' encoding of the Garibaldian parades analyzed here and their relationship to the final scene of the celebrations with which I am about to conclude: the 'historic' speech that 'unveiled' Anita on 4 June 1932.

Making the Past Present

It will surely surprise no one to learn that this concluding segment of the *Cinquantenario garibaldino* was orchestrated by Mussolini so as to present himself as the literal embodiment of the 'fascist mass subject' that had made the past present at the end of the Roman parade. Only after having been manifested by such a semiotic agent could the past be actively signified in its relationship to the present. And, indeed, this was the task assigned to the third and final scene of the Garibaldian celebrations. The speech the *Duce* delivered during the monument's inauguration revealed the ultimate aim of the entire rhetorical strategy. As all the front pages of the newspapers published the next day and the sound newsreels of the ceremony all convincingly show, this final spectacle was structured so as to highlight the contrast between the *energeia* of Mussolini's signifying words and the inert aesthetics of Rutelli's historical monument. The latter was left to function solely as a backdrop aimed at enhancing the speech's (re)presentational power.[29] Thus, when Mussolini finally pronounced the words 'le Camice Nere sono anche politicamente sulla linea ideale delle Camice Rosse e del loro Condottiero' (the Blackshirts are, also politically, in ideal continuity with the Redshirts and their Chief), the long postponed acknowledgment of the historical continuity between Garibaldianism and Fascism produced an unrestrainable surge of enthusiasm in the listening crowds which also extended to the readers of next-day newspapers and to the thousands who watched its sound newsreel or documentary.[30] Having been repressed throughout the celebrations, and being finally uttered by the prime representative of the 'fascist mass subject,' Mussolini's affirmation of historical continuity managed to assume its proper historic status. Like a Proustian *madeleine*, the historic speech functioned as an overcoded attempt to make the repressed signified 'Garibaldianism' suddenly present to the consciousness of the whole nation, thereby permitting nothing less than a reversal of historical legitimation and consciousness: it was not Fascism that gained legitimacy from the affirmation of its historical continuity with the Garibaldian past – it was this past that gained real presence and meaning only through the signifying word of the fascist *Duce*.

There is no denying the anomalous status of the Garibaldian celebration in the panorama of fascist ritual culture. However, if any microhistorical study is stimulated by the exceptionalness of its object and the desire to transform 'into a hypothetical monograph that which for another scholar could have been a simple footnote,' the conjunctural perspective privileged by all microhistories addresses questions not only to 'the comprehensive visions delineated by macrohistory,' but also to their theoretical assumptions (Ginzburg 1993: 22 and 27). My close reading of the Garibaldian celebrations shows that the centrality of image politics in the Italian-fascist phenomenon cannot be solely ascribed to a totalitarian 'logic' that sustained both Mussolini's aesthetic politics (Falasca-Zamponi 1997: 26) and the cult of the lictor (E. Gentile 1996), but must also take into account a rhetorical literacy of codes that subordinated the formation of fascist identity to the collective celebration of distinction. Positioned at the crucial nexus between intellectual modernism, fascist visionary politics and popular-cultural rhetorical codes, the Garibaldian celebrations suggest that, at the level of fascist imaginary, the fascist symbol (the lictoral *fasces*) may always have referred more to the immanent presence of a Mussolinian ax that hacked all the *fasces* from their roots than to the transcendental bundling of party, individual and state into a 'totalitarian community' of 'collective harmony' (E. Gentile 1996: 80–101). And, taking place at the apex of the regime's institutional self-confidence, the historic imaginary to which the celebrations sought to give visual form also refers us to the imminent translation of the 'historic' *Duce* into the 'epoch-making' imaginary that pervaded fascist culture in the 1930s. In this respect, the Garibaldian *Cinquantenario* constituted only the first act of a modernist historical spectacle soon to be completed with an astonishing final act: the historic representation of Fascism itself in the Exhibition of the Fascist Revolution which opened the commemorative frenzy of the fascist

Decennale on 29 September 1932 (Fogu 1996). And, from this perspective, the study of this composite historical spectacle – from the autotelic
annunciation of Anita's monumental birth, in 1929, to the autoctic
transubstantiation of *Cinquantenario* into *Decennale* in 1932 – opens a
window onto the collective visionary endeavor that sought to transform
the 'a-historical' (Passerini 1991) or 'immortal' (Falasca-Zamponi 1997)
image of Mussolini, into a cipher of fascist historic-ness.

Notes

1. As part of the official program of the *Cinquantenario* the Fascist
   government financed the traditional pilgrimage to Garibaldi's tomb
   in Caprera – which had been organized by the Roman association of
   Garibaldian veterans every five years since 1887 – a *Garibaldian
   Exhibition* to be hosted in the prestigious Palazzo delle Esposizioni
   in Rome, the publication of the first national edition of Garibaldi's
   writings, a special issue of commemorative stamps and a Garibaldian
   lottery. It also decreed a parliamentary commemoration before a
   plenary session of the two chambers, a day of celebration in all schools
   and universities, and another day to be set aside for public speeches
   by prominent members of the Partito Nazionale Fascista (PNF) in the
   main squares of most Italian cities.
2. Italian newspapers dedicated entire front pages to the celebrations,
   and L'Unione Cinema Educativo (LUCE) edited an astonishing 900
   meters of positive film to produce one silent documentary, one sound
   documentary, three silent newsreels and two with sound.
3. All of the documents regarding the government sponsorship of the
   Garibaldian celebrations are stored in the Archivio Centrale di Stato,
   Rome (ACS): Presidenza Consiglio dei Ministri (PCM), 1931–33,
   Cinquantenario Giuseppe Garibaldi, f. 14.5.701/1–34 (henceforth
   cited as ACS: PCM, 14.5.701/ #).
4. All requests for local activities received by the PCM were denied with
   a standard response which underlined their 'interference with the
   national events planned in Rome.' Not even the prestigious ad hoc
   Lombard Commemorative Committee was allowed to stage the series
   of planned commemorative events it had hoped to hold in Milan
   between June 2 and June 5. ACS: PCM, 14.5.701/23.

5. Anita died of illness and exhaustion near Ravenna, in November 1849, during Garibaldi's flight from the fallen Republic. According to sympathetic reports, Garibaldi was 'obliged' to abandon the dying Anita in a hurry because the French pursuers were closing in on them.

6. Following his father Ricciotti Garibaldi Senior and his older brothers Bruno and Costante, Ezio had been wounded during the celebrated Garibaldian 'expedition' of the Argonne (December 1914), which Mussolini himself had defined as the most heroic episode of all in the campaign to assure Italy's entrance in the Great War. On the symbolic occasion of the 1922 National Pilgrimage to Caprera, Ricciotti Senior and Ezio had returned Mussolini's homage by inviting the *camice rosse* (Redshirts) to follow the new *Duce* of the *camice nere* (Blackshirts).

7. In 1923, Mussolini had sent Ezio to Mexico as official plenipotentiary for all economic matters. And, notwithstanding their conflict over the organization of the *Cinquantenario*, in 1935 he entrusted Ezio with the very delicate task of carrying out secret negotiations with O'Hare and Laval to prevent British and French approval of economic sanctions against Italy in response to the military invasion of Ethiopia.

8. Maltese by birth, Sciortino was director of the Roman Accademia Inglese delle Arti. Notwithstanding his foreign nationality, he was 'un'artista di purissimo animo italiano' (an artist of the purest Italian soul) according to Ezio in an enthusiastic letter to Mussolini. This letter is preserved, together with the photographs of Sciortino's plaster cast, in a folder entitled 'Monumento Anita Garibaldi,' in the combined archives of the *Società di Mutuo Soccorso Giuseppe Garibaldi* (SMSGG) and *Federazione Nazionale Volontari Garibaldini* (FNVG), Rome, Piazza della Repubblica 12. I wish to thank the president of the *Istituto Internazionale Studi Giuseppe Garibaldi*, Countess Erika Garibaldi, as well as the president of the SMSGG, Dr. Giuseppe Garibaldi, for giving me permission to conduct my research in the archive and for allowing me to publish the photographs that accompany this chapter.

9. Compare the photographs with Garibaldi's narration: 'Even my beloved Anita, twelve days after she had given birth, was forced to leave the camp with her infant in front of the saddle, to confront stormy weather. Riding a fiery horse, surrounded [by the enemy] she did not surrender, . . . but, spurring her horse, she passed with a vigorous rush right through the enemy's fire and though grazed by a bullet which pierced her hat and burned a lock of her hair, she was fortunately unharmed' (Garibaldi 1932 [1872]: 175–7).

10. Rutelli's first plaster cast was seen and approved by Mussolini in December 1929. All documents referring to the building of Anita's monument are in ACS: PCM, 14.5.701/7a.

11. On the left side bas-relief Rutelli represented Anita leading a group of Garibaldians to battle at Coritibanos; on the right side, he sculpted Anita's desperate search for her husband on the battlefield. In both groups Anita was also characterized by the same representational signs exploited in the main statue: dress, long hair, female riding posture, horse without reins.

12. I am referring here to the radical differentiation between the scholarly attribution of *historical value*, and the sensory mass appeal generated by the aesthetic signs of *age-* and *newness-value* in monuments. These notions were first theorized in 1903 by German art historian Alois Riegl in his seminal essay 'The Modern Cult of Monuments: Its Character and Its Origin' (1982 [1903]).

13. In the European panorama of 'invented traditions' described by Eric Hobsbawm and Terence Ranger (1983), the Garibaldian tradition constituted an anomalous case. In the first place its birth coincided with a private act: the political will left by the dying General Giuseppe Garibaldi. In this he nominated his eldest son Menotti as military leader of his veterans and spiritual heir of his own brand of militant voluntarism. The general had been distinguished both by his support of peoples seeking freedom and independence, and by his goal of conquering all the *irredente* lands for the 'incomplete' Italian State (occupied by either France or Austria): first and foremost, Rome, but also his natal city of Nice and the regions of Trentino and Venezia-Giulia. A description of how Menotti and his successor Ricciotti Senior interpreted this will would constitute far too long a digression for the dimensions of my study; the crucial point is that in its original form the Garibaldian tradition was not embodied in any specific ritual or institution. It thus rested on the private attribution of a genetic right to military leadership which made the content of this tradition – what Hobsbawm and Ranger call 'the values and norms of behavior, which automatically implied continuity with the past' (1983: 1) – dependent on the political interpretation and public statements of the eldest family heir.

14. This journal was founded in 1903 by Ricciotti Senior and functioned as the official organ of Garibaldianism until it ceased publication during the war. In 1925, Ezio refinanced it and became its sole editor until 1939. In its heyday, between 1925 and 1928, *Camicia Rossa* attracted a sizable public, thanks also to the regular contributions of

Curzio Malaparte Suckert and several *Selvaggi*, including Mino Maccari.

15. Founded on the symbolic occasion of the second anniversary of the March on Rome (28 October 1924) the *Federazione Nazionale Volontari Garibaldini* (FNVG) opened its doors to all generations of Garibaldian veterans. That is to say, to the few surviving ones who had fought with General Giuseppe Garibaldi in 1860, 1867 and 1871; to those volunteers who had followed Ricciotti Senior and his sons in their military expeditions (the Balkans in 1897; Domokos in 1912; the Argonne in 1914); and to the many more who had fought in the *Brigata Cacciatori delle Alpi* during the Great War. Ezio was elected chairman of the federation by the representatives of the pre-existing Garibaldian societies, and entrusted with the right to be its sole authorized representative in all contacts with the government. A public invitation to all Garibaldian veterans was issued, and by February 1925 about 3,600 veterans had joined the FNVG, although their numbers – just like Ezio's symbolic capital – were destined to steadily decline during the 1930s, to reach fewer than 800 in 1939.

16. Ciotti's early opposition to Fascism was anything but symbolic. In 1926, he was arrested by the French police in connection with the famous Zaniboni attempt on Mussolini's life. Expelled from France, he wandered for some time through the U.S., England and Cuba, but, on the occasion of the 1932 Garibaldian celebrations, he was pardoned by the Fascist regime and allowed to return to Italy to resume some publishing initiatives under the watchful eye of the OVRA.

17. According to Calabrese's semiotic analysis of the image-cult of Garibaldi (1982), the worldly popularity of the general was the result of his literary and iconographic codification as *the* 'Legendary Hero.' This composite figure, in fact, was the result of a complex interaction among intentional factors and cultural conditions: first, Garibaldi's own self-fashioning as a heroic man, modeled on the literature (especially Sir Walter Scott) he himself had read and absorbed; then the literary production of the 'heroic figure' in the historical novels and memoirs he himself wrote; at the same time, there was the development of the literary and iconographic representation of the 'hero Garibaldi' by famous writers and painters (Victor Hugo, George Sand and Alexandre Dumas père among the former; Domenico Induno foremost among the latter); and, finally, the melding of all these 'figures' into the characterization of 'hero-types' in popular literature after his death (especially in Emilio Salgari's novels).

18. ACS: PCM, 14.5.701/9: letter Ezio-Mussolini dated 19 May 1932. The SMSGG – whose members were absorbed by Ezio's FNVG in 1924 – had not only proposed the Unknown Soldier initiative, but was also the acknowledged guardian of this secular temple. The direct involvement of this organization in the performance of a national commemoration had become its major claim to distinction. Certainly, no more fitting a prototype of this successful ritual could have been present in Ezio's mind as he drafted his requests to Mussolini.

19. ACS: PCM, 14.5.701/9: hand-written annotation on the right margin of Ezio's letter of 19 May 1932.

20. Here, and in the following paragraph, I am referring to the press accounts of the parade published by the main Genoese dailies *Il Secolo XIX* and *Il Lavoro* on 2 June 1932. Given the new competitive space for the mass representation of public events created by the production of sound newsreels in the early 1930s, I consider these press accounts as crucial decoders and recoders of fascist rhetorical strategies, rather than as mere propaganda pieces.

21. The term *macchiaiolo* refers to the impressionistic technique used by a group of painters who sought to portray – in addition to other more pastoral themes –– both Italy's Risorgimento and the more melancholic aftermath of independence and unification in the second half of the nineteenth century.

22. All the Roman newspapers published maps similar to the one reproduced in figure 6.6 as well as detailed instructions for the formation of the parade. The invited groups were told to start marching in unison towards the point where they were to join the parade, while the parade's beginning was marked by the funeral car followed by Mussolini and the Garibaldi family. Hence, functioning as the fulcrum of its spiraling movement, Mussolini's presence – he joined the parade only between the station and Piazza Esedra – foregrounded the symbolic resonance of the parade's synchronicity. The same newspaper articles also notified the non-parading crowds to converge on the curbs of Via Nazionale and along the route to the Janiculum. According to most newspapers, no fewer than 300,000 people accompanied Anita to her burial site.

23. My phenomenological reading of the 'Roll Call' performed at the end of the Roman parade seeks to highlight the ideological resonance of this ritual against its tout-court identification as 'the supreme rite of Fascism, the principal testimony of their religiosity' (E. Gentile 1996: 54). According to Gentile, this ritual represented the symbolic essence of Fascism as a political religion. However, in my view, Gentile

does not take into account the rhetorical thrust of this ritual, which cannot be solely reduced to an emblematic form of fascist religiosity, and must also be analyzed in connection with the different spectacles into which it was inserted.

24. For example the Italian expressions *un evento storico* and *un discorso storico* carry the same semantic charge of the English locutions 'a historic event' and 'a historic speech.'

25. Rhetorically speaking, our contemporary notion of 'historic event-fulness' is built upon an anti-historicist syntax of subject–object relations. We attribute to the object that we call historic the active faculty of signifying that we normally recognize only in thinking subjects, and, in the specific case of the signification of human events in time, to historians. The historic event, then, does not merely 'have an interest or importance' in the eyes of historians. It is significant both passively and actively, transitively and intransitively. It is signified by the subject which defines it so in implicit reference to narrative images of the historical process (historical imaginary). And yet, it simultaneously signifies by re-coding the very narrative structure of the historical imaginary in relation to which it is defined.

Let us take, by way of exemplification, the most popular and generally acknowledged historic event of our times, the 'fall of the Berlin Wall.' In order to signify that it is a historic event, all the possible signifieds which we could attribute in our sentences to 'the fall of the Berlin Wall' would not refer to its causal or sequential connections to other historical facts, but to their metanarrative forms in our consciousness: 'the (romantic) victory of capitalism,' 'the (tragic) defeat of communism,' 'the (comic) return of repressed nationalism,' 'the (farcical) vindication of history over historical consciousness.' By contrast, were we to say instead that 'the fall of the Berlin Wall caused the end of communist rule in Eastern Europe,' we would immediately signal our entry into a completely different signifying structure from that of historic-ness, one in which the speaking/writing subject signifies the relationship among discrete objects of discourse that he or she considers 'historical,' that is, 'facts' belonging to the past.

26. It might be worth noting that the above-mentioned development of modernist studies from a structuralist-nominalist towards a generational-historical perspective finds in the internal evolution of White's theory of historical modernism a most significant example. For a discussion of the evolution of White's conception of modernist history see Kansteiner (1993).

27. The term *autoctisi* was a neologism introduced by G. Gentile (1979 [1912]) to summarize the founding principle of actualism: absolute immanence of action and thought. Seen from the perspective of actualism's intended reform of Hegelian dialectic, for Gentile, autoctisis meant that every action is an act of thought and every act of thought was unmediated because it was a pure act of spiritual self-consciousness. In my reading of Gentile's participation in the creation of Italian modernist culture – defined by Adamson as a generational project of 'cultural regeneration through the secular-religious quest of new values' (1993: 360) – I consider *autoctisi* as a modernist translation of the myth of autogenesis (Falasca-Zamponi 1997) that correlated – on the religious side of the modernist spectrum – the secular-futurist myth of self-creation.

28. Following and connecting with Ginzburg's suggestive remarks on the rhetorical origins of modern historical culture and the modern concept of representation put forward in two separate essays (1989, 1991), I connect the evolution of modern historic semantics to the founding rhetorical figure of Greek historiography, *energeia*, and the Roman notion of *imago*, both of which referred truth and reality to a representational effect of presence. In this respect, I see the fascist attempt to give visual form to a historic imaginary as being in line with the long-term – and by no means extinguished – quest for fusion of signifier and signified that has dominated the evolution of Latin-Catholic visual culture and imagery (Freedberg 1989).

29. Mussolini's care in making sure that Garibaldianism's relationship to the present was obscured throughout the celebrations is perfectly symbolized by the indistinct figure of Anita Garibaldi on horseback behind *Il Duce* the Orator appearing on the front pages of most Italian newspapers on 5 June 1932.

30. In the ACS folder collecting all the documents regarding the *Cinqu-antenario* I have found an extraordinary document which occupies, alone, the last unmarked file in the folder. It is a handwritten letter to Mussolini from a Mr. Cotugno who wished to express to the *Duce* the uncontrollable enthusiasm which he felt upon reading Mussolini's speech in a local newspaper. In closing his laudatory note, Mr. Cotugno wrote to the *Duce*: 'While speaking about well-known and often "abused" events, [you] have succeeded in being ingeniously original, and have said things and produced judgments and drawn conclusions about which the most illustrious historians of the Risorgimento never had the faintest idea.' In my opinion, the isolation of this letter, in a file all to itself, constitutes a clue to its having been

considered by Mussolini as a precious relic: a document, that is, attesting to the success of his grand attempt to recode as a revelation a continuity that had been already codified in innumerable texts and rituals throughout the 1920s.

References

Adamson, W. (1993), 'Modernism and Fascism: The Politics of Culture in Italy, 1903–1922,' *American Historical Review* 95: 359–90.

Bann, S. (1990), *The Inventions of History: Essays on the Representation of the Past,* Manchester: Manchester University Press.

Benjamin, W. (1988 [1936]), 'The Work of Art in the Age of Mechanical Reproduction,' in *Illuminations,* ed. H. Arendt, trans. H. Zohn, New York: Schocken Books, pp. 217–51.

Berezin, M. (1997), *Making the Fascist Self: The Political Culture of Interwar Italy,* Ithaca: Cornell University Press.

Calabrese, O. (1982), *Garibaldi, tra Ivanohe e Sandokan,* Milan: Electa.

Cardano, N. (1984), 'Per una storia dei monumenti celebrativi a Roma dalla prima guerra mondiale agli anni '30,' in *Roma Capitale: 1870–1970. Architettura e urbanistica. Uso e trasformazione della città storica,* Vol. 12, Venice: Marsilio, pp. 216–27.

Croce, B. (1928), *Storia d'Italia dal 1871 al 1915,* 3rd edn, Bari: Laterza.

—— (1948), 'Vent' anni fa: Ricordo della pubblicazione di un libro,' *Quaderni della Critica* 4 (10): 111–12.

De Frede, C. (1983), 'Il giudizio di Mussolini su Croce,' *Storia e Politica* 23 (1): 123.

De Grazia, V. (1992), *How Fascism Ruled Women. Italy, 1922–1945,* Berkeley and Los Angeles: University of California Press.

De Vecchi, C.M. (1937), *Bonifica fascista della cultura,* Milan: Mondadori.

Fachinelli, E. (1979), 'Il fenomeno fascista,' in *La freccia ferma: Tre tentativi di annullare il tempo,* Milan: Adelphi, pp. 135–52.

Falasca-Zamponi, S. (1997), *Fascist Spectacle: The Aesthetics of Power in Mussolini's Italy,* Berkeley and Los Angeles: University of California Press.

Fogu, C. (1996), 'Fascism and *Historic* Representation: The 1932 Garibaldian Celebrations,' *Journal of Contemporary History* 31 (2): 317–45.

Freedberg, D. (1989), *The Power of Images: Studies in the History and Theory of Response,* Chicago: The University of Chicago Press.

Garibaldi, E. (1928), *Fascismo garibaldino,* Rome: Edizioni Camicia Rossa.

Garibaldi, G. (1932 [1872]), *Memorie*, Bologna: Cappelli.

Gentile, E. (1996), *The Sacralization of Politics in Fascist Italy*, Cambridge: Harvard University Press.

Gentile, G. (1979 [1912]), 'L'atto del pensare come atto puro,' in *Giovanni Gentile: Opere complete*, Vol. 3, Florence: Sansoni, pp. 310–21.

—— (1918), 'Politica e filosofia,' *Politica* 1: 39–54.

Ginzburg, C. (1989), 'Montrer et citer: La vérité de l'histoire,' *Le Débat* 56: 43–54.

—— (1991), 'Représentation: Le mot, l'idée, la chose,' *Annales ESC* 6: 1219–34.

—— (1993), 'Microhistory: Two or Three Things that I Know about It,' *Critical Inquiry* 20 (1): 10–35.

Greco, M. (1907), *Il Monumento ad Anita Garibaldi: L'Arte*, Rome: Lux.

Hobsbawm, E., and T. Ranger, eds (1983), *The Invention of Tradition*, Cambridge: Cambridge University Press.

Isnenghi, M. (1984), 'Usi politici di Garibaldi, dall'interventismo al fascismo,' in F. Mazzonis, ed., *Garibaldi condottiero: Storia, teoria, prassi*, Milan: Franco Angeli, pp. 533–44.

Kansteiner, W. (1993), 'Hayden White's Critique of the Writing of History,' *History and Theory* 32 (3): 273–95.

Koselleck, R. (1985), *Futures Past: On the Semantics of Historical Time*, Cambridge, MA: MIT Press.

Labita, V. (1990), 'Il Milite Ignoto: Dalle trincee all'Altare della Patria,' in S. Bertelli and C. Grottanelli, eds, *Gli occhi di Alessandro*, Florence: Ponte alle Grazie, pp. 120–53.

Longenbach, J. (1987), *Modernist Poetics of History: Pound, Eliot, and the Sense of the Past*, Princeton: Princeton University Press.

Macciocchi, M.A. (1976), *La donna nera*, Milan: Feltrinelli.

Mosse, G. (1975), *The Nationalization of the Masses: Political Symbolism and Mass Movements in Germany from the Napoleonic Wars through the Third Reich*, New York: Howard Fertig.

Mussolini, B. (1939a [1929]), 'Relazione alla camera sugli accordi del Laterano,' in *Scritti e discorsi di Benito Mussolini: Edizione definitiva*, Vol. 7, Milan: Hoepli, pp. 43–62.

—— (1939b [1929]), 'Risposta al Senato sui patti lateranensi,' in *Scritti e discorsi di Benito Mussolini: Edizione definitiva*, Vol. 6, Milan: Hoepli, pp. 107–22.

The Oxford English Dictionary, Vol. 7 (1989), eds J.A. Simpson and E.S.C. Weiner, 2nd edn, Oxford: Clarendon Press.

Passerini, L. (1991), *Mussolini immaginario: Storia di una biografia 1915–1939*, Bari: Laterza.

Riccoboni, A. (1942), *Roma nell'arte*, Rome: Mediterranea.

Riegl, A. (1982 [1903]), 'The Modern Cult of Monuments: Its Character and Its Origin,' trans. K. Forster and D. Ghirardo, *Oppositions* 25: 21–51.

Spackman, B. (1996), *Fascist Virilities: Rhetoric, Ideology, and Social Fantasy in Italy*, Minneapolis: Minnesota University Press.

White, H. (1991), 'Historical Emplotment and the Problem of Truth,' in S. Friedlander, ed., *Probing the Limits of Representation: Nazism and the Final Solution*, Cambridge, MA: Harvard University Press, pp. 37–53.

—— (1996), 'The Modernist Event,' in V. Sobchack, ed., *The Persistence of History: Cinema, Television, and the Modern Event*, London: Routledge, pp. 17–38.

Wohl, R. (1979), *The Generation of 1914*, Cambridge, MA: Harvard University Press.

Zunino, P. (1985), *L'ideologia del fascismo: Miti, credenze e valori nella stabilizzazione del regime*, Bologna: Il Mulino.

7

'Tramonto' and 'Risorgimento': Gentile's Dialectics and the Prophecy of Nationhood

Roberto Dainotto

... as soon as Italy was made [formata] all the intellectual and political world which had created it, suddenly unmade [sformato] itself. It would have looked like a dissolution, if one did not see in it, vaguely but already visible, a new horizon.

Francesco De Sanctis, *Storia della letteratura italiana*

On 15 April 1944, Senator Giovanni Gentile, Minister of Education of the moribund Fascist regime, and newly appointed president of the 'Italian Academy' that Mussolini has instituted in the last days of Salò, is gunned down in Florence. The partisans are overjoyed to hear of the death of the philosopher of Fascism – the *only* philosopher of Fascism in the whole of Europe, indeed, according to Zeev Sternhell (1984: 20). The Fascists, on the other side of the barricade, do not shed a tear either: Gentile, the haughty philosopher sometimes so scornful of the Law of the Duce, the rescuer of too many Marxists and Jews, has finally gotten what he deserved. But as the sun sets on that festive April 15, at the dim flicker of the lampposts, the mystery starts haunting Italy in the best tradition of a Sciascia novel: who killed Gentile – the Fascists, or the partisans (Canfora 1985)?

Fifty years later, in a good introduction to *The Italian Risorgimento*, the elimination of Gentile takes a new, mysterious turn. The author of the book, Lucy Riall, writes:

In the attempt to re-evaluate the mythology of national unification against the background of liberal Italy's collapse [after World War I], two conflicting accounts of [the Risorgimento] emerged, one published by the idealist philosopher Benedetto Croce in 1928, the other written during the fascist period by the imprisoned Marxist activist Antonio Gramsci (but published only in 1949) (Riall 1996: 2).

Croce (1928) and Gramsci (1996 [1949]) have offered the two alternative standards, according to Riall, between which Italy has imagined, and imagines still, its origin as nation. For Croce, this beautiful origin was the ideal of a bourgeois society to which Italy, now in the grips of Fascism, had to return. Gramsci, on the other hand, understanding the Risorgimento as a 'failed revolution' bent solely to bourgeois interests, and Fascism as a consequence of such failure, was calling for the necessity of a new, and truer, popular and national revolution. But what has happened to Giovanni Gentile in Riall's history of the histories of the Risorgimento? What has happened to that book, *I profeti del Risorgimento italiano*, written, like Croce's and Gramsci's, 'against the background of liberal Italy's collapse,' and precisely as an 'attempt to re-evaluate the mythology of national unification'? How can the book against which Croce wrote his, and from which Gramsci took his cue, be omitted from consideration?

There is something enigmatic in this recurring suppression of Gentile, and to say that repression has to do with the unease felt for this peculiar philosopher both by post-fascist nationalism and by Italian marxism (Erbetta 1988), is to spell only half a truth. Certainly, Gentile's philosophy is, as we will see, unacceptable for nationalism: as much as it pretends to legitimate a notion of 'Italian national identity' as the continuation of a project begun with the Risorgimento, it also insists on the dialectical necessity to undermine it as a necessary failure. And it might also be true that Italian marxism has often tried to suppress, with Gentile, the disturbing origin of its own 'philosophy of praxis' – Gramsci's *volontarismo* – that is, the idea that the will of the 'people and people alone,' not Marx's 'material circumstances,' can change history (Golding 1988: 558).

Yet, while Italian marxism has come to terms with its uneasiness vis à vis the philosopher of praxis (Comune di Roma 1995), and while Italian nationalism has started to reclaim Gentile as its own,[1] his suppression remains unconditional in books, like Riall's, devoted to the Risorgimento. Interestingly enough, however, it cannot even be claimed that Gentile's ideas on the topic are, in any way, marginal or inconsequential. Besides Gramsci's own indebtedness to Gentile's notion of the Risorgimento as a 'failure' (which I will discuss later), what *Gentile* thought about the Risorgimento has informed, since the school reform he designed in 1922, the entire educational system of Italy. Moreover, the entries concerning the Risorgimento included in the popular *Enciclopedia Treccani*, which Gentile had directed since 1925, have since been a point of reference for Italian culture at large. His repression can thus signal neither a historical nor a theoretical defeat.

It is more as if there were, in Gentile's idea of the Risorgimento, a traumatic kernel that had to be positively eliminated. All this looks like – to get into the business of clinical assessment – a bad case of theoretical repression. My first thesis would then be that the debate concerning the Risorgimento has confined itself within a couple of prefabricated questions and approaches which take for granted assumptions about 'identity' which Gentile shows in fact as being highly problematic. The first of these approaches – the Crocean one – imagines the Risorgimento as a beautiful movement from division to unity, from regional separation to a 'synthetic' national identity. The nation would then be the locus in which all local and regional tensions are resolved into a perfected form of national 'identity.' The problem with this approach is that it fails to explain the persistence of regional tensions in post-unification Italy – from the vexed 'Southern Question' to the resurgence of regionalist feelings in northern Italy with the 'Leagues.'

The second approach to the Risorgimento, which takes its cue from Gramsci's notion of the 'failed' revolution, rejects, in Riall's words, 'the national explanation of unification, pointing instead to the persistence of regional and local identities/conflicts in Risorgimento Italy' (1996: 65). Yet, at the moment in which local histories postulate an irreducible kernel of regionalist resistances to unification, they come to the impossibility of explaining, simply, how the unification of Italy could ever have happened, and how the question of nationalism *did* mobilize both public opinion and intellectual theorization.

Far from being a story of the progressive overcoming of regionalism as it merges into national identity, or else the myth of the persistence of local identities, the Risorgimento is for Gentile a dialectical movement registering exactly the failure of all such attempts. The 'trauma' that the omission of Gentile in effect represses is then the idea that 'identity' is an attempt at symbolic integration doomed, in the last resort, to failure. Both the regionalist and the nationalist solutions are provisional moments in the dialectical, endless postponing of an Italian 'identity' as a fundamental impossibility. Region and nation remain the dialectical moments of this very failure – historical moments, in other words, in which 'identity' alienates itself into the concepts of either 'region' or 'nation.'

I profeti del Risorgimento italiano is a very particular book on the Risorgimento. A pertinent description of it remains, in fact, the one given by Croce: '[Gentile's work] is a disgusting mixture of history and politics offered to a government [Mussolini's] which God knows what will do with it' (Croce 1947 [1923]: 260–1). In truth, much more than an understanding of history was at stake in Gentile's version of the Risorgimento:

through it, nothing less than the fundamental non-Italianness of Fascism's political adversaries – first of all, Croce's liberal coterie – was claimed. Conversely, the book tried to picture Fascism as a moment of continuity with an alleged Italian origin of *italianità risorgimentale*. Gentile's book is then part of a more general strategy through which the Fascist Party was trying to invent its own origins in the Risorgimento, and to legitimate itself as a new Risorgimento of Italy after the losses of World War I. Garibaldi's motto 'Rome or death,' after all, had been the slogan of the fascist 'march to Rome' that brought Mussolini to power. The inauguration of the monument to Anita Garibaldi at the Janiculum Hill in 1932, the foundation of the fascist journal *Camicia Rossa* in 1925, and the publication of Garibaldi's complete edition in 1936 are other symbolic moments of this instrumental appropriation (Isnenghi 1996).

Gentile's book begins with a series of short chapters on Giuseppe Mazzini. The instrumental role of this 'father of the Nation' is immediately obvious here. Mazzini's authority is called upon to unmake the liberal idea that 'the individual is . . . the goal of society,' and that 'the State is . . . a minor evil, whose role is merely to prevent that one individual damages another' (Gentile 1944 [1923]: 48). Passing quickly, almost inadvertently, from citation to commentary, and from commentary to assertion, Gentile tells us that liberalism 'has generated the egoism of a class' (ibid.: 31), and that parliaments represent not national, but partisan interests. The assertion reflects the epochal crisis of the bourgeois state organized around the idea of parliamentary democracy – a crisis that World War I had opened in the whole of Europe. The failure of such a state to avoid an international conflict doomed, from its very outset, to end with no winners was seen by many as a sign of its general inadequacy to solve any conflict at all. Lenin, for one, had theorized the necessity to move from state war to civil war, with the objective of destroying a state so ineffectual at resolving the social tensions within (Lenin 1952 [1915]: 15 *et passim*).

Not altogether differently, for Gentile the crisis is fundamentally the breaking of the original and moral unity of the state into partisan or class interests. Parliaments, for Gentile as for Lenin, do lack the moral authority to recompose this crisis into an original totality. In fact, they *represent* the crisis – they are the very symbol of a unity shattered into parties. But whereas marxism-leninism thought inconceivable the overcoming of class conflict, which remained instead the very motor of history, Gentile envisions the possibility of an original, unbroken, total idea of the state. Dialectics, which marxism-leninism identifies as a conflict between material, historically real social forces, is thus 'reformed' by Gentile: it is now short-circuited *within* the state as a tension – a dialectic of the same – between the ideal state and its realization. If the historical liberal state is a broken vessel, the ideal state prophesied by the Risorgimento, and to be realized in the unity of the *fascio*, is a wholesome idea: 'the *patria* is always above the individual' (Gentile 1944 [1923]: 57), above the party, and above the class as well.

The fascist idea of the absolute state is thus advanced: such a state requires Mussolini's famous 'spirit of sacrifice' – the alienation of individual interests for the sake of the total state. Through the Risorgimento, moreover, Gentile implicitly legitimates Mussolini's dismissal of the Parliament in 1923, the outlawing of all political parties except the Fascist, and the coincidence of the latter with the state on the one hand and with the figure of the Duce, the Leader, on the other. These historical decisions, Gentile maintains, are but a continuation of the project of the Risorgimento:

> After [World War I], the torch [of Italy] was almost dead. But it did not die, because the warrior spirit was kindled and survived in Mussolini . . . The same spiritual conception of the world [as in the Risorgimento]; the same opposition to individualism; the same concept of state and nation . . . the same postulate of a totalitarian understanding of human life . . . [came back with Fascism] (Gentile 1944 [1923]: 151–2).

The fascist notion of 'absolute state' thus finds a legitimating origin in the founding event of the nation – the Risorgimento. The problem remains at this point to understand what the Risorgimento is for Gentile.

Is the Risorgimento a historical fact *prophesied* by Gioberti or Mazzini, and which later happened between 1848 and 1870 with the unification of Italy? Or is the unification itself the prophecy of an event – a Risorgimento, a resurrection of Italy – which is yet to come? As Gentile states in his introduction, the Risorgimento, as a matter of fact, has not happened yet – or, at least, 'has not been totally accomplished on 20 September 1870, with Vittorio Emanuele.' A Risorgimento of Italy remains then an unrealized augury. Paradoxically, what history calls 'the Risorgimento' is for Gentile a series of events almost meaningless in themselves – until, that is, we interpret them as the omen of a *future* resurrection. Interpretation, here, is a prophetic act.

The most immediate effect entailed by this notion of 'prophecy' is that Fascism starts now appearing not as the heir of the Risorgimento project, but as the historical force called upon to realize it for the first time. More subtly, however, Gentile is operating, through this very notion, a quite radical revision of the traditional histories of the Risorgimento. This revision took the Risorgimento to be a 'revolution' of sorts. Prophecies, after all, see the future as nothing other than the realization of an original omen. Oedipus' destiny is all in Tiresias' words, and his story is the unfolding of the prophecy toward a realization of it. Not altogether differently, the history of Italy is for Gentile not a national revolution, but a return to an original end. It is the making real of a 'faith in a concept of life, proper to [the prophets of the Risorgimento], and which is, and must be, ours as well' (Gentile 1944 [1923]: 129). The realization of a prophecy *is* a return to an origin. It is not a leaping out, or a negation of history aimed at establishing a new revolutionary reality.[2] The Risorgimento becomes a *re*-surrection, a return, to what once was said, and to what in an ethical sense always *had to* be.

Gentile's thesis of a conservative, reactionary Risorgimento, was in itself a revolutionary concept, which Gentile defended as follows:

> no one can deny that around 1820, in Italy, there is a general movement of reaction which, if one looks at it from a certain perspective, seems to suffocate many of the fecund ideas which the French had brought to us. However, it is undeniable that, within this movement, a new civic sentiment is born . . . which leads to the assertion of national conscience and will (1985: 5).

This identification of the 'original' essence of Italian nationalism with a conservative, even reactionary logic of restoration, can be read historically as an attempt to reinvent Fascism as the party of law and order after the revolutionary *coup* of 1922. The period that goes from 1919 to 1922, Gentile once wrote, is characterized by the revolutionary phase of Fascism: 'In order to realize a superior regime, [Fascism] transgresses the laws of the regime that it wants to overthrow.' But, 'after 2 October 1922, Fascism no longer confronts a state to overthrow. Fascism is, itself, the state' (Gentile 1934: 34). While the irregular fascist militia is then 'regularized' by entering the new state's army, Gentile prepares, in his writings on the Risorgimento, the analogous theoretical move from revolution to conservation.

Gentile, however, is quick to translate this political change of direction of Fascism into some sort of epochal event. Revolution, he claims, ought to be followed by a moment of restoration, just as destruction has to be followed by edification: 'the liberation of a people is not simply a work of destruction; on the contrary, it is, mainly, a work of edification [*edificazione*] . . . This cannot be achieved if not by a doctrine which . . . lets us feel universal brotherhood' (1944 [1923]: 75). The metaphor of 'edification' implies, on the one hand, a catechizing return to that 'sort of Christianity' (ibid.: 71) which Gentile saw as animating the spirit of the Risorgimento. It also implies, however, a dialectical synthesis, a *superamento* of the very principles of the French Revolution: not only does the idea of state prophesied by the Risorgimento 'let us feel universal brotherhood'; it also 'contains within itself the principles of freedom and equality' (ibid.: 37).

If Mazzini could lament that 'The French Revolution weighs on us,' Gentile's philosophy prepares now the *Aufhebung*, the *superamento* of that age which the French Revolution symbolized:

> Now, that age is over. . . . Today we should aim at a higher goal; no longer the individual, but the association, humankind; the people in its moral and religious value. . . . Politics is no longer enough (Gentile 1944 [1923]: 141–2).

The *Aufhebung* of one age into another coincides therefore with a moment in which politics itself is transcended by a higher, spiritual and ideal impulse. 'Politics – said Mazzini – affirms men as they are: it defines their tendency, and attunes their actions. Only religious thought can transform tendencies and actions' (Gentile 1944 [1923]: 35). From now on, prophecies, not ideologies, will be able to transform men and their actions.[3]

Prophecy, as the restoration of an origin, thus inaugurates for Gentile the end of an epoch begun with the French Revolution (Del Noce 1978; Gramsci 1948: 241–2). As revolution makes room for restoration, the 'ideas which the French had brought on us' lose their hold, and are replaced by Italian ones, centered on the 'assertion of national consciousness and will' (Gentile 1985: 15). The 'moral and civil primacy of Italy,' which Gioberti had seen emanating from the Catholic Church (Gentile 1944 [1923]: 86), is plainly reaffirmed. The Risorgimento, however, is no longer the mere creation of the Italian nation; it is, rather, the assertion – a prophecy – of an Italian *concept* of national identity which is

> neither the elective principle of the French, nor the natural or racial one of the Germans. Nationality converges . . . with the general idea of life, of man, or, better, of the spirit . . . (Gentile 1944 [1923]: 30).

Once both French contractualism and German racism cease legitimating nations, what is left of the state is an ethical imperative. In this sense, as

Gentile puts it, 'this nation is a duty' (1944 [1923]: 21): it is the moral will of a people to make a prophecy real (Natoli 1989: 78). Auguries, like 'ideas, precede facts and make them' (Gentile 1944 [1923]: 41). 'So that, Ladies and Gentlemen, what else can faith in the future be . . . if not the will to create such future?' (Gentile 1934: 90).

In the Italian prophecy, the social antagonism exasperated by revolutionary politics is subsumed by an idea of total, wholesome unity. What Gentile calls 'nation' is, exactly, such an ideal of total unity – the synthesis, as Gentile quotes from Gioberti, of

'. . . stability and motion, conservation and progress, unity and variety, authority and liberality, centralism and diffusion, property and community, capital and labor, proletariat and bourgeoisie, city and family, town and country, nationalism and cosmopolitanism, concentric and eccentric action, private law and public law, and so on.' All the principles, in other words, which clash in the political struggle (1944 [1923]: 102).

In the *Italia una e indivisibile* of the prophets, in the augury of an Italian nation 'morally one' (Gentile 1944 [1923]: 90), Gentile seems to detect the omen of an original, mystical oneness to be regained. The proletariat in tatters which peopled the streets of revolutionary Europe will then make room for a new, sublime humankind: 'not the debased people of the present, but a different sort of people, the sublime one of the future [*quello sublime dell'avvenire*]; the people that will be, but that is not a reality' (ibid.: 51). Unity, not the dictatorship of the proletariat, will be the final synthesis of European history, and the Epiphany, in short, of a *futura umanità*.

'A new era has begun' (ibid.: 171). But it is an era which, simply, needs still to be realized in the future. As Hegel had seen 'the absolute end of history' (Hegel 1975: 197) approaching while the ideals of the French Revolution were getting older, Gentile's prophecy of a *future* Risorgimento indicated a new direction for a new history to begin. Now, at least, there *is* a future. While Hegel had remarked that 'world history travels from east to west' (ibid.: 197) and that Germany (the north) was the end of all, Gentile thus opposed Italy (the south) to the northern *Abendlanden* as the beginning of a new world-history. 'Italians, having begun a new history [with the Risorgimento], begin a new history not only for themselves, but for the whole world' (Gentile 1992b: 73). While the fear of a *finis Europae* and of a decline of the west haunted entire nations already fatigued by an ominous war and corrupted by an inept political class (Papa 1993), Gentile was thus proposing nothing less than a Risorgimento of *history*. The decline, the *Untergang*, the *tramonto* had been just a prelude to a new sunrise, to an immanent Risorgimento which the unification of Italy had begun, and which Fascism would have to bring to its zenith (Calabrese-Conte 1995).

Yet, are we sure that, for Gentile, the absolute state of Fascism could ever accomplish and realize this prophecy of oneness? Are we sure, to put it differently, that *nationalism* could? In Gentile's displacement of world history from a decadent north to a rising south, much more than a shift from the French age of revolution to a new 'moral and civil primacy of Italy' (Gentile 1944 [1923]: 86) is at stake. The movement south is a movement away, in fact, from that 'maturity' of world history that Hegel saw embodied in the ultimate synthesis – the *stasis* – of the state made absolute. A movement south, in other words, is the unmaking of an idea of nation grounded on the state, and a return, in Hegel's words, to a 'liquid,' local and provincial south. Parted at its center by the sea, Hegel had seen this south as something which 'does not have a clearly defined nucleus of its own, but is oriented outwards, looking towards the Mediter-ranean.' Without a center, Hegel's south, we remember, 'encourages individual autonomy' (Hegel 1975: 195–6). And it is to the 'individual autonomies' of the south that Gentile's prophecy, in fact, returns.

That is why Gentile, as Minister of Education, will realize the ideal unity of the Italian nation as a pervasive form of localism. Unity, after all, is the dialectic synthesis of differences. Or, to put it differently, national unity is an ideal than can only be made real as a coexistence of regional and local sentiments of unity, tradition and belonging. The new, idealist school imagined by Gentile for the instruction of Italy has, for this very reason, to 'renew, reinforce and promote the beautiful local traditions [*le belle tradizioni locali*] . . . in order to free Italians from foreign teachings' (Gentile 1992b: 77). What is national and 'Italian' only exists as a specificity rooted in the local. As Gentile laments the corruption of Italy by 'all dominant ideas coming from beyond the Alps' (Gentile 1992c: 104–5), he seeks to recuperate 'the good local tradition [*la buona tradizione paesana*],' and to replace a 'generic Italianness [*generica italianità*]' with a 'particular Italianness [*italianità particolare*]' (ibid.: 194). This new form of Italianness is 'implanted, so to speak, in the language and folklore of the land to which it belongs, in the region [*regione*] in which language and folklore have the first appearance of a determinate configuration; [it has to spring] from the regional dialect and culture . . . (Gentile 1992b: 345). The possibility of a Risorgimento coincides then with the quest for the 'sources' of *italianità*, for a 'particular' italianness 'isolated [*isolata*] and opposed to a general Italian spirit [*generale spirito italiano*]' (Gentile 1992d: 28).

Can it be mere chance that Gentile, while working on the idea of a redeeming Italian Risorgimento, starts also to write that 'curious regionalist book' (Del Noce 1996: 13) published with the intriguing title of *Il tramonto della cultura siciliana* – 'The Twilight of Sicilian Regionalism'? Or is not Sicily – provincial and isolated Sicily – the very emblem, for Gentile, of an 'Italy which did not suffer at a social level the impact of the French Revolution' (Gentile 1992d: 17)? Is not this Sicily, where Garibaldi's adventure, in fact, began, a model for the 'origin' (ibid.: 99) of an otherwise lost *italianità*, a 'primal island [*isola iniziatrice*]' (Gentile 1992a: 58) closer to the beginning? The most southern of the southern provinces, further from a north where 'stronger [is] the influence of French thought' (Gentile 1992d: 29), Sicily is not *an* island, but *the* Island, '*l'Isola*' as Gentile calls it with a capital 'I'. Capitalization, as Walter Benjamin puts it, 'is not only the aspiration to pomp,' but the very 'principle of the allegorical approach' (Benjamin 1977: 208). Sicily then becomes, allegorically, a geographical 'Island always sequestered . . . from the rest of the world' (Gentile 1992d: 5); and a symbolic one as well: 'it is not merely the geographical configuration . . . which sequesters the Island from the remaining Italy' (ibid.: 13), but an allegorical destiny makes it into a 'particular nation [*nazione particolare*]' (ibid.: 4–5) that will serve as an example to the entire nation.

The making of Italy is thus accompanied, throughout *Il tramonto della cultura siciliana*, with the cultivation of the 'tender affection of the mother island' thereby reconciled with the 'more vast horizon of the Italian nation' (ibid.: 26–7). The local is here the 'rightful originating motive [*motivo originario*],' the 'deep root' from which the sense of 'nationality' will, eventually, grow (ibid.: 85). The local, after all, was for Gentile nothing less than a microcosm containing in itself 'the problems of the other regions . . . the history of the nation, or, better, of the world' (ibid.: 108) – an ideal and 'particular' Italy whose example is 'to be incorporated and fused into the national unity' (ibid.: 103), just as his Sicily was to become the 'instrument and center of a new, superior and universal culture' (ibid.: 81).

Curiously enough, this moral example, as the title of *Il tramonto della cultura siciliana* implies, is now at its twilight. The 1917 preface of the *Tramonto* opens with an unmistakably elegiac tone: it mourns the death, between 19 March and 10 April 1916, of 'the triad of the most illustrious and representative writers of Sicilian culture in the nineteenth century': Salvatore Salomone-Marino, Gioacchino Di Marzo and, above all, the beloved and revered Giuseppe Pitrè. Especially the latter had been, for Gentile, the emblematic figure of a Sicily which 'yielded to local trends'

but 'always looked at the Italians beyond the Lighthouse [of Messina] . . .'
Gentile 1992d: 199–200). With his death, elevated to symbol, nothing
will remain of Sicilian culture on the face of the earth: Sicilian culture is
'a closed chapter . . . in the modern history of Italy.' From now on it 'will
be available only in the books of the dead.'

What has caused this twilight, this tramonto, this *Untergang* of a
particular, redeeming *italianità*? Augusto Del Noce, arguably *the* authority
on Gentile, has suggested that the causes of a Sicilian *tramonto* are in a
way the same in Sicily as elsewhere: 'materialism . . . naturalism,
scientism, *verismo* . . .' (Del Noce 1996: 163) have corrupted all cultures
alike. Yet, Gentile's own answer to the question is rather more explicit
than that: 'the rigid political and administrative unification' (Gentile
1992d: 21) of Italy begun with the Risorgimento – he claims – has initiated
'the dissolution of [Sicilian] regional culture . . . just after 1860' (ibid.:
28–9). The very same idea of a destructive national unification, in fact,
recurs in a speech of 1923, devoted to yet another twilight – that of the
local culture of the Abruzzi:

> After 1860, Italian patriotism depressed and almost erased the regional
> sentiment [*il sentimento regionale*]; but in the present reawakening of the Italian
> soul the need is felt to awaken all the sleepy local energies, stimulating the
> particular capabilities [*capacità particolari*] of the different provinces, to give
> the national soul, in the end, a concrete content consisting of all the memories
> and glories of the various regions (Gentile 1992d: 137).

In Gentile's dialectic prophecy, the only way for the sentiment of nation
and unity to exist is if it is transposed into a 'concrete' reality, rooted and
grounded in local soil. In a sense, there is no nation without regions: the
ideal – national unity – can become real only by negating, by alienating
itself into its opposite – into regional difference, that is. In this sense,
what the historians call 'Risorgimento,' having eradicated that 'concrete'
and 'originating motive,' is, in a Gramscian way, a 'failed restoration,' a
failure (Schechter 1990), a twilight. The Risorgimento, again, is a yet
unrealized prophecy.

Gentile's theory seems, no doubt, the fruit of some practical, even
opportunistic considerations: there could be no national feeling, in the
'liquid' reality of Italy, if not one rooted in a form of local sentiment.
Adopting on the one hand the flag of nationalism, Fascism yields to the
desires of the nationalistic, conservative bourgeoisie, and becomes the
defendant of national tradition. On the other hand, accommodating the
popular unease for national unification, Fascism subtracts the discomfort
of the masses from the control of socialism (Natoli 1989: 60).

Yet, there is more than *Realpolitik* at stake in Gentile's seeming paradox. What might look like an ambiguity, is instead the very kernel of Gentile's dialectic of nation. The nation has a 'concrete content' only insofar as it is the expression of a people. Yet, a people – which for Gentile does not coincide with a 'race' or with a social contract – only expresses itself in its own language, culture and rituals. Such modes of expression spring in turn from a physical space that is not, simply, the space of nation, but is instead the place which roots a local community. Now, the idea of a nation which confers unity to the indeterminacy of reality, and which bestows onto the people a sense of national *identity* is, exactly, just an idea – a prophecy. Any attempt at realizing it is doomed to failure. It will end up in a 'rigid unification.' The only way the idea of national identity can become real is as its opposite – as a form of contiguous regional identities. If 'our entire life is a continuous sacrifice, a continuous denying our particular being' (Gentile 1992b: 55–6), it is also a continuous realization of our national identity in a series of concrete, particular identities.

Neither nationalism nor localisms, in the end, exist if not through their continuous dying of one into the other. While regions supply their 'concrete content' to the nation, they set at the horizon of history; and while nationalism rises as a concrete entity, it dies into localism instead. Every *risorgimento* is a *tramonto*, every sunrise a sunset. In this dialectic, nationalism reasserts itself, *risorge*, through the several epiphanies of its opposite – by becoming, in fact, regional sentiment.

In our own times, as the fortunes of nationalism seem to have come to an end, and while the nation is repeatedly denounced as the invention of an 'imagined community' (Anderson 1983), Italian Studies, too, have been lured by the glitter of regionalism. While Croce's nationalist mythology has been relinquished, Gramsci's understanding of the Risorgimento as a 'failed revolution' has quickly been translated into the felicitous highlighting of 'local identities/conflicts in Risorgimento Italy' (Riall 1996: 65). Yet, in this attempt to unmake the national 'imagined communities' abhorred by this *fin de siècle*, and in the insistence on the 'concrete' historical experience of local *realities* alleged to exist, one can see, after all, nothing more than the realization of Gentile's disquieting prophecy.

In the new age of restoration prophesied by Gentile, the way in which the sentiment of nationalism survives, and resurrects itself time and again, coincides in fact with the possibility of transforming this very sentiment into its dialectical opposite. The Italian regions, as Gian Enrico Rusconi notices, revert to the same 'mythopoietic operations . . . that have forged the historical entities known as nation-states' (Rusconi 1993: 12). Confining itself within the false opposition between (Croce's) 'successful' national unification, and (Gramsci's) 'failed' unification of local realities, the discourse on the Risorgimento suppresses, with Gentile, the fact that such opposition is, in truth, only a dialectical *relation*. Disguised as love for the local and the particular, the blood and soil rhetoric of 'local histories' almost looks like the dissolution and unmaking of nationalism – but only if one does not see in it, vaguely but clearly visible, the *risorgere* of the same old nationalism that we thought had set at the horizon.

Notes

1. If nothing of scholarly interest has followed the 1994 declaration of Gianfranco Fini – that his nationalist and post-fascist Partito di Alleanza Nazionale would have considered Gentile as its own ideological reference point – one can register, at least, the formation of a few 'Circoli Gentile' (one, for instance, in the town of Castelnuovo di Porto) on the part of Italian nationalist youth. Frequent references to Gentile are also made in a curious, nostalgic internet page put together by nothing less than the surviving Repubblica Sociale Italiana (Italia-RSI 1998).
2. 'Because a revolution' – writes Gentile in 'La filosofia della prassi' – 'in fact, is a negation of history, it denies validity to all that history has consecrated as natural movement and development of the human society' (1991: 22).
3. It is according to this logic that we should read Gentile's understanding of the failure of the Neapolitan insurrection of 1799 because it had 'passively adopted' French revolutionary ideas. As politics fails in 1799, idealism will triumph with Mazzini in 1860 (Gentile 1927: 133).

References

Anderson, B. (1983), *Imagined Communities: Reflections on the Origin and Spread of Nationalism*, London: Verso.

Benjamin, W. (1977), *The Origin of German Tragic Drama*, trans. J. Osborne, London: Verso.

Calabrese-Conte, R. (1995), 'Recezione di Spengler in Italia,' in R. Calabrese-Conte and F. Jesi, eds, *Il tramonto dell'Occidente: Lineamenti di una morfologia della storia mondiale*, Parma: Guanda, pp. xxxi–xlii.

Canfora, L. (1985), *La sentenza: Concetto Marchesi e Giovanni Gentile*, Palermo: Sellerio.

Comune di Roma (1995), *Giovanni Gentile: La filosofia, la politica, l'organizzazione della cultura*, Venice: Marsilio.

Croce, B. (1947 [1921]), *Storia della storiografia italiana nel secolo XIX*, 3rd edn, Bari: Laterza.

—— (1928), *Storia d'Italia dal 1871 al 1915*, 3rd edn, Bari: Laterza.

Del Noce, A. (1978), *Il suicidio della rivoluzione*, Milan: Rusconi.

—— (1996), *Giovanni Gentile: Per una interpretazione filosofica della storia contemporanea*, Bologna: Il Mulino.

Erbetta, A. (1988), *L'eredità inquieta di Giovanni Gentile: Sentieri della pedagogia italiana*, Milan: Marzorati.

Gentile, G. (1944 [1923]), *I profeti del Risorgimento italiano*, 3rd edn, Florence: Sansoni.

—— (1927), *Vincenzo Cuoco: Studi e appunti*, Venice: La Nuova Italia.

—— (1934), *Origine e dottrina del fascismo*, Rome: Istituto nazionale fascista di cultura.

—— (1985), *Rosmini e Gioberti: Saggio storico sulla filosofia italiana del Risorgimento*, ed. H. Cavalletta, 3rd edn, Vol. 25 of *Opere complete,* 55 vols, Florence: Sansoni.

—— (1991), *Opere filosofiche*, ed. E. Garin, Milan: Garzanti.

—— (1992a), 'Il fascismo e la Sicilia,' ed. H. Cavalletta, 3rd edn, Vol. 45 of *Opere complete*, 55 vols, Florence: Le Lettere.

—— (1992b), *La riforma della scuola*, ed. H. Cavalletta, 3rd edn, Vol. 41 of *Opere complete,* 55 vols, Florence: Le Lettere.

—— (1992c), *Studi vichiani*, ed. H. Cavalletta. 3rd edn, Vol. 21 of *Opere complete*, 55 vols, Florence: Le Lettere.

—— (1992d), *Il tramonto della cultura siciliana*, ed. H. Cavalletta, 3rd edn, Vol. 30 of *Opere Complete,* 55 vols, Florence: Le Lettere.

Golding, S. (1988), 'The Concept of the Philosophy of Praxis in the *Quaderni* of Antonio Gramsci,' in C. Nelson and L. Grossberg-Nelson, eds, *Marxism and the Interpretation of Culture*, Urbana: University of Illinois Press, pp. 544–63.

Gramsci, A. (1948), *Il materialismo storico e la filosofia di Benedetto Croce*, Turin: Einaudi.

—— (1996 [1949]), *Il Risorgimento*, ed. V. Gerratana, 3rd edn, Rome: Editori Riuniti.

Hegel, G.W.F. (1975), *Lectures on the Philosophy of World History. Introduction: Reason in History*, trans. H.B. Nisbet, Cambridge: Cambridge University Press.

Isenghi, M. (1996), 'Garibaldi,' in M. Isenghi, ed., *I luoghi della memoria: Personaggi e date dell'Italia unita*, Bari: Laterza, pp. 25–45.

Italia-RSI, Associazione Storico-Culturale (1998), *Italia e orgoglio dell'italianità*, November 25, 1998, Web page, available: http://www.impnet.com/italia-rsi/orgoglio/orgoglio.htm. December 10.

Lenin, V.I. (1952 [1915]), *Socialism and War*, Moscow: Foreign Language Publications.

Natoli, S. (1989), *Giovanni Gentile filosofo europeo*, Turin: Bollati Boringhieri.

Papa, F. (1993), '"Finis Europae" e "Renovatio" del sapere occidentale,' in E. Sciacca, ed., *L'Europa e le sue regioni*, Palermo: Arnaldo Lombardi, pp. 121–36.

Riall, L. (1996), *The Italian Risorgimento: State, Society and National Unification*, London: Routledge.

Rusconi, G.E. (1993), *Se cessiamo di essere una nazione*, Bologna: Il Mulino.

Schechter, D. (1990), 'Gramsci, Gentile and the Theory of the Ethical State in Italy,' *Italian Quarterly* 31 (119–120): 43–56.

Sternhell, Z. (1984), *Nè destra nè sinistra: La nascita dell'ideologia fascista*, trans. G. Sommella and M. Tarchi, Naples: Akropolis.

8

Nostra patria: **Revisions of the Risorgimento in the Cinema, 1925–52**

David Forgacs

In 1948 the film critic Antonio Pietrangeli was running for parliament as a candidate for the Fronte Popolare Democratico, the joint platform on which the Socialist and Communist parties had agreed to stand in the general election of 18 April. He carried with him a print of Alessandro Blasetti's film *1860*, about Garibaldi's Sicilian campaign, to show at pre-election meetings. Pietrangeli claimed that the film, made in 1932–33 and originally released in March 1934, was a precursor of the neorealist cinema that had developed in Italy since 1945 and which had become broadly identified with anti-fascism.

This story is recounted by Gianfranco Gori in his book on Blasetti (1984: 39). Assuming it is true, it is of considerable interest because it means that a film about the Risorgimento, made under the Fascist regime, could be considered in 1948 not just ideologically non-fascist enough to be recycled but tendentially anti-fascist enough to be used for the left's political purposes and treated as of a piece with neorealism. Should we take this as evidence that there was ideological continuity, or common ground, between the two periods in their ways of representing the Risorgimento and the national past, or were the contexts thoroughly dissimilar and were different meanings being read into the film? This chapter tries to answer these questions.

Let us start by considering how Blasetti's film would probably have appeared to Italian audiences respectively in 1934 and in 1948. Such reconstructions are always necessarily conjectural, but they become more plausible if one takes care to reconstruct the ideological context of the two moments and pay attention to contemporary accounts. *1860*, which Blasetti co-scripted with Gino Mazzucchi and Emilio Cecchi (who also supervised production) from a text by Mazzucchi, is a Risorgimento story from below. It centers on the popular protests in Sicily which preceded and continued during Garibaldi's military expedition to the island, and its main characters are a peasant couple, Carmine (Carmineddu) and Gesuzza, played respectively by the non-professionals Giuseppe Gulino and Aida Bellia. It starts with a sequence in their village where a protest has just been brutally crushed by Swiss mercenaries hired by the Bourbon rulers. The dead and wounded lie on the ground. The priest Padre Costanzo (Gianfranco Giachetti), who has come from Palermo where he has been in contact with Rosolino Pilo, sends Carmineddu to Garibaldi in Genoa to give him information about the state of the Sicilian rising so that he will intervene. Carmineddu tearfully takes leave of Gesuzza and sets off. On his journey northward by calash and train he meets in successive caricatural vignettes the exponents of different political options: a Mazzinian, a Giobertian, a regional autonomist. In this way Carmineddu functions in the narrative as a sounding-board for the opinions of the educated. He is, like Walter Scott's central characters in Belinsky's description (cited by Lukács 1969 [1962]: 35), a 'hub' round whom the action and the opinions of others revolve, and a channel through whom information about the politics of the period is conveyed to the audience. At the same time the audience can see that in his passivity and silence he is morally above the bourgeois characters: they talk politics while he and his compatriots must fight for their lives. At Genoa he gives the news to Colonel Carini but he discovers that Garibaldi has decided not to sail to Sicily. Demoralized, he spends the evening at the Sicilian Association. The Sicilians there hear the Piedmontese across the courtyard singing 'Fratelli d'Italia' and think they are making fun of them. They go to protest, only to discover that Garibaldi has in fact decided to sail. We then see the embarkation at Quarto (see figure 8.1), the beginnings of the Sicilian campaign (where Carmineddu is reunited with his beloved Gesuzza, who during his absence had been captured by the Swiss soldiers and reprieved by a hair's breadth from a firing squad), and the battle of Calatafimi, on which the story ends. A peasant runs down a hillside shouting 'Garibaldi ha detto che abbiamo fatto l'Italia!' (Garibaldi said that we have made Italy!).

On its first release the film had a modern-day coda attached at this point. It consisted of two shots showing elderly veterans of the 1860 campaign saluting and saluted by parading Fascists in Rome. This sequence was cut from the film after World War II: when it was re-released theatrically in 1951 (and presumably also in the print shown by Pietrangeli in 1948) it ended with the central couple reunited followed by a montage of shots of victory and celebration: a bell is rung, a flag is waved, a bugle is blown and the title 'Fine' (The End) appears over a portrait of Garibaldi. This version has been the one subsequently shown on Italian television

Figure 8.1 Still photograph from *1860* (director, Alessandro Blasetti, Italy, 1934)
The Risorgimento as popular epic: the Thousand set sail from Quarto in 1860
Courtesy of Cineteca Nazionale, Rome

and released on home video. Elaine Mancini, who interviewed Blasetti
in 1979, claimed that the coda with the Blackshirts was added at the
insistence of Luigi Freddi, who in 1934 had assumed the newly-created
post of Direttore Generale per la Cinematografia (Mancini 1985: 112).
However it is not clear what the source of this claim is. Blasetti himself
had told Francesco Savio in 1974 that the coda was added in response to
criticisms (from fascist *gerarchi*, one assumes) that he had not alluded to
'the continuation of the *garibaldini* tradition among fascist youth' and
that he himself added it 'without any difficulty or any shame. I admit this
because I was a convinced fascist and I really believed it was right to
point to the new generation as continuing the tradition of the *garibaldini*'
(senza alcuno sforzo e senza alcuna vergogna. Lo dichiaro perché ero
convintamente fascista e credevo che effettivamente fosse giusto che la
generazione attuale fosse indicata come la prosecuzione della tradizione
garibaldina [Savio 1979: 1.128]). The two accounts are not necessarily
mutually incompatible, but Mancini's version of events seems implausible
given that Freddi's declared strategy in 1934 for rebuilding the Italian
film industry was not for the state to produce propaganda films, which

he considered crude, but to help private producers make quality commercial films which were aligned with the moral and political ethos of the regime (see Freddi 1949: 1.71, 156–7, 285–90). Indeed, Freddi disliked and nearly refused distribution to Blasetti's overtly propagandistic film about fascist squadrismo, *Vecchia guardia*, also released in 1934. As for Pierre Sorlin's remark, alluding to the addition of the coda, that 'The film-makers of *1860*, who were not fascist, tried to play their part in reconciling Fascism and the Risorgimento' (1980: 123), this is plain misleading. It suggests that Blasetti, Cecchi and Mazzucchi did not support the regime and the ending was a sort of reluctant and extraneous compromise. Yet one of the essential points about the film industry in Italy under Fascism is that it typically involved these kinds of more or less consensual alignment and mutual adjustment between private production companies, like Cecchi's Cines, state agencies like the Direzione Generale and Fascist Party activists, in which commercial calculations, artistic aspirations and political demands were juggled with one another.

In fact, even without its coda *1860*, which contemporary critics generally liked but which did poor box office, was easily readable in 1934 as a fascist film. Together with the other major Risorgimento film of the same period, *Villafranca* (Giovacchino Forzano, 1933) – about the events surrounding the 1859 armistice between France and Austria that temporarily thwarted the ambitions of the Risorgimento leaders to create a larger united Italy, and that, in the fascist context, suggested a parallel with the 'mutilated victory' of the Treaty of Versailles – Blasetti's film fitted into a precise strategy of reappropriation of the Risorgimento by the regime and by fascist intellectuals that was getting under way in the early 1930s. This was the result of the convergence of two sets of events. First there was a series of official state commemorations of Garibaldi, the fiftieth anniversary of whose death on 2 June 1882 happened to fall in the same year as the tenth anniversary of the March on Rome, the *Decennale*. In March 1932 Mussolini exhorted the editors of the national edition of Garibaldi's writings to have the first volume ready in time for the half-centenary, telling them that 'Garibaldi with his magnificent actions has always been closer than anyone else to the people, who feel deeply everything which emanates from him, choose him above all others and will always be enthralled by his spell' (Garibaldi è sempre stato più vicino di ogni altro al popolo nelle sue azioni meravigliose; tutto ciò che emana da lui non può che essere profondamente sentito dal popolo che lo predilige e sempre ne subirà il fascino profondo [1958a: 81]). On 4 June he inaugurated in the presence of the King and Queen a statue of Anita Garibaldi on the Janiculum Hill near the equestrian statue of her husband. In the ceremony, in which he made only the briefest of references to Anita, he hailed Garibaldi as 'a national Hero born of the people' (Eroe nazionale nato dal popolo) and drew a clear line of descent of the fascist revolution from his campaigns of the 1860s:[1]

> The Italians of the twentieth century resumed, between 1914 and 1918, under Your Majesty's command, the march which Garibaldi broke off at Bezzecca in 1866 with his laconic and dramatic 'I obey' and they have continued it to the Brenner, Trieste, Fiume, Zara, the peak of the Nevoso, the opposite shore of the Adriatic.
>
> The Blackshirts who knew how to fight and die during the years of humiliation, also stand politically in a line of descent from the Redshirts and their leader. All his life his heart was enflamed by one passion: 'the unity and independence of the fatherland.' He never let himself be deflected in difficult times from this supreme aim by men, sects, parties, ideologies and speeches in public gatherings, which he despised, ardent proponent as he was of 'totally unlimited' dictatorships.
>
> The true, sovereign greatness of Garibaldi lies in this character of his as a national Hero born of the people who always remained with the people, in peace and in war . . .
>
> If by a miracle the bronze horseman who rears up near this spot were to come alive and open his eyes I should like to think that he would recognize the descendants of his Redshirts in the soldiers of Vittorio Veneto and the Blackshirts who for ten years have continued, in an even more popular and productive manner, his volunteer spirit and that he would be happy to rest his gaze on this vast, luminous and pacified city of Rome which he loved with infinite love and from his first youth identified with Italy! (Mussolini 1958b: 109–11)

Secondly, there was in this same period a reaction by fascist intellectuals against liberal accounts of recent Italian history. The central texts here were Croce's two histories, the *Storia d'Italia dal 1871 al 1915* (1928) and the *Storia d'Europa nel secolo XIX* (1932), both of which proposed a continuity of liberal ideals from the Risorgimento to World War I, and Adolfo Omodeo's *L'età del Risorgimento italiano* (1930) which inserted the Risorgimento into a line of development from the Enlightenment through the French Revolution, a line which the *Enciclopedia Italiana* article on the doctrine of Fascism, signed by Mussolini but generally attributed to Giovanni Gentile, would represent Fascism as having decisively broken (1932: 14.847–51). Croce's *Storia d'Europa* lamented the dictatorships and dictatorial tendencies that had emerged after 1917–18 and the replacement of liberty by 'libertarismo attivistico,' the libertarian cult of action.

Liberty, which before the war was a static belief or a practice barely supported by beliefs, has disappeared from people's minds even where it has not disappeared from institutions, and has been replaced by a libertarian cult of action which dreams above all of war, upheaval and destruction, breaks out in disorganized actions and lays conspicuous and sterile plans. (Croce 1932: 352)

Fascism in these accounts was a break in the development of liberty, while the Risorgimento was 'the crowning glory of the liberal-nationalist movements of the nineteenth century' (il capolavoro dei movimenti liberali-nazionali del secolo decimonono [Croce 1932: 226]). This view underlay Croce's well-known definition of Fascism as a deviation or 'parenthesis' in Italian history which would be succeeded by a restoration of liberty. In 1931 the fascist historian Gioacchino Volpe published a searing attack on the *Storia d'Italia* in the preface to the new edition of his *L'Italia in cammino* (originally published in 1927), which covered a period similar to that of Croce's book: from 1870 to the end of World War I. In taking issue with Croce's defence of the liberal governments of the period from unity to World War I, Volpe reasserted the idea of the decadence and corruption of liberal political institutions and the failures of democracy and the parliamentary system (a judgement which was shared after World War I by Fascists, left-wing Socialists and Communists). By breaking the line of continuity established by Croce between the Risorgimento and the liberal state he could remake the line of continuity between the Risorgimento ideal of Italy and the fascist ideal (Volpe 1931: ix–xxvii). This reappropriation of the Risorgimento by fascist historians was capped by the fascistization in 1933 of the *Rassegna Storica del Risorgimento*, the journal of the Società Nazionale per la Storia del Risorgimento Italiano. The fascist intellectual and quadrumvir Cesare Maria De Vecchi was put in charge of the Society and appointed editor of the journal. In the first issue under his control he reproduced Mussolini's letter of congratulations, which alluded to these recent historiographical debates: 'The history of the Risorgimento needed to be removed from an excessively academic and sometimes factious environment, brought into more direct contact with the Italian people and looked at afresh with fascist eyes' (Era necessario togliere da un ambito troppo strettamente professorale e talora fazioso, la storia del Risorgimento, per portarla a più diretto contatto del popolo italiano e riguardarla con occhio fascista. [Mussolini 1933]). De Vecchi's reply confirmed how important historiography, and not only that of the Risorgimento, had now become to the regime's construction of national memory for the new generations:

We want the study of the past to generate life, youth, the spring-like flowering which has given spiritual and material life to Fascism. If history is life's teacher then it must radiate an eternal perfume of spring, not the musty smell which antiquarians may like but which is not suited to today's youth, who must learn to live in the sunshine, as fascist custom prescribes. (De Vecchi 1933)

In a fascist context, then, *1860* is part of this tracing a descent from the expedition of the Thousand to the March on Rome. It also belongs to its particular historical moment in other ways. In the period of rapprochement with the Catholics after the crisis over Catholic Action (1931) it gives prominence to a priest who fights for the national cause and to a Giobertian who ends up joining the Thousand. In the period of fascist ruralism – the *bonifica* programs, the policy of 'andare verso il popolo,' the promotion of local festivals by the Opera Nazionale Dopolavoro, the Ente Radio Rurale – it centers its narrative on a Sicilian peasant community which finds its salvation in Garibaldi and annexation to Italy. At the same time it is a pre-sanctions, pre-Pact of Steel, pre-World War II film in that the oppressors can still speak German (evoking the hated Austrians of the Risorgimento and World War I) and the British can still be shown working for the unity of Italy by making a donation to Garibaldi.

If we now move to the second context of reception, that of 1948, it is not too hard to see why the film, shorn of its original propagandistic ending, could have been viewed as compatible not just with a generic sort of patriotism but with a particular progressive version of national history. One needs to remember that there had been a widespread reappropriation of Risorgimento names and slogans by the anti-fascist movement since the mid-1930s. The liberal socialists of Giustizia e Libertà had carried forward Piero Gobetti's analysis, first published in 1924, of the Risorgimento as an incomplete or unsuccessful revolution ('rivoluzione non riuscita'; Gobetti 1964: 29) and in 1942 they named the political organization they formed in alliance with other anti-fascist groups the Partito d'Azione, like Mazzini's party. One of the new party's founders, Luigi Salvatorelli, published in 1943 the first edition of his pro-Mazzinian *Pensiero e azione del Risorgimento*, which denounced Fascism as an 'Antirisorgimento' that had suppressed all liberties and free political institutions (1950 [1943]: 189). The Italian Communist volunteers in the Spanish Civil War had organized themselves in a Battaglione Garibaldi; one of their clandestine radio broadcasts into Italy from Spain had declared in March 1937: 'Mussolini's policies are dragging Garibaldi's Italy into the mud.'[2] The Communists in the Italian Resistance likewise named their units Brigate Garibaldi. In Rome the single issue of the Confederazione dei Lavoratori broadsheet *Il Lavoro Italiano*, whose editorial team consisted of a Communist (Mario Alicata), a Socialist (Olindo Vernocchi) and a Christian Democrat (Alberto Canaletti Gaudenti), appeared on the streets on 10 September 1943, as German troops began occupying parts of the city, with the headline 'Garibaldi returns' (Torna Garibaldi) and a picture of Garibaldi by Renato Guttuso. The article, by Alicata, began:

> Today Garibaldi returns on his horse to Italian soil. He gallops again through the streets of Rome; he is the true leader of the people, dressed in battle uniform, who at long last takes up and aims his rifle in defence of their rights. As in 1849 he calls on the people to help defend their city. This true rebirth of Garibaldian spirit, which does not just consist of words but becomes concrete in actions, is, we feel, the best prelude to the future because finally popular democracy is being defended now, and with determination, by the people. (Cited in Spriano 1975: 21)

After 1945 various reappraisals of nineteenth-century history from below began to circulate. *Il Politecnico*, which took its name from the nineteenth-century periodical of the Risorgimento democratic federalist Carlo Cattaneo, published articles on the Socialist Carlo Pisacane (27 October 1945) and on Cattaneo (2 March 1946) as well as extracts from Cattaneo's account of the 1848 Milan uprising (23 March 1946). The communist journal *Società* serialized extracts from Emilio Sereni's analysis of rural capitalism after 1860, subsequently published by Einaudi in 1947, which showed how the spread of private landholdings had proletarianized or partially proletarianized masses of peasants without bringing significant economic benefits. This was followed in 1949 by the publication in book form of Gramsci's prison writings on the Risorgimento, which saw in the failure by the radical bourgeoisie to form a 'Jacobin' alliance with the rural masses the long-term origins of the subsequent degeneration of the parliamentary system, economic crises and the rise of Fascism.

In this context Blasetti's film could be seen as expressing a politics of 'popular democracy' and the Popular Front, or rather, these meanings could be easily projected back onto it. In the first place, it centers on a peasant community rather than on great individuals, who remain in the background, and it celebrates alliances between social classes and political groups against the common oppressor: the old regime and the foreigners, represented by the French troops in the Papal States and in particular by the Swiss mercenaries, who interrogate Gesuzza, threaten to execute her, and speak German (evoking now not the Austrians of World War I but the occupying Germans of 1943-45). Secondly, in this period after the selective purging (*epurazione*) of former Fascists and the subsequent amnesty declared in June 1946 by Communist Party leader Togliatti in his capacity as Minister of Justice in De Gasperi's first coalition government, it suggests that the film's director was not considered one of those ex-fascists who were irredeemable. Rather, the fact that his film could be recycled as politically neutral or even anti-fascist in 1948 is one piece of evidence that Blasetti was by then well on the way to being rehabilitated and recycled as a postwar progressive. Indeed, Blasetti (who continued to make feature films up to 1969 and television films until the early 1980s) was very successful in presenting himself after the war – and was presented by various film critics – as one of the few directors of the regime who, despite his commitment to Fascism, at least up till 1936, had retained his artistic integrity, a true man of the cinema, whose best work had already in the 1930s laid the basis for neorealism and had been fundamentally humanist and anti-militarist. Third, it can be interpreted to mean that the way the expedition of the Thousand was appropriated by the anti-fascist movement shared some common ground with the way it was appropriated by Fascism.

Let us consider this last claim, which is the most controversial. If Blasetti's film could work in a Popular Front context as well as in a fascist context, then it means that its narrative could be appropriated either way, that there was not a fixed political meaning permanently inscribed in the text of the film but that its meanings shifted according to how different people read it at different times. However this is not the same as to say that the film had the same meaning for Blasetti and his audience in 1934 as it had for Pietrangeli and his audience in 1948 or that the fascist Risorgimento was the same as the anti-fascist Risorgimento. The film, to repeat, seems to have been made with clear fascist intentions and to have been part of a wider ideological project of deriving Fascism from the Risorgimento. In a Popular Front context, the same elements are present but they are combined with different extratextual elements which change their meaning and allow the Risorgimento to be linked to the Resistance. Padre Costanzo becomes the progressive Catholic who defends the oppressed in his community and fights with the partisans of Garibaldi; in this he is like Don Pietro in Rossellini's *Roma: Città aperta* (1945) or the heroic partisan priest in Aldo Vergano's *Il sole sorge ancora* (1946). The film stresses the alliance between city (Palermo, Genoa) and country, and the expedition of the Thousand and the battles of the Sicilian campaign are a great melting pot of different classes and political factions. In both cases, certain elements are left out of the narrative: the ambiguous political aims of Garibaldi, his oscillating relations with Mazzini and Cavour, his own suppression of peasant risings at Biancavilla and Bronte.

The situation is reminiscent of Borges's story of 1939, 'Pierre Menard, autor de el Quijote,' about the French scholar who produces, by dint of immersing himself deeply in Cervantes's text, exact equivalents of two chapters of *Don Quixote*. These are not copies, the narrator insists, but different originals. One layer of this complex parable is that an identical text can have different meanings depending on the historical moment in which it is read. Take the example of the sequence in *1860* where the Sicilians who are in Genoa are angered by the Piedmontese across the courtyard singing 'Fratelli d'Italia.' In this sequence there are two brief shots of a picture of Carlo Pisacane on the wall. In 1934 Pisacane is evoked as the martyr of the ill-fated Sapri expedition (1857), which had become mythologized as a sort of dress-rehearsal for the expedition of the Thousand and emblematic of the nationalist movement in the south more generally. In 1948, at the time of the peasant occupations of the land in the south, he could also signify the struggle for socialism and collective land ownership. The second reading was not impossible in 1934, but it was not officially thinkable.

Clearly, the fact that the film is calculatedly not a biopic, not a cult of the hero film but a film about the common people (there are only a handful of glimpses of Garibaldi, mainly in long shot) facilitated its passage from a fascist to an anti-fascist context. Only at a few points is the parallel between Garibaldi and Mussolini made explicit. One of these is when the Mazzinian autonomist and the Giobertian who had been seen earlier arguing over politics on the train in front of Carmineddu meet up again: both are waiting on the shore at Quarto having joined up with the Thousand. The Mazzinian, surprised to see the Giobertian says: 'don't you know Garibaldi's slogan is "L'Italia e Vittorio Emanuele"?' The Giobertian replies: 'do you remember when we were on the train we were so busy arguing that we allowed those Germans to take our seats? Believe me, the time for discussion is over. It's time to act. He has taught us that,' and he points off screen to Garibaldi (si ricorda che laggiù in treno, a furia di ragionare, ci siamo lasciati prendere il posto da quei tedeschi? Credi a me, è finito il tempo di discutere ed è venuto il tempo di fare. Ce l'ha insegnato lui). Blasetti himself drew attention to this aspect of the film's narrative in pre-release interviews with the press. In *La Stampa* of 23 May 1933 he drew a parallel between 1860 and 1920–22, between the 'political tower of Babel' of pre-unification Italy and the parliamentary talking shop of the Giolitti, Bonomi and Facta governments, between Garibaldi and Mussolini, the man who could channel the forces of isolated nuclei of patriots and rebels.

In a nutshell what the film aims to do is evoke the atmosphere of 1860, which in many ways was like that of 1920–22: words flying everywhere, a political tower of Babel, people not realizing that any chance of uniting the fatherland is about to be destroyed. Isolated groups of patriots and rebels, silent, determined, sworn to fight to the death, hold out because they put their faith in a Man who will channel their strength and will inexorably attract the strength of others when he lifts politics from the plane of discussion to that of action. (Cited in Gori 1984: 41)

In *Il Mattino* of 2 June 1934 he talked about such parallels in a historical film providing warnings and encouragements for the present, as well as knowledge or understanding which could reinforce popular consciousness:

A historical film can recall moments which are perfectly analogous with those we are living through, or, which refer so obviously to them as to make us abolish the intervening centuries. From these analogies and references can derive warnings, exhortations and understanding which may serve to reinforce the popular consciousness of today. (Cited in Gori 1984: 41).

At the same time, given the reappropriation of the figure of Garibaldi by the anti-fascist movement, and in particular by the Communists, it is not surprising that these same allusions to Mussolini and to Fascism's often-reiterated myth of its own origins (replacing talk with action, division with unity, and so forth) should have become invisible, or at least hard to notice, by 1948.

Let us now consider the implications of what we have discussed so far and put it into a stronger theoretical framework. *1860* is not an isolated case but is one of a number of films made in the fascist period, dealing not just with the Risorgimento, which were re-released after the war in second- and third-run theatrical distribution and later on television and were able to enjoy a new life as 'non-fascist' or 'post-fascist' films. Most of the personnel involved in the making of these films (directors, scriptwriters, actors, etc.) also recycled themselves, like Blasetti, by disavowing their past, retrospectively adjusting it or selectively forgetting it. In fact the material form of motion pictures – shots joined together on an editing table, prints which can be restruck, recut and redistributed in alternative versions – makes them particularly well suited both to physical alteration and to that feature of ideological discourse which Ernesto Laclau called 'articulation.' Laclau used this term in *Politics and Ideology in Marxist Theory* (1977), which touched in passing on Fascism but dealt mainly with kindred forms of 'authoritarian populism' in Latin America, such as Peronism. The terms 'articulation,' 'articulate' and 'article' come from the Latin *articulus*, 'joint,' a diminutive of *artus*, 'limb' – the cognate terms in Italian are *artiglio*, 'claw,' and *arto*, 'limb.' Laclau revived the original meaning of 'jointedness' (which survives in such uses as 'articulated truck') and overlaid it on the figurative and now dominant meaning of 'articulation' as 'verbal expression' and 'articulate' as 'able to make well-formed speeches.'[3]

Articulation, as Laclau used the term, is that process, central to ideological discourse, by which two or more terms, between which there is no intrinsic or necessary connection, become joined together to form utterances that come to seem natural and unquestionable, so as to constitute the very fabric of common sense. Sometimes these utterances take the form of mottos, slogans or hackneyed phrases: 'a fair day's wage for a fair day's work,' 'a woman's place is in the home,' 'man is naturally aggressive.' At other times they may be mere ad hoc juxtapositions. Laclau stressed how ideological conflict takes place over competing combinations of key words. Different camps unpack (or 'disarticulate') key words from existing utterances and recombine (or 'rearticulate') them to fashion new utterances. He traces the first theorization of articulation back to Plato's allegory of the cave in *The Republic*, where the prisoners believe that the voices they hear come from the shadows they see projected on the wall:

> Common sense discourse, *doxa*, is presented as a system of misleading articulations in which concepts do not appear linked by inherent logical relations, but are bound together simply by connotative or evocative links which custom and opinion have established between them. (Laclau 1977: 7)

In the case of the Risorgimento we have an example of changing articulations in the vicissitudes of the key words *nazione*, *popolo* and *patria*. From the mid-1930s to the fall of Fascism in 1943 these became increasingly articulated not just with each other but also with *impero*, *Regno*, *razza*, *stirpe*, *guerra*. In the civil war of 1943–45, they became disarticulated from the latter by the various anti-fascist forces and rearticulated with other terms – *libertà*, *liberazione*, *democrazia* – as well as being counterposed to a set of negative terms like *barbarie*, *invasore*, *oppressione*. All these terms had a nineteenth-century, Risorgimento ancestry. The changing articulation of the word 'popolo,' for example, is evident if we compare the two passages above, one by Mussolini (p. 285–6) and one by Alicata (p. 289), which both describe the equestrian figure of Garibaldi returning to present-day Rome. The first evokes an organic relationship between the 'popolo' and the 'Eroe nazionale' ('nato dal popolo e ... sempre rimasto col popolo') who despised political assemblies and advocated dictatorship. The second also has Garibaldi as leader of the people preferring action to words, but the people he leads are bearers of rights and they will defend popular democracy for themselves.

The individual shots, or sequences of shots, which make up a film on a patriotic theme can be seen as so many elements of an ideological discourse. The joining together of these shots constitutes what we might call the system of articulation internal to the film. A second level of articulation is between shots or sequences in a film and images or concepts external to it: here the number and type of possible combinations is more arbitrary. Several silent films with Risorgimento subjects made in the 1920s, including *Nostra patria* (Emilio Ghione, 1925), *Cavalcata ardente* (Carmine Gallone, 1926), *Garibaldi e i suoi tempi* (Silvio Laurenti Rosa, 1926) and *Anita* (Aldo De Benedetti, 1927), contain articulations between images that draw on a pre-established iconic tradition of paintings, popular prints and so forth. In silent film the system of articulation is different from that of sound film (and the fascist period was bisected by the transition from silent to sound in 1929–32) in that silent films had developed a particular set of codes and conventions of gestural acting and facial expression – including what the film theorist Béla Balázs called the 'microphysiognomy' of the close-up (1952) – which would largely disappear with the advent of the sound film, along with the 'leaders' or intertitles which introduced new episodes or filled in dialogue.

Garibaldi e i suoi tempi is, like *1860*, an example of a recycled film and, again, of the elasticity of Risorgimento ideology which allows it to be variably articulated. The only extant print I have been able to find in the archives is not the original as it appeared in 1926 but a sound-dubbed version, a 'riedizione sonorizzata e parlata,' which was probably done in the late 1940s or early 1950s. The film tells the parallel story of Mazzini's exile and Garibaldi's exploits from the 1830s to Garibaldi's death in 1882. It relies heavily on superimposed titles to indicate dates and places, and it also uses a strongly gestural style of acting which looks very odd in a dialogue-dubbed version. For example, in one sequence of shots a hand (presumably that of Napoleon III or Franz Josef) writes the word 'Villafranca'; Garibaldi, silhouetted against the sea, points his finger towards Sicily, and a *garibaldino* takes leave of his wife before setting sail. This last image also evokes, by external articulation, the many painted and printed images of the Thousand embarking at Quarto on 5 May 1860. In another example, near the end of the film, Garibaldi on his triumphant visit to London in 1864 goes to see Mazzini, who is dejected by Italy's incomplete unification. The two embrace. Then Garibaldi (implausibly dubbed) tells Mazzini that, inspired by the latter's vision, he will throw down his crutch (from the wound in the foot he got at the battle of Aspromonte, 1862) and will try again to march on Rome (an allusion to the failed attempt he was to make three years later, in 1867). This is followed by shots of the successful taking of Rome, by French troops, in 1870. The sequence of shots thus emphatically links Garibaldi's throwing away the crutch in London to the image of Italian troops breaching Porta Pia in 1870. One can see from the pixillated motion of the characters where intertitles have been cut out and the film stuck back together.

The articulation in both these cases is a form of metaphorical association between discrete shots, which forms them into meaningful sequences in which there is an escalation towards action: the hand noting down the armistice, the pointing finger, the departing volunteer; the embrace between Risorgimento leaders, the throwing down of the crutch, the breach of Porta Pia. The patriotic music adds a further element to the articulation: 'Fratelli d'Italia' has been dubbed onto this sound print, but the same or a similar tune would almost certainly have been played by musical accompanists to the silent print. At the same time, the addition of spoken dialogue modernizes the film, albeit in a rather awkward way, and allows it to circulate to a later audience. The interesting point here remains the fact that this Risorgimento narrative was felt to be sufficiently ecumenical to survive the transition from Fascism to the postwar era. What was continuous were words like 'patria' and 'popolo' and some of the visual images associated with them. What changed was not so much the 'intrinsic meaning' of these concepts and images (as if such a thing could exist) but the sense they acquired through articulation, their collocation with other concepts and images in a politically-charged discursive context.

A postwar Garibaldi film called *Camicie rosse* (subtitle: *Anita Garibaldi*), directed by Goffredo Alessandrini and Franco Rosi and released in 1952, may be used to illustrate the workings of external articulation, both with other Risorgimento images and with other film genres. It is about Garibaldi's withdrawal across the Apennines in 1849 after the defeat of the Roman Republic and his heroic but failed attempt to ignite revolution in the Veneto. It is also about Anita's courage during her terminal illness during this campaign: again the images of the dying Anita evoke the many popular prints on this subject. Here we are dealing not with a recycled film from the fascist period but with a recycled director. Alessandrini had made among other features *Luciano Serra pilota* (1938), a fascist action picture, co-scripted by Roberto Rossellini, about a pilot demobilized after World War I whose life loses meaning in peacetime. He cannot be the father he wants to be for his son and his marriage consequently breaks down. He goes to South America alone to work as a commercial pilot. The story climaxes in the Abyssinian war when Luciano, played by Amedeo Nazzari, rescues his son, whom he has not seen for many years and who is now a pilot too. Luciano dies in the attempt but his son survives knowing his father was a military hero and that he sacrificed himself for him. Mario Isnenghi among others has asked what this eminently fascist director was up to in making a Garibaldi film in 1952.[4] He suggests that the film was perhaps a coded reference to the retreat of Mussolini and his few loyal retainers in the Salò period, in other words an expression of nostalgia for Fascism (1994: 394), but this seems unlikely. A more plausible answer is that Alessandrini was seeking relegitimation, by taking on a story by the young writers Enzo Biagi, Renzo Renzi and Sandro Bolchi and by using material which had acquired anti-fascist associations. Not only were there the associations of Garibaldi, through the communist partisan formations, with the Resistance, of the Austrians with the Germans and the guerrilla skirmishes in the Apennines with the partisan war; Alessandrini also used other associations, from those of the cast – Anna Magnani as Anita and Raf Vallone as Garibaldi both evoked the neorealist films in which they had played between 1945 and 1950 (see figure 8.2) – to that of the western: the figures on horseback, the rolling wagons, the music, all link this film by external articulation with the pioneer ethos and the idea of courage in adversity.

Other allusions are present in the film, notably to the tradition of nineteenth-century prints and paintings depicting Anita as a fiery Brazilian beauty and woman warrior and to miscellaneous other heroic women, from Bradamante to Odabella, from Joan of Arc to Marianne, from Annie Oakley to Calamity Jane. A sequence where Anita urges the men, demoralized, to continue, is a familiar topos both of westerns and of war films, where a sheriff or commanding officer rallies those who, surrounded or outnumbered by the enemy, are about to give up or lose hope. The point about articulation here is that the images of Garibaldi, Anita and their followers on screen become linked by external articulation to a set of absent images and memories of recent historical events and popular cinematic genres – the Resistance, the cowboy picture, the combat picture – which give them a determinate meaning.

Stylistically and iconographically, Blasetti's *1860* was also a curious mishmash of codes. Various commentators have seen in it echoes of Risorgimento prints and paintings – notably those of the *macchiaiolo* Giovanni Fattori – in the design of the closing battle sequences, though

Figure 8.2 Still photograph from *Camicie rosse* (directors Goffredo Alessandrini and Franco Rosi, Italy/France, 1952)
The Risorgimento as melodrama. Giuseppe Garibaldi (Raf Vallone) comforts the dying Anita (Anna Magnani)
Courtesy of Cineteca Nazionale, Rome

Blasetti denied having imitated these paintings consciously, as well as parallels with the camera and lighting style of films by Pudovkin and Dovzhenko. At the same time there is an odd switching between the code of 'realism'[5] and various codes of artifice and stylization, notably in some of the caricatural depiction of the bourgeois characters, which evokes Eisensteinian 'typage.' These caricatural features are even more strongly in evidence in *Vecchia guardia*.

The mixture of codes may be illustrated by a sequence where Carmineddu, on his way to Genoa to take news to Garibaldi, lies slumped and parched on a small boat between Sicily and the mainland. In the next shot we see him, rescued, surrounded by French-speaking soldiers. After being told he can go, he asks an Italian-speaker where he is and the reply comes: 'Civitavecchia.' The shots which follow throw us back to the codes of silent cinema. The word 'Civitavecchia?' appears superimposed on the screen, followed by the word 'Italia?' These are clearly from Carmineddu's viewpoint: they are what he is asking himself. The camera at this point zooms in on a portrait of Napoleon III, over which we hear French spoken, then the film cuts to another picture, of Maria Sophia of Bavaria, with German spoken over. The cut has taken us back to Sicily and we see Carmineddu's wife Gesuzza being interrogated by Swiss mercenary troops. The meaning of this very visible articulation of shots is clear: Italy is in the hands of foreigners, who speak a babel of languages, while across the sea the husband and wife, separated, must each face a set of trials.

The fact that films like *1860* or *Garibaldi e i suoi tempi* could be recycled from the fascist period to the Republic seems to confirm what various writers on nationalism have suggested, namely that nationalism is a slippery notion of which a 'scientific definition' is impossible (Seton-Watson 1977: 5), that nations are contingent artefacts (Gellner 1983: 6–7) or imagined political communities (Anderson 1983: 15), that 'core nationalist doctrine' is generic and adaptable because it depends on large categories (fatherland, nation, people) which can mean different things to different people and whose membership is indeterminate and fluid.[6] Of course, harsh struggles have been fought over particular political inflections of this idea at key moments in history, and not least in the history of united Italy: the intervention crisis of 1915, the Resistance, the 1948 election campaign, and most recently the conflict over so-called 'post-fascism,' the attempted revisionist healing of the historic division between Fascism and anti-fascism, which came to a head with the entry of Alleanza Nazionale into Berlusconi's coalition government in 1994 and the commemoration of the fiftieth anniversary of the Liberation in 1995.

It is when these struggles are fought that the work of articulation comes in, and the conflicts are often settled by new forms of consensus around the core. However, this does not mean that after each struggle over articulation the core ideology remains the same. On the contrary, there are clearly important differences between the Mazzinian idea of *nazione*, *patria* and *popolo*, the Mussolinian idea and the Popular Front idea; or, to take a more particular example, between Gramsci's notion of the *nazionale-popolare* in the 1930s, that of the nineteenth-century liberals in Italy and Russia from whom he probably derived the term[7] and the bolshevik writings of the 1910s and 1920s through which he rethought it. However, if there were not also some common ground between these different articulations of ideas of the nation there would be no room for political negotiation, no possibility of winning people over and constructing alliances, no chance of reclaiming terms that had become tarnished with negative connotations by giving or restoring to them

positive meanings. Above all, it may be argued, the existence of ideological common ground has been essential for a sense of continuity of
collective identity in Italy, as elsewhere. The need to retrieve a good
national history from the ruins of a bad national history, to suppress shame
and the guilt of complicity or failed opposition and to recover collective
pride, has proved to be powerful at all times of systemic crisis. The
transition from Fascism to the Republic was without question the deepest
of these crises in united Italy's history.

Notes

1. For the *Decennale* and the inauguration speech, see Chapter Six in
   this volume.
2. From the script reproduced in Monteleone 1976: 369.
3. The original metaphor was that of a speech being made up out of
   parts joined together, one of which is called appropriately the 'article.'
4. Alessandrini had also made the diptych of anti-Soviet melodramas,
   Noi vivi and *Addio Kira*, in 1942, and was briefly suspended from
   filmmaking in 1945 by the *epurazione* commission.
5. The use of dialect in the dialogue, the shepherds' costumes, the many
   location shots, the use of tracking camera and long takes, all led to
   the film's being claimed, by Pietrangeli and others, as a precursor of
   neorealism; for a dissenting view see Aristarco 1996: 109.
6. See Smith 1971: 20–1, who calls nationalism 'sketchy and incomplete.'
7. On *narodnost'* and the Russian populists see Venturi 1952: 1.35; this
   derivation was first suggested by Romeo 1959: 25.

References

Anderson, B. (1983), *Imagined Communities: Reflections on the Origin
   and Spread of Nationalism*, London: Verso.
Aristarco, G. (1996), *Il cinema fascista: Il prima e il dopo*, Bari: Dedalo.
Balázs, B. (1952), *Theory of the Film (Character and Growth of a New
   Art)*, trans. E. Bone, London: Dobson.
Croce, B. (1928), *Storia d'Italia dal 1871 al 1915*, 3rd edn, Bari : Laterza
—— (1932), *Storia d'Europa nel secolo XIX*, Bari: Laterza.

De Vecchi di Val Cismon, C.M. (1933), 'La "Consegna,"' *Rassegna Storica del Risorgimento* 20 (1): unpaginated.

Freddi, L. (1949), *Il cinema*, 2 vols, Rome: L'Arnia.

Gellner, E. (1983), *Nations and Nationalism*, Oxford: Blackwell.

Gobetti, P. (1964), *La rivoluzione liberale: Saggio sulla lotta politica in Italia*, Turin: Einaudi.

Gori, G. (1984), *Alessandro Blasetti*, Florence: La Nuova Italia.

Gramsci, A. (1949), *Il Risorgimento*, Turin: Einaudi.

Isnenghi, M. (1994), *L'Italia in piazza: I luoghi della vita pubblica dal 1848 ai giorni nostri*, Milan: Mondadori.

Laclau, E. (1977), *Politics and Ideology in Marxist Theory: Capitalism – Fascism – Populism*, London: NLB.

Lukács, G. (1969 [1962]), *The Historical Novel*, trans. H. Mitchell and S. Mitchell, Harmondsworth: Penguin.

Mancini, E. (1985), *Struggles of the Italian Film Industry during Fascism, 1930–1935*, Ann Arbor: UMI Research Press.

Monteleone, F. (1976), *La radio italiana nel periodo fascista,* Venice: Marsilio.

Mussolini, B. (1932), 'Fascismo: Dottrina,' *Enciclopedia italiana,* Vol. 14, Milan: Istituto G. Treccani.

—— (1933), Letter to Cesare Maria De Vecchi di Val Cismon dated 12 May, *Rassegna Storica del Risorgimento* 20 (1): unpaginated.

—— (1958a), 'Per l'edizione nazionale degli scritti di Garibaldi' (speech reported in *Il Popolo d'Italia*, 10 March 1932), *Opera omnia,* Vol. 25, eds E. Susmel and D. Susmel, Florence: La Fenice, p. 81.

—— (1958b), 'Epopea garibaldina' (speech reported in *Il Popolo d'Italia*, 5 June 1932), *Opera omnia,* Vol. 25, eds E. Susmel and D. Susmel, Florence: La Fenice, pp. 108–11.

Romeo, R. (1959), *Risorgimento e capitalismo*, Bari: Laterza.

Salvatorelli, L. (1950 [1943]), *Pensiero e azione del Risorgimento*, 3rd edn, Turin: Einaudi.

Savio, F. (1979), *Cinecittà anni trenta*, 3 vols, Rome: Bulzoni.

Sereni, E. (1947), *Il capitalismo nelle campagne (1860–1900)*, Turin: Einaudi.

Seton-Watson, H. (1977), *Nations and States: An Enquiry into the Origins of Nations and the Politics of Nationalism*, London: Methuen.

Smith, A.D. (1971), *Theories of Nationalism,* London: Duckworth.

Sorlin, P. (1980), *The Film in History: Restaging the Past*, Oxford: Blackwell.

Spriano, P. (1975), *Storia del Partito Comunista Italiano,* Vol. 5, *La Resistenza: Togliatti e il partito nuovo*, Turin: Einaudi.

Venturi, F. (1952), *Il populismo russo*, 3 vols, Turin: Einaudi.

Volpe, G. (1931), *L'Italia in cammino: L'ultimo cinquantennio*, 2nd edn, Milan: Treves.

9

Visconti's *Senso*: The Risorgimento According to Gramsci or Historical Revisionism Meets Cinematic Innovation

Millicent Marcus

The release of Luchino Visconti's *Senso* in 1954 had a doubly powerful impact on the course of postwar Italian culture.[1] The film brought a critique of official Risorgimento history into the cultural mainstream, and pushed cinematic realism to a new phase of its evolution. *Senso*, in other words, marked the convergence of historiographic and cinematic change, reaffirming the medium's long-standing link with the development of Italian national identity. In fact, Italy's first feature film, *La presa di Roma* (1905), took as its subject matter the final campaign of the Risorgimento, establishing the connection between the birth of the medium and the birth of the nation, and setting a precedent for the way in which the postwar rebirth of a nation would coincide with the surge of cinematic activity known as neorealism. This cinema of austere means and unflinching social commentary, whose founders included Roberto Rossellini (*Open City*, 1945; *Paisà*, 1946; and *Germany Year Zero*, 1948); Vittorio De Sica (*Sciuscià*, 1946; *Bicycle Thief*, 1948; and *Umberto D*, 1951) and Luchino Visconti (*La terra trema*, 1948), did not constitute a school in any formal sense of the term. There was no manifesto, no fixed set of rules or ideological program which demanded rigorous adherence on the part of its followers. But neorealist filmmakers can be said to loosely subscribe to a common code of practice, including the casting of non-professional actors; a penchant for on-location shooting, the use of unobtrusive camera and editorial techniques, a respect for the time-space continuum of experience, a focus on ordinary lives, the use of regional dialect, an attention to contemporary social problems, an aversion to dramatic contrivances, an invitation to active spectatorship, and the refusal of narrative closure.[2] Cesare Zavattini, De Sica's prodigious screenwriter and the movement's self-appointed theorist, along with Luigi Chiarini, director of the Centro Sperimentale di Cinematografia, set themselves up as arbiters of ideological acceptability, and the battles for neorealist rigor were played out on the pages of the important film journals of the time. It was on these pages that the critical controversy surrounding *Senso* raged in 1954, and it is here that the relationship between Risorgimento revisionism and cinematic innovation will emerge.

Based on the nineteenth-century novella of the same title by Camillo Boito, *Senso* tells the story of Countess Livia Serpieri, whose allegiance to the cause of Italian nationalism gives way to a guilty passion for Lt. Franz Mahler, stationed in Venice during its Austrian occupation. An idler and a coward, Franz flees the battle front to seek refuge in Livia's country villa where he persuades his lady to help him obtain a medical discharge from the service. In order to bribe an army doctor into compliance, Livia gives Franz a sum of money originally destined for the Italian rebel forces. Released from military duty, Franz sets up housekeeping in Verona where he amuses himself with women and drink. When Livia pays her lover a surprise visit and finds him in the company of a beautiful young harlot, she reports him to the Austrian authorities who preside over his immediate execution.

In making *Senso*, Visconti presupposed his audience's acquaintance not only with the events of the Risorgimento, but also with the official interpretations of the historical episode from which the film strategically departs. What made *Senso* a cinematographic and political event in 1954 was Visconti's audacity in challenging the received wisdom on the Risorgimento and in offering his own, variant reading of this seminal chapter in modern Italian history. The film is a bold example of the kind of historiography proposed by Gramsci in his essay on the Risorgimento where he challenged the 'sentimental and political interferences' and the 'prejudices of every kind' (Gramsci 1949: 44)[3] which turn Risorgimento history into hagiography and myth. Admitting that all history is really 'current politics *in nuce*' (ibid.: 114) which uses the past to legitimize the policies of the contemporary wielders of power and wealth, Gramsci calls for a reinterpretation of the Risorgimento as the basis for the intellectual and moral reform of the modern Italian state (ibid.: xiii). Such a reinterpretation must avoid the hero worship of standard histories and must expose the Risorgimento as 'conquista regia e non movimento popolare' (royal conquest and not a popular movement). 'The famous Italian minority, by definition "heroic" . . . that led the unitarian movement, in reality was concerned more with economic interests than with ideal formulas, and it fought more to prevent the people from intervening in the struggle and making it a social one . . . than against the enemies of unification' (ibid.: 65).

Gramsci's refusal to honor the romanticized version of Italian unification held dear by the heirs of the Risorgimento moderates is equivalent, in its iconoclasm, to Charles Austin Beard's 1913 *Economic Interpretation of the Constitution*, which portrays America's founding fathers as more financially than idealistically motivated, more concerned with consolidating their own interests than with championing the rights and freedoms of all citizens. Though there was no movie dramatizing Beard's revisionist insights into American history, the movie that dramatized Gramsci's was met with some distaste by Italian officials who hastened to censor the most damning passages and succeeded in removing the film's true revolutionary sting (Lizzani 1979: 219–20; Bondanella 1990: 99; Liehm 1984: 150). The offending scene occurs toward the end of the film as Roberto Ussoni, a leader of the volunteer forces for the liberation of Italy, is turned down by the authorities of the royal army who want to preserve the Risorgimento as 'conquista regia' and counter any efforts to make it 'movimento popolare.' When Meucci, the spokesman for the royal army, rejects Ussoni's volunteer corps, he claims to do so for strictly technical military reasons: 'Wars are fought with a faithful, resolute, compact army . . . Experience has always shown that volunteers enlisted in the regular army are of scant help, if armed and dispersed in skirmishes.'[4] Ussoni's answer unmasks the political implications of this supposedly strategic ploy. 'Let's speak frankly, Captain. The order that you have transmitted to me reflects the repugnance of the entire army, beginning with General La Marmora, for the revolutionary forces. It's clear that they want to exclude these forces from the war' (Lisi 1975: 863–4).

Without this scene, Visconti's criticism of the Risorgimento is considerably weakened, though elements of it survive in the opportunism of Count Serpieri, Livia's husband, as he endorses first the Austrian imperial rulers' claims to power in Venice, and then the Italians', when it becomes clear that his compatriots will ultimately win out (Bondanella 1990: 99). The count makes a conciliatory offer to the patriots, explaining, 'I'm a Venetian born and bred, and you know perfectly well that all my interests and affections lie in this city. Now it's obvious that whichever way the war ends, Venice will certainly go to the Italian government . . . As you see, this is a very practical proposal and has nothing to do with passions or ideals or dreams that I do not share' (Visconti 1970: 139). Visconti levels his most virulent attack on the 'official' reading of the Risorgimento by making the Serpieris of Italy, with their *Realpolitik* approach to conserving power and wealth, prevail over the Ussonis with their selfless devotion to a nationalistic ideal (Nowell-Smith 1973: 90). Ussoni's impassioned sermon to Livia – 'We haven't any rights any more, Livia, only duties. We must forget ourselves, Livia. I'm not afraid of sounding rhetorical. Italy's at war. It's our war . . . our revolution' (Visconti 1970: 140) – is betrayed not only by her own guilty love for an Austrian soldier, which puts the self and its desires before all else, but also by Serpieri who will salute any flag and mouth any slogan in the interests of maintaining his class superiority.

In Serpieri's triumph, Visconti exemplifies Gramsci's thesis that the Risorgimento was indeed a 'passive revolution' wherein the power redounded to an already formed state, that of Piedmont, rather than to a new political group capable of radically revising the social contract. (Gramsci 1952: 106). The leaders of the old order simply became the leaders of the new, assimilating, through the process of 'transformism' (ibid.: 100), the revolutionary Partito d'Azione led by Garibaldi into the fabric of a constitutional monarchy, shaped by Cavour and governed by the Savoy dynasty. Visconti's findings in *Senso* well accord with Gramsci's own condemnation of the Risorgimento leaders who 'said that they would propose the creation of the modern state in Italy and they produced something bastard, they proposed to give rise to a diffuse and energetic ruling class and they did not succeed, [they proposed] to insert the people in the governmental picture and they did not succeed' (ibid.: 94).

But this by no means exhausts Visconti's Gramscian polemic against established interpretations of the Risorgimento. By making heroes out of the leaders of the Partito d'Azione, the standard histories divert popular attention from the collective actions and the subversive threat of this radical party, attributing its success to single, larger-than-life figures rather than to its ideological stance. Visconti, instead, resists any temptation to indulge in such Risorgimento hagiography by banishing Garibaldi and La Marmora to the edges of the story and concentrating on what Lukács calls 'maintaining' rather than 'world-historical' individuals (Lukács 1962: 43). Visconti's indirect reporting of Garibaldi's whereabouts and his various military successes through messengers allows him to subordinate epic action to personal reaction in a strategy which Lukács considers to be the very essence of the historical novel. What interests Visconti in *Senso* is not the Italian victories at Gaeta or Calatafimi, for example, but the irony of Livia's indifference to her country's military fate or her resentment of any combat that might endanger her beloved Franz. Perhaps most indicative of Visconti's revisionist strategy is his decision to make the Italian defeat at Custoza the military centerpiece of his film, rather than its victories at Gaeta or Calatafimi. It is as if a Hollywood filmmaker were to make a movie about the American Revolution, dwelling on the British victory at Brandywine as a way of challenging the standard histories of the USA's national birth. Visconti makes explicit his polemical reading of history in explaining the importance of Custoza to the original design of the film.

> It is towards the historical aspect that it was oriented first of all.
> I even wanted to call it Custoza after the name of a great Italian defeat. The battle therefore had originally a much greater importance. My idea was to draw a comprehensive portrait of Italian history against which the personal adventures of Countess Serpieri would stand out, though she was, basically, no more than the representative of a certain class. What interested me was to tell the story of a badly waged war fought by a single class and leading to disaster (Armes 1971: 109).

This passage is counter-factual in its implications, suggesting that Italy lost not only the battle of Custoza but also the entire war of independence. Indeed, for Visconti, the Risorgimento may have been a military victory, but it was a political defeat – the 'conquista regia' that precluded the 'movimento popolare' of the radicals' dreams. In *Senso*, Custoza bears a synecdochal relationship to the entire unification campaign, revealing in miniature the failures that Gramsci ascribed to the Risorgimento as a whole and to the newly emergent nation-state.

Not surprisingly, *Senso*'s interpretation of the Risorgimento generated considerable controversy. There were detractors not only in official circles, where the threat to the myth of Italian national identity called forth drastic defensive measures, but also among the marxists themselves who were made uncomfortable with implied parallelisms to the failures of the Resistance movement (Sitney 1995: 105–6), and whose reverence for Gramsci did not always override their monomaniacal devotion to neo-realism. What incited the controversy among film critics on the left was not Visconti's historical reading, but the fact that the film was a reading at all – that it stood several removes from its subject matter in a violation of neorealist imperatives to contemporary themes and unobtrusive style. Though *Senso* was obviously aesthetic worlds away from *Open City*, *Bicycle Thief* and even Visconti's own *La terra trema*, such was the intellectual authority of the neorealist precedent that politically progressive critics felt compelled to relate every artistically serious film to it. Thus, neorealism constitutes the absolute standard against which *Senso* is measured, and found wanting, by Luigi Chiarini and Cesare Zavattini, who fault Visconti for abandoning the contemporary subject matter and stylistic transparency of the postwar movement (Chiarini 1975: 882–8; Zavattini 1975: 888–92). When the film's primary defender on the left, Guido Aristarco, refutes such charges, he does not deny the relevance of the neorealist standard, as we might expect, but broadens and alters that standard to fit the aesthetic requirements of *Senso*. Hence he argues that Visconti's film represents an evolution of neorealism, not its negation, as Chiarini claimed, marking the passage to a full-fledged realism in the nineteenth-century literary sense of the term (Aristarco 1960: 19–22; 1975a: 861; 1975c: 895 ff). Aristarco's argument implies a criticism of neorealism as necessarily superficial, purely descriptive, and limited to documenting a static present, whereas realism involves a deeper analysis of the dynamic forces that shape the historical process. In opposing Zavattinian neorealism to Viscontian realism, Aristarco is simply renegotiating the tenuous truce reached by Italian thinkers of the nineteenth century between French naturalism, with its purely materialistic, scientific approach to phenomena, on the one hand, and the vestigial classicism of Italian culture, which holds to abstract, philosophically inflected notions of virtue and truth, on the other.[5]

The very elements that most distance Visconti's film from unmediated neorealist reportage – his withdrawal into history and his use of extra-cinematic conventions – are not only justified by Aristarco's broadened definition of realism, they are celebrated by it. An analytic mode which is to narrate rather than describe, probing beneath the surface rather than limiting itself to purely material phenomena, must have the depth, breadth, fullness of characterization, and polemic stance that is best exemplified in literature by the novel.[6] For Chiarini and Zavattini, however, the immediacy of neorealism becomes a moral imperative, so that any abandonment of contemporary subject matter or direct cinematic reportage amounts to an abdication of the filmmaker's ethical responsibility to raise the level of public consciousness and to motivate corrective social action. Chiarini deplores Visconti's intrusive style because it detracts from the film's moral impact, while Zavattini argues that only contemporary themes have the power to educate and politicize the film-going public. 'The most substantial merit of neorealism was precisely this,' wrote Zavattini, 'to propose only subjects which were near in time and space, and in order to develop these, it was indispensable to insert oneself even physically into the fabric of the country, increasing, in geometric progression, the exchange of reports of knowledge among Italians' (1975: 890).

It is, of course, Gramsci who offers the best counter-argument to Zavattini's criticism of Visconti's retreat into the past. If the moral and intellectual reform of modern Italy must be predicated on a reinterpretation of the Risorgimento as 'conquista regia e non movimento popolare' according to Gramsci, then the neorealists' reformatory mission can be inestimably advanced by such historical inquiries as Visconti's.[7] Lukács's studies of the historical novel further suggest how neorealist didacticism can be reconciled with forays into the past, when informed by what he calls the 'necessary anachronism' – that is, the characters' expression of 'feelings and thoughts about real historical relationships in a much clearer way than the actual men and women of the time could have done' (Lukács 1962: 63).

In Serpieri's affiliation with the leaders of the occupying forces, and in Livia's passion for one of its officers, Visconti supports Gramsci's challenge to the major premise of Italian historiography. All Risorgimento history, Gramsci argues, indeed all Italian history, is predicated on the myth that Italy has forever been a unified nation, and that foreign forces have simply suppressed the political manifestations of that unity (Gramsci 1952: 44). What Visconti's film suggests is that indigenous class influences have divided Italy all along, inviting foreign occupation and resisting, for economic reasons, reunification. Indeed, the Serpieris have far more in common with the Austrian aristocrats than with inferior classes of Italians. Livia's initial loyalties to the movement for Italian independence stem more from her attraction to her aristocratic cousin Ussoni than from any innate devotion to nationalistic ideals. When her patriotism succumbs to the superior force of romantic passion for Franz, she is merely reverting to type, enacting the imperatives to courtly love which are the natural prerogatives of her class. Indeed, the scenes of her courtship and seduction by Franz, which could be criticized for their preciosity and their indulgence in literary clichés, constitute an important index of the tastes that define the European social elite. The couple's odyssey through the nocturnal city is a virtual repository of courtly love motifs, which create the illusion of a self-sufficient poetic cosmos, obedient to its own laws and exempt from the forces of historical change.

Livia has just bid farewell to her cousin Ussoni who has been consigned to a year's exile when she tells us in a voice-over, 'I had a strange foreboding . . . of what his departure might mean . . . for me' (Visconti 1970: 120) as if his presence were necessary not only to sustain her patriotism, but also to keep her in touch with her best self. The terminal qualifier 'for me' suggests that the story is now leaving the objective, public realm of history and moving into the private world of sentiment and sensuality. Livia's nocturnal odyssey through the streets of Venice in the company of Franz becomes a metaphor for her moral errancy as under his aegis she abandons the virtuous path of chaste love and political commitment and becomes prey to her worst inclinations. Franz's strategy in seducing Livia away from Ussoni's cause is to transform all political issues into erotic ones and to empty his own military presence in Venice of its partisan implications. 'Don't you think it would have been much better if you had told me the other evening at the opera that Ussoni was your lover?' (ibid.: 121) Franz asks, attributing her anxiety for her cousin's safety to sexual motives alone. Though Livia resolves to maintain her honor and pride in the face of Franz's vulgarity, she capitulates by answering, 'There's one thing I'd like you to know. Roberto Ussoni is not my lover,' thus accepting the ground rules of his seductive game by deigning to refute him on his own terms. When they stumble upon the body of a murdered Austrian soldier, this too is emptied of its political significance when Franz offers a strictly erotic interpretation of the problems of the occupying forces. Though the dead man is a victim of the Italian resistance, Franz makes this politically charged murder an excuse for more sexual self-advertising. 'You can see that . . . it's not very pleasant to be part of an army of occupation. One has to live among people who hate one. And as for us younger men, far from home, all alone, we end up courting their wives and their daughters' (ibid.: 124). The corpse ceases to function as a historical sign and becomes instead a poetic one: a *memento mori* which bids the lovers to seize the occasion in the face of an uncertain tomorrow. When Franz quotes Heine's verses, 'Tis the Judgment Day / the dead rise to eternal joy, or to eternal pain. / We still embrace, heedless of all, both Paradise and Hell' (ibid.: 126), he is revealing the generic conflict between the courtly love story of Livia and Franz and the historical novel that provides the larger literary context of *Senso*. The Heine passage suggests the a-historicism of the courtly love code, which removes the couple from the realm of the ordinary and places it in a transcendent sphere of permanent, metaphysical desire. Yet the apocalyptic allusion in the Heine verses is not without historical force, for it reflects Franz's awareness that his class is doomed to extinction, that the Risorgimento will be an Armageddon for his kind.[8] 'In a few years Austria will be finished,' he tells Livia when she finds him drunk and debauched in Verona, 'and a whole world will disappear. The one you and I belong to' (Visconti 1970: 179).

The mediating position of Livia's maid Laura, who helps hide Franz, protects the secrecy of the couple's affair, and facilitates their meeting, is another index of the literary and class origins of this love. Laura descends from a long line of officious but efficient ladies' maids, from the Duenna in *The Romance of the Rose* to Juliet Capulet's Nurse, and she seems to have assimilated all the practical wisdom of her literary predecessors. Indeed, Laura is always several steps ahead of Livia, anticipating her mistress's needs and acting on her own initiatives to further the adulterous plot. When Livia finally realizes that Laura has discovered the affair, she naively fears for her own reputation. 'So what,' Franz reassures her. 'That's what ladies' maids are for' (Visconti 1970: 157), thus confirming the literary stereotype to which Laura so well conforms.

Another literary indicator is the allusion to Narcissus during the couple's nocturnal wanderings through the streets of Venice. When Franz perches on the edge of a well and admires his image in a mirror, this way of saying that he is vain and self-loving may strike us as overly artful until we realize that Visconti is forging yet more elaborate links between his characters and the courtly love tradition which is their class inheritance. Narcissus has provided the informing myth for much courtly love literature, be it the celebratory kind that finds in the lady's eye an idealizing mirror for the lover or the condemnatory kind that sees in such worldly desire man's love of himself in preference to his divine creator. It is significant that in adapting Boito's novella, Visconti has transferred the mirror fetish from Livia to Franz, thus giving it to the character who has the clearer consciousness of class destiny. Just as Narcissus came to self-knowledge by contemplating his image in the well, so the aristocracy came to know itself through this special kind of loving – secret, passionate, adulterous, accountable to no higher authority and to no other law – which became a kind of caste trademark, distinguishing it from inferior classes whose loving was ruled by religious, legal and practical restraints. Thus when Livia becomes an initiate of the cult of courtly love, she is merely claiming her literary birthright as a lady of the titled nobility.

Yet in the very enactment of the code that defines their class ideal, Livia and Franz fall short of it. The courtly lover must be a warrior as well as a suitor, spurred on to deeds of military prowess by the desire to please his lady. Since Franz, instead, uses Livia's love as a way of exempting himself from battle, and she complies, they are both guilty of violating their courtly imperatives: he to military proofs of his manhood, and she to inspiring them. Franz's desertion is not only emasculating, but socially degrading, banishing him from that class to which the practice of courtly love and his former military position had entitled him. 'Look, I'm not an officer any more. And not even an gentleman,' he rails at Livia. 'I'm a drunken deserter. What a stink' (Visconti 1970: 175).

Courtly love is not the only ideal which is subject to deterioration and inner collapse during the course of *Senso*. Indeed, the entire film may be seen as a study in the process of decline, as Visconti's strategy in adapting the Boito novella suggests. Most of the filmmaker's changes are made in the direction of 'mobilizing' a static portrait of a certain social class by linking its fortunes to the historical forces at work in mid-nineteenth-century Veneto and analyzing the reciprocal effects of historical, cultural and personal degeneration on this once splendid elite.[9] 'What is important, Calvino says of *Senso*, 'is the drama of decadence in times of revolution, the "cupio dissolvi" of a society, seen with the participation, together with the hatred, of one who knows it too well' (Calvino 1975: 879).[10] Boito's novella is an a-historical love story that simply happens to take place on the eve of the Venetian independence from Austrian rule and could have just as easily been set during any other era of foreign occupation (and there are many to choose from). The vexed political situation has no bearing on the affair and serves merely as a technical device for resolving the plot – Livia can denounce her lover as a deserter to Austrian authorities and thereby exact revenge for his infidelity. Visconti's story, on the other hand, lives up to Lukács's definition of the historical novel wherein the 'personal destinies of a number of human beings coincide and interweave within the determining context of an historical crisis' (Lukács 1962: 41).

A comparison of Boito's Livia with Visconti's reveals how the film-maker has transformed a static, a-historical character into a typical one, in Lukács's sense of the word, embodying the salient conflicts of her era and exemplifying the process by which the old order passes into the new. The Livia of Boito's novella is a vain and frivolous woman who remains unchanged by the historical storms breaking around her as well as by the death-dealing emotions of her own private life. History is more a source of annoyance to her than of partisan concern. 'Garibaldi, con le sue orde di demonii rossi, voleva scannare tutti quelli che gli sarebbero capitati in mano' (Garibaldi, with his hordes of red demons, wanted to slaughter all those who fell into his hands [Boito 1971 (1882): 397]) she writes in a text that is otherwise indifferent to the burning historical issues of the times. The story is told in the first person as Livia commits to her memoirs the account of her sordid affair with an Austrian soldier named Remigio Ruiz. This narrative is framed by her diary entries about a current flirtation with 'the little lawyer Gino' who is first rejected by Livia, then becomes engaged to a respectable woman of his own social class, before returning to the countess's embraces.

The framing situation reveals two things about Boito's Livia: that her treacherous affair with Remigio has not changed her at all; and that she merely uses it as a standard against which all subsequent suitors must be measured. When she looks back on her grand passion with nostalgia, it is Remigio's violence and vulgarity she misses most of all: 'Mi stringeva alla vita in modo da stritolarmi e mi mordeva le spalle facendomele sanguinare' (He squeezed my waist so as to crush me, and he bit my

shoulders, making them bleed. [Boito 1971 (1882): 390]). Such reminisc-
ence leads to inevitable comparisons between Remigio's virile seductions
and Gino's pale, anemic ones. By having her speak in the first person,
Boito allows Livia to damn herself. Not only is the brazen tone of her
confession a judgement on her moral deficiencies, but so too are the
misunderstood allusions and inappropriate responses with which the
journal abounds. When Livia compares herself to the Roman matrons of
Parini's 'Ode on Dressing for the Guillotine,' she mistakes the poet's
critical stance for an admiring one, inadvertently revealing what kind of
a target she herself is for authorial satire. In another witty misunder-
standing, Livia obeys the Socratic injunction to 'know thyself' by
assiduously studying her image in the mirror – an activity that qualifies
her for the title of 'filosofessa perfetta' (perfect philosopher-lady).

  Perhaps the most damning entry in her journal is the final one, in its
juxtaposition of inappropriate commentary and misunderstood event. A
witness to the execution of Remigio, she is momentarily dazzled by his
naked torso, stripped for the sharpshooters' fire. But when Remigio's
whore throws herself on his corpse, Livia regains her composure,
remembering the wound to her vanity that prompted this quest for revenge.
'Avevo la coscienza del mio diritto . . . tranquilla nell'orgoglio di un
difficile dovere compiuto' (I was aware of my rights . . . calm in the pride
of a difficult duty accomplished [Boito 1971 (1882): 422]). In this utterly
improper use of moral language, Boito conceals his own judgement of
Livia's character. Perhaps this vocabulary of duty and conscience was
suggested to her by the military honor code to which Livia had appealed
in her vindictiveness, or perhaps it bespeaks the 'all's fair in love and
war' philosophy to which she obviously subscribes. Nonetheless, Boito
makes Livia her own worst judge by putting moral language to the service
of a woman who prides herself on defying standard morality. The
Bohemian soldier who spits in her face as Livia leaves the execution site
constitutes a further authorial judgement on this murderess whose journal
leaps to the present to report, with characteristic levity and detachment,
that the new suitor Gino embraces her '[q]uasi con la vigoria del tenente
Remigio' (almost with the vigor of Lieutenant Remigio [ibid.: 422]).

  Though Visconti borrows Boito's first-person narrative technique, he
does so to entirely different effect. Where the novella's narrative mode
serves as a distancing device and as an internal judgement on its protagonist, Visconti uses Livia's voice-overs as a way of establishing
our shifting relationship to a character who undergoes a precipitous
negative change. At first, the voice-overs command our sympathies and
draw us into an identification with Livia, but gradually, as she descends

into self-degradation and treason, they function as a measure of how involved we once were with this character who is now so morally repellent. Unlike Boito's Livia, who is never admirable, and therefore cannot fall in our estimation, Visconti's begins on a moral pedestal so lofty that her decline occasions surprise as well as distaste. To maximize the dimensions of her fall, Visconti adds a political element to it, making Livia a traitor to the patriotic cause from which she embezzles funds to finance Franz's desertion, whereas Boito's Livia has no public trust to betray and no audience expectations to disappoint.

In establishing the heights from which Livia will eventually fall, the film begins with the suggestion of a love story far different from the one she ultimately enacts with Franz. From her box at La Fenice theater, Livia looks down into the orchestra and catches the eye of a handsome civilian who rewards her attentions by tossing up a bunch of tricolored flowers. When Livia lifts the bouquet to her lips, she gives the stamp of a possible love interest to this token of patriotic fervor from her cousin Roberto Ussoni. At the same time, another man exemplifies a radically different approach to the floral demonstration of patriotism which takes place between the acts of *Il trovatore*. 'How entertaining!' remarks Franz Mahler: 'This is the kind of war that suits the Italians: showers of confetti to the sound of mandolins' (Visconti 1970: 109). It is their differential response to the patriotic gesture that sets the plot in motion, precipitating Ussoni's challenge to Franz, Franz's consequent denunciation of Ussoni, and Livia's attempt to intercede on behalf of her cousin. The proposal of a duel (which Ussoni would fight but Franz would not) represents, in germinal form, the military future of the entire story: Franz will flee combat later on while Ussoni will seek out battle against all military-bureaucratic odds. Indeed, Ussoni's long and circuitous journey to the battle front parallels and reverses Franz's odyssey through the nocturnal city which wins him the very love that will save him from combat.

Were the film to develop the love interest of Livia and Ussoni, it would resemble the high melodrama of the Verdi opera that constitutes the background of the opening scene. Like his operatic exemplar Manrico, Ussoni promises to excel in battle and to pursue a selfless ideal. 'He seems to be the type who's born to sacrifice for some noble cause!' (Visconti 1970: 121) Franz says of Ussoni in acknowledging his rival's qualifications for Verdian heroic stature. Manrico's performance of 'Di quella pira' as Visconti's expository titles fade suggests the fixed hierarchy of values that governs the world of *Il trovatore* and that would presumably apply to the love story of Livia and Ussoni as well. Manrico's aria subordinates the claims of love (even those of a 'casto amore' or chaste love) to a higher ideal – that of filial piety – when he delays his marriage to Leonora so that he can defend his mother's life, or die with her, just as Ussoni tells Livia 'we must forget ourselves . . . Italy's at war. It's our war . . . our Revolution.' If we add the standard metaphor of maternal Italy with her citizenry of 'figli buoni' (good children [Gramsci 1952: 68]) into the equation, then the analogies between Manrico's and Ussoni's hierarchies of value become more obvious still. For the Italian audience of *Il trovatore* in *Senso*, this metaphor was alive enough to arouse patriotic choruses of 'all'armi' (to arms), in response to Manrico's own battle cry on stage.

Visconti sets up this operatic paradigm of high melodrama only to show how far short of this ideal his own story will fall. *Senso* may be considered a degraded melodrama in its violation of the moral laws that govern the Verdian world.[11] The heroics of the sort which typify *Il trovatore* are explicitly renounced by Franz who confesses, 'we like elegant uniforms because they make us look good . . . we're all eager as long as it's only a matter of toasting our future victories, but we don't feel up to paying the price for what those victories cost' (Visconti 1970: 151) – Franz is like the 'little boy playing soldier with a wooden sword' (ibid.: 149) of the dream he recounts to Livia when she gives him sanctuary at the Serpieri villa in Aldeno. Like a child, he enjoys the fancy trappings of military service but dreads its bloody realities. 'I'm not your romantic hero' (ibid.: 179), he finally tells Livia, echoing their first interview in the Serpieri box of La Fenice. 'I like it [opera] very much,' Livia had told him: 'I don't care for it offstage, though, or for people who act like melodramatic heroes' (ibid.: 116). What Franz insists in his final orgy of drunken lucidity in Verona is that Livia does care for opera off-stage and that she wants to be a Leonora to Franz's Manrico. During the episode in Aldeno when she resolves to give Franz the money destined for Ussoni's volunteer army, she enacts a twisted version of the melo-dramatic heroine's self-sacrifice. The heightened emotionalism of the lovers' encounter, and the lady's anguished choice between two opposing claims on her loyalties, give this scene a superficial likeness to melodrama while reversing the hierarchy of values implicit in the true melodramatic mode.

By introducing *Senso* with a spectacle within a spectacle, Visconti announces his interest in the relationship between staged melodrama and its offstage counterparts: 'I love melodrama because it is situated right on the border between life and the theater. I have tried to render this predilection of mine in the first sequences of the film *Senso*' (cited in Fink 1977: 88).[12] Not only in the opening scene, but throughout the film,

Senso inhabits that boundary line between life and theater,[13] which explains Visconti's preoccupation with uniforms and veils, and the questions of personal identity underlying the costumes and political labels that the protagonists wear. Is Livia the Leonora of her melodramatic fantasy, or is she simply the older woman clinging to the self-delusions that Franz exposes when he tears off the veil during their encounter in Verona?[14] Is Franz truly a soldier who degenerates into a drunken nonentity when deprived of his epaulettes, or is he a coward who never merited the prestige of his uniform in the first place?

Indeed, the Risorgimento itself becomes a melodramatic performance with heroes, villains and high-minded principles requiring a theatrical scenario of its own. It is no coincidence that the patriotic demonstration staged by Ussoni and his fellow activists takes place in La Fenice theater and is precipitated by Manrico's on-stage call to arms. Not only did Verdi's operas constitute the cultural vehicle for the country's burgeoning nationalistic sentiments, but its power to stir the democratic masses was analogous to the Risorgimento leaders' own propaganda campaign to capture the popular imagination. Thus La Fenice serves as the arena not only for a cultural performance, but also for a political one whose success is registered both by Ussoni who gloats, 'they're waking up, they're waking up!' (Visconti 1970: 112) and by Serpieri who fumes, 'we cannot allow the Venice Theater to become a stage for revolutionary demonstrations' (ibid.: 114).

But just as *Il trovatore* creates expectations and illusions about romantic love that the offstage affair of Livia and Franz cannot equal, so the Risorgimento myth propagated by the opera house demonstration falsifies the realities of the campaign for unification.[15] The messenger Luca's political fantasies are analogous to Livia's melodramatic ones, when he insists, 'we'll free our land ourselves without anybody's help' (Visconti 1970: 156) in a naive belief that the Risorgimento will indeed be 'movimento popolare' and not 'conquista regia.' Livia's degraded melodrama is thus the erotic counterpart of the degradation of the Risorgimento ideal as Gramsci exposed it.

For this reason, Visconti chose to make a movie about Livia and Franz rather than one about Livia and Ussoni. What Visconti argues is that Verdian melodrama is not possible in a fallen, post-Risorgimento world where myths of absolute good, absolute evil, self-sacrifice and heroism have given way to a reality of moral compromise and disillusionment. Franz's attraction for Livia proved the superior pull of class identity over the claims of nationalism – Livia would rather consort with another of her class and enjoy her literary-erotic birthright than burn with a chaste love for a man who would put her second to his political-moral vocation. It is the very survival of these class interests, as Livia embodies them, which subverted the Risorgimento ideal of 'movimento popolare' and assured its preservation as 'conquista regia,' free from the true revolutionary threat that participatory democracy would entail. Thus the primacy of the Livia-Franz plot over the Livia-Ussoni one constitutes a Gramscian criticism of the Risorgimento in melodramatic terms.

Visconti had originally envisioned a very different opening for his film. The first scene was to take place in a Veronese hospital where a madwoman would spill out her story of a 'sad and guilty love' (Visconti 1970: 147; see Doniol-Valcroze and Domarchi 1959: 2). Such a beginning would solve the problem of the narrative present from which Livia's voice-over derives – a problem that leaves the story as we have it disturbingly incomplete.[16] What happened between the final episode in Verona and the present, which motivates Livia to tell her desperate story? Has she resumed her former privileged status, like Boito's Livia, or has she undergone some irreversible change in identity and quality of life? The confessional genre to which Livia's first-person narrative belongs demands that we know the narrative present that determines and explains the speaker's perspective on the past. Without such information, Livia's voice seems to be suspended in some post-narrative limbo which tells us nothing about the personal and political consequences of her 'sad and guilty love,' nor how we are to judge her narrative perspective on it. To be sure, open-endedness is a legitimate structural ploy, as the neorealists argue, but it is to be regretted in a story whose generic affiliations with the confession require that the narrative point of departure be rigorously established.

Though Visconti's original opening would solve this interpretive problem, I would prefer it on no other grounds to the present beginning with its virtuoso staging and its intricate positioning of the story on the 'border between life and the theater.' In the confluence of Verdian melodrama, Risorgimento idealism and romantic love which animate the first scene, Visconti has created a golden age moment of perfect reciprocity and balance between the public and the private, between culture and history. But to continue his story in this high register would be to write Verdian melodrama in an age when it was no longer appropriate, when to do so would be to falsify the real historical forces that shape post-Risorgimento Italy. Verdi must be corrected by Gramsci, Leonora must become Livia, before the Risorgimento can yield a politically useful subject for twentieth-century Italian art.

The Gramscian argument is perhaps the most successful in reconciling *Senso* with the neorealist precedent which still, in 1954, held theoretical sovereignty over the Italian cinema. By invoking Gramsci, Visconti is exonerated from charges of an irresponsible retreat into the past and is vindicated as a historical novelist – in Lukács's sense of the term – who puts history to the service of a modern political consciousness. But this argument fails to address the most troublesome objection to *Senso* raised by its detractors – that of the film's spectacular elements, which ally it with the more retrograde examples of prewar production: the costume films of the silent era, and later the calligraphic exercises in pure style.[17] This criticism of *Senso* is especially hard to refute because it rests on the assumption that aesthetic choices are inherently ideological, and that a luxurious, self-congratulatory style full of extra-cinematic conventions will necessarily compromise any aspirations the artist may have to a politically progressive stance. Aristarco defends Visconti's aestheticism as a realistic extension of the lovers' own world view (Aristarco 1975d: 874); and argues that the director's appropriation of pictorial, literary and operatic codes provides a formal analogy to the film's thematic conflict between the old order and the new (Aristarco 1975c: 898). Aristarco's defense rests on the valid assumption that Visconti uses the film's spectacular elements strategically, that he self-consciously manipulates his own spectacle from a critical distance that enables him to see it as a function of the very sensibility that he condemns in Livia and Franz.

Thanks to its risky marriage of spectacular form and revolutionary content, *Senso* served to broaden critical tolerance for film styles that did not exhibit the usual neorealist austerity. The use of color, calligraphic effects and extra-cinematic conventions would no longer be grounds for immediately dismissing a film as regressive and ideologically suspect. Visconti was to perfect this balance between material spectacle and progressive ideology in another Risorgimento film, *The Leopard* (1963), whose Gramscian critique of the unification as 'conquista regia, non movimento popolare,' was to find poignant expression in the decaying palaces and tragic awareness of Don Fabrizio Corbera di Salina.

Notes

1. Directed by Luchino Visconti; Assisted by Francesco Rosi, Franco Zeffirelli; subject by Luchino Visconti and Suso Cecchi D'Amico, based on the eponymous novella by Camillo Boito published in 1882; screenplay by Luchino Visconti, Suso Cecchi D'Amico in

collaboration with Carlo Alianello, Giorgio Bassani, Giorgio Prosperi, dialogues in consultation with Tennessee Williams and Paul Bowles; edited by Mario Serandrei; photography by G.R. Aldo and Robert Krasker; scenery by Ottavio Scotti; costumes by Marcel Escoffier and Piero Tosi; music by Anton Bruckner (Seventh Symphony, first and second movements). Acted by Alida Valli (Countess Livia Serpieri), Farley Granger (Lt. Franz Mahler), Massimo Girotti (Marquis Roberto Ussoni), Rina Morelli (Laura), Marcella Mariani (Clara), Heinz Moog (Count Serpieri).

2. This 'check-list' of neorealist attributes is my own. The very notion of neorealism as a coherent cinematic movement is highly controversial, providing fuel for decades of academic debate. See the overview of the problem in Marcus 1986: 21–3.

3. Not only was Visconti conversant with Gramsci, he considered the historian a kind of mentor whose example provided the filmmaker with the historical-political analyses that would typify his cinematic approach. See Visconti's remarks in 'Da Verga a Gramsci' (Lizzani 1961: 449). On *Senso* as a Gramscian interpretation of the Risorgimento, see Brunetta 1982: 400.

4. For the text of the censored scene, see Lisi 1975: 863–5.

5. For a fuller discussion of the nineteenth-century background of this debate, see Marcus 1986.

6. Hence Aristarco calls *Senso* a 'romanzo cinematografico' (1975b: 91). On Visconti's preference for a novelistic filmmaking mode, see Chiaretti 1975: 285 and Armes 1971: 120. On the appropriateness of the novel for the filmmaking needs of post-neorealist Italy, see Carpi 1975: 902–3.

7. Accordingly, Vittorio Taviani writes, 'it was inevitable, after having turned his gaze to the present, that he try to arrive at the roots of the political and social phenomenon . . . that is he met with the Risorgimento as the historic moment that marks the birth of Italy as a modern nation' (Taviani 1975: 881–2).

8. On Franz's class consciousness, which makes him far more self-aware than Remigio, his counterpart in Boito's novella, see Aristarco 1975c: 897, and Calvino 1975: 880.

9. Accordingly, Laurence Schifano argues that Visconti shifts the emphasis from the two characters of the novella to history itself, which serves as the protagonist of the film (1987: 304).

10. Visconti's own aristocratic background may be what generates his fascination (and identification) with the historical spectacle of upperclass decline.

11. Hence Geoffrey Nowell-Smith calls *Senso* an 'impure' melodrama in its absence of clear-cut moral categories (1973: 83). Similarly, Guido Fink sees the film as a mediocre compromise of the melo-dramatic ethos (1977: 91).

12. Much critical attention has been devoted to Visconti's self-conscious use of melodrama in *Senso*. Lino Miccichè sees melodrama as the organizing principle at work on all levels of the film, from the structure of duets, trios, quartets and chorus, to the diegetically appropriate use of the music of Anton Bruckner, to the ending in which story and history are inexorably divided (1996: 78). Henry Bacon sees in *Senso* a constant tension between melodramatic exaltation and the ironic truth of the historical context – a tension which gives rise to Bacon's application of the label 'melodramatic realism' to the genre of the film (1998: 78–9). Laurence Schifano argues that in *Senso* Visconti seeks to rescue melodrama from critical and cultural disrepute and restore its original dignity and appeal (1987: 306).

13. Pierre Leprohon reveals how the high-angle camerawork of the opening theater scene, which makes us share the spectators' point of view, is continued throughout *Senso*: 'The screen becomes a stage and is treated as such visually' (1972: 148).

14. The importance of this 'unmasking' cannot be overestimated. Visconti explains how his films are born from single obsessive images which then give rise to full-fledged narrations, and this is the one that inspired *Senso*: 'I had constantly before my eyes, a woman dressed in black, presenting a face streaked with tears to the insults of her lover. That was to provide the determining scene of the denouement of the action: the encounter in Verona of Livia and Franz.' Translated from Visconti 1960: 84.

15. Angela Dalle Vacche concurs. Her comments on the relationship between melodrama and historical context, reinterpreted in terms of the link between the body erotic and the body politic, are extremely illuminating (1992: 134–55).

16. As Nowell-Smith observes, 'the story is left in suspense and never reconnected with the hypothetical present tense of the voice-over' (1973: 87).

17. This, in fact, is the position taken by Miccichè, who argues that the film does not represent the passage from neorealism to the next stage of realism so much as a return to 'realismo colto, carico di accent-uazioni liriche e di invenzioni spettacolari, ritorno motivato dalla crisi profonda, e ormai non più separabile, del neorealismo' (1996: 31).

References

Aristarco, G. (1960), 'Esperienza culturale ed esperienza originale in Luchino Visconti,' in G. Aristarco and G. Carancini, eds, *Rocco e i suoi fratelli*, Bologna: Cappelli, pp. 13–47.

—— (1975a), 'Dal neorealismo al realismo,' in G. Aristarco, ed., *Antologia del 'Cinema Nuovo' 1952–1958*, Florence: Guaraldi, pp. 859–61.

—— (1975b), 'Del senno di poi sono piene le fosse,' in G. Aristarco, ed., *Antologia del 'Cinema Nuovo' 1952–1958*, Florence: Guaraldi, pp. 1–151.

—— (1975c), 'E' realismo,' in G. Aristarco, ed., *Antologia del 'Cinema Nuovo' 1952–1958*, Florence: Guaraldi, pp. 892–9.

—— (1975d), '*Senso,*' in G. Aristarco, ed., *Antologia del 'Cinema Nuovo' 1952–1958*, Florence: Guaraldi, pp. 869–79.

Armes, R. (1971), *Patterns of Realism*, South Brunswick and New York: A.S. Barnes.

Bacon, H. (1998), *Visconti: Explorations of Beauty and Decay*, Cambridge: Cambridge University Press.

Boito, C. (1971 [1882]), '*Senso,*' in *Storielle vane*, Rome: Silva.

Bondanella, P. (1990), *Italian Cinema from Neorealism to the Present*, New York: Continuum.

Brunetta, G.P. (1982), *Storia del cinema italiano dal 1945 agli anni ottanta*, Rome: Riuniti.

Calvino, I. (1975), 'Boito, un punto di partenza,' in G. Aristarco, ed., *Antologia del 'Cinema Nuovo' 1952–1958*, Florence: Guaraldi, pp. 879–80.

Carpi, F. (1975), 'Finita l'inchiesta si trova il romanzo,' in G. Aristarco, ed., *Antologia del 'Cinema Nuovo' 1952–1958*, Florence: Guaraldi, pp. 899–903.

Chiaretti, T. (1975), 'La maniera di Visconti,' in L. Miccichè, ed., *Il neorealismo cinematografico italiano*, Venice: Marsilio, pp. 284–7.

Chiarini, L. (1975), 'Tradisce il neorealismo,' in G. Aristarco, ed., *Antologia del 'Cinema Nuovo' 1952–1958*, Florence: Guaraldi, pp. 882–8.

Dalle Vacche, A. (1992), *The Body in the Mirror: Shapes of History in Italian Cinema*, Princeton: Princeton University Press.

Doniol-Valcroze, J. and J. Domarchi (1959), 'Entretien avec Luchino Visconti par J. Doniol-Valcroze and J. Domarchi,' *Cahiers du cinéma* 16 (March): 1–10.

Fink, G. (1977), 'Conosca il sacrifizio: Visconti fra cinema e melo-dramma,' in A. Ferrero, ed., *Visconti: Il cinema*, Modena: Comune di Modena, pp. 84–97.

Gramsci, A. (1949), *Il Risorgimento*, Turin: Einaudi.

Leprohon, P. (1972), *The Italian Cinema*, trans. R. Greaves and O. Stallybrass, New York: Praeger.

Liehm, M. (1984), *Passion and Defiance: Film in Italy from 1942 to the Present*, Berkeley and Los Angeles: University of California Press.

Lisi, U. (1975), 'Non dissero solo obbedisco,' in G. Aristarco, ed., *Antologia del 'Cinema Nuovo' 1952–1958*, Florence: Guaraldi, pp. 861–5.

Lizzani, C. (1961), *Storia del cinema italiano 1895–1961*, Florence: Parenti.

—— (1979), *Il cinema italiano 1895–1979*, Rome: Riuniti.

Lukács, G. (1962), *The Historical Novel*, trans. H. Mitchell and S. Mitchell, London: Merlin Press.

Marcus, M. (1986), *Italian Film in the Light of Neorealism*, Princeton: Princeton University Press.

Miccichè, L., ed., (1975), *Il neorealismo cinematografico italiano*, Venice: Marsilio.

—— (1996), *Luchino Visconti: Un profilo critico*, Venice: Marsilio.

Nowell-Smith, G. (1973), *Luchino Visconti*, New York: Viking.

Schifano, L. (1987), *Luchino Visconti: Les feux de la passion*, Poitiers: Librairie Académique Perrin.

Sitney, P.A. (1995), *Vital Crises in Italian Cinema: Iconography, Stylistics, Politics*, Austin: University of Texas Press.

Taviani, V. (1975), 'Tre giudizi su *Senso*,' in G. Aristarco, ed., *Antologia del 'Cinema Nuovo' 1952–1958*, Florence: Guaraldi, pp. 881–2.

Visconti, L. (1960), (*no title*), in *Le livre blanc du cinéma,* special issue of *La Table Ronde*, 149 (May), pp. 82–6.

—— (1970), *Two Screenplays,* trans. J. Green, New York: Orion.

Zavattini, C. (1975), 'Una grossa botta in testa al neorealismo,' in G. Aristarco, ed., *Antologia del 'Cinema Nuovo' 1952–1958*, Florence: Guaraldi, pp. 888–92.

Part IV
The Character of a Nation

10

National Identity or National Character?
New Vocabularies and Old Paradigms
Silvana Patriarca

Although not completely dismissed, the concept of 'national character' has today to a large extent lost scholarly legitimacy.[1] Scholars prefer to talk of national identity, and even popular culture shows signs of having adapted to this new vocabulary. In an essay published in 1991, Perry Anderson observed that these two notions are not interchangeable although they are often treated as if they were. The concept of national character refers to a community of culture and is 'self-sufficient' while that of national identity is relational and has a reflexive dimension that the other lacks: 'If national character was thought to be a settled disposition, national identity is a self-conscious projection [. . .] Memory is crucial to identity, as it is not to character. So too is mission . . .' (1992 [1991]: 270). In his view the rise of an interest in national identity in Europe in the 1980s was to be connected to anxieties generated by mass immigration from non-European areas and to the furthering of the process of integration between the member states of the European community. Anderson's reflections were in particular spurred by the last and unfinished work of Braudel, *L'identité de la France*, and thus concerned primarily the case of France as well as the other 'core' countries of Europe (the usual ones, that is: Britain and Germany). He observed that in that same period Italy, in contrast with the core countries, had been little touched by the rise of interest in the question of national identity.

It is one of the typical ironies of history that if Anderson had waited only a couple of years, he would have had to say something quite different about Italy. First spurred by the increasing visibility of the Northern League on the political scene and by its secessionist threats, the Italian production on issues of national identity has in the past ten years been considerable, and it continues to grow. The titles exhibit in a vivid way anxieties and concerns about the dangers of disintegration in which Italy seemed to find itself: to recall only a couple of the titles which most directly express these anxieties, one can mention political scientist Gian Enrico Rusconi's *Se cessiamo di essere una nazione* (If We Cease To Be a Nation [1993]) and historian Aurelio Lepre's *Italia addio? Unità e disunità dal 1860 a oggi* (Farewell Italy? Unity and Disunity from 1860 to the Present [1994]). Historian and commentator Ernesto Galli della Loggia, author of the controversial *La morte della patria* (The Death of the Fatherland [1996]), has just inaugurated a series of volumes entirely devoted to 'Italian Identity' with the explicit purpose of strengthening the idea of nation in Italy.[2] The question of national identity has clearly become a major concern of Italian scholars and intellectuals. But what do Italian intellectuals mean when they talk about national identity? How is this notion being used and deployed in today's growing literature on the topic of the Italian nation?

My contention is that in the current Italian debate the notion of 'national identity' has often replaced without much substantial change of meaning or problematic the notion of 'national character.' When they deploy the vocabulary of identity, educated Italians today appear to express many of the same concerns which filled previous Italian writings about national character. These often were and are primarily concerned with the question of the modernity – or better, the lack of modernity – of their country, and this is why to talk of the identity of the Italians is to talk of the 'vices' of the Italians. Thus, along with works focusing on the fragility of the national construction, we find titles such as *L'Italia è un paese civile?* (Is Italy a Civilized Country? [1995]) by journalist Piero Ottone, *Le Italie parallele: Perchè l'Italia non riesce a diventare un paese moderno* (Parallel Italies. Why Italy is not Able to Become a Modern Country [1996]) by commentator Sergio Romano, and *L'identità civile degli italiani* (The Civic Identity of the Italians [1998 (1993)]) by political scientist Umberto Cerroni. Italian national identity is described almost exclusively as a problem: as we learn from one of the most recent essays on the subject, Italians do not really have a nation, but have a character all the same, and it does not make for a pleasant sight (Schiavone 1998).

Of course the Italy of the 1990s seems to be particularly suited to this kind of soul-searching. In the past ten years or so Italy has had to face a number of momentous political changes culminating with the crumbling of the party system which had governed the country since World War II and the challenge of the European Monetary Union. Whether Italy could confront this challenge and avoid falling into 'third-world status' is what explicitly worried commentators especially in light of the 'Italian anomaly,' namely the disturbing presence of media tycoon Silvio Berlusconi in the political party system. But the concern about modernity is not a new preoccupation. As a matter of fact, the question of how Italy compares to the Europe that matters, namely its most 'advanced' core, has been a constant preoccupation for the patriotic elites of the country at least from the Enlightenment onward. This has not escaped perceptive observers: before the onset of the recent debates, Tim Mason already noticed that Italian intellectuals have a tendency to see their country as backward and to inflect the term modernity only in positive terms (Mason 1988).

This intellectual and political entanglement is what largely impedes the emergence of fresh ways of looking at Italian identity. Not by accident the text that has become an obligatory point of reference in critical literature on *italianità* is completely informed by the modernity/back-wardness problematic. I am referring to the pioneering essay by the late Giulio Bollati, 'L'italiano: Il carattere nazionale come storia e come invenzione' (The Italian: National Character as History and Invention) which originally appeared in the first volume of the *Storia d'Italia* published by Einaudi in 1972, and was later reprinted in a collection bearing the same title (1996 [1983]). In the article previously mentioned, Perry Anderson refers to this essay as almost the only example of Italian meditation on the question of identity to appear in the period he examined. A graduate of the prestigious Scuola Normale Superiore di Pisa, Giulio Bollati was not an academic, but had the highest intellectual credentials as first a collaborator of publisher Giulio Einaudi (from 1949 to 1980), and then as the managing director of another prestigious publishing house, the Bollati-Boringhieri of Turin.[3] 'L'italiano' is his best known essay. Although, or better because, this text has rapidly acquired the status of a classic, its main assumptions have not been questioned. This questioning is what I intend to offer in the following pages, along with some reflections on the shaping of the Italian discourse on Italian character and identity, past and present.

It is not surprising that Bollati's essay should be so frequently cited. It is a groundbreaking work which combines uncommon flair, erudition and stylistic elegance. In his approach, Bollati anticipates (the essay, let's remember, first appeared in 1972) the emphasis on the artificial or constructed nature of nations which has become the centerpiece of innovative thinking about nationalism in the 1980s (as seen in the work of B. Anderson 1983, Hobsbawm and Ranger 1983, Hobsbawm 1990). While maintaining that national character has an objective basis in history, Bollati looks at it as an ideological construction. Early in the essay he points to historical roots of a resilient 'pathological form of Italian consciousness,' a self-representation of identity based on a 'simultaneity of primacy and decadence, of objective inferiority overcompensated by an invincible sense of superiority' (Bollati 1996 [1983]: 41). But noticing the role of intellectuals in the making of this self-representation and the importance of this debate in the period in which the nation-state was made, he focuses the bulk of the essay on the ideological construction of *italianità* in the nineteenth century.

The author's background as a historian of literature partly accounts for the choice of the main objects of his analysis: a variety of texts – mostly political pamphlets and treatises – produced primarily during the central years of the Risorgimento by some of the most important intellectuals of that period: from Vincenzo Cuoco, historian of the 1799 revolution in Naples, to the romantics of the Milanese journal *Il Conciliatore*, to Alessandro Manzoni and political philosopher Vincenzo Gioberti. Bollati argues that the definitions of the Italian character that these 'engineers of Italianness' provided, far from being accurate descriptions of it, were projects for the creation of Italians suitable to their own convictions and their own needs, needs that amounted essentially to the preservation of their power in the midst of social and political unrest.

It is in this light that Bollati reads Gioberti's claim in *Del primato morale e civile degli italiani* (Of the Moral and Civil Primacy of Italians that the Italian people were 'a desire and not a fact, a premise [*presupposto*] and not a reality, a name and not a thing [. . .] There is in fact an Italy and an Italian stock [*stirpe*] united by blood, religion, a written and illustrious language, but it is divided by governments, laws, institutions, spoken language, mores, affections, habits.' reported in Bollati 1996 [1983]: 44 [my translation]). In this passage Gioberti argued at the same time for the need to 'make' Italians through the creation of an independent confederation of states, and against any project of involving them in the political struggle by means of revolution. (The polemical target was of course Mazzini and the radicals.) By focusing on the work of Gioberti and other moderates such as Vincenzo Cuoco and Alessandro Manzoni, Bollati wants to emphasize the moderate origins of the Risorgimento which in his view had not attracted the necessary attention. Even Mazzini did not escape the ambiguities and paternalism of what Bollati calls the 'Italian ideology' (1996 [1983]: 44, 120), the sum of cultural and ideological attitudes prevailing among the educated elites and informing their ideas about Italy and *italianità*. Privileging land and agriculture both moderates and radicals shared a fundamental distrust towards the economic changes which were taking place in the more 'advanced' countries of Europe.

Given the pedagogical vocation of Risorgimento culture, the nature of the ideological convictions and preferences of Italian intellectuals could not but have important consequences for the new state. For Bollati, Risorgimento culture left 'a "heritage of ideas" which, if one looks at it dispassionately, and after recognizing its patriotic function and its moments of cultural dignity, [contained] a *basic reservation about modernity*' (1996 [1983]: 112–3; my emphasis). Not surprisingly this analysis ends with the indictment of the Italian elites of the Risorgimento as a whole. The unwillingness of these elites to accept and support a full economic and political modernization of the country, their fundamentally conservative attitude and their rhetorical culture constituted the roots of other, later evils plaguing the transition of Italy into the twentieth century: the slowness of the process of industrialization, the continuing predominance of a rhetorical humanistic culture, the elites' distrust of democracy. All these phenomena would culminate, after the shock of the war, with the deadly invention of Fascism, final product of the 'modernity deficit,' so to speak, of the 'Italian ideology.'

It is not difficult to identify the roots of the interpretative paradigm which Bollati applies to the analysis of Italian culture. In his emphasis on the moderate origins of the Risorgimento, Bollati developed insights from Antonio Gramsci's thesis on the hegemony of the moderate liberals during the Risorgimento (1996 [1949]).[4] Bollati's claim about Italian intellectuals' reluctance to embrace modernity is echoed in marxist literary scholar Alberto Asor Rosa's conviction that an 'anti-industrialist vein of pre-capitalist nostalgia' runs through nineteenth- and twentieth-century Italian culture carrying profoundly negative consequences (1975: 829). For the latter too, the humanistic (in the sense of a-, and even anti-, scientific) and fundamentally 'backward' mentality of Italian intellectuals at the turn of the century predisposed them to a destructive *deprecatio temporum* and impeded an understanding of the needs of the modern industrial world and a realistic approach on their part to the problems of the country.

Hegel too looms large behind Bollati's analysis. In the preface to the 1983 volume in which the 1972 essay was reissued, Bollati recognized explicitly that for him modernity was the only 'yardstick with which we can construct a non-abstract and not purely verbal historical sequence; the only sequence which allows us to evaluate different hierarchies of values, projects, aspirations, rebellions, proposals' (1996 [1983]: xxi). This is the iron law which gives a clue to the movement of history. Not only Marx, but also the historical sociology of modernization (in the more critical version of Barrington Moore (1966) and Reinhard Bendix (1996

[1977])) shape this interpretive paradigm. Bollati's idea of modernity was predicated on a normative view of the process of modernization in which Britain constituted the model of modern economic development, and France a model of modern political development, with which all other nations should be compared. It is precisely this view which has been under a lot of questioning by historians in the past twenty years or so. Today Britain's path to modernity is no longer seen as a model, and many in fact look at nineteenth-century Britain as a peculiar mix of old and new when social relations and institutions and even the economy are concerned.[5] As for France, its status as a model of political development has always been much more contested.

It is not my purpose here to blame Bollati for holding views and conceptions which were widespread at the time of his writing. The fact that his general interpretive framework continues to inform the discourse of many participants in today's debate on Italian identity is more troublesome, but I will elaborate on this later. Now I wish instead to examine the main claim made by Bollati concerning the substantial 'reservation about modernity' which characterized Italian culture in the Risorgimento and even after. If we take modernity to mean industrialization, as Bollati does, this reservation certainly existed, but it is incorrect to make into a 'national peculiarity' what was in fact a phenomenon also to be found elsewhere in continental Europe. The wariness of the Italian educated elites vis-à-vis the process of industrialization which was taking place in some areas of northern Europe was the expression of the awareness to be found among all the dominant classes of the so-called late-comers (namely all European countries except England) that an unbridled process of industrialization could lead to social disruption and could pose a threat to their domination. Nothing peculiarly Italian therefore, since a preference for a slower transformation of society generally characterized the European continental elites after they had witnessed the British industrial revolution.

If we take modernity to mean something beyond 'membership in the industrialized world,' to be inclusive also of a willingness and openness to change in other fields, and we widen our scope of observation to encompass authors also engaged in the task of imagining Italy and not considered by Bollati, it is more difficult to assent to Bollati's verdict. An examination of these other authors and their works shows that in that particularly intense moment of 'identity quest' which was the Risorgimento, the intellectuals who actually positively embraced 'modernity' were more numerous than Bollati suggests. I have in mind here the writers who during the Risorgimento collected and published 'positive,' that is quantitative, information on the state of the country or of any of its particular subdivisions, those who called themselves statisticians in homage to the science that they considered fundamental for promoting 'civilization.' They espoused diverse political outlooks and wrote in a variety of periodicals which were supposed to favor the process of 'improvement.' They attempted to rectify what they perceived as contemporary misperceptions of Italy and aimed to show that the Italians were already a quite 'civilized' people, or had the potential of becoming a fully civilized one. They rejected the image of Italy as a 'southern country,' and as such determined by its climate, which had been circulating in Europe at least since the Enlightenment. In other words, if we consider the work of this type of admittedly 'minor' intellectual operator, we clearly see the diffusion of what we could call a 'culture of things' developing along with that of the 'rhetoricians' in nineteenth-century Italy (Patriarca 1996). This type of culture, oriented towards the acquisition and use of precise and practical information which could help increase the productivity of the body social and politic, must surely be seen as a component of a 'modern' outlook. The work done by these researchers in the pre-1861 period contributed to create in unified Italy a terrain in which a lively positivist culture could flourish.[6]

In light of these observations, to speak of 'Italian ideology' in terms of a basic reservation about modernity means to create a fictitious creature, and to participate in the process of articulation of that very 'national character' which Bollati would seem to have set out to deconstruct in the first place. But the fact is that Bollati actually believed in the existence of a national character and in the possibility of studying it more or less scientifically, and he thought that history can provide us with a fundamental clue to its traits. What are these traits? In the preface to the 1983 collection, Bollati points to 'an Italian trait with profound structural and cultural roots' and 'a constitutive element of [Italian] history' (1996 [1983]: x): *trasformismo*. As known, *trasformismo* entered the political vocabulary during the tenure of prime minister Agostino Depretis (1876–87) to indicate the formation of governmental majorities with members of the opposition. Other statesmen and governments after Depretis are believed to have resorted to it (Giolitti for example), although there is no consensus among historians on who should be placed in this category and even on whether it is appropriate for historians to use the category at all (Carocci 1992; see also Tranfaglia 1994).

The term almost immediately acquired negative connotations, indicating a generalized political practice that reflects lack of principles, a constant resorting to compromise for purposes of political self-preservation.

Bollati uses the term in this way and is certainly not alone in the belief that transformism, erected by the Italian elites into what he calls an 'art of government,' is a fundamental key to understanding Italy. Indeed this is a belief that he shares with many Italian as well as non-Italian intellectuals and politicians, from the early passionate critics of the Italian state in the ranks of the opposition, to writer Giuseppe Tomasi di Lampedusa (whose *gattopardismo* represents a kind of extreme variant of 'transformism' [1971 (1957)]; see Mondo 1993), to historian Denis Mack Smith who finds the first premonitory signs of this national trend in Cavour's *connubio* (1959: 30–1), to anthropologist Carlo Tullio-Altan, who has further elaborated on the idea of an 'Italian ideology,' choosing transformism and populism as the two main components of it (1989). In his weekly column, 'L'antitaliano,' in the popular *Espresso* magazine, the influential commentator Giorgio Bocca operates with exactly these ideas.[7] It is a view which was recently best summarized in the headline and subhead of the daily *Corriere della Sera*'s review by Claudio Magris of a reprint of Bollati's *L'italiano*: 'Italians a People Under a Mask All Fearful and Transformist [subhead:] In Search of One's Conscience: Giulio Bollati's Essay on Our National Character from the End of the 18th Century to the Present is Back. From Peasant Culture to the Rejection of Industrial Modernity: A Merciless X-ray of the Eternal Vices of the *Belpaese*' (1996; see also Parlato 1996).

To make transformism into one of the distinguishing features, if not *the* distinguishing feature, of Italianness means transferring to the whole of the Italian people a trait which has characterized the practice of its governing classes at specific historical junctures. From a historiographic standpoint this is a questionable operation, although it reflects a real frustration with which I completely sympathize – the frustration of those who desire a substantial change that never seems to arrive. The term 'transformism' brings with it heavy historical and ideological baggage and does not allow us to appreciate how those characteristics which appear as national peculiarities are often the outcome of an excessively narrow dialogue between the historian and his *national* sources. If one looks beyond the national boundaries, one may consider how 'transformisms' of various kinds can be found in other countries too, particularly from the era of mass politics onward. (Third-Republic France is a case in point in this respect [cf. Carocci 1992: 10].) By saying this I am not trying to find a justification for Italian transformism, as many liberals have done: I am simply pointing out that linking transformism and 'national character' is a risky business leading to overgeneralizations and unwarranted conclusions. Transformism is a powerful weapon in political practice and discourse (and today it saturates political discourse both on the left and on the right), but it is highly problematic when made into a transhistorical category.

I would argue, moreover, that the popularity of the notion of transformism in the definition of Italianness is not only a product of the history of Italy and of the central place the notion has in current political discourse, but also of the very negative connotation it carries, a negative connotation that fits well with what Bollati calls the 'dark side' of the stereotype of the Italian and of which a Machiavellian attitude towards politics – seen as a mere struggle for power in which all means are legitimate – is a fundamental and time-honored component. Since the idea of transformism fits with a widespread stereotypical representation (and self-representation) of Italianness, it rarely gets to be questioned. I will not dispute the 'kernel of truth argument' about stereotypes, but again we must pay attention to the price we pay in forgetting how one-sided they are.

Transformism is not the only notion which treads on the fine line between 'reality' and stereotype. If in his diagnosis of the 'vices' of the Italian character Bollati tends to focus on the responsibilities of the political and cultural elites who have acculturated the Italians into their values, other authors are inclined to shift the burden of responsibility onto the Italian population as a whole. In one of his recent essays, Sergio Romano claims to see '[a] strong desire for modernity among the most dynamic part of the national society and [a] strong resistance against modernity among its "families"' (1996: 170 [his quotations marks]). By referring to these otherwise unspecified 'families,' Romano manages to introduce yet another component of the dark side of Italianness, 'familism.' Familism is a word vague enough to accommodate a variety of prejudices and commonplaces about what is or is not modern or conducive to modernity. The term was first introduced – preceded by the adjective 'amoral' – in a study by the American political scientist, Edward Banfield, in the late 1950s and has gained more currency among Italians themselves in the last two decades. The considerable international success of political scientist Robert Putnam's *Making Democracy Work: Civic Traditions in Modern Italy* (1993), which operates with categories and assumptions similar to those of Banfield, is witness to the resilience of this view.[8] In recent Italian works on national identity the traits that Banfield (1958) thought to have identified in his study of a small southern community (strong attachment to the family, lack of 'civic spirit') are now taken to be representative of the whole Italian *mentalité* (e.g. Gambino 1998; Galli della Loggia 1998).

The issue is of course quite controversial: in a recent investigation aiming at critically analyzing the idea of familism and its linkage with the alleged lack of civic spirit of the Italians, and in particular of those in the south, sociologist Loredana Sciolla has shown how in fact there is little empirical basis to the idea that Italians have an abnormal attachment to the family. (According to recent surveys, it would appear that the citizens of the US place more value on the family than the Italians.) Nor is civic spirit the antithesis of familism (1997).[9] One of the best students of the south, historian Gabriella Gribaudi, has pointed out the distance between the paradigm of familism and the reality of families and family life in the south (1999).

I have mentioned familism here because of the common ground that it shares with transformism. Beside the fact that both notions easily become stereotypes, they are both linked to an idealized representation of the modernization process according to which modernity eradicates the features of 'traditional' or 'backward' society such as the importance of kin and family networks, the presence of patron-client relationships and so on, and establishes in their place a society based on the impersonality of state and market. In fact, we are becoming increasingly aware that categories such as 'backward' and 'modern' are very problematic as descriptive and/or explanatory tools and must themselves be accounted for.[10]

If we problematize the notion of modernity, it becomes clear that the frequent debates on national character in which Italian intellectuals – Bollati included – have been engaged in the last two centuries of Italian history deserve to be analyzed with a fresh approach. Since this in itself could be the topic for a whole book, I will limit myself to a few observations on some of the major moments and aspects of the discourse on national character in Italy. But first we must recall that this discourse is an important component of any process of nation-building. It may or may not focus on issues of ethnic identity, but it invariably implies comparisons with other countries, with models to imitate and negative examples to avoid. Thus the discourse on national character has a relational quality which can scarcely be overemphasized. Moreover, it always occurs in the intensely populated space of intertextuality, while it also points to the specific history of the nation in which it emerges and reflects the culture and ideology of the intellectuals who articulate it. Hence the repetitiveness of the discourse on national character and its tendency to acquire a life of its own. It will not suffice, however, to analyze this discourse within the boundaries of the nation itself: we must also pay attention to its transnational political and intellectual environment.

Although the origins of the discourse must be traced back to the Enlightenment and even to the end of the seventeenth century, it is during the Risorgimento that most clearly a desire for membership in the Europe that mattered, namely its 'advanced core,' was fully articulated. It was this desire that spurred many Risorgimento intellectuals and politicians to advocate the national cause and shaped their arguments and rhetorics. Vincenzo Gioberti's lofty and emphatic claims about the primacy of Italians cannot be isolated from his eagerness to re-introduce Italy into the circle of Europe's 'great' or 'universal' nations by appealing, as Stuart Woolf has observed, to 'all shades of moderate opinion by a clear and simple message based upon rhetoric about Italy's great past' (1979: 344). While praising the virtues of Italianness, Gioberti also castigated the 'idleness' in which youthful energies wasted away, energies which could have been put to better, namely patriotic, use (Gioberti 1932 [1843]: 200–7). Behind the inflated rhetoric, the political moderatism and the paternalism of its author, it is the modernity and perhaps the banality (as nationalist tracts go) of the *Primato* that should call our attention today. Buried in it is for example the very modern talk about the 'civilizing mission' of Italy once it achieves nationhood.

After unification, the problem of Italy's international location did not go away and was added to the domestic issues that the new political entity immediately had to face: soon statesmen and commentators began to worry about the strength of the new nation and its ability to survive and indeed prosper in an increasingly competitive international arena. In the late 1860s and the 1870s the issue of character was discussed with reference to the moral qualities that Italians needed in order to be a strong nation, namely in the sense of the famous (but generally misreported) quote from Piedmontese statesman Massimo D'Azeglio: 'Italy's prime need is to educate Italians who know how to do their duty, that is to say Italians with strong, lofty characters. Alas! Every day we are going in the opposite direction' (1966 [1867]: 17–18).[11] To participants in this postunification debate (moderate supporters of the historic right, but also strongly anti-clerical members of the historic left), the word character meant essentially moral strength, stamina. Proponents of what Samuel Smiles at the time was advocating in England, they aimed at instilling in all Italians the values that would be conducive to a strong character, namely, love of work, family orientation, honesty and so on (e.g., Alfani 1876; Carpi 1878). The making of Italians 'of character' was what the authors of this literature thought necessary to ensure the common good of the country. Those of more radical views added to their recipes for change the appeal to an eradication of the pernicious influence of the

Catholic Church (Mazzoleni 1878). Without this, a country which had been born without a true and 'regenerative' revolution was headed toward certain ruin.

Later, with the growth of empirical investigations and the consolidation of a biological and evolutionary anthropology in the 1880s and 1890s, and in a context of increasing imperialistic tensions, the meaning of character and the discourse on national character were inflected differently. No longer understood purely as stamina, character became more of a stable attribute of whole peoples or races: Pasquale Turiello's *Governo e governati in Italia* (Government and the governed in Italy [1889]) is indicative of this new climate. In this work, the author made proposals for a stronger executive on the basis of an analysis of Italian character which stressed its extreme individualism and its lack of discipline. Although it was still seen as the outcome of history and milieu (physical and socio-historical), national character had a less plastic nature. The issue was further complicated by the contemporary consolidation of the image of the 'Two Italies' namely the idea that two profoundly diverse civilizations confronted each other in Italy, one in the North and one in the South, the latter being the embodiment of all that was backward and uncivilized, the internal Other that 'infected' the whole.

With Fascism, elements of both conceptions – character as stamina and sense of duty and character as ethnological traits – were combined. Mussolini, who did not think much of the actual character of the Italians (in his view, in fact, it required a total reform [*rifacimento*]) – attempted to make Italians into a new people, nothing less than the 'Romans of modernity' (E. Gentile 1994: 87). The project, as we know, fortunately failed and Italians again were left to reflect pessimistically on their character as a nation after the disaster of Fascism and the war (e.g. Cusin 1945, Fenoaltea 1945 and Guarnieri 1948).

Ideas of national peculiarities and the study of national character were to receive a big spur by World War II particularly in the Anglo-American world with anthropologists, historians and political scientists engaged in trying to forecast first German and Japanese behavior during the military operations, and then the prospect of democracy in the countries which had experienced dictatorships in the interwar period (Hoebel 1967). Although Italians do not seem to have contributed much to this research, echoes of it are to be found in the 1960s reflections on the transformations the country was undergoing in the era of the 'economic miracle.' At that juncture a question frequently asked was: how well can the Italian 'character' adapt to the changes connected with economic development and a mass society? Will Italians – a people, according to several commentators, burdened by its antiquity, by its strong inclination towards individualism and by its lack of social spirit (E. Croce 1962 [1961]; Golino 1964)[12] – will they be able to deal with these challenges?

Bollati's critical essays on Italian character are themselves an instance of this tradition of intense self-examination. To insist, as he does, on the negative legacy of a predominantly humanistic culture and to call attention to the scarcity – in the Italian literary landscape – of 'explorers in the unknown land called modernization' (Bollati 1996 [1983]: 202) means to point to the inadequacy of Italian culture and society vis-à-vis the requirements of an advanced industrialism. The weight of the old humanistic tradition and the pernicious legacy of idealism could be defeated only through a sustained injection of modern scientific culture.[13] This profound conviction informed Bollati's life-long work in the publishing industry. His collaboration with Giulio Einaudi first and then his work in the Bollati-Boringhieri publishing house were always inspired by a desire to place modern European culture and knowledge in the service of the transformation of Italian society. As he stated in an interview he gave a few weeks before his death in 1996,[14] 'linking cultural life and the problems of the country' had been his life goal.

But there is more: by the early 1980s when *L'italiano* was published, an increasingly disillusioned left was waging a battle against the corrupt political practices of the parties in power while fully realizing the difficulties of changing the political system. The fact that Bollati makes transformism the distinguishing trait of the Italian character in the preface to his 1983 collection is certainly also a reflection of this climate. The peculiar pathos of this and of the other pieces in the collection which were written in the late 1970s must be linked to the widespread feeling that all that remained to the left were the campaigns for a 'moralization' of public life against a rising tide of corruption and political opportunism.

Far from being – and I say this in admiration – a purely academic exercise, Bollati's critical work is thus the expression of a militant critique of the Italian political classes and of the culture that they have generalized to the whole of Italy. Indeed Bollati's own work of unveiling the historical determinants of the 'Italian character' was fully part of a cultural and political struggle for changing it and making the nation, and in particular the culture of its elites, more 'modern.' In his own critical work, Bollati mirrors what he claims the writers he analyzes were doing when discoursing about the Italian national character: as they were attempting to make an Italian more suitable to their projects, he too is attempting to reshape Italian culture to make it more suitable to his project. In doing this he expresses a passionate longing for the wholesome modernity denied to Italians, a longing which he even projects onto the poet he most admires, Giacomo Leopardi – whose posthumous *Discorso sui costumi degli italiani* (Discourse on the Mores of the Italians [1906]) has significantly been the object of several reprints and re-readings in recent years.[15]

As I historicize Bollati's interpretation, I should make clear that I am not disputing the objectives of his project, which I share, but its interpretive underpinnings based as they are on an uncritical view of modernity. The same modernist paradigm reappears today under the new guise of the problematic of Italian identity in the crop of titles mentioned at the beginning of this chapter, which point to the 'modernity' that was absent from the construction of the nation. They perpetuate arguments and conventions of a discourse which, because of its long history, has become increasingly entangled and self-referential. All this does not help to renew our understanding of the meaning of identity, national or otherwise.

The Italian intellectuals' 'fixation' with national character need not be construed as yet another Italian peculiarity. Countries in similar structural positions or with histories characterized by similar experiences (relatively late transition to nationhood, authoritarian regimes, war defeats) are likely to face analogous predicaments and produce analogous debates and self-representations. One may think of Argentina where a succession of authoritarian regimes has spurred intellectuals to reflect gloomily on the peculiarities of national traditions and culture (e.g. Garcia-Hamilton 1990). Germany may also fall into this category although the heavier burden of its past combined with the economic successes of the postwar period has made the debate on identity largely 'frozen' at least in the period before 1989 (Jarausch *et al.* 1997: 37).

If we consider these cases and look at the content of actual debates, the distinction Perry Anderson makes between the concepts of national character and national identity starts to blur. In other words, the shift from one terminology to the other is certainly significant, but we need to pay closer attention to what is being said: we may discover that the novelty is not that great after all. Moreover, we should look out for cases of what I would call 'concept transmutation.' It is interesting in this respect to consider when exactly the idea of 'national character' has exited the field of the social sciences. This has happened, I would argue, only when scholars found a substitute for it in the vocabulary of 'culture.'

I am intentionally using the word 'substitute' here in order to point to a specific, historical process of intellectual filiation. In the early 1960s political scientists studying comparatively the political attitudes of different countries developed a new approach which they called 'political culture.' The 'political culture' approach was based on the use of a new survey research methodology and on the adoption of the conceptual framework of anthropology and social psychology. This made it possible to establish – in the words of one of its inventors – 'whether there were indeed distinctive nation "marks" and national characters . . .' (Almond 1980: 15).[16] Needless to say they found some. The notion of 'political culture' indeed differs only slightly if at all, at least in this research tradition, from the notion of national character as developed by contemporary social psychology.[17] The study of culture, political and non, may thus turn out to be just another way of inscribing national character, of re-creating more sophisticated versions of a national peculiarity discourse with the risk of reproducing stereotypical representations of human collectivities and of conjuring up the figure of the Other.

The same could said of studies of cultural or national identity which do not problematize the elusive notion of identity. As this type of study proliferates today, we must remember with sociologist Zygmunt Bauman that identity is never a stable entity, but a project: 'identity has the ontological status of a project and a postulate [. . .] neither is there nor can there be any other identity but a postulated one. Identity is a critical projection of what is demanded and/or sought upon what is . . .' (1996: 19). Interestingly, this statement echoes what Bollati says à propos the discourse of natural character, but without the ambiguity of Bollati's position.

Bauman looks at identities as constituted in the realm of representations, of images calling subjects to life.[18] 'Character' too belongs to this realm and here perhaps lies, deeper than the difference claimed by Perry Anderson, the similarity which links the notions of national character and national identity. Thus one should be careful when operating with these notions in a 'realistic' or referential mode. I mentioned one reason, the risk of conjuring up the figure of the Other. But there is also another reason which concerns specifically the political impact of the discourse on national character and identity which is currently taking place in Italy. The emphasis on the vices of national character does not make for wise politics. The term 'character' tends to naturalize and psychologize sociocultural traits and attitudes and this certainly does not boost hope for change and it may even have a paralyzing effect. It also elicits purely reactive and contrary responses from those who look at the insistence on national vices as anti-patriotic. Moving the discourse beyond the old paradigms is thus all the more necessary.

Acknowledgements

Earlier versions of material in this chapter have been presented at the UC Berkeley conference on 'Making and Unmaking Italy' and at the annual meeting of the American Historical Association in Seattle, January 1998. I would like to thank the editors of this volume as well as John Davis, Arno Mayer, Anders Stephanson, Mack Walker and the audience of those conferences for their valuable criticisms and suggestions on the earlier versions.

Notes

1. 'Die-hards' to be sure still exist especially in the field of social psychology: see for example Inkeles 1997.
2. The first volume is authored by Galli della Loggia himself and bears the same title as the series (1998). For an explicit statement about the objectives of the series see Valensise's interview with Galli della Loggia (1998).
3. For a profile of Bollati's career see articles in *La Repubblica* 19 May 1996; *Il Manifesto* 19 May 1996; *La Stampa* 19, 21, 23 May 1996.
4. Gramsci, however, had a more positive attitude towards this moderatism because he saw it as an example of hegemony at work, as his 'Notes on Italian History' (1971) make clear.
5. The literature is extensive. Arno Mayer's provocative *The Persistence of the Old Régime* (1981) has greatly contributed to the re-examination of commonly held views about the modernity of England (and more generally Europe) in the nineteenth century. For a critical discussion of the behavior of nineteenth-century economic elites see Harris and Thane 1984. See also the discussion in Sked 1987, ch. 2.
6. More recent interpretations of the attitudes of Italian cultural operators in the post-unification period tend to emphasize their aspiration to be modern: see for example Lanaro 1979 and E. Gentile 1997.
7. Even he, however, seems to be increasingly at a loss in understanding what goes on in the Belpaese: see his latest volume, significantly entitled *Italiani strana gente* (1997), where the categories such as 'paradox' and 'complication' pop up quite frequently. The meaning of these categories, however, is ambiguous: while it can point to the

crumbling of the old certainties of modernization theory (or at least to a more cautious approach), the idea of Italy as a 'complex reality' may just be an inflection of the view that Italians are a people difficult to understand because of their love of theater and dissimulation as Barzini, a compendium of stereotypes about Italianness, tells us (1965: 100).

8. See especially chapter 4 of Putnam for an open acknowledgment of Banfield's views: 'data show that in the efflorescence of their associational life, some regions in Italy rival Tocqueville's America of congenital 'joiners,' whereas the inhabitants of other regions are accurately typified by the isolated and suspicious 'amoral familists' of Montegrano [the name given by Banfield to the community he studied]' (1993: 91–2).

9. Sciolla's is a very useful essay, even though the evidence she provides is not always as strong as one would like it to be.

10. Already Weber and exponents of critical historical sociology warned that 'modernity' and 'backwardness' should be seen merely as heuristic devices and not a 'reality,' a warning that, as they were aware, was usually forgotten (see for example the important discussion in part 3 of Bendix 1996 [1977]). Adopting a postmodern approach, John Agnew goes so far as seeing 'modernity' and 'backwardness' as metaphors which can turn into myths, and claims that the ideas of 'backward Italy' is one such myth (1997). This may be justified, but a fuller discussion of the implications of abandoning altogether this vocabulary would be necessary.

11. I am quoting from the translation. Soldani and Turi 1993 have pointed out how this quote has been misreported.

12. Elena Croce (1962 [1961]), however, also found a positive and redeeming side in these burdens, namely their being a barrier against the negative tendencies of 'mass society' (civiltà di massa).

13. There are echoes here of the 'two cultures' debate whose main outcome in Italy was a work by Preti (1968).

14. As reported in the book reviews section of *La Stampa* 9 March 1996: 3.

15. For Bollati's view of Leopardi see 'Il modo di vedere italiano (note su fotografia e storia)' (1996 [1983]: 136–40). Leopardi's *Discorso* (first published only in 1906) has recently been re-edited by several publishers: Marsilio in 1989, Feltrinelli in 1991, Mondadori in 1993 and Rizzoli in 1998.

16. The pioneering work in which the study of political culture was first pursued is Almond and Verba 1963.

17. Inkeles (1997: 40–1) alludes to the reciprocal influences between these two research traditions.
18. A very critical approach to identity can be found also in Prasenjit Duara who has pointed out the 'network of changing and often conflicting representations' (1995: 7) in which the self and identity are constituted.

References

Agnew, J. (1997), 'The Myth of Backward Italy in Modern Europe,' in B. Allen and M. Russo, eds, *Revisioning Italy: National Identity and Global Culture,* Minneapolis: University of Minnesota Press, pp. 23–42.

Alfani, A. (1876), *Il carattere degli italiani,* Florence: Barbera.

Almond, G.A. (1980), 'The Intellectual History of the Civic Culture Concept,' in G.A. Almond and S. Verba, eds, *The Civic Culture Revisited,* Boston and Toronto: Little, Brown and Company, pp. 1–36.

—— and S. Verba (1963), *The Civic Culture: Political Attitudes and Democracy in Five Nations,* Princeton: Princeton University Press.

Anderson, B. (1983), *Imagined Communities: Reflections on the Origin and Spread of Nationalism,* London: Verso.

Anderson, P. (1992 [1991]), 'Fernand Braudel and National Identity,' *A Zone of Engagement,* London and New York: Verso, pp. 251–78.

Asor Rosa, A. (1975), 'La cultura,' *Storia d'Italia,* Vol. 4, *Dall'unità a oggi,* Turin: Einaudi, pp. 819–1664.

Barzini, L. (1965), *The Italians,* New York: Atheneum.

Banfield, E.C. (1958), *The Moral Bases of a Backward Society,* New York: The Free Press.

Bauman, Z. (1996), 'From Pilgrim to Tourist – or a Short History of Identity,' in S. Hall and P. Du Gay, eds, *Questions of Cultural Identity,* London: Sage, pp. 18–36.

Bendix, R. (1996 [1977]), *Nation-Building and Citizenship: Studies of Our Changing Social Order*, Enlarg. edn., New Brunswick and London: Transactions Publishers.

Bocca, G. (1997), *Italiani strana gente,* Milan: Mondadori.

Bollati, G. (1972), 'L'italiano,' in R. Romano and C. Vivanti, eds, *Storia d'Italia,* Vol. 1, *I caratteri originali*, Turin: Einaudi, pp. 949–1022.

—— (1996 [1983]), *L'italiano: Il carattere nazionale come storia e come invenzione*, Turin: Einaudi.

Carocci, G. (1992), *Il trasformismo dall'unità a oggi*, Milan: Unicopli.

Carpi, L. (1878), *L'Italia vivente: Studi sociali*, Milan: Vallardi.

Cerroni, U. (1998 [1996]), *L'identità civile degli italiani*, Lecce: Mauri.

Croce, E. (1962 [1961]), 'Che cosa significa essere italiano,' *Tempo presente* 7: 871–7.

Cusin, F. (1945), *L'italiano: Realtà e illusioni*, Rome: Atlantica.

D'Azeglio, M. (1966 [1867]), *Things I Remember,* trans. E.R. Vincent, Oxford: Oxford University Press.

Duara, P. (1995), *Rescuing History from the Nation: Questioning Narratives of Modern China*, Chicago and London: University of Chicago Press.

Fenoaltea, G. (1945), *Storia degli italieschi dalle origini ai giorni nostri*, Florence: Barbera.

Galli della Loggia, E. (1996), *La morte della patria*, Bari: Laterza.

—— (1998), *L'identità italiana,* Bologna: Il Mulino.

Gambino, A. (1998), *Inventario italiano: Costumi e mentalità di un paese moderno,* Turin: Einaudi.

Garcia-Hamilton, J.I. (1990), *Los orígenes de nuestra cultura autoritaria*, Buenos Aires: Albino y asociados.

Gentile, E. (1994), 'La nazione del fascismo: Alle origini del declino dello Stato nazionale,' in G. Spadolini, ed., *Nazione e nazionalità in Italia*, Bari: Laterza, pp. 65–124.

—— (1997), *La grande Italia: Ascesa e declino del mito della nazione nel ventesimo secolo,* Milan: Mondadori.

Gioberti, V. (1932 [1843]), *Del primato morale e civile degli italiani*, ed. G. Balsamo-Crivelli, Turin: Unione Tipografico-Editrice Torinese.

Golino, E. (1964), 'Il carattere degli italiani,' *Tempi moderni* 7: 99–106.

Gramsci, A. (1971), 'Notes on Italian History,' *Selections from the Prison Notebooks*, ed. Q. Hoare and G.N. Smith, New York: International Publishers, pp. 52–120.

—— (1996 [1949]), *Il Risorgimento*, ed. V. Gerratana, 3rd edn, 1977, Rome: Editori Riuniti.

Gribaudi, G. (1999), *Donne, uomini, famiglie: Napoli nel Novecento,* Naples: L'Ancora.

Guarnieri, S. (1948), *Carattere degli italiani*, Turin: Einaudi.

Harris, J., and P. Thane (1984), 'British and European Bankers, 1880–1914: An "Aristocratic Bourgeoisie"?,' in G. Crossick, P. Thane, and R. Floud, eds, *The Power of the Past: Essays for Eric Hobsbawm*, Cambridge: Cambridge University Press, pp. 215–34.

Hobsbawm, E. (1990), *Nations and Nationalism since 1780: Programme, Myth, Reality,* Cambridge: Cambridge University Press.

——— and T. Ranger, eds (1983), *The Invention of Tradition*, Cambridge: Cambridge University Press.

Hoebel, E.A. (1967), 'Anthropological Perspectives on National Character,' *The Annals of the American Academy of Political and Social Science* 370: 1–7.

Inkeles, A. (1997), *National Character: A Psycho-Social Perspective*, New Brunswick and London: Transaction Publishers.

Jarausch, K., H.C. Seeba, and D.P. Conradt (1997), 'The Presence of the Past: Culture, Opinion, and Identity in Germany,' in K. Jarausch, ed., *After Unity: Rethinking German Identities*, Providence and Oxford: Berghahn Books, pp. 25–60.

Lanaro, S. (1979), *Nazione e lavoro: Saggio sulla cultura borghese in Italia 1870–1925*, Venice: Marsilio.

——— (1988), *Italia nuova: Identità e sviluppo 1861–1988,* Turin: Einaudi.

Leopardi, G. (1906), *Scritti vari inediti dalle carte napoletane*, ed. G. Mestica, Florence, Le Monnier.

Lepre, A. (1994), *Italia addio? Unità e disunità dal 1860 a oggi*, Milan: Mondadori.

Mack Smith, D. (1959), *Italy: A Modern History*, Ann Arbor, MI: University of Michigan Press.

Magris, C. (1996), 'Italiani popolo in maschera: Tutti paurosi e trasformisti,' *Il Corriere della Sera* 15 September.

Mason, T. (1988), 'Italy and Modernization: A Montage,' *History Workshop* 25: 127–47.

Mayer, A. (1981), *The Persistence of the Old Régime: Europe to the Great War,* New York and London: Pantheon.

Mazzoleni, A. (1878), *Il carattere nella vita italiana*, Milan: Galli e Omodei.

Mondo, L. (1993), 'Gattopardismo,' in G. Calcagno, ed., *Bianco rosso e verde: L'identità degli italiani*, Bari: Laterza, pp. 92–5.

Moore, B. (1966), *The Social Origins of Dictatorship and Democracy*, Boston: Beacon Press.

Ottone, P. (1995), *L'Italia è un paese civile?* Milan: Mondadori.

Parlato, V. (1996), 'Vizi d'Italia: Il trasformismo principe dei nostri mali. Una parabola del carattere nazionale,' *Il Manifesto*, 18 September.

Patriarca, S. (1996), *Numbers and Nationhood: Writing Statistics in Nineteenth-Century Italy*, Cambridge: Cambridge University Press.

Putnam, R. (1993), *Making Democracy Work: Civic Traditions in Modern Italy*, Princeton: Princeton University Press.

Preti, G. (1968), *Logica e retorica*, Turin, Einaudi.

Romano, S. (1996), *Le Italie parallele: Perchè l'Italia non riesce a diventare un paese moderno*, Milan: Longanesi.

Rusconi, G.E. (1993), *Se cessiamo di essere una nazione*, Bologna: Il Mulino.

Schiavone, A. (1998), *Italiani senza Italia: Storia e identità*, Turin: Einaudi.

Sciolla, L. (1997), *Italiani: Stereotipi di casa nostra,* Bologna: Il Mulino.

Sked, A. (1987), *Britain's Decline: Problems and Perspectives*, Oxford: Basil Blackwell.

Soldani, S., and G. Turi (1993), 'Introduzione,' in S. Soldani and G. Turi, eds, *Fare gli italiani: Scuola e cultura nell'Italia contemporanea*, Vol. 1, *La nascita dello stato nazionale*, Bologna: Il Mulino, pp. 9–33.

Tomasi di Lampedusa, G. (1971 [1957]), *Il gattopardo,* Milan: Feltrinelli.

Tranfaglia, N. (1994), 'Trasformismo,' in P. Ginsborg, ed., *Stato dell'Italia,* Milan: Mondadori, pp. 95–8.

Tullio-Altan, C. (1989), *Populismo e trasformismo: Saggio sulle ideologie politiche italiane*, Milan: Feltrinelli.

Turiello, P. (1889), *Governo e governati in Italia: Fatti*, 2nd edn, Bologna: Zanichelli.

Valensise, M. (1998), 'L'Italia è sfatta ma ci sono gli italiani,' *Panorama* 28 May: 150–3.

Woolf, S. (1979), *A History of Italy 1700–1860: The Social Constraints of Political Change*, London and New York: Routledge.

Index of Names

Abbiati, Franco, 106–7, 115n2
Adamson, Walter, 237n27
Agnew, John, 315n10
Aleramo, Sibilla (pseudonym of Rina Faccio), education of, 160, 181, as female writer 15, 158, 176, 181–4, 186, as transgressive writer 170–1, 190, autobiographical writing of 181, 183–4, 189–90, bisexuality of 195n39 & 195–6n40, compared to Serao, 183–5, image of self as writer in, 164, 181–2, 184, 186, depicted by Serao, 184–5, 195n36, epistolary novels of, 190n2 , image of androgyne in, 195–6n40, influenced by Ibsen, 179, photographs of, 181–3, 184, 186, possible influence on Pirandello, 188, relations with Boccioni and futurism, 179, 181, use of pseudonym by, 194n25, work: *Una donna*, 158, 179, 181, 187–9, 191n2
Alessandrini, Goffredo, 270–1, 274n3, works: *Addio Kira* [Kira, Farewell] 274n3, *Camicie rosse* [Redshirts (co-*directed with* Francesco Rosi)], 270, 272, *Luciano Serra, pilota*, 270–1, *Noi vivi* [We the Living], 274n3
Alexander III, Pope, 48–9, 67n28
Alfieri, Giuseppina, 150n38
Alfieri, Vittorio, 80–1, 86, and Dante, 78, 80–81, 83, 86, and the decline of classical drama, 32–3, 65n9, and the idea of 'Risorgimento,' 6, 14, 78, 80, compared with Schiller, 33, 65n9, Mazzini on, 78, 80, Petrarchan attitude of, 81, works: *Agamennone*, 80, *Filippo* [Phillip II], 33, 65n9, 80, *Parigi sbastigliato* [Bastille-less Paris], 80, *Del principe e delle lettere* [*On the Prince and Literature*], 80, *Saul*, 80,

Della tirannide [*On Tyranny*], 80
Alicata, Mario, 264, 268
Almond, Gabriel A., 313, 315n16
Amari, Emerico, 138–9, 148n30
Amari, Michele, 55–7, 68nn40–42
Amendola, Giovanni, 90
Anderson, Benedict, 252, 273, 301
Anderson, Perry, 299, 301, 312–13
Anita, *see* Garibaldi, Anita
Apollinaire, Guillaume, 99n11
Aragon, House of, 53
Arese Lucini, Count Francesco Teodoro, 38–40, 68n37
Aristarco, Guido, 274n4, 281–2, 292, 293n6
Armes, Roy, 281, 293n6
Armstrong, Nancy, 176, 194n29
Arnaldo da Brescia, 63
Artom, Isacco, 142, 144n1
Asor Rosa, Alberto, 303

Bacon, Henry, 294n12
Balbo, Cesare, 45, 58, and Risorgimento historiography, 45–6, 60–1, 70n49, attitudes toward women of, 164, 169, work: *Lega di Lombardia*, 47, 112
Banfield, Edward, 307, 315n9
Banti, Anna, 184
Banti, Cristiano, 50
Barbarossa, Emperor Frederick, 30, 47, 49, 67n28, 112
Barbi, Michele, 101n17
Baretti, Giuseppe, 86
Bauman, Zygmunt, 313
Beard, Charles Austin, 279
Beccaria, Cesare, 43, work: *Dei delitti e delle pene*, 43
Belgioioso, Cristina Trivulzio di, 66n18
Bellia, Aida, 258
Bembo, Pietro, 78–9

Index of Names

Cattermole, Evelina, *see* Contessa Lara

Cavarero, Adriana, 173, work: 'La passione della differenza' [The Passion of Difference], 173

Cavour, Count of (Camillo Benso), 14, 18, 126–8, 138, 143, 163, 170, 280, and the 'connubio,' 306, and Garibaldi, 266, 280, and a northern Italian Kingdom, 124, and southern Italy, 8, 12, 125–6, 137, 142–3, 144n1, 145n14, 146n21, 147n24, 148–9n30, letters from, 14, 122, 125–6, 143, 144n1, 145n14, letters to, 122, 125–6, 137, 139–41, 143, 145nn12 & 16, 146–7n22, 148n28, on making Italy European, 123

Cecchi, Emilio, 90, 194n31, 257, 260

Cecioni, Adriano, 190n2, work: *La zia Erminia* [Aunt Erminia], 157, 178

Cena, Giovanni, 181–2, 195n34

Cerroni, Umberto, 300

Charlemagne, 45

Charles Albert, *see* Carlo Alberto

Charles of Anjou, 46, 51, 52

Chateaubriand, François-René de, 158

Chiarini, Luigi, 277, 281, 282

Cialdini, General Enrico, 150n36

Ciccarelli, Andrea, 7, 8, 13, 14, 16

Cola di Rienzo, 67n29. *See also* Faruffini, Federico

Colajanni, Napoleone, 92

Collegno, Ghita, 127

Colombi, Marchesa (pseudonym of Maria Antonietta Torriani), 158, 176, 178, 191n3, 194n25, work: *Prima morire*, 158, 190–1n2

Colonna, Prospero, 58

Compagnoni, Giuseppe, 47, 67n27

Confalonieri, Federico, 33, 38

Constant, Benjamin, 43

Contessa Lara (pseudonym of Evelina Cattermole), 171, 176, 194n25

Cornali, Pietro, 108, 114, work: *Canto degli italiani* [The Song of the Italians], 107–9

Creuzé de Lesser, Augustin, 121, work: *Voyage en Italie et en Sicilie* [Voyage to Italy and Sicily], 121

Crispi, Francesco, 58, 125, 126, 138

Croce, Benedetto, 10, 18, 224, 228, and G. Gentile, 90, 228, 242–4, gendering of authorship by, 187, 195n32, 196n42, historiography of attacked by Mussolini, 224–5, interpretation of the Risorgimento, 10, 241, 252, 253, 262, letter to Aleramo by, 187, liberalism of, 70n49, 244, 261–2, on abuses of 'Dantism,' 101n17, on Fascism as 'parenthesis,' 10, 262, on Neera, 195n32, on representations of southern Italy, 120, 146n20, on the 1848 Revolution, 70n49, opposition to Lateran Pacts, 224–5, works: *Letteratura della nuova Italia* [The Literature of the New Italy], 187, *Storia d'Europa* [History of Europe], 261, *Storia d'Italia* [History of Italy], 224, 261–2

Croce, Elena, 315n12

Cuoco, Vincenzo, 302, work: *Platone in Italia* [Plato in Italy], 44

Dahlhaus, Carl, 105

Dainotto, Roberto, 10, 15, 16

Dalle Vacche, Angela, 294n15

D'Annunzio, Gabriele, 60, 101n18, 194n25, 228, and Serao, 184, 194n26, work: *Giovanni Episcopo*, 194n26

Dante Alighieri, 7, 12–14, 46, 51, 68n41, 77–101 passim,183, and Alfieri, 80–1, 83, 86, and Dante criticism, 88, 92–5, and Foscolo, 81–4, 88, and Leopardi, 80, 82, 84, and Manzoni, 80, 84–5, 92, 93 96, 98n3, and Marinetti, 95–6, and Mazzini, 78, 91–3, and neo-Ghibelline thought, 46, 51, 84, and Papini, 93–4, 96, 101n19, and Prezzolini, 93–4, 101n19, and Slataper, 91–2, and Società dantesca, 89, 92, 101n19, and V. Monti, 97–8n3, as icon of Risorgimento, 7, 13–14, 77, 86, 87–8, 92–3, De Sanctis on, 14, 86–8, 94, monuments to, 77, 92, on 'courtly vernacular,' 68n41, Parodi on, 92–3, vs. Petrarch, 78–80, 83, 86, work: *Divina commedia* [The Divine Comedy], 51, 79, 85, 95

David, Jacques-Louis, 49

Gilbert, Sandra, 191n3, 194n29, 196n45
Gillis, John, 10
Ginzburg, Carlo, 230, 237n28
Gioberti, Vincenzo, 18, 44–7, 116, 162,
  245, 247–8, 302, 309, and historical
  origins of 'Italy,' 44, 309, as neo-
  Guelph, 45–6, 116n10, 247, as prophet
  of Risorgimento, 245, on 'Italian
  character,' 18, 302, on Italians as
  'chosen people,' 45, 47, 247, 309, on
  women, 162, work: *Del primato morale
  e civile degli italiani* [Of the Moral and
  Civil Primacy of Italians], 44–5, 247,
  302, 309
Gioia, Melchiorre, 193n20
Giolitti, Giovanni, 174–5, 266, 305
Gladstone, William, 124, 145n18
Gobetti, Piero, 263
Goethe, Johann Wolfgang von, 32, work:
  Sorrows of Young Werther, 81
Goldoni, Carlo, 97n2
Grajano d'Asti, 69n45. *See also*
  D'Azeglio, Massimo
Gramsci, Antonio, 10, 18, 242, 247, 273,
  314n4, as reader of *La Voce*, 99–
  100n12, debt to G. Gentile of, 242, idea
  of 'volontarismo' in, 242, influence on
  Bollati, 303, influence on Visconti's
  Senso, 17, 279–81, 283, 290–2, 293n3,
  interpretation of Risorgimento as
  failure, 7, 17, 241–3, 251–3, 264,
  277–83, 290–2, 293n3, 303, on
  historical realism, 282–3, 292. *See
  also,* Gentile, Giovanni
Gribaudi, Gabriella, 308
Grossi, Tommaso, 35, work: *I lombardi
  alla prima crociata* (poem [*see also*
  Verdi, Giuseppe]), 35, 65n11
Guacci, Maria Giuseppina, 193n20, work:
  'Canzone per le donne italiane' [Song
  for Italian Women], 193n20
Gubar, Susan, 191n3, 194n29, 196n45
Guerrazzi, Francesco Domenico, 51–2,
  63, 69n47, 116n7, works: *Assedio*
  [Seige], 59, *La battaglia di Benevento*
  [The Battle of Benevento], 51–52, 59,
  67nn33–4, 69n47
Guizot, François, 66n24
Gulino, Giuseppe, 258
Guttuso, Renato, 264

Hapsburg, House of, 38, 43, 55, 68n38.
  See also Ferdinand I, Franz Josef, Josef
  II, and
  Maria Theresa
Haskell, Francis, 42
Hayez, Francesco, 18, 35–8, 54–5, 60,
  66nn17–20, 68nn38–9, and Grossi, 35,
  65n11, and historical painting, 36–8,
  111, and Manzoni, 35, 38, and
  Milanese liberalism, 38–41, changing
  politics of, 54–5, 68nn38–9, influence
  of Amari on, 54–5, influence of
  Byron's *The Two Foscari* on, 60,
  influence of Machiavelli on, 68n20,
  influence of Sismondi on, 36, 43,
  66n20, patrons of, 38, 41, 53–5,
  66nn17–19, praised by Mazzini, 35,
  praised by Stendhal, 65n12, works:
  *Allegory of the Political Order of
  Francis I of Austria*, 68n39, *La
  congiura dei Lampugnani*, [Conspiracy
  of the Lampugnani], 40–1, 66n19,
  Pietro l'eremita predica la crociata
  [Peter the Hermit Preaches the
  Crusade], 34–6, 54, 66n17, *Pietro
  Rossi*, 36–8, *Ritratto del Conte
  Francesco Teodoro Arese Lucini in
  carcere* [Portrait of Count Francesco
  Teodoro Arese Lucini in Prison],
  39–40, *I vespri siciliani* [The Sicilian
  Vespers (1822)], 52–4, *I vespri siciliani*
  [The Sicilian Vespers (1829)], 111, *I
  vespri siciliani* [The Sicilian Vespers
  (1844)], 54–5, 68n37
Hegel, Georg Wilhelm Friedrich, 248,
  249, 303
Heidegger, Martin, 227
Heine, Heinrich, 284
Hobbes, Thomas, 82
Hobsbawm, Eric, 28, 233n13, 301
Hohenstaufen, House of, 46, 51. *See also*
  Frederick Barbarossa, Frederick II,
  Manfred
Hroch, Miroslav, 28–9
Hugo, Victor, 234n17
Huyssen, Andreas, 188, 196n44
Hypsypops rubicundus, see Garibaldi fish

Ibsen, Henrik, 179
Induno, Domenico, 234n17